THE LIVING LIGHT DIALOGUE

Volume 8

THE LIVING LIGHT DIALOGUE

Volume 8

Through the mediumship of
Richard P. Goodwin

Living Light Books

The Living Light Dialogue Volume 8
Copyright © 2016 Serenity Association

Through the mediumship of Richard P. Goodwin.

All rights reserved. Printed in the United States of America. No portion of this book may be reproduced—electronically, mechanically, or via internet transmission—without advance, express written permission of the publisher except in the case of brief quotations embodied in critical articles and reviews. No derivative work—games supplemental material, video—may be created without advance, express written permission of the publisher. For information address Living Light Books, P.O. Box 4187, San Rafael, CA 94913-4187.

Cover design copyright © 2016 by Serenity Association

Cover photograph by Serenity Association, 2014; copyright © 2016 by Serenity Association.

www.livinglight.org

Library of Congress Control Number 2007929762

FIRST EDITION

This volume of teachings is dedicated to the spirit friends who brought to Earth the Living Light philosophy. With eternal gratitude, we pray that we may demonstrate these principles and continue to bring to publication these teachings.

CONTENTS

Acknowledgement ix
Preface xi
Introduction xv
Consciousness Class 219 3
Consciousness Class 220 15
Consciousness Class 221 24
Consciousness Class 222 52
Consciousness Class 223 71
Consciousness Class 224 91
Consciousness Class 225 103
Consciousness Class 226 116
Consciousness Class 227 132
Consciousness Class 228 154
Consciousness Class 229 165
Consciousness Class 230 175
Consciousness Class 231 196
Consciousness Class 232 215
Consciousness Class 233 226
Consciousness Class 234 247
Consciousness Class 235 260
Consciousness Class 236 273
Consciousness Class 237 287
Consciousness Class 238 299
Consciousness Class 239 315
Consciousness Class 240 339
Consciousness Class 241 353
Consciousness Class 242 369
Consciousness Class 243 385
Consciousness Class 244 408

Consciousness Class 245 429
Consciousness Class 246 449
Appendix. 471

ACKNOWLEDGMENT

Grateful acknowledgement is made to the many friends and associates for invaluable aid in compiling this book, for their helpful suggestions, for their loyal interest and encouragement.

Special acknowledgement is due to those who painstakingly and selflessly transcribed and proofread the text.

PREFACE

It was through the mediumship of the Serenity Association founder, Mr. Richard P. Goodwin, that a philosophy known as the Living Light was given in more than 700 classes over a twenty-five-year period.

To be specific, the philosophy was imparted through Mr. Goodwin by a magistrate who had lived on Earth some 8,000 years ago. The former magistrate is known to Living Light students as "the Wise One," and he narrated the journey of his soul on the other side of life, the experiences—especially the difficulties—he encountered in having to face himself, as well as the teachings he earned to help himself through the realms in which he traveled. It was his decision to share the teachings with souls on both sides of "the curtain."

Prior to the advent of the Wise One, Mr. Goodwin had prayed for a teacher from the realms of light. Mr. Goodwin, since age fourteen, had been the instrument through which spirit was able to communicate with those seeking help. But he saw that his mediumship brought only temporary solace, because the people he was trying to help soon became fascinated with the phenomena and ignored the help that spirit was imparting. He prayed for someone who would bring forth teachings that would benefit any soul seeking a path to a greater awareness of himself and of God.

His prayers were answered in 1964 when the Wise One came through for the first time. Mr. Goodwin, at first apprehensive about what this new teacher would impart, was taken into deep trance and not able to control what was being revealed through him. Upon hearing the recorded classes afterward, however, he became convinced of the goodness of the teacher and of the value of the simple, beautiful teachings he had to impart. This, then, was the beginning of the Living Light philosophy given to Earth through the mediumship of Richard P. Goodwin.

In carrying out the request of the Wise One and Mr. Goodwin, students of the Serenity Association transcribed from audiotape the classes that had been brought through. Because most are in the form of teacher-student interaction, the classes became known as *The Living Light Dialogue*; and the students were instructed to publish the classes as a multi-volume set of the Living Light philosophy. *Volume 1* was published in the autumn of 2007.

The present book, *Volume 8,* completes the publication of the series of spiritual awareness classes known as Consciousness Classes and includes CC 219 through CC 246, covering the time period of August 5, 1982, through May 9, 1985.

The foundation of the classes—the foundation of the Living Light philosophy itself—is the Law of Personal Responsibility which states, in part, that we are responsible for all our experiences, and that our experiences are the return of the laws that we have established with our thoughts, acts, and deeds. Through greater awareness of our thoughts and by exercising our divine right of choice, we may choose to establish laws of greater harmony and goodness.

The Living Light Dialogue teaches that we have come to Earth to learn the lessons that are necessary to free us from the dictates and limits of our own thoughts and judgments, which are the mental patterns that we follow through our own lack of awareness and are so very potent, forceful, and limiting. These teachings guide us in making the necessary changes in our thinking in order to free ourselves from those patterns and to express our soul consciousness.

The choice of guiding the direction of our life, as stated by the Wise One when he speaks of being with a person, place, or thing, is, in essence, of being in this world and not a part of this world. He further explains that no matter what experiences we encounter, no matter what we do or do not do, we—our spirit—may view the experience in objectivity from a soul level of consciousness where peace reigns supreme.

The teachings of this volume help us to restore harmony or balance in our life by flooding the consciousness with spiritual affirmations and prayers, a few of which can be found in the appendix. When reason is restored, by balancing our sense functions with our soul faculties, we will consciously experience peace. Without annihilating our ego or our sense functions, we will find a pathway of expression for our soul. Where there was once disturbance, now there is acceptance. Where there was disease, now there is poise. And where there was hopelessness and despair, now there is reason, divine neutrality; and peace shows the way.

If you make the effort to apply these laws, such as, "If man is a law unto himself, what are you doing with the law that you are?", and demonstrate the wisdom of patience, the truth of this philosophy will be your living demonstration.

As the teacher states in CC 130, "My journey of many centuries and much experience has brought me here to Earth to share with you these simple teachings that have come as the effect of a long, long, long journey. Let not *your* journey be so long in the realms of illusion. For it is not necessary for you. For in your evolution, you have earned an awakening. But it is up to you to do something that is constructive and worthwhile."

INTRODUCTION

[This introduction was written by Mr. Goodwin and originally appeared in *The Living Light*, which were the first teachings of the Living Light Philosophy published in book form. The entire text of *The Living Light* was republished in *The Living Light Dialogue*, Volume 1.]

> "Think, children. Think more often
> and think more deeply."

The teachings in this book were given as a progressive series of lessons to a group of four students who were sitting for spiritual unfoldment with me beginning in January of 1964. The communications were regular until October of that year, when nearly a seven-year silence ensued, and resumed in 1971 to the present. They were received in three ways by me as a channel. The main text was taped from a direct control of my voice in deep trance at special sittings of our group, during which I had no experience of the voice or what was being transmitted. A few scattered verses were given independently when I was privileged to see and hear our teacher clairvoyantly. I have also been a channel for this communicant when speaking from the podium at church and in answering difficult questions at our public seminars.

Nearly all we know about our teacher is contained in the lectures. He reports that he had tried for sixteen years to break through an interference barrier that the channel had to deep trance. When our conditions were in resonance with his patient wisdom, he came through ready to teach his understanding. I have seen him as an old man dressed in white with long flowing white hair. He has blue eyes, slightly smiling and deeply compassionate. I have always called him the Old Man. The students liked to call him the Wise One. He is surely one of those often called a Teacher of Light. I do not know his country, although he indicated at one time that he was from 6000 B.C., and a form of a judge in his time.

The text is often difficult, but it is complete, having been transcribed word for word from the original tapes recording the trance voice. It is presented with a minimum of punctuation to be freer for the individual interpretation of each reader. The lessons given before the long silence are phrased with many allegories often paradoxical. There are repetitions and renewals of theme, but it is explained that if an understanding is not perceived, compassion dictates that it be said again. Some of the topics have but a simple mention with little development but all are revealed, we are told, according to merit.

The Old Man is a fine teacher. He has in a hundred ways intertwined his allegory, progressive explanations, unfolding exercises, and timely references to reach a multitude of levels of individual understanding. A notable change is his more direct style of presentation beginning in 1971.

There is an endearing intimacy of person that can be felt through his lectures, a meaningful and loving encounter with a wise friend. Like an old man, he makes a mistake and conscientiously corrects himself a few paragraphs later. He listens often and carefully to our earnest discussions of his words. He consults with a group of experts on evolution and cites their learning in his lesson. His use of the direct address "children" or "my children" is not patronizing but infinitely loving and supportive.

A word must be said about the teachings. The Old Man makes clear that his lessons are not dogma, a creed or a narrow way, but simply his own understanding offered to us as a form of instruction to aid us in our own individual progression. When he speaks of Laws, he does not refer to man-made rules or moral traditions but to the cosmic and atomic way-things-are, the natural world of what-is, the universal laws of life, part of the original creative design and through which creation is fulfilled. These laws are beyond the possibility of being changed, suspended, transcended, or destroyed but they are ever a tool of mankind, not his master. First, through our awareness of the universal laws and then slowly through our developed understanding, the powers of creation are accessible to us. Not power over men's minds or circumstances, but power over whatever is selfish and imperfect in ourselves is the way up the eternal ladder of progression. When the Old Man cautions us concerning the Law of Responsibility or gives us a thinking exercise to explore the Law of Identity in a dynamic manner, he prepares us to take another step. And all move in accordance with the Law of What Can Be Borne.

Our teacher shows us how the two worlds are drawn together. In his realm, he describes, there is a great diversity of thought, many schools of understanding; but the Light is always known by the Light. Because of the interdependence of the two realms, listening to our discussions helped to clarify his teaching to others on his side of the curtain. His love and gratitude he humbly equates with ours.

The lessons to be perceived are not new, they are very old, but they are new to certain levels of our being. I would personally advise the reader, after reading this volume of discourses in full, to make a daily habit (or when there is a feeling or need) to sit quietly with the book. Open it at random and be guided to the Light by the passage that is there for the day. This technique is still used by the original students who were given the lessons and by many students after them who have studied in unfolding classes with me through these teachings.

Go beyond the words into feeling, into the immediate meanings for you. Touch into the inspiration that flows into the form of this book. It is from the Divine.

RICHARD P. GOODWIN
San Geronimo, California
June, 1972

CONSCIOUSNESS CLASSES

CONSCIOUSNESS CLASS 219 ✤

Now, this evening's class will be a bit on the introductory side, because we do have a few students who are here for the first time.

I'll have to get used to the height of this table, but I'm sure that I will. Like anything that is new, the mind does not readily or easily accept it.

On the path of truth, you will have to give the most precious gift that you have. Now, that is the law that demands that most precious gift that you have. And that most precious gift, of course, is that which we value the most. It is not our money that we value the most. It is not even our health that we value the most. But it is what we call our time. Now, our time, or what we call our time, is that which we have the greatest value for. But it is not just any time. It is not the time that we have to work and earn a livelihood. It is not the time that we have to do any specific other thing. But it is that particular time that we judge is our time to do what we judge is our thing.

Now, that time, when we analyze it and investigate what that time is, we readily see, is wasted timed. Now, wasted time is time that is nonproductive. It is energy utilized to create forms in the atmosphere through desires; forms that do not fulfill the purpose of their creation. In common language, one would call that daydreaming.

Now, we spend much of our so-called precious time in what is known as daydreaming or wishful thinking. When we think, we create, in a mental world, a form. Now, ofttimes a person may say, well, they wish that their financial situation was much better. And they dream about that; they think about that. But they are not aware of what the form is that is being created. If they were, they'd soon stop thinking about how they *wished* things were better in their mundane and material world. Now, the vehicle or the form that is created is created by what we spoke of, in a much earlier class, as the primitive mind.

We are all subject to, and victims of, what we understand to be fear. We fear that which we do not understand because we know by not understanding something, we cannot control it. And so we fear what we cannot control. And the reason that we fear what we cannot control is simply because there's something inside of us that knows what we cannot control is, in truth, controlling us. And there is a something inside of us that finds it repulsive to be controlled by something outside of ourselves.

In this, the most precious gift you have to give (the gift of wasted time) in order that you may have the truth that frees you, takes a conscious moment-by-moment effort to gain control over the vehicle of your mind through which your soul is expressing. Unless we are willing to do that, we must then be willing to be the victims of those things that, from our lack of effort, from our lack of understanding, [which is] the effect of our lack of effort, are in truth controlling us.

We have spent, over these many, many years, much time on the vehicle of mind because it is the mental realm that stands between our conscious awareness and our spiritual world in which we are living and are not yet aware. The reason that we are not aware of the spiritual world in which our spirit is this moment, all moments, is simply because we are identifying with a mental realm. And a mental realm cannot offer to us that which is spiritual and a part of a spiritual realm of consciousness.

To awaken to that which is truth is to awaken to that which is formless and, therefore, that which is free. And to awaken to that which is formless and that which is free, we can no longer identify. For when we identify, we have to first have in our consciousness the thought of I. Without the thought of I, it is not possible to identify.

Now, I'm going to, in this introductory class, in a few moments, give you some time to ask your questions in reference to this discussion of the most precious gift you have—that which we value above all things. But before so doing, we want to spend a few moments on the process of death.

We are dying and being born moment by moment. And that process, someday, takes place on all eighty-one levels of consciousness. And then, we understand that to be the transition—the leaving from this world to another world. When we pass through the portal of death, which we are passing through on various levels of consciousness moment by moment, when we pass through the portal of death, that which calls us from the Light that frees us, that is, the Light within us, the Light of Truth, is called temptation.

Now, all of us, I am sure, will agree that nothing tempts us that is not a weakness within us. And so by awakening inside of ourselves to that (those things that we love) will reveal to us what our weakness is. Anything that we awaken to that we love more than we love truth is the weakness that we shall be tempted by as we pass through the portal of death.

Now, as I said a moment ago, that passing through the portal of death is taking place moment by moment on various levels of consciousness. So we can relate to this moment, this moment of which we are consciously aware. We take a look and we see the things that we want to do. We have [an] intent of doing those things, for we know that by so doing they are in our best interests. They are constructive. They are beneficial. They will reap a good harvest and they will, in turn, produce for us the good that we are sincerely and honestly seeking. And so we do have the intent. But when it comes to the energy, which is called effort, that is necessary to establish the Law of Application in the intent that we have in consciousness, we ofttimes stumble and we fail. We quit before the victory.

Now, why do we, with these good intents, these motivations, why do we—what is it within us that quits before the victory? We do not sustain the energy necessary for a long enough period of time to walk through the gates of victory, for the hissing hounds of hell, they tempt us before we reach our goal. Now, as I said a moment ago, we can only be tempted by the weaknesses within us. These weaknesses or frailties, through which we are tempted and, therefore, distracted from the fulfillment of our soul's purpose here on Earth, are the effects not of a short, a very short span of life here on this Earth planet. They are the effects of failures for untold centuries. And so we enter this earth realm with these certain weaknesses, these certain tendencies. And unless we make the effort early in life to correct these, to strengthen our character, to stay with something that we intend to accomplish until it is accomplished, then we only perpetuate the law that we have for centuries been the victim of.

Now, that, of course, is taking place for us every day in every way. But it is a rude awakening when we pass from this physical world through the portal of death and we find that, once again, after so very many centuries of effort, once again we must serve in those realms of consciousness until our next incarnation. Only to try again and again and again and again.

We are fortunate here to have received this beautiful, demonstrable truth that clearly teaches and demonstrates that repetition is the law through which change is made possible. Now, we must remember that repetition is not the law that makes change possible. Repetition is the law through which change is made possible. You can repeat many things many times to many people, that does not deprive that person, or persons, of their divine right of choice. We always have this divine right of choice.

Many of us in receiving these classes—and I'd like to draw a similarity, because I find a great similarity between becoming a student of the Living Light philosophy and getting married. There's a phenomenal similarity there—very, very similar. They both have, if you want to be successful, the Law of Responsibility—the ability to respond. Now, a person makes the conscious choice and they work very hard. And they do everything that their mind has to offer. And the day arrives that they get married. And it isn't long before they forget how hard they worked, how many years of effort they have already spent, how much energy they've poured in to getting what they want. And it's just amazing how short-lived, sometimes, it is.

And so it is in our efforts and in our choice to seek the truth within us that frees us we try many philosophies and we try many schools and we try many classes. But then we reach that point in our understanding where we know—and no one has to tell us—that we've got to make some kind of a change. And fortunately for us, our conscience clearly dictates what that change is. But then there is something else that rises and it doesn't want to make that change, though we know that someday that change for us shall have to be.

The realms of temptation serve the king of procrastination, for through the function of procrastination our weaknesses become weaker and we become more tempted in our life. Whenever we enter the realm of self-thought, the realm of the thought of I, but not the I—and such a difference between delusion, illusion, and truth. When we enter those realms, we find ourselves under what is commonly referred to as a great, heavy weight of time pressure. Of course, it is revealing to us that our weakness is getting, yea, even greater in our consciousness, that we are so easily tempted and so easily distracted from the things that we consciously intend to do. And that which had eternal value to us a moment ago no longer has any value today. Only to fall to someday to rise again, to begin over and over and over, again and again and again.

The identification with the computer known as the thought of I offers us nothing, absolutely nothing but the experiences that have already been. So here we find ourselves moving through this illusion called time and space. We find ourselves seeking something better, the key to success, the abundant good that is rightfully and justly ours. And yet, when, through those moments of effort, we earn the opportunity to accept the personal responsibility for our lives, that we are, in truth, captain of the destiny that we are moving on, that we and we alone have established the laws, the effects of which we are experiencing this moment, when that moment comes, my friends, stop, pause, and think. Try to think a little more deeply than the momentary level of consciousness that has risen up to take control.

Long ago we spoke to you about desire; desire being the divine expression, the expression of the Divinity itself. There is no mind in any universe that is greater than the Divinity known as God. And because desire is an expression of God, the Divinity, it is greater than the thought of man. Therefore, in keeping with that truth we have spoken to you, never, ever suppress desire. We have spoken to you on the process of educating or fulfilling. The choice is ever yours. But educating a desire does not mean to eliminate the desire. For you have permitted yourself to be receptive to the Divinity, the expression of the Divine, and your mind has recorded that and you are experiencing that urge called desire. But your choice in fulfilling it has been limited by your short earthly experiences. Therefore, time and time again, you suppress: you force down into the deep recesses of your subconscious mind that energy, that power of God itself. Someday it is guaranteed to rise.

Now, when you force that energy into the depths of your being, those patterns of mind, those created forms in your aura are the ones who feed upon it. So the expressing or the fulfilling of this desire is limited by what your minds have already experienced in Earth life. That puts you under the control and the victim of circumstances. And it ofttimes seems that due to circumstances beyond your control, your desires cannot be fulfilled. By suppressing that energy of the Divine, you have indeed placed yourself the victim of so-called circumstances. They guarantee someday to rise to have their way. The more you suppress the energy, the stronger those patterns of mind become. Until someday the floodgate opens and your life becomes a disaster.

Now, how does that happen? First of all, the energy is phenomenal that you've been pushing down into those depths, those recesses of your mind. When the floodgate opens, there is only desire. There is no light of reason, for the flood of desire is such a great force in your consciousness. Therefore, that which is reasonable, that which is in your best interest, for your own health, wealth, and happiness, is not even considered. Only desire is considered—the mountain you have created in the depths of your mind.

One of the very simple ways of educating desire is to discuss, through the spoken word, that which you desire: to communicate. For in communication there is a release, an exchange of energy. When there is communication and discussion over the things in life that you desire and think or believe that you are not getting, when there is discussion, the light of reason begins to shine. And it is the light of reason that, in time, will transfigure you and will bring about the things that you are seeking in life.

But to hold this energy and to suppress it, to believe for an instant that your desire is not worthy, that it will be ridiculed, that someone else will not understand, and to place all of those restrictions upon that which is divine, is to place you into a realm of denial, guaranteeing the destiny of that which you do not want. Surely, that is not the path of freedom, let alone the path of truth.

We are ofttimes so conscious of what other people think about us. We are so conscious of what people think about us only because we're not so happy about what we think about ourselves. Now, we say that no one sleeps for us and no one eats for us. Why then should we allow them to think for us? But pause and think for a moment. We cannot be so concerned about what other people think about us unless we're so concerned of what we think about ourselves. If we do not make the effort to be a friend to ourselves, then we will never find anyone or anything to be a friend to us.

We must learn to be good company so that we don't have to have our ears bombarded with noise, our eyes blinded with visions in order to be at peace alone with ourselves. So often, you know, we have to be constantly doing something, constantly moving or constantly having something move for us, because not to have that constant charging of our senses, we become aware of thoughts in our mind and feelings that have been suppressed that we don't appreciate. But is it not better to pause and become aware of these thoughts and these feelings, to have a talk with these levels of consciousness, to come to terms and be good company with oneself? We live a long time with our self. For when we leave this physical world, due to our identification with our self, the self does not easily leave us. It is very tenacious. It is very determined. It is very persistent. And it can accomplish a great deal of good if we will permit it, through a little bit of conscious guidance, to do so. But that, of course, is going to take some effort on our part.

Now, the key to success is something you already have. I can only share with you the laws involved in your turning the key in your own consciousness. Life is ever going to be, for us, the way we make it. If we choose to make it dependent upon things beyond our control, then that's the way our life is going to continue to be. It does not have to be that way. But if that's the way we need it to be for us, then that is the way that it will be.

Many times a person wants something to change in their life. And they go through the mental computer and they try everything that that computer has to offer to bring about the change that they desire. And they find that it just doesn't work. Well, of course, it doesn't work, for if it worked, you would already have had the experience and you wouldn't need the change from what you find yourself in. It doesn't work. It's only a repetition of what has been.

Now, there's something that does work and it works without limit, without time, without demand. It works by a simple request. When you free yourself from that which keeps you in a mental world, for a moment, and you place your request, your request shall be fulfilled in keeping with laws that your mind shall never control. That's known as giving it up. Give up what it is that you think you want. If you will give it up on all levels of consciousness, you may be rest assured there is something that works in ways that you can never figure out, because it is not working in mental substance. It is that which is beyond mental substance. It is that which sustains mental substance. Therefore, it is far greater than mental substance, of which the human mind is composed. That is my interest in life, for this short mental realm in which we are presently existing is very short indeed.

Become aware of what it is in creation that tempts you. Do not deny it, for it will become your master, your destiny in time. But look at it and look at it honestly. See what it has to offer you as far as endurance, as far as consistent benefit, as far as improvement with your health, your wealth, and your happiness. Is it something that sustains you in your hour of greatest need? Or is it something that demands that you serve it and serve it and serve it to get a moment's sensation, a moment's awareness of a charge of energy? And is it a selfish thing that is demanding your energy? Does it consider your responsibilities in life? Does it consider what your other levels of consciousness want to do? Or is it so greedy and so selfish that it only considers itself at its convenience at its time? Look at it for what it really is, not for what you think it is. It is not you. It is true it is something that you have created, but it is not you. It is form. It is a child that you have created that has grown and matured and treats you as the child. And you follow it, when it calls, to do its bidding.

I assure you that is not the fullness nor the benefit of the divine expression known as desire. That is when the human mind steals desire from the Divinity and in that stealing places it into the limitation of form. And it's known by all philosophies as the greatest sin of all: the thought of lust. The thought of lust. That, my friends, is a bondage we all seek to be free from. It demands not only our time, but it demands our energy. It demands our vitality. And it demands it when it sees so fit to demand it. It does not matter whether it humiliates us, disgraces us, whether it robs us of our very sustenance of life. It comes, it calls, it demands, and we follow. Let us awaken to what we choose to follow. Let us not blindly follow the call in the wilderness. Let us pause and let us become aware of what it is.

For only when we separate truth from creation shall we be free. Never shall we be free as long as we believe the illusion that we are the form. Never shall we be free as long as we believe the illusion that we are the desire, that we are that thing that is calling us. We cannot be free that way. We can only be free when we put creation in perspective by separating it from truth, by looking at it for what it really is: a form of birth and a form of death. We are not the form. We never were the form. We never shall be the form. We are that which uses the form. Let us awaken to what we are, for in that awakening shall we make the necessary changes that will free us. As long as we remain in the belief that we are the forms, that we are the images, that we are the thoughts, as long as we believe that illusion, we must pay the price that it shall extract from us.

That is not the intent nor the purpose of our journey here on Earth. Each part of the temple in which our eternal being now resides is revealing to us—from the color of our eyes, to the tip of our toes—is revealing to us the lessons we have to learn.

So many of us suffer from so-called discord, known to man as disease. We suffer because we do not understand the laws that we are blindly following. We suffer because we have entered a temple in which certain changes have to be brought about and we do not see what those changes are. We do not see them clearly. We do not understand why we have the form we have. We do not understand what we're supposed to be doing with the form that our soul is now residing in. We're under the delusion that we need to improve on the temple that we have merited. We need to bring about some changes because there's something inside of us that no longer wants to see what the temple, the house in which we live, is telling us and showing us. We don't want to look at it anymore. Our conscience is beginning to rise. We no longer want to see the house. So we do everything possible that we can to bring about certain changes so we won't have to look at the lesson that is revealed in the temple of God, the human form.

We are the way we are because of what we're doing. If we do not like the way we are, we can change what we are doing and see something new and something different.

It does not benefit us to think of what has been unless, in so doing, we are not emotionally attached, that the magnetic field is not in control, and we are objective and we can view, as you would view pages of a book you've already read.

And so it is with what we have to do, as we move forward in awakening that which is within us, for that's where truth is. Truth is inside of us. It has always been there. These classes will not bring you truth. No classes can do that. They will bring to you, through revelation, the demonstrable laws of life, which, through your own personal effort, if you will apply, in time, in keeping with the laws you establish, will awaken that truth that lies within you. But that, of course, is up to you—what you choose to do.

As we open our eyes, we are first saddened to see how we follow these forms throughout creation. We follow them by the delusion that we are them. We really do believe that it is us that wants to do this, that it is us that wants to do that. And time passes and we say, "Now, why did I ever think I wanted to do that? How did I ever get involved in that mess? What happened to me that I stepped over the cliff the day I got married?" Because some people, you know, do feel that way, now and then—not always. If that was the case, we would have no marriages in the world at all. But we look at things and we wonder why we ever did such a thing. But that part of us that is wondering why we ever did such a thing was not the level that was in control at the time the decision was made.

And so it is in making any decision, unless you allow yourself seventy-two hours from the first thought of your desire before making your final choice, unless you allow—that's what it takes to go through the levels of consciousness—unless you allow that duration of time, my friends, be rest assured all your levels were not awakened, let alone agreed. And you guarantee what is called regret. You guarantee the thought of, "Whatever made me so stupid that I did such a thing?" You guarantee regret. You guarantee disappointment. If you want to be freed from disappointments and discouragements and regrets and all of those choice functions, then weigh out in consciousness for seventy-two hours. Weigh it honestly and sincerely. And give yourself the opportunity to pass through the many realms of consciousness. So that when the day comes you will know. "Yes, this did work out this way. But I did have a feeling. If I didn't have the thought, at least I had the feeling." And so you're not unhappy then. You're not disappointed. You're not discouraged.

My friends, they say that enthusiasm means to be in God. It means a lot more than that. It means the power of God, the Divinity itself. Now, some people say "Well, I use to be enthused.

I'm not enthused anymore. I can't get encouraged anymore. I can't get enthused about anything anymore, because if I even think about getting enthused, this mountain of disappointments of past events rises up." It takes vitality to be enthused. It takes the full activity of the vital body to be enthused. And it takes that to be encouraged and to be inspired. It takes that much energy.

Now, if your vital body is not getting the energy necessary to be fully active, then the energy that should be going to your vital body is going to something else. And what is the something else that's taking your energy, that's robbing you of the enthusiasm, the vitality, the success, that is your right? Well, I'll tell you in a very simple word, before we conclude our class this evening. It's called wasted time. And I do hope that you will make the effort to consider the class this evening, especially that which is known as wasted time.

Thank you.

AUGUST 5, 1982

CONSCIOUSNESS CLASS 220

Good evening, class.

Before we get into our class this evening, I think it is very important to understand the spiritual principle of promptness. It not only respects oneself, but it respects and considers others. Now, without respect, which is a spiritual soul faculty, there is no consideration. Without consideration, there is no understanding. Without understanding, there is no wisdom. And without wisdom, there is no truth. So I do feel that we should understand and make the effort to have some degree of self-respect.

When we conducted these classes before, at the [American Legion] Log Cabin, we always locked the door promptly. On some occasions, we did have some people wait outside till class was over and come in and have refreshments. Now, our policy has not changed. If, for some reason, you feel that you are unable to be prompt, then this is not the class that you should be in. Because this is a spiritual class to help guide you inside yourself to find the path of freedom. And we cannot find the path of freedom without respect for ourselves and consideration and understanding and truth. So let us make great effort, because, otherwise, I will see that the doors are locked—the bathroom doors—if it's going to cause us to have disrespect for ourselves and lack of consideration for other people.

To those of you who are new to our classes, it has been, in the past, our policy to give trance classes. To the degree of trance, it is very important to try to be still, to just let yourself be still. In fact, we had given a class some time ago on what happens when we move. We cannot move without the process of thought and the process of thought is the creation of form. A medium—no matter who they are—is sensitive and receptive to forms that are in the atmosphere. And therefore, the higher the teachings, the greater the stillness. So as you're at peace, so, those higher teachings will come through for your benefit and also, of course, when I hear the tapes, for mine.

So we have these nice zappit lights *[electronic bug zappers]* out there for you. And I've done my part in talking to all the mosquitoes—telling them how they can get to the other side quickly and peacefully. And hopefully they will leave you alone. *[This class was given on the lanai at the church home, with the doors and windows open, which permitted various insects to enter the lanai.]* So let us just be at peace, please, for a few moments.

[At this point, Mr. Goodwin goes into a trance.]

Greetings, fellow students on the path of Light. This evening we will discuss the principle of life.

We think we are the thinker and therefore believe we are the thought. As you know, man *is* an idea. An idea is that which is [and] is not dependent upon the Law of Becoming. The difference between a thought and an idea is the attachment, from need, which is the Law of Mental Substance, the need to form. And so it is that man, the idea, becomes, through the Law of Identity, which is the Law of Attachment; he believes, becomes, and lives the illusion of creation.

And so it is with all of your experiences in life and all of the struggles that your experiences seem to offer, the struggle is only the effect of identifying, through the realm of thought, to the bondage of form. This process takes place moment by moment and is known to your mind as birth and death. For that which is, that you are, is not bound by the world of mental substance. It is because you think you are the thinker. It is because you believe you are the thought. It is that identification that is the suffering, that is the struggle, that is the obstruction, which, someday on the path eternal, you will, once again, be freed from.

In entering your present realm, the earth realm, you entered in keeping with identification of the life and experiences of what had been. You entered that way, through identification and attachment, to the journey of your eternal being. We can move from the bondage in the moment of our choice. But it takes a little practice, a little effort on your part to still, which is to control, that known as the mental world. The effects and experiences, known as man is a law unto himself, is totally dependent upon your belief that you are the thought that you think you think. And life, the short life of Earth, has already revealed to you on many, many, many occasions that you, in truth, are not the thought.

The statement which declares, "I think, therefore I am," is the necessary step in believing and becoming. It is known to your world as self-awareness. The awareness of self, of course, is dependent upon the identification with self. And the more we identify with self, the more bound we are by the thoughts and the mental world in which we are moving and breathing. To be in the world and not a part of the world is dependent upon your own effort at any moment in what you do and how you control the mental world in which you have identified.

You have made that choice to move from the idea, which you are, to the thought, which you believe—a choice from freedom to bondage. For in the realm which you are, in truth, an idea, there is fulfillment. In the realm in which you believe you are, there is satisfaction. The difference between an idea and a thought is a simple word known as need. Because thought is form—an idea is form*less*—thought knows need, for it knows form and, therefore, knows boundary and limit. Because it knows limit, it ever seeks to gather, to garner, for it has, as the very basic ingredient of its own survival, it has the insatiable want, need, and desire to become, which it knows is the essence, the principle that truly sustains it.

So often we ask for many things; for being identified with a mental world, we know need of many, many things for we know limit and we know lack. We know form. We know restriction. We know those things. We know them because we *believe*. And in that belief, we become the denial of truth, the destiny of bondage.

To be aware of what you are is the effect of your efforts of controlling what you are not. He who does not control one thought controls no thought. Tell the thought, the form that you are aware of, to be still, to be still. For a thought cannot be still. Only an idea is stillness, for only an idea is formless. Only an idea can fulfill. Only an idea can awaken, for only an idea is the principle of life. A thought, which is a form, is the illusion, the covering, the sensing.

And so it is in these experiences in life, it is our senses that suffer. And they suffer and serve a good purpose, for when the suffering is intense and sufficient enough unto the need, we then shall be still. We then shall be free, for freedom [is] the effect of self-control, the control of a mental world that you have, through error in evolution, over-identified with. That is where the pain [is]; that is where the dual law binds the eternal free soul.

Let us enter that moment in consciousness. Enter the stillness and the peace that *is*. But that is only possible when you no longer believe the thought that moves. Because thought, its nature, its life, which is birth and death, is dependent upon motion and because motion is a vibration that is constantly changing, man finds the need for constant change to sustain, to maintain his identification with the mental world that he has identified with and believes that he is.

Out of the void is Life herself. The void is not nothing. The void is everything. When everything is in a perfect state of unity, harmony (the Law of Peace) is the void. Beyond thought is beyond question. Beyond thought and beyond question, that you are. And because you are that great void, that everything your eyes see, everything your ears hear, everything your senses sense, because you are all of that in perfect unity, you are the Law of Harmony and peace is your soul.

To believe that you are the thought, the name, the thing, is only to bind you for the duration of the belief.

The journey through your planet is a great journey filled with much opportunity. The restoration of your health, your wealth, and your happiness is totally and completely dependent upon your willingness, your ability to gain control of the mental world that you have and are identifying with.

When you ask and receive not, you ask from the thought of I and receive from the thought of I. It returns unto you and does not accomplish what you speak it forth to accomplish because it does not go beyond a mental world. Because it is formed in your consciousness, it goes out to form to return to the limit of the forms that you have already identified with.

One asks the question, "Shall I give all I know for something I do not know?" You have already given all you know for something you do not know times beyond number in your evolution.

And so it is not new for you. It is only new for the limit of your identification with a few short years that you permit yourself to be aware of. Horizons cannot be broadened until we are ready to permit that process to take place for us. It is not easy to let go of what we think we are. But it is necessary and it is a process that is taking place moment by moment. We ofttimes refer to that as, "Circumstances have forced me to make these changes in my life." The circumstances, of course, are the lack of our understanding of the laws we set into motion and reap the harvest thereof.

My freedom in this great eternity came with much struggle and great effort. At least my over-identification with my own self-importance was my greatest bondage in eternity because I had always been what I understood to be a self-reliant person, dependent on no one for what I needed, wanted, or desired. And so it is in the process and the evolution of identification with self, we all reach the final point of saturation. And in this great self-reliance and self-dependence, the greater is our self-reliance, the greater is our self-dependence, the greater is our denial of the Source that is.

To receive from anything we must first become the thing. And so it is we ask. And we ask from a level of consciousness that we are identified with, and we receive like kind. For that which is, we must pause to be—not to become, but to be.

We have spent many years and much time on understanding—be not concerned *[At this moment, a large insect enters the zappit light and the process makes a loud noise that lasts many seconds.]*—on understanding the mental world. And so it is the time has come to move beyond these forms and things to be formless and free, to pause more often that we may know beyond question and, therefore, beyond doubt, for that which is beyond question is forever beyond doubt.

One cannot question the formless and the free, for there is nothing to question. Truth cannot be questioned. Truth is.

Questions are for the children who play the mental games in the kindergarten and nursery schools of creation. Question will serve its purpose if you permit it to be instrumental in graduating from the kindergartens of life. But if you permit yourselves to be dependent upon answers to your questions that serve only to support judgments already made, then it will only bind you to what has been.

Let all go, for in letting all go, you rise in consciousness and know who you are. You live, therefore, in rising to those realms of freedom, you live in the perfect balance, the perfect harmony of Life herself. One cannot, in creation, remain in those realms of consciousness for long durations and yet remain in form. For without attachment, the effect of identification, you leave this world and enter others. And there is a duty and a responsibility to your house of clay and the millions of forms that you serve. There is a responsibility and then there is the greater responsibility to your eternal being. Therefore, break the shackles of attachment by controlling the thought that identifies that you may experience *you* in the course of a day and night, that you may have those moments of awareness and, in so doing, once again take charge over all creation.

We all know when the obstruction seems the greatest, we are over-identified with the self, the mental world. If, in those moments, we will pause and we will permit ourselves to be freed from that mental realm—it's only a moment that's necessary to move the obstruction that seems to block your path. So whatever the obstruction may *appear* to be, remember, it is only an obstruction to you. It does not exist in truth. It is not the Light that is. It is only the light that appears. For the Light that is does not appear and, therefore, does not disappear. So the obstructions on your path—only an effect of your thought and your identification with the thought. That's all, my good friends, they ever were. That's all they are. That's all they can ever be.

So whatever it is that your mind tells you, you are seeking, pause when it tells you those things and declare the truth: "That which my mind seeks, I already am. And because I already am and my mind does not know, then I have a great responsibility to educate my mind." That, my friends, is a responsibility of your eternal journey. For that which rises to declare need, want, and desire, that which rises is that which is darkness, that which needs the Light that is that it may awaken, evolve, refine its vibration and someday know.

For it is the rise and fall that is the refinement of all form. That that rises, destined to fall, is ever refined to answer the call of the Light that is. So be not so concerned with identification of that which is falling. Be not so concerned with identifying with that which is rising. View it for what it is: a process that is taking place constantly throughout all universes of form, a process that is taking place to evolve, to refine, that all vibration, in time, in eternity, shall be united.

Power is very different than force. Power, which is the Divinity that you are, is the perfect balance of all vibration. Power *is* in the moment of your stillness. Power *is* when thought does not exist. Power *is* peace itself. Force is that which drives in a mental world, in a vibration to conquer, in a vibration of insatiable need. That is the Law of Force: to gather, to garner, to destroy.

And so it is that man, through self-thought, is destroying the vehicles that his eternal being is using to express. The more thought of self, the more the thought of I, the more rapid the destruction of the forms for which you all are responsible.

We all seek, in our true being, to express harmoniously in ways that are beneficial to ourselves and, therefore, beneficial to all who come in contact with us. But to do that, to truly express that, we must make greater effort to control the illusion and delusion of the thought of I. Only then shall we be clear and receptive to our true being.

Shadows of the past, they haunt us as we move on the path of Light. They haunt us with the call of temptation. We are tempted only when we think of self. We cannot be tempted when we do not think of self. And so he who is easily tempted lives much of his life in the thought of I. The something greater, that we all know is, comes to all of us and knocks at the door of our conscience day after day after day. There are moments we hear the knocking. There are moments we act accordingly and in those moments, the goodness of life is expressed.

And so, my friends, because it is important in your evolution, I shall take a few moments for you to speak with questions that may be instrumental in helping you to help yourself to move along the path to greater realms of freedom. And so I will ask my good chairman here to respond when you raise your hand that you may speak forth your questions.

Anyone with a question may raise their hand. [After a pause, the chairman speaks to the Teacher.] *There are no questions.*

Oh, but there are many. But we shall discuss them another time. Let us encourage ourselves when we awaken. Let us encourage ourselves as we go to sleep. Let us spend more effort, more time to see the abundant good and beauty that surrounds us.

Many have said that beauty is in the eye of the beholder and, of course, for the beholder, it is. For the beholder and the beauty that they see, of course, is dependent upon what past experiences and the identification with them will permit for them. Beauty, a soul faculty, like harmony, *is*. Remember, my good friends, beauty *is*. And that which is beautiful is harmonious. And that which is harmonious is united. So for health, wealth, and happiness, flood your consciousness with beauty, harmony, and unity. Be united as you are identified with the mental realms of thought. Be united in your thought, you will be harmonious in your act and beautiful in your expression.

Good night.

AUGUST 12, 1982

CONSCIOUSNESS CLASS 221

This is our third class of this semester of eleven classes. And so it's important that we have an exchange of thought and understanding about what we're studying.

Now, many, many words have been given about this philosophy and how it is applicable to our daily activities and what we do with it and what we don't do with it and why we do anything with it, if anything at all we do, do with it.

Everyone, of course, here understands that like attracts like and becomes the Law of Attachment. And we all understand, I'm sure, personal responsibility; that doesn't seem to be too tasteful to some of us sometimes. And yet, we seem to continue, off and on, in rather a cyclic pattern of having struggles and difficulties. We find change in our thinking, in our patterns of mind, very difficult. We find them extremely difficult when we want to change our attitude about anything, because we know only through changing our attitude can we change our experiences. We often slip into blaming others for our frailties in life and continue on with our struggles because we have yet to accept that demonstrable truth.

We seem to have a struggle and difficulty upon awakening in the morning and telling ourselves what a beautiful day it is because we know the truth: that the day, and life, it's ever the way we make it and it's always as we take it. And so if we don't make those little, simple efforts in life, the time comes when the struggle of life becomes more than we are willing to bear. It's called the weight of responsibility has exceeded our love of God.

It is important, in the study of anything, to express one's understanding of what they are studying, because our understanding in the studying of anything in life may be far different than what it is we're really studying. Because we are expressing through these eighty-one levels of consciousness and because these levels of consciousness react to the dictates of our mind, it is our mind that we must concentrate upon. Because only with the power of concentration can we ever gain control over our mind, which is the instrument that permits varying levels of consciousness to express.

Now, without control over the human mind and the thoughts that it expresses, there can be no freedom or abundant good. We never know just who we are because one level acts one way and another level in another moment acts an entirely different way. And because of our error of attachment and belief that we are the level at the moment of its expression, we have real problems. And we think, of course, that is us. We take a slight for an injury because we believe we are that level at that moment. We do not pause to think, to consider, and to question the mind itself, which is a constant instrument of questioning. We understand the mind is ever in need. And, of course, it is in need because it is a vehicle that gathers and garners; it is the very principle on which it operates. And therefore, an attachment to it is a life of struggle and is certainly not a life of peace nor of harmony.

One does not escape from the human mind. One educates the human mind. To attempt to escape from the human mind is to deny the responsibility of the human mind that we have earned in our evolution and all that it has to offer and is waiting to be educated. So escaping from it is not the path of the Living Light philosophy. Working with it, understanding it, and educating it is the path of peace and the path of prosperity.

The centuries untold that we have passed through—many lives prior to this one and many lives yet to go—can only be awakened within the consciousness when there is control over the vehicle of mind. Because only when there is control over the vehicle of mind can you stop the echoes that you hear when you try to be still. So the benefits, of course, of gaining control over the vehicle of the mind that we are expressing through are eternal benefits. They're not something that are just temporal.

And it is our destiny in eternity to awaken to the eternity that we are, not by believing some book that we read, not by believing what someone tells us, but by awakening within ourselves to what we are and who we really are, not what we think we are and, therefore, believe we are. Because we think one moment and we believe the next and we become the next only to learn at a later time that that really wasn't us at all. And then we question how we ever got into such a mess in the first place. How could we have been so ignorant and how could we have been so stupid?

And so we are not all of those things. And I'm sure we are aware of that. But what can we do with this moment, this day-to-day routine that we seem to permit to become the mountain that we have to climb? Only through our own personal effort, only when we see the value of making that daily effort will those mountains that we seem before us, slowly but surely, melt away.

Because we continue in this world of creation to find the better half of ourselves and because we've always looked outside—and the last place we want to look is inside—we're always looking outside for something, for someone to fill the gap. The gap that we all know exists within our consciousness. We know it's there. We certainly demonstrate it's there, because we chase creation everywhere to try to fill that gap. Time and again, we delude ourselves and we think the gap has been filled, only to realize, at a later time, that didn't fill the gap at all.

There's something missing. And it is true, there is something missing. And we're looking in the wrong place to find it. We're looking beyond ourselves. We're looking out at a world of creation and there it does not exist. It never did exist and it never will exist there. That is not where the fullness is. And it is only a waste of time, a waste of energy, and a waste of effort to chase the world over to try to fill that gap because you will never find anything or anyone that can fill it. It is not possible, for it does not exist out there.

Time and again, when I have asked students to spend the time to be still and to listen, to listen attentively, they don't want to hear what they hear. For the first thing we hear are the echoes of the uneducated ego. We hear the echoes of unfulfilled desires. We go through the seeming struggles of life and we do not permit our minds to see the good that is there. We do not see the opportunity, the opportunity for change.

Whatever we find in life that we find distasteful, that we find difficult, that we find such a struggle and so much to endure contains within it a golden opportunity to bring about a change in our consciousness. Now, if we look, we will see what that experience is offering to us: that someday we're going to have to make a change in our consciousness so that we can live more harmoniously and more abundantly. But we fight that. We resist that, for we find security in what has been. We find security in what has been only because we are familiar with it. And that which we are familiar with takes no effort to learn anything about it. We already know it. We're familiar with it.

Now that reveals to us that our security is based upon laziness. We don't have to make any effort to investigate, to research, to find out. So our security is based on what we already know and what has already been. Our security is based upon the shadows of life, for that's what the past is: an event that has come, that has gone, and only the shadow is left.

And if I find any of my students sleeping, I will ask what any decent teacher would ask: that they stand during class so that they may have value for what is given or be excused. Now, many people think I'm a bit of a strict teacher. I never knew anyone benefit and learn self-discipline without some degree of what you call strictness. If you cannot gain control over your mind long enough to be in a half hour or forty-five minute class without sleeping, then you have a great deal of work to do for the sake of your own soul, for your own life eternal. So I'm going to ask my students who are awake to nudge those who can't seem to stay awake long enough for the class to be given. It's known as the sleep of satisfaction.

I am very well aware of this blanket of sleep that comes over people, especially when you get a little close to the level of consciousness that's putting them to sleep. Stop and think, my friends. If you believe you are the one that is sleeping, you are in the wrong class. If you have awakened that you are permitting, through your own lack of effort, you are permitting yourself to be the victim of a thought form that you alone have created in your days of ignorance, *then* you have entered the right class. If you believe you are the thought that passes through your mind, then you have yet a long, long ways to go.

I am sufficiently in a mild trance to be well aware of who is sleeping and who is not sleeping. What classes and what teachings you receive, how high those teachings may be is dependent upon 51 percent of you, you people, you students, and your value, through demonstration, of what you are given. For only a fool casts their pearls before the swine of life. And I have never considered myself to be such a fool.

So if you want to sleep, we can make arrangements for everyone to take a twenty minute nap. I will go and walk the dog. I will return after your twenty minute nap, which will be deducted from the time allotted for your classes. And then we will finish up. Now, if that's what you want, I will be more than happy to accommodate all of you. If it is not what you want, then you, as students, will make the effort to stay awake. And so I excuse our chairman to turn the lights on in the lanai here and turn them on bright.

From now on, the lights will be on as an aid to you to help you, as individualized souls, to gain control over your mind long enough that you may endure a forty-five [minute] or an hour or half hour class meeting. That is why we are here. We are here for truth and freedom. That, my good students, is the effect of self-control. To think for one moment that you can receive truth and freedom without the demonstrable Law of Self-Control is total folly and you're wasting your time, your energy, and your effort in life.

Now, if you want to do your part in helping your co-students to stay awake to demonstrate some value for what you are receiving, then, yea, shall you receive more. If you do not have the consideration and care to do so, in keeping with the law that you alone are demonstrating, you will receive less.

Now, those of you who wish to have a nap for twenty minutes and I'll go walk the dog, as I said, please raise your hand. And we'll have a class recess for that time. Now, if you want to stay awake, if the class has some value to you, then I will continue to share these teachings with you. If you do not want to stay awake and demonstrate your value for them, then they shall not be. Perhaps now you understand in forty-four years of this work, I have never relied upon my spiritual work for my material sustenance in life.

Now, I'm going to permit you here, perhaps, to help you to awaken and once again gain control over your mind—the sleep of satisfaction—to ask your questions. You may do so by raising your hands. *[After a short pause, the Teacher continues.]* No questions? Then we can have our—

There's a question in the back.

Yes, please.

How does one dis-identify from the I?

How does one disassociate from the identification of the I?

Yes.

That is a very important question, a very, very important question. Because we, in our evolution, have entered the earth realm by the Law of Identification, by the thought of I, because of that, it takes a constant, constant process, a constant process of gaining control over the mind, that our soul has entered, to declare the truth, the demonstrable truth that you are an inseparable part of a whole. And because you are an inseparable part of a whole, you are a part of everything you see, hear, sense, feel, and witness; that you are, then, the witness of life, that you are that which views life. You are not separate from it, but you are the viewer of it.

Now, when the effort is made every day to declare the truth of what you are—the witness of life, that you are inseparable from it, but the viewer of it, that you are not affected by it, because you are in that position of viewing it—then you will, slowly but surely, free yourself from the bondage and the illusion of the thought of I. For the thought of I is that which limits you. It is that which builds all the struggles in life itself.

Because, you see, when you entertain the thought of I, in that process you deny, you deny the whole. You immediately put yourself into a separate position and therefore, in that separatism, you experience what is called need. Now, you cannot have want and need, you cannot experience that until you identify with the thought of I, which separates you from all that you are. Does that help with your question?

Yes.

You see, man chases the world of creation in need of this, in need of that, in need of sleep, in need of everything you can think of. It's a constant process of need because it is a constant process of identifying with the I, with the separate, with the limit. Does that help with your question?

Yes.

You're welcome. Yes, please, the gentleman over here on my right.

To my understanding, they say our adversities become our attachments. OK. Would you expound on that? And also, expound on how they show themselves or manifest in our everyday encounters or actions?

Thank you very much for your question. Our adversities become our attachments. The only reason and the only way that we can become adverse is through a lack of effort of understanding the cause of anything we are adverse to. Therefore, what happens is, from the laziness and lack of effort to understand a thing, we become intolerant. From that intolerance—that lack of effort, that laziness, that lack of understanding—we build up an adversity. We become adverse to the person, place, or thing. Because this has been born and takes place in the error of our own ignorance, in our own laziness, we have established that law unto ourselves. We direct energy to that form we have created, that form of our adversity. And that directed energy, creating that form, lives in our universe. And it's known as the chickens come home to roost. It knows its home. It knows where it was born. And it becomes our attachment. It is with us day and night, like a shadow. And so our adversities become our attachments; they are our own children.

Now, we may be adverse to a child we've given birth to, but only for a time, because in the adversity is the attachment. And also in the attachment to anything in creation do we become adverse. Now that very process keeps us free from the bondage, the limit, and the struggle of creation. You see, a person becomes attached to a person, place, or thing, and when the degree of attachment touches the eternal soul—and it's known, in man's thinking, as selling out your soul—the adversity comes in to save him. Does that help with your question?

Yes.

Yes, you're welcome. Yes, please. I'll be right with you.

It has happened many times where we think of an individual and somehow, either in a short while or perhaps that very same day, we're driving along the freeway and all of a sudden we see that individual. And I know it's by the law of—through imagination or visualization of seeing something. How can we apply that same principle, like in our everyday life, say for health, our wealth, or whatever goodness in life that we can visualize? What is the key or what is the principle?

Thank you very much. The key and the principle is quite simple: it's known as the divine expression. It's called desire. It is always interesting, I find in life, to note that when the desire for anything is sufficient, it always finds a way of fulfilling itself. Always. Now, we may think that, oh, we desire this and we desire that and etc., etc., but those are all those passing desires. There's a multitude of them. But when you have a desire for something or someone, you may be rest assured—and it becomes a priority in your consciousness—you may absolutely guarantee that it comes to pass, for that is the principle and the key through which it works.

Desire is a release of a phenomenal amount of energy out into the universe. And so whatever it is we really want in life, be always rest assured we really do get it.

I noted this evening—and I found it very interesting. I spoke to one of my students to speak to another one of my students on the divine principle and soul faculty of self-respect. And so I witnessed this evening with great interest, as I entered this class and the moments passed and I found some of my students snoozing off into those realms of the sleep of satisfaction.

Well, those of you who know me, know me well enough to know I have no problem speaking up. That has never been one of my problems. And I am very grateful for that. So the more of my students that seem to have a problem with sleeping, they'll sit up here next to me. And be rest assured, I'll have someone else to sit up here. Perhaps we'll get a special stick, like they used to have in the olden days to tap them on the head to keep them awake. Because if that's what is necessary, we have a very fine cabinet shop. And I guarantee you, I will have one made. Perhaps one for each hand, depending on how many students I have to have up here to keep awake to show some degree of self-respect and demonstrate that there is some value for this philosophy that has taken centuries to enter this earth realm. Thank you.

Now, this lady here, please.

I noticed within myself that there is a struggle, like two beings in one. And it seems to me to be an immense struggle that I deal with. And I was wondering if you might be able to tell me how I can—what would help.

Thank you very much. You are very fortunate: you only have conscious awareness of two that are in different directions? *[Many students laugh.]* Most of my students have about twenty! You never know which one you have to deal with. But, no, seriously, you see, it is a lack of control over the mind. You see, when you feel that you are—usually, these are direct opposites: one wants to do the good things in life and maybe it's just a little bit too good, and the other wants to do the bad things in life and maybe it's just too bad. Because they're quite extreme. So they've got to be brought together.

You see, we are spiritual beings expressing through animal form. Now, if we'll only understand that this human form of ours is an evolved animal—we call it a "human being." It is an animal with animal instincts. And the strongest instinct of the animal is survival. And very high on that list, very high on that list is food. And next to that—and high on that list—is procreation. So we're dealing with these very basic animal instincts. Now, here is this spiritual essence. Here are the soul faculties flowing through this animal being. And they kind of mix like oil and water.

And so it takes some talking to the animal side. Now, many philosophies will call it the lower self or higher self or this or that. Well, we like to look at it from a different view and see that this is the animal form of this particular planet. It has evolved through eons of time. And we are the spiritual beings that are expressing through it. Now, we've got to make friends with that animal side inside of us. And we can't make friends with it without communicating with it. And if we're not willing to face that this animal that we're expressing through has these various basic instincts that we find so distasteful, then we're not being honest with ourselves. So if you will work with those animal instincts and you will talk to them as you would a little child, you will, slowly but surely, educate them. Does that help with your question? And that's the way all people are. Remember, the greater the sinner, the greater the potential of sainthood.

Yes. The lady here, please.

Yes. I understand that when we sleep too much, we're serving the realms of, well, you said, self-satisfaction just now. But I understand the forms really take all our energy from our vital body at that time.

How do you feel when you wake up?

If I've slept too long, I feel terrible. The thing I was asking about is when a little dog is left alone, he seems to sleep all the time. Does that happen to him the same way?

He is a different type of an animal than you are. Thank you. You will find that most animals, when they're bored, [when] they have nothing to distract them, like most human animals, they go to sleep. Now, I find that most human animals if the TV, they decide, is not interesting and the panorama of pictures and sound isn't interesting, sitting in their chair, bored, they go to sleep. Would you not agree?

Yes.

So if a person decides that they're bored with anything, the first thing that you find them doing is going to sleep. They enter another dimension where there are all kinds of interesting things, known as their suppressed desires. So, you see, if we're not happy with life as we have made life, we find ourselves, slowly but surely, sleeping more and more and more and more and more. Because, you see, my friends, we're bored with what we have done to life. However, you have no conscious control when you are sleeping. And so you enter those realms of all the multitude of varied forms of suppressed desires. But that I would not consider living, for living is a conscious awareness of Life herself. Does that help with your question?

Yes. Thank you.

Thank you. Yes, the lady here, please.

Could you please distinguish between thoughts and ideas?

Yes, indeed. Well, it is very important to understand thoughts and ideas. An idea is best put as the essence of the principle of the Law of Fulfillment. The essence of the principle of the Law of Fulfillment. We will consider that an idea, for that, in truth, is what it is. Now, we will consider thought. Thought—a form gathered and garnered from experiences past, ever in want, in need, to reach its limits of satisfaction. Now, a thought will satisfy your senses, but an idea will fulfill your soul.

So many people, of course, have many thoughts of many things and they experience a multitude of temporal satisfactions. And they're always hungry, they're always hungry. I've yet to find a person who lives in the realm of thought that wasn't hungry. But ideas, you see, fulfill you, for they are that which is. A person can experience ideas through the effort of contemplation. Because when one contemplates a flower or an object, they move beyond the form to that which sustains the form. And that is what an idea really is. Does that help with your question?

Yes. Thank you.

The lady back of you, please.

Yes. I had a question about the balance of our spirituality in creation on the mundane plane when we're in the mundane plane every day of our work day and the balance of that, of the higher and lower self. And as we evolve more spiritually, how do we deal with that?

Thank you very much. Well, we're dealing, so to speak, with that every moment of every hour. Because we can be in the mundane world—and should be in the mundane world—there to serve the purpose of the mundane world and never without the spiritual world that we are. Now, we have a simple teaching that states clearly, "Put God in it or forget it." So put God where your thought is. Put God where your mundane job is. You see, it's up to you. It is within your power to put God in your work. It's in your power. It's in your decision, whether you want to do it or not. You can put God there or you can put man there and all that man and his mind has to offer. That's entirely up to you.

You see, we can put God in the class, as we are here, this evening, or we can put man and his sleeping and all the foolishness and the judgments and everything else that that has to offer, you see. The thing is, my friends, to do what you have to do because it's right to do it, but not be controlled by it. So you can do any job that you have in this old, mundane world in any way, shape, or form, and by putting God in your consciousness, you will not be controlled by what someone else is doing or not doing. You will be able to speak the truth, you see, if it is within your particular right that you have earned at that time in your evolution to do so. Because one must always use discretion in working in a mundane world. Discretion does not mean selling out, but when we're in Rome, we do as the Romans do, without being a Roman. Now, that's the vast difference, you know, in working in a mundane world: to do as the Romans do, while you are in Rome, you don't have to be a Roman to do it.

Close the door for the people, please. *[The Teacher gives an instruction to his assistant.]*

Does that help with your question?

Yes, it does. Thank you.

You see, if you know where you are, you don't have to be concerned about where someone else is or isn't.

[As the automatic door begins to close, the students realize that the door is closing upon them and they, along with their chairs, are forced to quickly relocate.]

Ah, are all the chairs in? Sorry. I didn't set the chairs [properly]. We must consider that situation back there for the next class. *[Speaking to a director, the Teacher continues.]* I'll check with you later who set the chairs that close to the door. You notice that there's plenty of room over there [on the other side of the room]. All right.

Yes, the lady here, please.

If the appearance of ill health is manifesting in form, which one takes personal responsibility for that manifesting because of attitudes of mind that one is not really in touch with—what they are—does one need to understand what those attitudes of mind were that we were holding that is manifesting the appearance of ill health? Or does one just need to put their attention on the affirmation and who and what we are in truth and hold to that?

Thank you very much. Yes, you are absolutely right. By declaring who and what you are in the eternal moment, which you have power, will have its effect upon the attitudes of mind that caused the problem in the first place. Now, to permit the mind to search through the computer to try to find out which attitude caused such and such, and such and such only strengthens the attitude as it prepares for its defenses. Do you understand?

Yes.

So, you see, by declaring the truth in the eternal moment of which you are consciously aware—those attitudes and things, they have an effect. They become affected by your new attitude of declaration.

Now, when you have evolved to the point where you are free from the condition, you may search your computer if you are in the Law of Disassociation and not attached to that which has been, you understand, and you can search out and see those various patterns that have brought about the condition. But never do that while you're going through it, because you only prepare those forms, those armies, for their defenses to fight you.

You see, it's like a person going on a diet. Now, they will work diligently and they will suppress all of those forms and desires and they may lose a lot of weight. But it does not last, because, you see, those forms that caused the problem in the first place, they all rise up and they retaliate. And then you're worse off than you were before you ever started. So it's the same thing in working with your health.

Be not concerned with those shadows that have been, but work with what you are this moment. Does that help with your question?

Yes. Very much. Thank you.

You're welcome. Yes, the gentleman in the back, please.

Yes. I have a question about, first of all, desire is the expression of the Divine. If I should have a goal or an objective and a desire, I have a choice of either fulfilling or educating that particular desire. And as I look at my goal or objective, which is also a desire and, in my heart, I have a desire, my mind says, "Well, do not fulfill this desire at this particular time." Am I correct in doing that and attempting to educate that desire to put it aside in order to do what I think I need to do in order to attain that goal or objective?

Yes, that's an excellent question. You see, first of all, you must understand that you have decided and established the law, as man is a law unto himself, that such and such shall take place in order to attain your objective or your goal. Do you follow me?

Yes.

Fine. Anything that interferes with that must be educated as a desire or fulfilled. Now, if, in the fulfilling of it, it simply puts your goal, your objective farther away from you and you do not want to wait that long, then the only thing to do is to educate the desire. Now, the desire—to educate it, you know, doesn't mean to suppress it. To educate the desire is to be consciously aware of it and talk to it and work with it. You see, a person may say, "Well, I educated a desire." And every time you turn around, the thing is haunting them. It's popping up in their mind. That is not an educated desire. But it is the absolute revelation of a suppressed desire. Does that help with your question?

Yes.

Certainly. The lady in the back, please.

On that same subject, I have a great deal of difficulty in understanding what it is you say to a desire that makes it not be suppressed.

Thank you very much. Now, well, let's take a desire—well, let me see, here. Well, let's take apple pie a la mode. It seems a lot of people like hot apple pie a la mode. Now, say that we have a desire for hot apple pie a la mode. And we say to that desire, "Now, just a minute. No, I'm not going to have that apple pie a la mode. No." That didn't get a bit educated. It sure got suppressed. Nothing was done to educate it.

Now, to educate a desire, you must never leave it without hope, because hope is essential to the education of desire. Now, hope is eternal and truth is inevitable. You do not leave desire without hope. Because to leave desire without hope, you only suppress it. You guarantee its retaliation inside yourself. Now, so the apple pie a la mode desire has risen up and you say, "No, not now." That's not a bit of education. There's not an ounce of hope. It's total suppression.

Now, you talk to the apple pie a la mode and you say, "Not at this time because I am in the process of losing weight. And I do not wish to have that. However, I do feel that in a few months, we will be able to have a piece of apple pie a la mode." Now, you've got to be a little bit clear about that, because the little apple pie a la mode says, "A few months?! Oh, my God. Well, what day?" *[Many students laugh.]* And it goes through all this. Because you have to understand it's created by your mind.

So depending on what type of mind—is your mind very specific about things with your desires? If it's very specific, then those desires of yours are very specific. And you've got to treat it as you treat yourself, you understand? You believe it's you, so you've got to treat it that way. So if a person is very general, you say, "Well, within a few months." And it has no problem: it still is left with hope, because it knows you. You gave it birth. It's your mind. Do you understand that? Now, if your mind is very specific and it is very detailed, you say, "Three months on the twelfth day of such and such hour," that it may continue to live. It must have hope that it may live, grow, and be educated.

Now, most people in their efforts to educate a desire do nothing but suppress it and live in total frustration. You see, it's like a student here in class—or students. And they think they are sleepy. Well, they could tell the desire, "Now listen, at such and such a time you can bomb out. There's no problem at all. But right now, you'd better stay awake or you know what's going to happen around here." Don't you see? That's educating the desire. You must talk to it as the type of mind that you have. Does that help with your question?

Thank you.

Then you won't have any problem. You won't have any problem at all. Any other questions? Yes, the gentleman here, please.

In our book, The Living Light, *there's a discourse that mentions the soul faculty of duty, gratitude, and tolerance, corresponding sense function of self, pity, and friendship. And could you please explain how friendship corresponds with tolerance?*

Well, I have never ever in my life experienced a friendship that didn't require a phenomenal amount of tolerance. Now, perhaps someone else has. I just never have. Because, you see, my friends, without tolerance, there is no friendship, because friendship, being use and not abuse, respects the rights of difference and will weather any storm. Now that takes a phenomenal amount of tolerance. Would you not agree?

Correct.

At least it does for me. Is there any other question about tolerance and friendship?

Thank you.

You're welcome. Yes.

If one is trying to accept everything around oneself as a demonstration of God, how come we have so many tests to show that we don't have acceptance of all these levels that come bombarding us?

Thank you very much. The test, of course, is our lack of tolerance. All tests reveal to us the degree of our tolerance in life. Now, we might meet a person and say, "Oh, my God, are they a real test! Indeed, they are." As our tolerance starts to grow and expand, they become less and less of a test. So it is entirely up to our efforts in expanding, you see, and broadening our horizons in gaining understanding of why people do the things that they do.

Now, when we understand—it's like a person sleeping in class, or persons—when we understand why they do things (what is it in their character and fiber that created this weakness), then we don't have any problems with our tolerance anymore. Because through our investigation and effort to understand how they got to be the way that they are, we immediately open up the door to compassion. You can't make the effort to understand a thing—understanding, the very foundation of all the soul faculties—without experiencing some of the soul faculties, including compassion. It's not possible. So as you make that effort to understand a person, place, or thing—you really make that effort—your compassion and all of those soul faculties begin to awaken. And the test becomes nonexistent. Does that help with your question?

Oh, yes. Thank you.

Yes, please, the gentleman there.

And then, are you saying in the end result we are free of judgment?

Oh yes, we most certainly are. You cannot have understanding and still have judgment. The moment you understand a thing, there is no judgment left. There is nothing to judge when you understand. See, our teachings, of course, as all teachings, say, "In all your getting, get understanding," ah, but in all your giving, give wisdom. So when you understand, you cannot judge. We judge what we do not understand. And that's the only thing we ever judge. The only thing we ever did judge, the only thing we ever will judge is that which we do not understand.

You've heard many philosophers teach God is not a judge. How could God be a judge when God understands, for it is the very essence and principle of all life? Only man, in his laziness and lack of effort, does not understand and, therefore, judges. You cannot understand a thing and judge it at the same time. Yes.

Well, am I to understand, then, that when one has tolerance and gains understanding and then so-called, in the vernacular, our buttons will not be pushed by anything around us? We could be with a thing that we found that we had a lack of tolerance before and it just—our rapport, we no longer have rapport. Therefore, it really doesn't matter where we are or what we do, because, in truth, we would be at peace anywhere.

That is correct. Absolutely and positively correct. Because, you see, there are no buttons to push if there is understanding. You see, he who understands a thing controls the thing. There is no need when there is understanding. There is no want when there is understanding. There is fulfillment, but there is no satisfaction. Yes.

Then, in truth, we would never have to—am I correct in understanding that we would never have to move from job to job, from mate to mate, from house to house? We could be at peace right where we are always.

Always. Where you are, wherever you are, because it's in consciousness where you are. You see, the physical move or the physical change is only necessary as a reinforcement of the effort to change in consciousness.

Now, for example, it's like a person—they want to make a change. Say, they want to stop, well, whatever habit pattern they may have. People have varied ones. And they want to stop it. Well, as long as they have support in making the change, they're able to stop. So the physical movement of anything is only the support to keep the effort going in consciousness to bring about the change.

Now, you can bring about the change through the powers of concentration. Say that you want to be in Hawaii. Well, you can be in Hawaii this instant, this minute. And you can actually be there. That takes a great deal of concentration, which is the control of the human mind, but that is really all that's necessary. Now, a person has—they have the thought, "I would like to go to Honolulu." All right. Now, when they have that thought, associated with that thought is a multitude of varying changes, which causes a physical movement to support those changes so they can be there. That is not necessary. Man has made that necessary. He made all of those different steps necessary to have the experience. The law doesn't make it necessary; only man's law made that necessary. Yes.

May I ask one more question, please?

Certainly.

If one finds themselves in a business dealing that does not seem to be an optimum thing and does not appear to be, do we need to remove ourselves from that or would a change of our consciousness, if it appears that we are being taken advantage of—

Depends if we have control. If we have control, then we can make all the changes in consciousness. If we do not have control, then there are other laws and factors involved. You see—for example, if we are involved in a business situation, or any kind of situation, and we do not have the control over it—that means over 51 percent of the entire operation; we must have 51 percent or more—if we do not have that, we do not have it in consciousness and, therefore, cannot bring about the change in consciousness because we have someone else who has that in consciousness. Now, if we do have that 51 percent in consciousness, we can bring about that entire change in consciousness. Absolutely and positively. However, if we are on the other side and we only have, say, 49 percent, then physical steps are necessary to bring about that change for us.

Thank you.

Yes. You're welcome. Yes, the lady here, please.

If we were totally free—

If? We are. We are. We're just not aware of it. Thank you.

Thank you. If we had total control of our mind—is that a better way of putting it?

Yes.

And we imaged ourselves, let's say, in Hawaii, as you said, would it be possible to literally physically move ourselves there by apport?

Absolutely. It wouldn't be the first time it has happened. I am sure it won't be the last.

Thank you.

But before we enter those steps, I think we should consider the multitude of laws necessary before getting that far, because maybe we'll get there and can't get back. And I wouldn't want to see that happen to you. *[Many students laugh.]*

Are there any other questions? Yes, the lady here, please.

In situations and relationships, how do we gain the understanding in order to be more compassionate?

Thank you very much. In situations and relationships, how do we gain understanding in order to be more compassionate? By not placing the person in the involvement that we are attached to, by not putting him on the throne that belongs to God. See, man's biggest problem, or woman's biggest problem—by "man" I mean humanity—is in the attachment. God, the very power that frees us, gets moved off the number one throne almost immediately. And that's when the problems really begin, because we put form on the throne that belongs to the formless free Spirit. That's the only time the problem begins, is when we make that error.

Now, you can have all kinds of relationships and involvements and if you won't make that error, then you'll never have a problem. Never. And they'll understand it from the word go. And by understanding it: otherwise, there is no involvement; otherwise, there is no situation whatsoever to be concerned about. Does that help with your question?

Yes. Thank you.

Well, if it doesn't—I think you wanted to hear a different answer. But why waste time and energy in an involvement with anyone if we're going to move from the throne the very power that will free us from our own errors? Would that be very beneficial, do you think?

I'm sorry.

Form must never take the throne of the Formless.

Right.

Thank you. There was someone else who had a question. Right there. Yes.

Could you explain the difference between serenity and peace?

Well, that's the first time I've ever been asked the question between the difference of serenity and peace. It's as different as the sun and the moon. That doesn't help your question too much, I'm sure, because you want to know where the sun is. Well, of course, the sun is the light and that is the peace, for peace is the power that passeth all understanding.

Now, peace is the power that passeth all understanding. We've heard that many times, haven't we? And so that's the question. Well, then, what is serenity? We mean by "serenity"— we're now speaking of the word *serenity*, not a church or an organization. I would say in speaking of the word *serene* that it is an experience that is both fulfilling and satisfying. And that is a very narrow margin—to have both. Because a person—if they feel serene, they feel a bit satisfied, I would say. Don't you feel satisfied when you're serene? Perhaps a little bit fulfilled. But I wouldn't necessarily say that one was in a state of peace in order to have serenity. Many people feel serene while they're doing a multitude of different things. I wouldn't call it peaceful. I hope that has helped with your question.

Yes. Yes, the gentleman here, please.

I don't have a clear understanding, but I would like you to clarify the phrase, I guess you would say, "divine heritage."

Yes?

That's what I—

Your divine right? I don't recall using the word *heritage*. I may have, but—

I . . .

Pardon?

OK. I've seen it "divine right." And I've seen it "divine heritage."

Good. Well, you show it to me someday—won't you?—that word *heritage*.

Yes.

I'm sure it may be there, but your divine right—

OK.

You want an understanding on your divine right?

Well, I was—

What do you feel is your divine right? Do you feel you have any divine rights?

Yes, the ones—the natural and physical laws.

Those are yours?

Well, that's what comes off the top of my head, yes.

Those are yours. I see. Is there anything that you feel is not your divine right?

That's not my divine right?

Anything at all?

That's not my divine right?

Yes. Do you feel that there is anything that is good for you that is not your divine right to have?

I won't say "have," but I say "to do." There are some things, I feel, that it is not my divine right to do, especially when it involves another. But if I just think singularly about myself, then maybe not.

Well, anything that is good for you is your divine right. But that that is good for you does not involve another. Because if it does involve another, then you just limited your divine right. Now, if you don't understand that, you speak right up. All that is good for you is your divine right. The problems exist when you dictate how to get it. If you say, "This is good for me—now this involves another person," you have just limited your divine right. And that that's limited no longer is divine. Is there some further questions on that?

I still very clearly see this word—you said there's no mention of "divine heritage." I know I wrote it down because I didn't understand it—divine heritage. But divine right, yes, OK. That's pretty clear.

Well, we can—you show that to me after class that word *heritage*. It is possible it has been used. I just do not recall that word. But remember that anything and everything that is good for you is your divine right. But don't walk down the street and tell some lady, "Yes, you're my divine right," because it's no longer divine at all. *[Many students laugh.]*

Yes, the lady here, please.

There is a statement that truth is individually perceived. And the level that each of us perceives truth on, as I look at you, I would say you are north of me and you look at me and I am south of you and we're both right. Is it important that we go within ourselves? And to the best of our ability at that time perceive our truth for ourselves? Is that part of our growth—to know what is our truth?

That *is* our responsibility.

And if it differs from another—we can't take another's truth. We must take ours until we gain that understanding.

Absolutely and positively, because, you see, it is not ours until we perceive it as ours. It must come from within ourselves. All teachings, all truth, everything *is* within us. Now, this class is an instrument through which, through your own effort, you may awaken varying levels of consciousness and perceive *your* truth. Because truth *is* individually perceived. That is the only way we can know truth, is from within our own being. No matter how much studying that we do.

Yes, the lady here, please.

I'd like to know when we do have our own truth, how can we just keep ourselves from infringing upon another's right to their own truth?

By accepting what your truth is. It needs no defense. So, you see, truth does not have need and want, for truth *is*. So if you have your truth—which everyone has their truth: the truth is within them—you have no need to impose it upon another. You see? Truth is shared, as it is solicited. And that's a fine line of discernment. But it has no need and therefore one does not impose it upon—truth—upon another. It's contrary to its very nature—freed from need. Yes, the gentleman here, please.

OK. You're saying, then, that truth is understanding.

No, I didn't say that.

OK.

I said, in all your getting, get understanding and in all your giving, give wisdom. You can get understanding. You cannot get truth. You *are* truth. You are truth. You can get understanding.

OK. We use terms such as evolve and evolvement.

Evolvement?

Yes, sir.

Oh, in reference to the lady's situation of an involvement with another. Yes, I see.

No. Evolve. Evolvement. In other words, there is a progression and a transgression.

Ah, evolution. Yes, I see.

OK. Evolution. In gaining understanding from another individual, will we transgress and regress? Will we go, I mean, I hate to say, up? Or, well, will we have to come down to understand someone or will we go up? Or would that be making a judgment to say that?

You will always, always climb to fall. And the climb will be never higher than the fall as long as you identify with form. As long as you identify [with] the thought of I, you will experience the rise and fall of creation, for it is the Law of Creation. Now, one can live serenely in creation through the Law of Disassociation. Being with a person, place, or thing, never a part of a person, place, or thing, does not free us from personal responsibility, but it does give us the balance, the harmony, that is the beauty of life itself.

When we understand that all things, including thoughts, they come and by that very law and nature of coming, they also go, and when we let things, thoughts, attitudes, judgments go as freely as they have entered, we will live a more balanced life. But, you see, we hold to what has been rather than make the effort to be aware of what is. We think of yesterday and what some wrong someone might have done to us, but that puts a dark shadow on our today. We think of what someone said a half hour ago that might have hurt our feelings, instead of thinking of what is happening this moment, right now.

You see, this is—in the moment of your conscious awareness is the fullness of life. The fullness of life does not exist for you in yesterday. It does not exist for you in the thought that has just passed. It does not exist for you in the thought that is yet to be.

The fullness of life is that moment of now. And that is a moment by moment by moment situation in all eternity.

By gaining control over the mind, you can put it, with all its fullness, into the eternal moment and, in so doing, experience the joy of living. We exist because we think of what has been. We *live* when we think of what is. Most people, unfortunately, are existing. They are not living. There are too many shadows that drain their very vitality. "Oh, if I had done this," and "If I hadn't done that," all of that thinking (that type of thinking) is what has been. You can't do any good back there. There's nothing that you can change. That has already—you see, life is a stream of consciousness.

Now, you can allow this Intelligence, this Divine Intelligence to flow through you unobstructed or you can create obstructions in the river of consciousness. And you create obstructions and dams in that river by thinking of what has been or what is yet to be. Now, each time you do that, you dam up the river of consciousness and then things do not flow freely through you. You have a difficulty receiving and you have a difficulty giving, because you build all these dams by permitting your mental world to hold to forms that have gone. Those [forms] build dams in your river of consciousness.

And so you live in want, need, and desire because—you see, desire *is* the divine expression; that you cannot escape. But as desire enters through this river of consciousness, here is the obstruction, one right after another, as your mind thinks of what has been and what is going to be. Here are all these obstructions. And that you experience as want and as need, you see? That is not the divine plan of life itself and its fulfillment. It is because we have lost control of the mind. And it lives in the shadows of what has been and [is] creating shadows of what may be. Therefore it does not experience the fullness of what *is*.

We are missing life, the river of consciousness, because the energy is directed to that which has passed. And we are not conscious of the great joy that is. We live in pity, the pity of self, because self is so emerged in what has been, in all the frustrations of the mistakes that it made and what it could have done and what it didn't do and what it should be doing. And that is not the joy of living. But I do admit, it is existing. It is survival, the miracle of life. Does that help with your question?

Yes.

Any other questions before class concludes? Because we're running over. Yes, please.

In perceiving truth, is it perceived—is it received by the mind after it's, it's . . .

The mind—

It's the soul, isn't it?

The mind conceives and the soul perceives.

And then, I have a second part to the question. As the soul perceives, it registers on the mind, right?

As much as the mind will permit it.

And that's what I was going to say. Then, we're only perceiving on the level that we are permitting it to come through.

That is correct. Whatever the mind will permit.

Thank you.

And as the mind thinks less of what has been, more gets through in the river of consciousness, because there is less obstruction.

Thank you very much.

That, of all of these teachings in all of these years, is perhaps one of the most important of all things to try to understand, is the river of life, the stream of consciousness, and what our thoughts do in blocking that stream and why we have such great struggles and difficulties of getting or giving. Because, you see, we have difficulties on both ends. And in the getting and in the giving, there's an obstruction, because we're constantly, constantly relating to what has been.

Let go of what has been. There's nothing there for you. It has already served its purpose. Take control of your mind. And every thought that is related to what has been, let it go. Because in the moment you let it go, this river of consciousness of Infinite Intelligence will flow unobstructed through your being and you will be amazed at what you see that *is*, that *is*, that you could never see before because it was obstructed by your very thought processes of what had been.

Thank you very much. Have a wonderful dinner. Thank you.

AUGUST 19, 1982

CONSCIOUSNESS CLASS 222

Good evening, class.

Looks like I have plenty of water here. For this evening's discussion, I am sure we all realize and we all know that these problems that we seem to have in life are the effects of our lack of understanding. And we lack in understanding because, for some reason or another, personal to each and every one of us, we fail to communicate. And when we fail to communicate, of course, the effect is a lack of understanding, a narrowing of our horizon, and the problems, of course, in life, they seem to increase.

Now, what is one of the major reasons for our unwillingness to communicate? Well, when we stop and we look at these things, we quickly see that we all have an image of what we think we are. And that image, we cherish and we guard and we protect to the very best of our ability, because we believe that that image is us. And when something happens, through laws we set into motion, and the image we have of ourselves (that we believe *is* ourselves) becomes tarnished and scratched and damaged, we experience that suffering and those effects.

Now, we know, as we look through our life, that the image we hold today is different in many ways than the image we held years ago. So the demonstrable truth is that we are not the image. We never were and we never can be. So it is not reasonable, practical, nor sensible to continue to believe that we are the image that we hold in consciousness, because it is not a very reliable thing at all.

We base this unwillingness to communicate upon the experiences we have had in the past. We immediately judge that we tried in the past—and many times—to communicate with someone and the results, we judged, were not beneficial. Consequently, we continue on with that attitude of mind and we continue to suffer and we continue to struggle through life, when that certainly is not the divine plan. It certainly isn't a plan of any intelligent being to have to live that way.

To make a change from that type of thinking requires some degree of honesty with oneself. First, we must decide whether or not we want to live the way we think that other people think that we should live. Now, when we start to make these changes to be freed from the images of ourselves that we hold in consciousness, we have to use a degree of reason and wisdom. Otherwise, we find ourselves acting and thinking, "Well, I don't care what anybody thinks or does. I will do my thing!" And in that type of thinking, we totally disregard the Law of Personal Responsibility.

Now, we've heard through all of our classes through many, many, many, many years about the Law of Personal Responsibility: that all experiences we alone have set into motion. Someone else didn't do it to us. Only our thinking does it to us. Our thinking is so very important because the mental realm is what we have over-identified with. Therefore we must take an honest view of what our mental world is. And the experiences in our daily activities reveal to us, beyond a shadow of any doubt, what our mental world is. It is what we have created. It does not have to remain that way. It's entirely up to us whether or not we feel we want to change.

If a person feels they want to make a change, that is the first law necessary to establish, because without the feeling and the desire to make the change—any change that you so choose—the change cannot be made. It takes the force of desire to bring about a change in a person's life. Whatever change it is you want, you must remember, the desire must be there. And the desire must remain there until you experience the result. That takes some degree of control of the mind, because we desire something and then, the next moment, there is some other desire and, the next moment, there is some other desire. And this is the great problem and what is called, "Fools quit before the victory."

As you get closer to reaching your goal (the fulfillment of the desire) whatever it is—the desire—that you choose, as you get closer to the fulfillment of it, many things will distract you. You will find your mind going off in many, many different areas of consciousness. And the force needed to bring you to the finish line, no longer is there because it's being dissipated, now, into other desires. Now, we find that happening to us all the time. We start a job. We're great starters and certainly we find in life we have proven to be, too frequently, very, very poor finishers. Because we do not go to work on our mind and keep the force of desire on the goal that we have set for ourselves.

And therefore, everyone of us is successful. I'm happy to see that I have only successful students. Though some may feel they are failures, that's only success in the negative. What is failure to one person is a great success to another. So let us take a look at the law itself and see how beautiful it works: impartially, it does exactly what we ask it to do. We say we start this and we do this and we do that. And we've had one failure upon another failure. And once that pattern gets established, we are absolute experts in being successful failures.

Now look impartially at how that works. It isn't what anyone wants to experience—starting something and being a failure at this and failure at that. And everything they touch does not turn to gold; it turns to something else. And that seems to be the way their life goes. But look at the law itself. It is doing your bidding. It is doing exactly—not what you consciously are asking it to do, no, no, no—what you have put into your computer, your subconscious: what you have programmed. We always do get what we really do want. I said that years ago. It seems to be a hard pill to swallow. But it is the truth. We are experiencing today, each and every day, what we alone really want. And when we make the effort to be very honest with ourselves, we'll see, "My gosh, I don't like this. I don't like it at all. But being honest with myself, yes, this is what, somehow in my thinking, I've set into motion. I'm really getting what I want."

Now, many times early in life, as children, we learn to get affection; we learn to get attention by doing things that we are trained and taught not to do. We grow up and we become adults and we don't educate that level of consciousness, and we find ourselves doing things just like we did when we were children because we need the attention, the affection, that we get. And that's the only way we ever learned of getting it. That's very sad, but it happens to untold millions of people. They have—when they have a feeling that they need affection, they need attention, why they go right out and they have one disaster right after another. And there's always someone to give them the attention that they are seeking. Someone, somewhere is going to stop and listen to their tale of woes. And in that listening, they feel a little better that there's somebody who cares enough to listen to all these horrible disasters that they are having—how tough times are for them, that they're losing everything and everything's falling apart in their life. And they feel better after they have expressed their horrible tale of woe. But if there were no ear there to listen, I assure you there would be no tale of woe.

So going beyond these seeming effects, going beyond these experiences, we see a great need—a great need to be wanted, a great need to feel important. Because it *is* important to feel important. If a person doesn't feel important, if they don't feel good about themselves, be rest assured they do not live a life of goodness. You see, we must feel good in order to experience life. Feeling good, as I have said before, is not a luxury. It is an absolute necessity. For good is God. And God, we must experience in order to live.

We go through life surviving and living and surviving and living and spend most of our time, energy, attention in surviving. A little of that time, energy, and attention is in living. We live when we feel good and we survive when we feel any other way. Now, we all have, unfortunately, censored and restricted the way we will permit ourselves to know God or feel good. Knowing God, feeling good is one and the same thing.

We have, from our own experiences, judged that when certain things happen in our life, we will feel good. And when certain things happen in our life, we do feel good. And when certain things don't happen in our life, we don't feel so good. There's no law beyond our control that dictates that that is the way that it has to be. It doesn't have to be that way at all. We have made it that way. Because we have made it that way, we can change it.

Now, if someone else had made it that way, then it would really be a tale of woe. And it would really be a sad day. But we all know that we've made it that way. And we all know, because we've made it that way, we can change it *if* we are ready. First of all, take a look at the many things that your mind tells you that will make you feel good. See if the list is a short list. See if it's a long list. First, be sure you look to see if it is dependent on anyone else. Now, if your feeling good, knowing God, is dependent upon another person, you really have a tale of woe. You really have a terrible struggle in life because you will never control another person, how they think, how they act, and what they do. You have placed yourself in a very difficult level of consciousness.

So the first thing to do is to see on your list of what you will permit for you to feel good or to know God if there is any person there. If there's a person there, go to work on that judgment in consciousness and get them rooted out of your consciousness. Root them right out immediately. Because you are in bondage, a slave and a victim.

Now, that doesn't mean that a person should not be married. That does not mean that they should not, as they say, love another person. But what is love? It's only the reflection in another of the goodness in oneself. And that reflection is totally dependent upon your own judgments. A person loves you or doesn't love you dependent upon your judgments. If you say, "Now, this person loves me because they act like they love me. They do this. They do that." And, of course, it's totally in keeping with your judgments. And when they stop doing this and they stop doing that, or possibly you start changing your judgments, they fell out of love with you. You can't imagine what's happened, but there has been a change: they don't love you anymore. What it is [is] you no longer experience the reflection of the goodness in yourself. That's what it is. You see, love is the reflection in another of the goodness *in yourself*. So you can no longer experience this, what you call love, because your judgments have closed it off.

Now, it's not the other person. It never was the other person. It never will be the other person. It's all your own mind and what you do, or you don't do, with your mind. Therefore you go to work immediately, if you see on your list of how you will experience God or feel good—which is one and the same—you go to your list and see if there's a person there. That's what you must root out in consciousness. Because that places you in your own bondage.

Now, to root a person out of your consciousness is really a very simple thing: you put God, which is that love and that experience you need, where you've got that person. And you keep that *[God]* there and that form (that person) will disappear in your consciousness. That does not mean a person should not be married. That does not mean that a person should not experience the reflection of goodness in another, you see, this thing you call love. But it does mean that if you want to live a life of freedom, a life of truth, and a life of abundant good, you must be honest with yourself and you must take a look at your list of judgments of what you will and will not permit for God to enter for you to live more abundantly and more fully.

Once you have done that, it is necessary to check your list every day—sometimes several times a day, because the bondage of judgment that the soul has already been trapped in for eons of time does not disappear just because one day you take a check to see where all of these chains of bondage are in your consciousness. That took eons of time for those to have control over you. But you do check each day, several times a day, and you gradually, slowly but surely, become aware of all of those things that stand in your way.

There is no limit, there are no impossibilities to the eternal soul and what can or cannot be done. There are no obstructions outside of the mental world that we alone have created and continue to create. Each time that you decide that you want to bring about a change in your life, you have to face all of those forms that are surviving from your directed energy: your children. You must face them. Now, you don't just tell them to go away, because it doesn't work that way. They have been created in a mental world. They have no eternal life. Their life, their creation is totally dependent upon the energy directed to them, through your attention.

This is why when you place your attention, your energy, upon the obstruction in your life, the obstruction becomes, yea, even greater. That's how the law works. Because, you see, for example, the obstruction in whatever you are endeavoring to do has been created by your mind. Now, you can say all you want about the economy or what someone else did, but that does not change that you alone have created the obstruction in your consciousness in the world in which *you* live. Therefore, you are not only responsible for the world that you alone have created in that mental world, but by placing your energy, directing your energy, through your attention, to the obstruction, you only strengthen the obstruction. For he who sees the obstruction never finds the way. There is no energy to find the way. It is all going to the form of the obstruction. Now that takes not only daily effort, it takes practice on controlling the mind.

You see, my friends, the soul cannot experience into your consciousness its true freedom until your mental world is under control. And the mental world—your mental world, my mental world, everyone's mental world—is not going to get under control until the effort to put it under control is made. And that is an effort that is every single day of the week. Now, if you feel that that just takes too much of your energy and that takes too much of your effort, then you have made your choice to serve the forms of your creation. But someday, we all can be rest assured, someday we will get very tired of serving those things.

By not placing your attention, which is your energy, on the obstruction, the form of the obstruction begins to disintegrate in consciousness. And the day comes, for you, it no longer exists. The seed is always there, you see. It's always there, but you don't have to water it and feed it and have it grow again unless that's what you want to do.

Now, we're going to take a little time here, this evening, for you to communicate. It is very important that you speak forth that which you feel, or don't feel. It doesn't matter how important or unimportant it may seem to someone else, because that's what this class is all about. You're here to awaken in consciousness, to declare your own divinity. The only thing that stands in our way is what *we* think about what someone else thinks concerning us. Now, as long as we live in that realm of consciousness, we are going to be bound, we're going to suffer, and we're going to have to pay the price.

I am trying to share with you the freedom, which is yours—that you already have—that isn't expressing itself, yet, because of what, through error of thought, our minds are doing to us. They don't have to do these things. There is no law in the universe that makes it some kind of an inevitable experience. It is not necessary to suffer. It is not necessary to do without. It is not necessary to have these failures. It is not necessary to have these disasters in life. It is not necessary. We, through an error in our thinking, only we are making it necessary.

We understand—and it is demonstrable—that God is goodness; that we must feel good in order to live; that none of us, in truth, want to just survive. Because what is survival? Who wants to just survive in life day in and day out? We make robots that could do those jobs. We're here to live, not just to survive. But we cannot *live* without feeling good. And we cannot feel good until we gain control over what we call our reality, our mental world.

The spirit world is in the here and now. It is viewed and it is known when our mental world is in control. And we set it there to keep its mouth shut, by keeping its mind shut, so we can be still, so we can pause, so we can experience that which is eternal, that which we are. But we cannot experience that until there is control over the mental world and all of the things it has to broadcast into our consciousness.

So we will take a few moments here, if you'll raise your hand, I'll be happy to share with you anything in reference to your questions. Yes, the lady in the back, please.

Can you tell me how do you know, when you're doing creative work, whether or not it's coming from spirit guides or whether it is something that is your own creation or development?

Thank you very much. The feeling that comes during the work—not what is after, but during the actual process of the work—reveals to the channel, to the person, the source from whence it cometh. Now, no one can tell you, looking at the result, if that was out of your brain or that was out of your soul or that was a spirit guide or teacher. Do you understand? But your feeling that you experience during the actual work—if that feeling is a good feeling and you have a harmonious experience in the process, you can be rest assured, that is coming from something beyond the mental world. And that's what's important. Yes. Because, you see, you must remember, when something is viewed, it is viewed and it is judged by the limits of the human mind. All of history has shown us that which had no value centuries ago has risen in great value. But in its day and time, the minds of men saw no value to it. So we must go by the experience we are having at the time that the work is being done.

Thank you.

You're welcome. Yes, the lady here, please.

Would that hold true for any situation?

Yes, it holds true for all situations. Now, let us discern between the difference of being satisfied and feeling good. There's all the difference in the world. Now many people have a multitude of experiences. They are very satisfied. But one thing about satisfaction—it doesn't last. Feeling good is something that endures. Satisfaction rises you to this great self-importance and drops you and you live in regret. So we must discern between the difference of satisfaction and goodness, for there's all the difference in the world in feeling good and being satisfied. Now, a person can eat and eat and eat and eat and eat and say, "Oh, I am so satisfied," and a half hour later have such a stomach ache they don't know what to do with themselves. They were satisfied; they weren't feeling good. There is quite a difference. Yes.

Thank you.

You're welcome. The lady here, please.

Can any endeavor be made successful by continuity of effort or are there some things that, once they do not seem to be going right, should just be dropped and perhaps a different path taken? And how could you know the difference?

Thank you. That's a very, very, very important question. Can any endeavor be successful through the Law of Continuity? If, in asking the question, you are referring to the Law of Continuity, which is indispensable to the Law of Evolution, which is indispensable to the Law of Change, then, yes, any endeavor, through the Law of Continuity, can be successful. But remember, as I said a moment earlier, in the Law of Continuity is the ingredient of the Law of Evolution, which is the Law of Change. All right. Now, understanding that any endeavor, through that Law of Continuity, the ingredient of evolution and change, can be successful, the question must arise, Are we willing or do we desire to pay the price?

Now, creation has a very high price tag, a very high price tag. And we must honestly ask ourselves the question, Do we want to pay that price? Now, if the answer is affirmative, then we go on through the months, days, weeks, or years paying the price, knowing that the change is inevitable: that through the Law of Continuity we and what we are responsible for are evolving. Ofttimes—most times, people do not want to pay that high of a price in creation. And therefore they let go—it has served its purpose—and they move on to something else.

Now, I understand you are referring to a situation in creation—is that correct?—of a material world.

Yes.

Yes. This is what is so important. We ofttimes have a desire and we are very enthused and we make mistakes and the years pass and we find ourselves in situations that it seems we must make a change to survive. One does not throw the baby out with the bathwater. But if one has something that they believe is worthwhile, is good and circumstances and conditions are such that energy is needed in other areas of consciousness, then they direct energy into other areas of consciousness; they keep the baby and throw out the bathwater. I hope that has helped with your question.

Yes. Thank you.

You're welcome. Yes, please.

I would like to know, does any part of judgment enter into the decision making process?

Thank you very much. There's a vast difference between decision and judgment. Decision contains within it the Law of Consideration and it considers all things. And judgment, it considers all things for itself alone. Judgment never considers the price of creation. Decision does consider the price of creation.

Now, a person makes a judgment based upon patterns of mind that they have served for a long time. A person, faced with a situation, who makes a decision has the intelligence, the wisdom, and the reason to wait [and] weigh out in their consciousness for a minimum of seventy-two hours, that all levels may rise to speak. And then they can weigh out whether or not they want to do this or they want to do that. A person faced with a situation who does not weigh out in consciousness for a minimum of seventy-two hours—it takes that long for the average person to go through the eighty-one levels of consciousness—who does not take that necessary seventy-two-hour time to weigh out is controlled by a few levels of consciousness. And when the other levels of consciousness rise up—and they're guaranteed to rise someday—they live in regret; they live in regret.

Now, ofttimes, making a judgment, we do things that later we're sorry we did and we wish we could change. We can change them, but usually our pride will not permit that to be. Sometimes a wife has a fight with her husband. She makes a judgment and tells him that's it (in that moment). And the next day she's very sorry and she wished things could be a different way. Now, if she has grown, or he has grown, in any degree, spiritually, they have a talk, a discussion, and they move on. But if pride is in the way, it is not possible for understanding to express itself. Does that help with your question?

Thank you.

You're welcome. Yes, please.

What if there aren't seventy-two hours? What if the choice has to be made sooner than that?

Well, it is most interesting. Many years ago I was asked the same question. You will find in all life's experiences there is always seventy-two hours. Always. For the law is very clear: we are ever and forever forewarned. You will never, in life, face a situation in which you have not had seventy-two hours to make your decision. Now, it may appear that, out of the blue, seemingly accidentally, you have to answer right away. But if you are honest with yourself, you will see that you did have, up to that point, at least seventy-two hours in which you could have prepared yourself. Do you understand that?

Yes.

Thank you. You're welcome. Yes.

When one has the feeling of letting go of something and the feeling is good and yet the mind, at that particular time, seems to get in right away and says, "Well, that's not the way it's supposed to be," but yet the feeling is there. And it's a different feeling—that it could be possibly, I guess, with the continuity. I can't understand that feeling, but sometimes it is there. And the mind fears something of letting go.

Yes. Thank you very much. The mind always fears. You see, that's how the mind, that's how the mental world controls the spiritual world, in the sense the spiritual world is not freely expressing itself until the mind is under control. You see, it's fear. What you call fear—what anyone calls fear—we understand to be, of course, faith in the negative. But what you call fear is the patterns of mind rise up and they tell you, you are not going to annihilate them. It means when, in your experiences in life, you are about to do something that is contrary to the patterns of mind, the forms of creation in your particular mental world that you have been feeding and you have been serving—you see, they're created in a mental world by your mind. They are mental substance.

Now, because they are created by you—you are the father and the mother—they are aware of all mental thoughts you have. They are aware of what you're going to do, of what you have done, and what you are doing. They are very alert and very aware, because their survival is dependent on what *you* do. Now, when you are about to make a change and do something that is contrary to their getting the necessary energy from you for their survival, they rise up and you experience what is known as fear. That's how they control you. That's the only way they do control you. This, my friends, is why change is so difficult for people to make.

Show me a person who has little or no control of their mind and I will show you a person who it's almost impossible to bring about a change. The more discipline, self-discipline, the more control you have over your mind, the less fear in life you will experience. So if you're not willing to make the effort to gain more control over your mind, then you must suffer the experiences of what is known as fear.

You see, as the gentleman said, when you're about to make a change, you feel good about doing a certain thing, but it's not the way it's supposed to be. Well, now who is telling you that? Who is it that says, "Well, now, this isn't the way it's supposed to be." Well, those are the patterns of mind, the forms, you have created. First, they tell you this isn't the way it's supposed to be, because they know that you're going to start directing this energy, this life-giving energy, to something else. They're a part of your mind, my friends. And then, if that doesn't work, if their forewarning doesn't work and you continue on to make this change that you feel good about making, then fear rises. Fear—the final battleground.

Why does man fear death? Man believes in death. He fears it because, you see, my friends, when your soul finally pulls itself free from the mental world, the forms of the mental world no longer survive. So-called death, transition, is a terrible experience to those who are over-identified with the mental world of self because it's all the forms—they all die. That's what dies. You don't die. You can't die because you weren't born. Because you're not born, you can't die. But if you permit those forms within you to constantly get you to direct energy, through attention, to them, through the greatest of all magnets, called belief—you see, remember that the magnetic world is the world of belief. Without belief, form, you cannot experience. You can only experience form because of the magnet of belief, which is the Law of Identification.

You want to be free from fear? Only through self-control can you be free from fear. You know, a person says, "Well, I'd like to do this. I feel good about going and doing that," you see. And all the fear rises up because it's a total change. And those other forms, they will no longer get the energy that they are after.

This is what happens—like I spoke earlier in reference to your goal in life, in reference to getting something worthwhile accomplished. Just before the victory come the hissing hounds of hell. Well, the hissing hounds of hell—the only thing those are, are the forms created from past experiences. And they rise up screaming their heads off because, you see, your energy now is going to go to feed new forms: the forms of your new success. They do not die easily, for man does not let a thought in his consciousness go easily.

Stop and remember the times when you wanted to let something go, that a thought was plaguing your mind and you didn't like the thought. You didn't want that thought. How easily were you able to root it out of your consciousness? Not very easily.

Only through the Law of Transmutation, only by desire, the divine expression. When you have an experience that you do not wish to have and it continues to repeat itself in your consciousness, use the Divinity to redirect. Because that's the only thing—that's the great power flowing through the mental world known as force, the force of desire. Desire will keep you awake. Desire will do many things for you. It's the expression of God, the Infinite. Learn to use desire for the greater good and not to feed the forms that have gone, that brought you no good.

I mean, after all, there were things twenty years ago you desired that you certainly would not desire consciously today. Yet they rise up and you feed them energy. For what? They are shadows. They are not that which is constructive and good. Take a look. That that has been served its purpose. Why call it forth to feed it energy, to shadows that are not constructively working?

Remember, the effect of your directed energy, through the vehicle called the mind, creates a form. Now, it's these forms in creation—your creations—they go out into the universe, you see, and they bring back to you—they are your workers. You see, we're not using our mind in the way that it has been designed to be used. You have a thought. It is a form. Now, that form has your life-giving energy. Now, if you're paying an employee to do a job, don't you supervise what the employee is doing? Do you just automatically just tell them, "Oh, go, now that's what you do," and you go on and do your thing? Because you're not a good business person if you do. You've got to monitor them. You told them to do that. Now, is that what they are doing? And you periodically check. Well, it's the same thing with all these forms you create by your thought. Now, you have this thought; it is sent to a form; it goes out into a mental world. Do you check to see if that form is doing what you sent it to do? No, my friends, that's the great failure and sadness of life.

Speak your word forth into the universe knowing it shall not come back to you void but accomplish that which you send it to do. How do you know if it's accomplishing that which you send it do? You don't know because you don't monitor. You're not aware of your thoughts. Therefore, these armies, created—constantly being created—the ones that have been created are draining your very lifeblood. You don't know what they're doing unless you're honest with yourself and say, "This is my experience. Look at this mess that I'm in. Ah, I did not check to see what these workers were doing. And they've been goofing off and look at the price I'm now having to pay!" Don't you see? That's the way it works in that world—the same way that it works in this world!

You don't give a person a job and expect them automatically to do it the way you want it done when you don't make the effort to monitor them and see that it's done the way you want it done. But you have a thought, you create a form. That worker—are they goofing off? Have you checked to see what they are doing? There's where the problem really lies. We are not making the effort to monitor the forms of our own creation.

Now, you don't have to be a bit psychic to see whether a person is monitoring those realms. All you've got to do is look at this physical world. Do we tell a person to do a job and then go on about our selfish little desires doing our thing or do we tell a person to do a job and ten minutes, an hour, a half hour later, do we repeatedly go back and check to see that their doing the job the way we instructed them? Well, if we don't, then we must expect the disasters of life, because that's what we're doing in our mental world with our thoughts, you see?

Thoughts are forms, be they angelic or the opposite. If they are angelic, then you have made them so. And if they remain angelic, then you have kept them so through your own personal efforts to monitor them. Now, most people don't want to be bothered with what [has become of] the thought they had and what's happening to it. They don't want to be bothered with that, you see. That's why they don't want to be still and become aware of what's speaking in their heads, because, you see, they come back and they've got to be fed. What person would feed a human being that is not doing the job that they sent them to do? No, that's not a bit practical. Don't believe in that at all.

You know, I realize that publicly not much is said about the forms of creation, but most all philosophies are very well aware of it. They call them all kinds of different things—demons and everything else. But you've got to remember what they're talking about are soulless creatures. And soulless creatures are not of a spiritual world. They are of an astral world, a mental world. They're soulless. They exist only from your energy. Without your energy, without your attention, they return into the substance from whence they were created.

Now, there are many ways—and that has been one of my responsibilities of life—[of] working with those forms to return them to the substance from whence they were created. That's part of my daily work right here with students. It has been for forty-four long years of my life. And it still is. Sometimes students will say, well, when they're finished, they feel much better. Well, I often have said to myself, "I wish it was in order that they could see what is really taking place." It isn't what you say. It's what you do while you say it.

Now, most people, they can say many things. That's not where it is. It's what *you* are doing in consciousness. I have students who come—they feel good or they don't feel so good. They have this, they have that. Well, it has been my job in life to send the armies back to where they came from. Then the soul rises. It feels great for a time, until they return and call them forth again and feed them.

We must—my friends, that's why we are in these classes—we must face that truth someday and stand guardian at the portal of our thought. Someday we must face that truth because, you see, here is your best chance. Here you do not consciously see them, feel them, hear them, smell them, and sense them.

You leave the physical buffer and that's where we live. And it's much more difficult. *Here* is where your real chance is. *Here*, on Earth, is your great opportunity—that you don't have to battle for the centuries in those realms.

The Catholics call it purgatory. Someone else calls it the astral realm. Go down the list of the names, it's still the same. It's still the same. Many artists have depicted them on canvas—all those different forms. Of course, they exist. But they are soulless creatures. But they can do—and *do* do—anything your mind is capable of doing. They know what you're about to do, for they are a part of your thought process. And if you're about to go contrary to what they want for their survival, then you've got to be diligent and you've got to put God in it or forget it.

Now, it's a beautiful truth. But it means a lot more than those few words: you put God in it or you forget it. And where you put God is in your thought. You put God in your thought or forget your thought, for the act is nothing but disaster. Now, a lot of times people say, "Well, I put God in my thought." Well, we know very well whether or not we put God in our thought because we are not stupid. We know what the result is. And the result is the revelation and the demonstration of whether or not God—goodness—was in our thought and stayed in our thought. Then we see very clearly.

So by putting God—don't you see, what you do when you put God in a thought—say you have a thought, well, maybe you have a thought of strawberry shortcake or something. Well, if you put God in the thought of your desire for strawberry shortcake, then it doesn't matter whether you have it today, tomorrow, next year, or the year after, because you know you're going to have it. And because you know you're going to have it, it doesn't matter what minute, what hour, what day, or what year. That's when you've put God in it. Now, you can always tell when God's not in it, because you've got the thought and the desire, and you're panting like a dog waiting for it to happen!

God's not in it. God's nowhere near it. So when God is in it, you know and you're grateful that you've got it. It doesn't matter what day it happens. It doesn't even matter what century it happens. Because you know beyond a shadow of any doubt that it happens.

Thank you very much. And have your refreshments.

AUGUST 26, 1982

CONSCIOUSNESS CLASS 223

Well, good evening, everyone. This is class number five, I believe. Is it?

Yes.

Well, like they say, five down and six to go. *[The Teacher laughs.]* I take that in a positive vein.

Now, this evening we want to discuss, for a little while here, about the importance of thinking. We've been talking about that directly and indirectly for some time.

But I'm sure if we're honest with ourselves, we will soon realize that we are very, very interested in what other people think about us. That makes a very difficult life. It is never, and should never be, important what other people think about you. It should be extremely important what you think about yourselves, for your experiences in life are totally dependent upon what you're thinking about you.

Now, if you are thinking about yourselves in a negative state of concern, an interest of how other people will react to you, what they will think about you, etc., etc., and etc., then you do have indeed a very, very difficult path to trod through this Earth journey and hereafter.

So we must spend a moment or two to analyze and to consider why we are so interested in what people think about us. It obviously reveals a need within us—a need to be wanted, a need to be liked, a need to be desired. But what is it within us that creates these needs that are so dependent upon what other people think and other people do? It's because we have not yet made the effort to find ourselves—who we are, what we are, and what we should be doing.

We go from one to another and we talk, but we do not communicate. See, communication is a two-way situation. Many of us talk and we say many, many things. It is a very rare person that communicates, because communication, if it is communication, is dependent upon understanding. And with understanding, the soul faculties have to be expressed.

One of those soul faculties being honesty. Therefore, when we talk to people, there is a part of our mind that is constantly censoring what we will say and how we will act and react. And it is censoring our efforts to communicate because we have such a high priority of what the person we are talking to is going to think about us that moment or some moment thereafter. Therefore, we are dependent upon the fluctuations of the thoughts of other people because we are demonstrating a dependence upon the fluctuations of our own thoughts.

Now, ofttimes a person, in meeting someone and becoming acquainted with them, the first thing they do is to go to work to see how the person reacts to what they say and what they do. And all of this information gets stored in a computer of our mind. And when it comes time, later, to communicate with a person, there is no communication: there is total censorship.

We ofttimes make great effort to please someone or ofttimes many people. We make the effort to please them because there is something that we want that we have already judged that they have. Now, we cannot consider that putting God in it, but we certainly can consider putting the cunning and the deception of the human mind into the experience. When we put cunning and deception and those various devices of the human mind into those things, that's what we get back. And so we go through life, some days and some moments we feel very good, but more frequently we feel very bad.

We have experiences in life—they are negative experiences. Something falls apart in our life and we don't pause to relate that we fell apart inside ourselves, that the outward manifestation—the demonstration is the revelation of where we are in consciousness. No experience can be changed, no life can be improved unless we're willing to make the changes in the thought patterns that we are expressing in our daily activities. Certainly, to the mind that has yet to make the effort, it seems like a phenomenal job—to pause moment by moment, to become aware of what we're thinking, for most people are not aware. We entertain our mind with a multitude of distractions. We do that because we have already found when we do not entertain our mind with a multitude of distractions, we do not like the experiences of the thoughts that rise up within us.

We all know that when there have been moments that we sit quietly, for every positive thought, there seems to be ten thousand negative ones rising up in our own consciousness. For every positive thought of goodness and declaration of our divine right of abundant good, there is a multitude of justifications, a multitude of fears that follow right behind it. It wastes no time at all. That, my friends, is what we must become aware of more often on a daily basis, because those patterns, they are the creators of the law that we must follow. Now, we have said before that man is a law unto himself. What are we doing with the law that we are?

We can't do anything with a law that we are not aware of. Now, we can and are definitely and positively aware of the effects. We are aware of the effects of the laws we set into motion. That we are aware of. But the cause? No. No, we rarely ever are aware of the cause. It is always someone else that has done something. It is always someone else or something or circumstances or conditions. It just happened to us. That's the level of dependence.

That's what it has to say. It is dependent on people and what they think about us. It's dependent on people and what they do concerning us. Consequently, we have these experiences. "Well, it's people—or some person's fault." It's not the Law of Personal Responsibility. That is immediately denied. Because to accept, in those moments, the Law of Personal Responsibility, we could not be dependent on what someone else has done or someone else is not doing.

If you ask a person to do something, you must accept the demonstrable truth: what is the experience, the reaction that you get? If you have made the effort to use some degree of understanding, of which the many soul faculties are inseparable from, then you will speak from a level of consideration. And in speaking from a level of consideration, you will never leave a soul worse than you have found them. For whoever meets a soul and leaves them worse than they have found them incurs a debt to the Divine Principle. And they will have to face that debt. They will have to pay that debt someday, somewhere. And that someday and that somewhere, my good friends, is here and now.

One, ofttimes, does not relate. They are aware that they have left certain people, surely, worse than they found them, but they don't see any debt being paid to those people. But they totally lose sight of the principle of the law. The debt can be paid to what you call a perfect stranger, but the debt *will* be paid. For every act, there is a react, for that is the Law of Duality; that is the identification that we presently have; that is the identification that we tenaciously hold to.

So, my friends, you know, there are many ways to get to the mountaintop. And you use the way that you are ready for. Not all people are ready to understand the law given in one particular way. But then, they are ready to receive the same law given in a little different way.

So if you cannot, or are not ready, to take control of the human mind and its tenacity of identification that places you in the blindness and the belief that you are it, then work with this Law of Identification. Use it to its best advantage for your own good. Now, that's quite simple. You insist upon being identified with the realm of consciousness in which you live, the present state of evolution, then make the best of the realm. You see, nothing's either good or bad, we all know, but thinking makes it so. And bad is only undeveloped good. Therefore, if you are in the state of evolution where the identification is—you are so bound to it—then turn that seeming bad experience into good results. You do that through the control of your own mind.

Now, we have these experiences that we do not consciously look for. Now, no one consciously looks for a disaster in their life. But there was a moment, there was a moment they were conscious of the thoughts that they set into motion to establish the law to bring the disaster. But you can turn that into [a] good result through the discipline of the human mind. But you must, in looking at the experience, you must look for the good that's in it. There is no disaster that does not contain the Divine Principle, known as God, for there is no life without God.

So an experience has the breath of life in the moment of its birth. And because experience has birth, it is destined, by the Law of Birth, to have death. Now, when you hold to an experience, you are not only holding to a shadow, but you are holding to something that, by the very law of nature, is dying and disintegrating. So when you permit your mind to hold to that that has been born, has grown, and has died, you are identifying with a disintegrating principle. So a part of you, through the Law of Identification, which is the bondage of attachment, begins to die and to disintegrate. Now, it is that dying and disintegrating process within your mind that is the emotional trauma, that is the upheaval. That's what takes place.

You see, my friends, there is nothing to worry about in so-called transition or death, because you are dying and being born in consciousness moment by moment by moment. But you hold to that that is dying. That is the suffering of life. Stop and think, without identifying, attaching, and being bound to that which has passed and is dying, you could not suffer. He who lives in the eternal moment, in which the power flows—and that's the only moment in which the power flows. It flows in the eternal moment. All other moments are a passing process in consciousness. So he who holds to that which is passing, passes with it. A part of yourself is dying.

So remember what happened a moment ago, it had birth, it grew, it had—you had experience and it is dying. And as you hold and identify to that that is dying, you die with it. That is the suffering of the human being. That is not the design of the life of abundant good, but it is what we, in our error, in our error of ignorance, have chosen to do.

That does not mean, of course, that one does not take care of their responsibilities, for one cannot escape or deny and be freed from the Law of Personal Responsibility. We know that denial *is* destiny. And for everything we deny, we destine ourselves to experience. For every adversity that we permit to grow in consciousness, we guarantee the attachment thereto. For that *is* the law. That is the law that we have made and therefore we alone experience it.

Now, the human mind, the great creator—as we understand, there is no Divine Principle that is creating. There are the nature spirits, the forms, the creators, the human mind, the mental world that creates. Form exists. Form is bondage. Therefore, all thought is an instrument of bondage, for all thought is a forming of a formless substance.

Now, that that is, which we call Spirit, exists only in the eternal moment of now. Our view, which is a created form, can exist for us as long as we identify with form. But as we insist upon identifying with form, as we permit ourselves to believe that we are the thought, then we will suffer, for we are the ones who are limiting, who are creating, and who are forming.

Truth is not truth in form. Freedom is not freedom in form. For form is the Law of Limit. And the Law of Limit is the Law of Denial. You cannot, in consciousness, limit anything and then think the delusion that it is free. So as long as man believes he is the thought, he will not have the awareness of truth and freedom.

So the first step—and the most important step daily—is to talk to yourselves. Know that you are not the thought you just had. You are not the thought of what you're thinking about and you will not be the thought of what tomorrow will bring. Though that exists in a realm of thought, it is not *you* until *you* identify with it.

Now a person, of course, can take this beautiful truth into total license and go do their thing and say, "Well, that wasn't me." But you will not escape from the divine law, because, you see, by the very thought and the very act that you can do something and that is not you and escape from the reaction and the payment of the law reveals to you, you are identified with that realm of consciousness and, therefore, shall pay the price of that realm of consciousness, which is known as an eye for an eye and a tooth for a tooth. That is the mental world. That's the way it is. That's the way it has always been and that is the way it will always be.

To be freed from that realm takes what is known in this philosophy—and any other philosophy that has the understanding—it takes daily, constant control.

We taught before in classes that truth is an effect of self-control, for what you control, you free. Now most people think what they control, they have. That's the furthest thing from the truth: that is the illusion that the mind has to offer. Whatever you control, you understand. Whatever you understand, you do not bind. And whatever you do not bind, you free. So control is freedom. So when you control yourself, you will free your soul. That is the law and that is how it really, simply works.

Now, you go out into the jungle, so-called, and into the world and you have all kinds of experiences and all kinds of thoughts and all these different emotions and things. You have emotion only through the Law of Identification. If you do not treat yourself well in consciousness, you shall not be treated well in life. Therefore, if you do not think well of yourself, there is no way you will be thought well of. But to be thought well of is not to be concerned of how people think. If you know how you think, you have no interest nor concern how others think. Because you know how you think. You know that you are responsible for you, and you are responsible for the laws that you alone have set and are setting and will set into motion. You alone are responsible for that. No husband, no wife is responsible. No parent is responsible. You and you alone are responsible.

Responsibility, the ability to respond—the ability to respond to what? This is what we are here [for and] interested in: responsibility, the ability to respond. The ability to respond to each and every law that you alone set into motion. That's responsibility. Now, we all have within us the potential of the ability to respond without emotion, without fear, to all the laws that we alone set into motion. Each time we deny, each time we deny—and we deny by blaming others. We deny by finding scapegoats for our own weaknesses. Each time that we do that, each and every time we do that, we move farther and farther away from the ability to respond to the laws we set into motion.

So the first step, of course, is to stop blaming outside for why someone does this and why someone does that and why did they react this way and why don't they do their share of this in life and why don't they carry their weight of the load and on down the list. My friends, if we are really applying this simple and beautiful philosophy, we are so interested in doing *our* part, there is little or no time or energy left to concern ourselves with everyone else. If we have, in our evolution, merited the responsibility of a job that requires, in keeping with the law that we alone established, to supervise, to consider, and to understand and to see that work is done, then that's the law that we set into motion. That is what we have evolved to. And we should accept it joyously and not be emotional about it.

Now, we all, of course, are here because, in truth, beyond all the varied, seeming motivations, we have come here, an effect not of days, months, or years, but an effect of centuries. We enter many schools along the path in our evolution, and we have entered this one. Some of us have been here for some time in this school here on earth. And some have arrived recently. But you've been in school before. It doesn't matter what name they call it. It does matter that it is a school, a spiritual school, that you have entered and left and entered again more times than your mind has numbers for. And so we enter again and once again we start upon the path. The teachings are so simple: on the spiritual path of light and freedom and truth, many things will distract you. And, of course, they will. They distract you because you identify with them. Your mind tells you, you have a need, you want, and you desire. And you let your mind, from lack of discipline, you let your mind take control.

Your mind is born and dies thought by thought, feeling by feeling, moment by moment. Be reasonable, my friends. Who would rely on something that is so demonstrably unreliable? How can we rely upon an instrument that has repeatedly revealed [that] to us year after year after year? If you have forgotten the centuries of evolution, just relate to the earth realm and look at the *years* of your dependence upon an instrument known as the human mind that is so fickle, that is so tenacious in its wants, needs, and desires, that is so undependable, unreliable, you never really do know what it's going to do.

You may be going out and you're headed for someplace and you meet someone you used to know and that someplace that you were headed for, you never get there, at least that day. Stop and think. If the human mind is allowed to do its thing with the multitude of distractions with all of the wants that are contained within this computer bank, you'll never reach your goal. There's no way possible unless you have the daily discipline of controlling it.

Just before the victories, we always seem to turn back, with rare exceptions, only because we live in what has been and cannot experience, to its fullness, what is. We think we are here this moment and a part of us—that is true—a part of us *is* here. But we have to be honest and see it's a very small part. But it is some part and that's better than no part. But if you be still a moment, you'll see that it's a very small part that's here. Listen to your thoughts and your mind. Listen quietly and you will hear them rise up with all the suppressed desires and different things and all the distractions while you are trying to experience the Light that frees you.

Very few—it is a rare student in these many years that I lived to see still having their morning meditation. It is a difficult path because we make it so. Because we identify with that which is difficult and cannot experience more often that which is beautiful, that which is harmonious, that which is beneficial. But as I have said before, and I say again, that is not necessary. There's a way of turning all of that around. But it will take moment-by-moment.

When the Spirit said moment by moment—you can only live moment by moment if you are living. Those who live, live moment by moment. Those who exist—it could be twenty years ago or fifty. They're dying, for they hold to that which has gone and, therefore, are dying with it. You had an experience a half hour ago. It came to you in keeping with the law you set into motion. You had the experience. It finished. It's in the process of disintegration and dying. And you hold on to it and die with it. That's the suffering. You die with your thought because you don't know when to let it go. Upset yesterday with your boss? Die with it because it was yesterday. And you will suffer and suffer and suffer and suffer. Is that the way to live? We can only live in the eternal moment. Therefore, that is moment by moment.

Now we have some time for your questions. If you'd like to raise your hand, I'll be happy to share with you. Yes, please.

I understand that we live in the eternal moment of now, supposedly—well, I'm trying to understand that. But can we make peace with our adversities before they—before we have to actually experience them?

Oh, yes. Yes, through the Law of Understanding, we can make peace with our adversities. Now, what you have to remember in that question is simply this: a great deal of energy has gone in to creating an adversity, and when it turns, as it's destined to and becomes an attachment, it takes an equal amount of energy to neutralize that before it becomes an attachment. Say that you have poured in, for example, a hundred thousand tons of energy to create a certain adversity. It is going to take a hundred thousand tons of energy to neutralize that before it becomes a hundred-thousand-ton attachment.

Now, there is, of course—through the Law of Identification, that only takes place in a mental world of consciousness. But I know very few people on Earth that can sustain moving from a mental world of identification for a very long period of time. Therefore, it behooves us, of course, to make friends with our adversities before they become attachments, because they're guaranteed to do just that. Does that help with your question?

One cannot just say, "Peace, adversity. Peace." You didn't create the adversity by calling it peace. You are not going to change the adversity by calling it peace. And the way out of a thing is the way we got into the thing. And there is only one way out because there is only way in. You do understand—

Yes, sir.

That only a judgment can create an adversity. You do understand that, don't you?

That only a judgment—
Only a judgment can create an adversity.
Yes. Well, a denial is a judgment.
Why, it most certainly is. And it becomes our destiny. And only a judgment can create an attachment.
OK.
And what creates a judgment?
An uneducated ego.
Yes, indeed. An uneducated ego creates a mountain of judgments. And a titanic ego even creates more of them. Thank you. The gentleman in the back, please. Yes.
Yes. In controlling the mind and living in the eternal moment of now, moment by moment, in controlling the human mind, is it useful to focus the mind on a specific thought or a specific thing?
Yes, indeed it is. Indeed, indeed it is. You see, peace is the power and you are peace. That's what you are. You think many things and believe you are many things. Everyone does. But what you are is peace, and peace is the power. That's what you are. You can call yourself "soul." That is the covering of spirit. Then there is the formless, free spirit. And that is the peace that passeth all understanding. So what we really are is peace.

Now, many people have many different understandings of what peace is. And peace for one is not the same for another. But that, my friends, is not peace at all. That is the formation of what peace means to the human mind. And that is not the peace that we are. The peace that we are is beyond understanding, which is expressed through the human mind. That is why peace passeth—and is beyond—all understanding. Does that help with your question?
Yes. And, also, how does one control the human mind?
One controls the human mind by first becoming aware of what it is and what it has to offer. One cannot control what one does not understand. Therefore, the first step in controlling the human mind is to become aware of it, that one may learn and

understand it. And after learning and understanding about the human mind, then one places oneself in a position, from that effort, to gaining control over it. Once one gains control over something, they can move beyond it.

So it's going to take a moment-by-moment awareness.

Absolutely. Because the law has been established in our earthly journey of moment-by-moment unawareness. And because we have established the Law of Moment-by-Moment Unawareness, the way out is the way we got in. And we got in by moment-by-moment unawareness. And the only way to get out is by moment-by-moment awareness. That help with your question?

Yes.

Yes. Yes, the lady here, please.

Can one retract a judgment? Let's say moment by moment you have a judgment and then, upon having a judgment, you realize that. Can you do that?

If you have entered the soul faculty of forgiveness, you can free your identification from it. That is true. To forgive is to free or to give forth. Now, if you enter in your consciousness, that realm of consciousness, if you make that effort and enter that realm, then you can give forth the error of ignorance that you have identified with and be free from [it]. Does that help with your question?

Yes, the lady here, please. You had a question?

Is it possible to think of a past experience without the Law of Identity or attachment being involved?

Only through self-control. Now, one will know right away whether they have any degree of self-control when they entertain in consciousness an experience that they have had that had a great impact upon them. If there is any feeling, any emotion, then you may be rest assured there is not self-control and there is the danger of, once again, becoming bound.

Now, you know, it's just like working with people. You work with people—if you over-identify with the obstruction, you never find the way, you see. So the thing to do is to work with that which they have totally identified with and move quickly on to something else to lift them up. That's how you lift the soul and lift yourself at the same time. You see, if you permit a person who is having a struggle or difficulty or problem—first of all, they've got the problem because they're over-identified with it and that's why they're falling apart. You understand? And so you can work with them—"All right. That's fine. That's identified."—and then move on. You've got to move them out of that realm of consciousness. Otherwise, what happens is, they continue dying because an event has passed and they are totally identified with it.

It's difficult to let go only because we have made it so difficult to gain. We've made it difficult from our own judgments, from our own negative experiences. And so we hold tenaciously in keeping with our judgment of how difficult it was to get. Therefore, we must make sure that it's difficult to let go because we've made darn sure how difficult it was to get. Now, I'm sure if you will think about that, you will understand why it is so difficult to let go, especially when you believe it's a part of yourself.

Yes. Now, the lady over here had a question, please. Yes.

If one is experiencing the effect of suppression of thoughts and one accepts personal responsibility for that suppression, then what is the next step to get out of the effect of that—the effect it has on the body?

Yes, absolutely. You see, first of all, one has accepted the Law of Personal Responsibility of an experience that has passed. Correct?

Yes.

And a suppression. Now, one must talk to those levels of consciousness, which are deeply rooted within, in our so-called subconscious, kindly, but firmly. And in so doing one will cast the light of reason over that area in consciousness. And if it tries rising again—now, a person may talk to a certain level of suppression, and it rises up again and it rises up again and again and again. Then, you must, through control of the human mind, each time you speak to it firmly, kindly, but you don't spend much time with it. Because the more time you spend with it, the more bound you become. And you move, with your identification—because you're now in a realm—you see, if you have the experience of the thought and the feeling, you're already in a realm of mental identification. Therefore, you must identify with something you want and desire that has a higher priority than the shadow that is screaming and tearing you apart. Now, you do that through a degree of control of the mind: you choose something that is desirable to you and something that you are able to do, something that you want to do and you *do* that.

Because this is the great danger—a great deal of danger in the different therapies and counseling: they identify upon the obstruction. And in so doing, the individual becomes totally bound to that which has passed and reexperiences. Now, remember, it is indelibly recorded in the memory par excellence—all experiences. And they reexperience through reidentification until finally—you see, they think they're freed from it? No, the form created of the experience has simply eaten a feast and will give you a break *for a time*, you see.

This why I have always taught, "May God save me from the reformer." Because the reformer is one who has suppressed, by sheer force, a certain pattern, whatever it is—or habit—and has an insatiable need, in order to keep that desire suppressed, to convert every person that they see. That is why I always said, "May God always save me from a reformer." Because it is a very dangerous level of consciousness. It is an extremely detrimental level of consciousness. Suppressed desire is very detrimental to the human mind. It must be educated or fulfilled. And if one chooses the education, then one must work with it and free themselves from it through redirection and identification with something that has a higher and stronger desire than the shadow itself. I hope that's helped with your question.

Yes. Yes, the gentleman there, please.

You said "redirection." It seems like it's kind of a thin line between redirection and suppression. So you have to be careful with what you redirect. I mean . . . redirect and suppression. Would you give me something specific when you say redirect my thoughts to something else?

Yes. Say, for example, you have a desire that you have suppressed and that desire rises up and demands that it be fulfilled. Do you understand that?

Right.

Fine. You have a choice in that moment to talk to the desire—the suppressed desire—to make some effort to fulfill or to educate it. And then to redirect: to direct your attention, which is your identification, to something else. Because if you don't do that, that desire that you have suppressed only gets stronger, for energy follows attention. And that that you place your attention upon, you have a tendency to become in keeping with the Law of Identification. So if you keep thinking about your suppressed desire and you keep directing energy to it, someday, be rest assured, it will consume you. But you have conscious choice. You can choose to direct that energy flowing through you to some other desire. Do you understand?

Yes. OK. Don't you think it's probably working in your subconscious?

Pardon?

It's still living in your subconscious.

It has life every moment that you identify with it. You alone give it life. You alone give it life. You alone gave it birth. You alone give it death. You alone give it rebirth. For it is recorded in memory par excellence. You may awaken it any moment you choose to do so.

Now, you see, my friends, if we do not make the effort to become aware of these things—we go out on our jobs and we say, "Someone pushed my buttons." Well, the only way someone can push your buttons is from your laziness of not pushing your own. Now, if you want to call them buttons—you have all kinds of buttons. Goodness sakes—and they're yours! You can't go out to work and out into the world and say, "Well, somebody pushed my buttons" and you are all emotional and all upset. That certainly is not accepting the law, the demonstrable Law of Personal Responsibility. And how sad. I tell you, it does my ego no good at all to think that someone can push my buttons. My goodness sakes, that I can't have enough control to push my own buttons if I want to push a button. That someone I may walk by pushes my buttons. What! Why, I would think your ego alone would rise up furious that you are so weak, so weak that you have no control over your mind that someone may walk by and push one of your buttons and you're miserable! Well, you best go live in a Faraday cage, where they can't get to your buttons.

Yes. Now the lady in front, please, had a question. Yes.

It seems that we have a lot of trouble with changes and still, we enjoy changes because it's something new. Why are we so attached to the old? And why don't we just let it go and go on to the new? Why do we struggle with changes?

Thank you.

Even though we want to change it.

Thank you very much. There is a part of us that knows that life is an evolution of form. And we know that deep inside of us from untold eons of experiences. We rely upon what we call self for our survival and "self" means many, many, many, many things. Self means all the experiences we've had in life, all the hopes, and all the fears. Self means all the security—emotional, material—that we had or we have.

Now, when we are identified with self, we have an unbelievable struggle with changes, because what we rely upon, in the thought of I, the thought of self, is being threatened. There is something new that is happening. A part of us is joyous about the change and the breath of fresh air, but the other part of us, identified with self, reliant and dependent upon what has been, begins to shake. It is threatened. It does not yet have the experience within its computer bank of exactly what it's going to be like. That is what fights. It is fighting for its life, for it believes that it shall die. It does believe that.

You see, change to those forms of yesterday—any change—represents annihilation. That's what they understand it to be. They're going to be annihilated. They will no longer live. You see, a thought form only lives as long as it receives energy from you. When it no longer receives energy, it lies in limbo in the memory par excellence in the computer bank. It can be recalled at any time in all eternity that you identify with those realms of consciousness, but it doesn't want to go into limbo.

You see, it is created by the human intellect. It has access to everything your intellect has—everything. And it knows that there's this change coming. It doesn't have any experience to directly relate to this change. It is not so sure that it may get moved out and be sent off into the computer banks in limbo. You understand? And that, it's fighting. That's what fights. Now, you won't have the fight, you won't have the struggle, you won't have the pain, and you won't have the suffering if you will stop and not identify with self. Then the change will come about very harmoniously. Because it is not really *you* that is going through all that, but it's all those forms in which, through identification, you are bound by. But you can—anyone can—change that at any moment of their choice by, as I said earlier, through redirection, which is identifying with something else.

You see, the first thing in the process of healing, which we will get to, hopefully, in our coming classes, the very first thing is to remove the person from the identification with self. When they are removed from the identification, all these forms disappear. Then the true healing and the restoration of one's health can, and does, take place. But as long as the person is identifying with the self, they have created a mountain of obstructions of past judgments, thoughts, [and] feelings. And those stand in the way to any good, beneficial healing power.

Because if you can visualize a flow of energy coming towards you—and you are receptive depending upon how many forms are standing in the way. Now, what happens is, this energy moves through to you [and] all of these forms take their share. Every bit of it, you see. And then, after they've all had their feeding and they go on their way, there may be one-millionth of the amount of energy directed through you that actually gets to you for the healing process. All of the other has gone to feed the forms, the judgments, because the individual is identified with the self and with that realm of consciousness.

The most important thing for healing in any hospital, any place, any type of healing, is to use whatever method legal, as the motive is pure, to get the patient to identify with something besides self because it's the self that stands in the way and those armies use up all of that energy.

Now, you will find a person who is not well or seemingly not well, you will find, if you will listen carefully, they are totally identified with self. They are so identified and locked into the disease that it's just unbelievable. Now, they may not say much, but if you listen carefully, you will soon find out they're over-identified.

Now, take a person that has a cold. Some of my students are fortunate. They have learned over the years when they get a sniffle, they ask the doctor—Dr. Waltham—for some help. And time and time again, they've had wonderful help and they don't have to have these so-called colds. Then I have other students who—well, I don't want to say that—but partially ask for help. They get censored help, you see—censored by their judgments, their identification with self of what they have had to offer in the past. So they have to go through whatever that law is going to take them through—maybe a week, three weeks, a month, whatever. But, you see, that's our choice. That is totally dependent upon ourselves: what we want to do.

Now, once a person has been helped, in the sense they've had a positive experience—because they got their ego out of the way long enough. They headed for a cold, they made the effort, and they got freed from having the cold, for example. Then that is now registered in the computer bank. So each time it happens, you understand, it gets easier and easier and better and better and better. Because this thing back here says, "Whoops, oh, I've got to get rid of this." And that just gets right out of the way. The obstructions get right out of the way and the healing completely takes place. And then, sometimes they slip and the healing is partial because we only made it partial. You get a full healing, but you only let a part of it in because your judgments ate up all the rest. There wasn't too much left. Now, that's just the way that it is.

It isn't that I have no tolerance for people who are sickly—I don't even care for that word—or puny. It's just that I know, as I know for myself, great effort has to be made. There is an over-identification and it has to be corrected. I am not a Christian Scientist, but I am a firm believer: control the human mind and you'll free the soul. Because that's just the way that it is. And I never, in all my experiences through this realm and the next one, have I ever, ever seen, heard of, or known a sickly soul.

Thank you. Good night.

SEPTEMBER 2, 1982

CONSCIOUSNESS CLASS 224

Good evening, everyone.

I want you to know that I am on time. We just found out the grandfather clock is four minutes fast, which will be corrected. Considering that I have always made great effort to see that others are on time, I wouldn't want you to think that I'm late.

Now, last class, we were continuing on with our discussion in regards to the human mind and how it works. And we also mentioned a bit to be discussed on healing.

Now, first of all, if we understand to some extent how the human mind works—because no one is ever qualified to control anything that they don't know how it works. Now, we're all familiar, I'm sure, with making the effort to study anything that we're interested in. So that we can, after our full study and investigation, gain some degree of control over it. A person studies to be an engineer; so that in time he will be able to control what he knows about engineering.

And so it is with the human mind. We must first learn how it works: its benefits, its detriments, and how to use it wisely in order that we may gain control over it. No one would even think of stepping into a car without knowing something about the process of driving it to take them where they want to go. But we have not—most of us—in our life, yet, made the effort to study how the mind and the thought process works; so it can do, for us, what we want it to do.

In anything, we are one of two things. We are either the victim or we are the victor. And, of course, none of us appreciate accepting the possibility that we are the victim. But as we begin to make the daily effort, hopefully, in time, the moment-by-moment effort, to see what is happening with our life—the experiences that we do not appreciate, the trials and tribulations and the difficulties—then we are, slowly but surely, preparing ourselves for some degree of incentive to learn how this is happening to us.

So it is with healing. Now we have taught, and continue to teach, that self-thought is self-destructive. We must understand and learn something about that. Why is it (self-thought) self-destructive instead of self-constructive? There has to be a reason. Whenever we permit our mind to think of what we call self, we must understand that we *think* we are many things. We think that we are happy. We think that we are sad. We think that we are wealthy. We think that we are poor. We think that we are healthy. We think that we are ill. And so it is that we identify with these various levels of consciousness, formed and deformed, and experiences that are already passed in our life.

We've also taught that it is human to forgive and it is divine to forget. I'm sure we will all agree whenever there is something unpleasant that happens in our life, we would like to forget it. We don't like the feelings that we have in remembering it. And when we want to forget it, we usually find great difficulty in doing so. And the reason that we find difficulty in experiencing the divinity within us, so that we can forget an unpleasant experience, is really quite simple: it is indispensable to enter the realm of consciousness known as the Divinity with identification—it is not possible to enter the Divine and hold to identity.

Therefore, it is absolutely necessary to forgive what you want to forget. You understand what forgiving means: it means to give forth. So unless you are ready, willing, and able to forgive an unpleasant experience—to give it forth—you cannot enter the realm of consciousness where you can forget it.

Now, we understand that the thought of I is the problem that we have, for the thought of I is necessary to identification. It is sad, but true, that we identify or dent the I. And we dent it all the time. And that causes us a lot of problems. It causes us a lot of problems because we find ourselves ofttimes in a state of frustration. We don't really know what we want. We think we do and then something takes place in our life and we decide, thank God, we never got that because we never did really want it. And this process is going on all the time in the human mind.

Now, what does all of that have to do with healing? Well, this philosophy teaches that the demonstrations in life are the revelations in life. And we find that self-thought is self-destructive, for we find, as we pause to think, that people thinking of themselves are most destructive people. They destroy things. The destruction continues day by day in their lives. The destruction manifests itself in many ways. They break things. They tear things. Then you have the other expression of the destruction of self-thought: the gradual, slow but sure destruction of what you call your health.

There are people who vent, they say, or express their feelings rather freely. Then there are those who express their feelings under great duress. Then there are those who you never see express their feelings. The ones who express their feelings with some degree of control, that is, they choose the time and the place—[with] some effort to pause and to think they express their feelings. The feelings being nothing more than the expression of created forms in the human consciousness. Those things can be worked with.

And there are those who never discuss their feelings. And that is the most difficult of all. For that energy becomes grounded in the consciousness of self and, slowly but surely, it begins to destroy the harmony of the human being.

Now, we understand that harmony is health. Therefore, in order to be receptive to what we understand, and call, the healing vibration or the healing power, it is absolutely necessary that one be free from the vibration of discord. And that is not possible until one makes the effort to be free from self-thought. Because self-thought is discordant thought and because we have yet to understand what we call the self—and therefore, not yet fully understanding it, we do not have yet full control of it—we have discordant thoughts. We have discordant feelings and emotions, contrary to the vibration that is necessary for the restoration of one's health: the absolute vibration of harmony.

Now, a person who feels that they are in need of a restoration of their health must take the first step. They must, out of sheer necessity and survival, forgive that they may forget what is known as the self. To the extent that the effort is made—that they are able to forgive and forget the self—shall the healing, to that degree and extent only, take place.

Now we have all had those experiences in our life. We have had poor health at various times in our life. We have become extremely interested in some particular object or subject of our choice and in those moments, in those moments we have realized a freedom from the discord and the so-called poor health.

Now, long ago we revealed to you that cancer, what man calls cancer—discord and disease that seems to be so prevalent, that has always been in all forms—it grows and prospers, within the form, through disturbance, through discord, through frustration. And the healing thereof, of course, is dependent upon the recipient, the individual, entering a state of harmony through an absence of self-thought. Without the daily effort to be freed from this identification process, man cannot, once again, experience, through his right of claim, his divinity—the divinity in the moment of his choice to be free from the discord and disturbance of creation.

We have bound ourselves to a dual law through our own error of ignorance. And that bondage is the payment that we experience today. Because so much energy, so much effort has gone in to the creation of the error, equal effort, equal energy must go in to neutralize it and to, once again, bring about a balance.

Now, remember, friends, that harmony is balance. And that that is harmonious is healthy. And that that is healthy is wealthy. You see, most people relate wealth to a brick of gold dug up from the earth. But there is the wealth of many things: the wealth of peace, the wealth of happiness, the wealth of joy, the wealth of health, the wealth of good.

We should not permit ourselves to seek, through ignorance, the wealth limited to gold from the planet, because in so doing we ofttimes seek what we call money, when really what we are truly seeking is health, happiness, and the good of life. But we limit it, through our ignorance, and that indeed brings to us a great deal of sadness. For whatever we rely upon that is subject to the dual laws of creation, we are victim of frustration. For duality is discord, not harmony.

Nature ever seeks to reach a state of balance. But remember, nature ever seeks and does never accomplish. For to do so, we would not experience what we call comparison, contrast and, therefore, would not have this duality taking place in our life.

We are in creation. Our efforts must be made to be in it and not a part of it. Because the struggle of life is that illusion and it is that error. When we go about our daily jobs and activities, we must learn to be aware of where we are. Now, we all know where the physical body is, but we really do not know where our mind is. Now, our experiences will reveal to us, if we will pause to think, where our mind is. We can look at our jobs and the things that we do and we can see if it was constructive or destructive, if we were in self or out of self, if our health is improving or doing the opposite.

We do not have to wait to make the change. There is nothing to wait for. For that that one needs to experience—the restoration of good in their life, the restoration of health and happiness—is available in whatever moment you choose to be receptive to it. Now, if you choose to go down a long path and across the waters to China to get what is available to you in the eternal moment of your choice, then, of course, that is the way that you must go. But I assure you, that path, that way is not necessary. But what *is* necessary is your efforts to accomplish what is known in this philosophy as the power of concentration—the key to all power: concentration. But how can man concentrate when man has yet to learn how his mind is working? It doesn't do all these things by itself. It does all these different things through our lack of effort to find out what's going on.

I have spent many of my years working diligently to help people to stop destroying themselves and everything around them. For some time I have known that it is through their lack of effort to gain control over their mind—that their minds are constantly entertaining self-thought—that they are not only destroying things they touch and around them, but they are destroying their own health, their own wealth, their own happiness. And it is only, I know, an error of ignorance.

I have for some time revealed to some of my students to become aware of how, when you permit your mind to entertain the functions of self, your budget soon goes haywire. When you think your budget is bad, watch the law go to work and make it worse for you. When you think you have not, watch the beauty of the law work for you to take even that which you think you have not. Because the laws of the universe are impartial laws—they have no personality; they are the principle itself—they work in any way that we choose them to work. And we are never left without those choices.

We do not need to go on in life the way that we have. But it's up to us, when we're ready to make the changes so that we can experience broader horizons and more abundant good in our life.

Now, in reference to health, when we start to make the effort to stop thinking of self that we may be restored through the Law of Harmony, we soon discover that there are some problems: thoughts rise up to plague us, to stop us so that they—the forms of yesterday—may continue to be served.

All disease or discord of the human body is dependent upon discord of the mental body. And the discord of the mental body is a lack of the light, the light of reason that transfigures us, shining fully over our mental world.

Our teachings demonstrate, Keep faith with reason, she will transfigure thee. Our teaching does not say keep faith with reason, *he* will transfigure thee. It specifically states *she* will transfigure thee. The feminine aspect of nature—it is the reason that must shine over the emotional body, the subconscious mind. That is the magnetic field. That is the field that attracts in keeping with the law. All those chickens come home to roost. So it is the magnetic field in our consciousness that the light of reason must be permitted to shine [over]. And in so doing, the transformation shall come to pass.

When we believe that there is nothing but what we call the self, then we have serious problems in life trying to get free from the self. For what mind will walk to something—from something to nothing? So it is that we believe what we think we are, as difficult as it is. And it seems almost an impossibility to get freed from the thought of I, because there is no acceptance that there is something else.

Now, you can demonstrate to yourself, in a moment, how great is your faith that there is something greater than your thought, than your identity to what you call the self. Just pause a moment and tell your self to take a nap; you're going to something better. I guarantee you the multitude of thoughts that rise up from what you think is the self will not let you be in peace, which, of course, is the personal demonstration to ourselves that we would like to believe that there is something, but when it comes right down to the choice of giving up that which we are familiar with to that which we have made no effort to become familiar with, we, of course, for the ignorance of security, choose that which we are familiar with. So we have permitted ourselves in this life to be familiar with creation. And so instead of being in it, we become a part of it. And we're tossed from shore to shore ever in keeping with our love of self.

It is the nature of the Divine expressing through all form to love all life. That *is* the law. And if we believe there is only our self, then this divine law to love all life is not only limited, but restricted to the love of self, for if self is all we believe in, if self is all we rely on, then self is all we can love. And so we use this great power to love the self until it's loved to death—absolutely smothered. And that's sad.

You see, one loves a thing too much when one begins to possess it. The philosophy teaches "Love all life and know the Light." It does not teach love all self and know the opposite. But that's what happens. Because you cannot take this great Power, known as God, the Infinite Intelligence, the Divine Principle, known to man as Love, and limit it to one person, place, or thing and expect to experience abundant good.

And so we try very diligently, sometimes, to forget a thought, to be free in our consciousness from an experience and it won't go away. How can it go away? For that which holds it—the house of self in which it lives—we love so very much.

It does not mean that we should not love the vehicle, the life principle of the vehicle through which we express. But our problems begin when that's all we love. And sooner or later we find out how detrimental that really is. Now, some people would call that, I suppose, vanity. It goes far beyond vanity because it destroys the whole being, not just portions thereof. Vanity is a function. And when the energy is directed to that function and it becomes imbalanced with its corresponding soul faculty, then a particular part of the house, a part of your anatomy, begins to experience the discord and the disease and the imbalance. And that's how it works.

So I'm going to take a few moments, now, to permit your questions on healing. And there's a lot more to heal besides the physical body. I'm sure you'll all agree. Some people would like to heal their business. Some people would like to heal their boyfriends. And some people would like to heal their animals. And there's a whole list of things that the human mind would like to have healed. Some people would even like to heal the weather. Well, there's all kind of things that our mind thinks about that should be healed, but whether they should or not—whether they're sick or not—could well be our own perspective. And we mustn't forget that.

So if you have any questions, you can feel free, at this time, to raise your hands. Yes, please.

I have a question about dental healing. It seems that I've known many people in my lifetime who were able to keep their bodies healthly with spiritual, metaphysical healing, but I've never known anybody that could keep their teeth healthy.

Through spiritual healing. Well, that is a very good question. You're asking about spiritual healing in reference to a person's teeth. Is that correct?

Yes. Is it the same order as the decay of eyes with age? In other words, is this something that we resign ourselves to or can we work on it metaphysically or . . .

If we begin before the law is so firmly established that it would take a dangerous amount of energy to correct—by that I mean a drain of the energy necessary for the vital body. Now, let us first understand what the teeth represent. Do you understand the meaning of teeth in this philosophy?

No, I don't.

The teeth, a part of the house of clay, are representative of the determination. Now, I'm sure we'll all agree we all have determination.

Now, remember, a person who has and expresses—we all have determination. But a person who expresses a great deal of determination—perhaps in their business, perhaps in their spiritual work, or whatever they choose to direct it into. Determination, a great amount expressed—the potential is always there to express the same amount of determination when they enter the realm of self-thought. And the destruction can be quite detrimental because they have already demonstrated their ability to release a great deal of determination in a constructive way and that potential, of course, exists also for them to release it in a destructive way, by entering the realm of self-thought.

Now, the teeth or the eyes of which you speak are just as receptive to healing as any other part of the anatomy. But we must understand that the minds of men have identified with, and accepted, in their realm of belief that they are more difficult to heal. Now this isn't something that we chose to accept (that it is more difficult to heal the eyes or the teeth or etc., etc.) It is the mass consciousness that has accepted that over a period of many centuries.

Now, this is a good—I'm glad you brought the point up. Because, you see, my friends, when we enter self-thought, the thought of I, the self, we also enter the mass consciousness. And the mass consciousness is a very powerful, potent force. The mass consciousness in our country today is the direct cause of the seeming economic situation. It is the mass consciousness that has created it. It is the mass consciousness that is sustaining and supporting it.

Now, if you get two people to believe a certain way, you have available, in those moments when they are truly in harmony in their belief, you have the power of the universe in its potential. You have all the force available to all human minds. Now we must think, that's two people. Because, you see, it must be two or more, because that is the Law of Creation. It must be two or more. Well, you're talking about *millions* of people; millions thinking a certain way and then proving to themselves that they are right.

Whenever you enter the realm of self, you must remember, your mind, like all minds, goes to work to prove that you are right. Because, you see, that's the way the so-called uneducated ego really works. You see, the uneducated ego knows that if it doesn't prove to you that it is right, you will not believe in it or rely upon it. So even though your mind says, "Whoops, now that's really a terrible thing"—a mistake that you're about to make—if your uneducated ego is in control, it will justify that out. It's the best excuser in the whole, wide world. Show me a person filled with excuses and justifications and I will show you an ego that's truly uneducated; I will show you a victim, a soul in the total bondage of self-thought. The more that we justify, the more that we excuse ourselves—we do that because we are so attached to the thing, that image, that is doing that.

And so we find ourselves, every time we do something and are corrected, we get emotional, we get frustrated, and we start immediately to defend our self, to blame someone else, to always look around to see who is close at hand that we can put the blame on. Because we cannot permit our self to face that we are relying upon an instrument that is not reliable and is not dependable; that it is getting us from the frying pan right into the fire every time we turn around. Now, no one wants to depend on that kind of an instrument. So we have to constantly prove to our self someone else made the mistake, someone else was wrong, someone else fell asleep, someone else did all these things. We do that because, unfortunately, we are our own worst enemy. And we will be that way until we learn what we really are and who we really are and not what we think we are, that causes us so very, very many problems.

Let's look at the constructive and positive side: the things that we can do, the things that we can accomplish. We can restore our health in anything in this the eternal moment. But how long can you sustain that acceptance? It's only—if you can sustain it at all—it's only for a fleeting moment. Therefore, we teach you must work moment by moment by moment. Because you can only hold that possibility for a moment. That's the reason, my friends. You want the restoration of health, wealth and happiness? Then you must go moment by moment by moment by moment. Because if you don't go moment by moment by moment by moment, the law never gets off the ground and you never have the experience of the greater good. You must learn to go moment by moment by moment.

Now, moment by moment, you don't hold it in your consciousness. It never accomplishes the good. You keep broadcasting it out constantly. If you have difficulty being at peace, always thank the powers that are that you *are* at peace.

You see, you must open up the soul faculties to enter the cosmic realms of consciousness. You can't enter cosmic consciousness with limited consciousness; they mix like oil and water. There's no way possible that you can enter that realm with your intellect, your thought. You don't enter that way. You must enter—and the only way to enter is—through one or more of the soul faculties.

Now we teach the first soul faculty, a triune faculty of duty, gratitude, and tolerance; that through entering, opening up the door of gratitude—you see, what happens, you open that door, you move with duty and tolerance into the cosmic consciousness and experience the good that is waiting for you. But you only can do that by sending out that beam into the vibratory waves through the Law of Repetition.

See, the human mind is constantly, from the mental world, twenty-four hours, moment by moment, right around the clock, it is broadcasting something. Your experiences in life are the revelations of what your mind is moment by moment broadcasting. That's what it is. So you know by your experiences what your mind is broadcasting. And [if] you don't like it, then take control of the broadcast station and start broadcasting vibrations that will enter you into limitless consciousness where you can experience limitless good.

You see, there's a vast difference between the realms of the cosmic consciousness of limitlessness and the payment and attainment of the mental world for the good that you seek. You can play the mental gymnastics and you will have to pay every step of the way. Do you understand?

Now remember, friends, when you enter those cosmic realms and experience the good, remember, your payment is always when you return to the delusion of the thought of I.

Are there any more questions? *[After a short pause, the Teacher continues.]* Thank you. The meeting is concluded. We will have our refreshments now.

SEPTEMBER 9, 1982

CONSCIOUSNESS CLASS 225

Tonight's class—if you'll recall, we had a class once here on the refrigerator. And I'm sure that benefited all you people who have listened to it in respect to applying the philosophy. Now, if we don't have application of what we study, then, of course, we're wasting our money. So tonight, we have a class on the disappearance of one of the chairs that you have paid for.

Several months ago I asked my students—so that we could have these classes—for you to donate to the cost of tables and chairs so you would be able to have a place to sit, to have a chair to sit in. And our records reveal that we purchased fifty-six chairs. On my regular, daily inventory check this morning—of course, with so many things to check I can't check chairs seven days a week. But today was my day to check the inventory of the chairs. And my investigation revealed that there were chairs missing. Tonight, under thorough investigation, we find that instead of six chairs missing, you only have one chair missing. Therefore, I'm asking all of you to donate a dollar to the replacement of that chair.

Now, if anyone feels that they don't care to donate a dollar towards the replacement of that chair, please raise your hand, because it is not a compulsory thing. But it is an opportunity for you, as students of this philosophy and in this class, to demonstrate your personal responsibility to care for the things in life that you use, including a chair.

And so tonight's class will be on the need of our mind to lose, to destroy property. What is it inside of us that doesn't seem to care? We must awaken to that. For you will find in life that today's waste is a guarantee of tomorrow's want. And we all know how much "want" we have in life.

Now, a person could say, "Well, how could a chair disappear?" Well, the same question was asked of me when we had to raise hundreds of dollars to replace the silver in order that you people would have knives, forks, and spoons to be able to eat food in the church. How do all those forks disappear? Well, it's quite simple: it reveals people responsible, using the forks—it wasn't that they were putting them in their pockets. No, they didn't have that much care. They were putting them in the garbage can. And hundreds of dollars had to be raised and spent to replace the silver.

Now, how does a chair disappear? Well, I think it's a wonderful question. It's no problem. Thank God, the store still sells this particular chair and we will go and replace it.

Now, those of you who feel that you are in financial straits or for some unknown reason, or known reason, do not care to donate your fair share of one dollar to the replacement of the chair, I will do my best to put in your share out of my weekly allowance. Now, are there any questions? *[After a short pause, the Teacher continues.]* There are no questions. Is there anyone—how many are willing to take care of their fair share this evening of one dollar to the chair? Please raise your hands. Those who are not, please just raise your hands. Fine.

Why do we seem to constantly set our self up for all these different experiences? This is a question we must ask our self. What is our need to destroy the things around us? A person may say that we're suicidal. Well, in that sense, we are. But there is so much to consider.

If you think that leaving this physical world, what you call death and transition, is some kind of an automatic process dictated by some Divine Intelligence, then you're far from seeing the light of truth. Our stay here on this planet in this physical body is entirely dependent upon the laws that we alone set into motion. We set these laws into motion, of course, in errors of ignorance and unawareness.

We have what we call good health and then we have poor health. We have what we call happy days and we have what we call sad days. And it just seems to happen to us. Well, it seems to happen to us because we're not aware of what's really going on. It doesn't mean we have to stay unaware. We can become aware of what we're doing if we are interested. And, of course, we have shown some degree of interest in becoming aware of how things work in our life. That, of course, is why we're here.

When we go along in life and we make a judgment of how we want things to be and then they don't work out the way we want them to be, we have a lot of problems, a lot of problems. We get very emotional and we get very upset. We find our self experiencing, usually in the course of a day, some degree of rejection. Someone didn't do what we felt they should: they didn't treat us the way we thought they should treat us. And we all are familiar with what we call the feelings of rejection. But then, being honest with our self, at least attempting to be, we clearly see that our feeling of rejection is the first line of defense, the first line of defense to protect and defend that which we are attached to. We all realize, of course, that we cannot have the feeling of rejection without a judgment. And we cannot have an attachment without a judgment.

So very early in life we learn the device that if we feel rejected, there is a fair chance we'll get what we're attached to. And when we permit our self to think of our self, then we guarantee these feelings of rejection in order to defend whatever we are attached to in our consciousness. No one likes to feel rejected. And then there is the stage of growth in our life that no one really likes to feel attached. Because, slowly but surely, we awaken to the truth that frees us within our self that to be attached to person, place, or thing is to be the victim of something beyond our control. And none of us wants to be the victim of anything that is beyond our control.

And so the philosophers of ages past—and present—have taught and continue to teach the Law of Non-Attachment. For there is no way that we can experience truth and its effect, known as freedom, as long as we permit our mind to be attached. For in that type of thinking is the bondage and the opposite of truth and freedom. Whenever we permit ourselves to think of the thought of I, of the self, we immediately enter a realm of consciousness—in that instant—that offers to us rejection, the defense of attachment, and all the limits that the mind can possibly conceive.

We know already what we think we have. That, we know. We know what we think we have. We are yet to awaken to what we do have. We know what we think we are, but we have yet to know who we are.

When we think who we are, the experiences, the attachments and adversities of yesterday rise up to tell us who we are. And if we are patient with our self, we will see, in those moments, that we are not that which first spoke within us. We are not that which spoke the second time or the third time or the fourth. We are passing through the panorama of experiences that have passed in our life. They have passed and left their mark. They awaken whenever, through the Law of Association, that we, once again, direct energy to them.

It is the birthright of the souls entering this planet, it is the birthright to dictate, in keeping with its evolution, that we may consciously choose the moment that we have completed the lessons that the planet has to offer us. But we cannot be consciously aware of that until the effort is made to consciously control what we call the self, that is the storage house of all the experiences that we have had in our journey here.

Now, when you go through your daily experiences and through the laws of association, these patterns of mind, these forms that have been created by your mind, they rise up demanding the life-giving energy that flows through you that is needed for your vital body, that is needed for your health, your wealth, and your happiness. They rise up and take more than what one would consider their share. For they take all that they can get. They are all consuming. They are born in a realm within our consciousness of blind desire. And I want us all to think of how consuming blind desire really is. You show me a person in blind desire and I will show you a person to whom, at that moment, nothing exists but the desire that they're serving.

So when the human mind, a vehicle of creation, steals the divinity known as desire, it becomes, in the human mind, all consuming. In the birth, which is truly the limit of the divine expression—for when the mind steals the divine expression, which is desire, it is an all-consuming force within the mind. You see, when power, formless and free, when power is taken by a vehicle [of] mental substance, it then becomes force. The mind does not have power. For power is force in a mental world. And force is all consuming in a mental world.

And so we have a desire and we create a form. The form and its creation is ever dependent upon what has been. It is dependent upon what has been for us because unless it is harmonious with what already exists in our experiences in life, it cannot enter the human mind. It immediately gets kicked out.

So we direct the divine, infinite, formless, free intelligent energy to this desire of the moment that we now have. As we do so, the forms of the past that are in harmony with it, they begin to grow; they begin to consume this energy. Because we have yet to separate truth from creation, we think and we believe that that desire, that form, that compulsion, we believe that is us. And in accordance with the Law of Belief—total identification—for us, it *is* us.

Casting the light of reason upon that type of feeling and reviewing our experiences that we have already had in life, we clearly see that there is no way possible that that particular desire, that all-consuming, compelling desire, could possibly be us. Because we go through life and after we have some degree of satisfaction of that compelling desire, we say, "Huh! That wasn't so good after all. Why was I so stupid?" We have now entered a different level of consciousness and really cannot understand why we acted in such a stupid way.

That is the proof and the demonstration unto our self that that form, that desire, is not, and was not, us. But it is, it was, and continues to be something, in our ignorance, that we continue to serve.

Now the question must be asked, why do we continue to serve these various created forms that are proving to us their total selfishness, their absolute lack of considering anything else in our life? What inside of us insists upon serving these forms that we have created?

We all know what it's like to feel compelled to do something. We have a thought in our mind and it tells us we're starved to death. And we eat and we eat and we eat and we eat and we eat. And then, we suffer and we suffer and we suffer. And then, perhaps we'll go a day or two and we go through the same thing! And we do it again and again and again and again and again. And then we have moments of telling our self, "Well, this is ridiculous. What am I doing to myself? And why am I doing this? It is not sensible. It is not practical. It is not reasonable. What inside of me—what am I doing to myself? What is it that I have no self-control?"

Now, we seek truth and we seek freedom, its effect. And we all know, from our own demonstration, that without the control of self, there is no truth and there is no freedom. And yet, we enter these realms of consciousness where we totally lose control of the self.

Now, we lose control of the self when we identify with the self and believe that what the self is composed of is us. That's when we lose control of the self, for we then become the self. And you cannot control that which you become a part of. You can only control that which you understand, not that which you are. There's a vast difference in life.

Now, you want to help yourselves to have this light flow in your consciousness that you may see clearly? Then make some effort, my friends. When these things strike a blow to your mind, before your body reacts, pause and listen attentively to what's taking place in your mental world.

As recent as—I believe it was yesterday, wasn't it?—yesterday, that I had some spiritual work to do that our chairman didn't seem to understand. And I will share that with you because it is one of the ways that you can awaken and be free. I had had a little bit of dental surgery and I decided that I would like to have something sweet to eat, something to chew on. And there wasn't anything in the house that I found desirable. So I went to the store to take a look.

Our chairman says that I spent two hours there. Well, I will agree that it may have been, perhaps, an hour, but it doesn't seem quite sensible to me, with all I have to do, that it was two hours. But I did spend a little time and, of course, it was most beneficial to me. Considering that I spent most of my life eating sweets and especially chocolates, I was naturally attracted to the chocolate department in the store. Anyway, I took a look at *everything*. And, of course, I had spent years eating Cadbury chocolates and all those other seeming goodies that the stores have to offer.

So, as our chairman said, I picked up everything. I looked it over. I fondled it. I put it back, but—and I did do that. And I was listening very attentively to the voices of the forms of yesterday that rose within my consciousness. And how clever the human mind is. Of course, it told me, "I hadn't been feeling too well. It had been *years* since I had all these chocolates. A little bit wouldn't hurt me at all. I *deserved* it. After all, I had already lost over a hundred pounds and there was no reason in the world why I shouldn't have some." So that's how clever they are. That's the first voices that spoke.

And like a movie, I saw all those many years when I could just eat ten or twenty of those candy bars and still, of course, be hungry. And I put each one back and I checked out all these new goodies that they have. And I put them all back. In fact, I must have gone through perhaps a couple hundred of them. I went to two different stores.

I did, however, go and purchase the things that I was supposed to purchase at the same time. So nothing was lost. In fact, everything was gained! So I went through the whole thing. And I said to our chairman, "I don't know what I'm doing here looking at all of this stuff. Why should I buy this cheap junk? I should go to See's and get five pounds of decent chocolate." I heard the thing speak.

You must learn objectivity. And I stopped and I said, "How interesting." Well, needless to say, I did get the other items I had gone for and I—the Friends agree, it was about two hours—and I came back minus all chocolate and minus all goodies.

What is important, my friends, is to be aware. And you cannot be aware without making the effort. To go blindly like some type of a machine and follow the desire that strikes a blow to your mind—it has no interest in you. It is only interested in the vibratory wave that gave it birth. You are an eternal being expressing through eighty-one levels of consciousness. What is it that you would permit one level of your consciousness to dictate your entire life even for a moment?

Time and again I have mentioned to students, when you have a decision to make, do not permit yourself, whatever you do, to make that decision without the minimum of seventy-two hours. For that is the law. That is the maximum time, the maximum time that it takes for your soul to pass through all eighty-one levels of consciousness. So that your decision may be based on the very foundation of reason and wisdom.

Unless you are willing to make the effort, when desire strikes a blow to your mind, to pause in those moments—and even if it takes two hours, what does it matter if you're going to be free?—to pause in those moments and listen to those things speak to you, [you will remain bound].

You see, you will not hear them until you've separated truth from creation. You will feel them and you will think that that is you! But as you gain control over your mind, you will, then, instead of feeling them—the compulsion of these things—you will hear the voices speak, so subtle, so clever. And if you are patient and you are strong, you will clearly hear how demanding they will get. And then, when they get demanding and angry, you will realize beyond a shadow of any doubt the thing, and things, that, through error, you have permitted yourself to be a victim of.

It is creation. The prince of darkness, the prince of death, the king of death, works with creation. From creation your vehicle has come, to creation it shall return. But you must remember that thoughts are forms. They're living things of creation. Given birth in your consciousness, they are your children. They have grown up and you are serving them. They were given birth to serve you. They have turned the tables. It is creation; that's where death is, for that's where birth is.

So your health, your wealth, and your happiness is totally, wholly, and completely dependent upon you being the victim of the forms you have created or being the master of the forms you have created and are creating. Are they doing what you gave them birth to do or are they doing what they want to do and you are serving them? You cannot be free until you separate truth—that which you are—from creation—that which you believe you are. And it is the over-identification with creation that is the bondage and is the lie that we live. We are truth living the lie. Because we believe we are creation, we have become creation. Desire, the divine expression, has lost its divinity because no longer does it serve us. We serve it, the form of our creation. It robs us of our health, our wealth, and our happiness.

And the only reason that they are able to do that is because we gave them birth and we have not given them the discipline that is necessary that they continue to serve the purpose for which we gave them birth. [If] you give a child birth and let him do his thing, you guarantee the day the thing he chooses to do, you will not like. And so it is, my friends, you cannot give something birth and just let it go. For having given it birth, it knows you are the mother and the father. And when it wants something, it shall come to you and take it, for it knows you have that responsibility. And it knows it can take whatever it wants to take whenever it wants to take it, because you've made no effort to instruct it, to discipline it, and, therefore, [you] can no longer control it.

And so it is we find our self compulsed, possessed, obsessed to do so many different things, knowing, in the moment of doing, that they are not beneficial to us. And then we say to ourselves, "Oh God, what happened to me? Why did I do this? What's the matter with me? I've bombed out somewhere." My friends, it's only because you are not listening to what's happening in your world. And if you don't start making that effort to listen, to become aware, then you have no alternative but to continue to serve the lie of life—the belief that you are creation.

When these forms, that we all have created, do not get what they want when they want it, they show you what they're capable of doing.

Now, let's go back to little children. When we had a desire, as little children, and we did not get the desire fulfilled, we did many things to try to get it fulfilled. We felt rejected, we expressed anger, we had tantrums, and, as a last ditch effort, we got sick. We made sure we got sick. And think about that because it's very important to your health today. In fact, it is indispensable to good health to be aware of what we did. When we didn't want to do something, when everything else failed, getting sick had a way of working. And sometimes it took quite a bit of effort to have a stomach ache, to get a cold, to do a multitude of different things so we could have our way.

Now many years have passed since that day. The little baby, you know, it has to be burped, and it gets all upset when its little mind doesn't get its way. So you have to understand that even during the embryonic stage—stop and think—even in those nine months, science, the day will come when they will prove beyond a shadow of any doubt that that intelligent being, from the very moment of conception, is doing things inside the womb when it doesn't get its own way. So it is registered indelibly within the consciousness.

And the years pass and we become adults. And we make many judgments and many forms are created and being served, and we don't get our own way. And so what happens is quite simple: we don't get our own way; we get upset. We don't serve the forms that we, in consciousness, opened the door to, because we see clearly that to do so, that will not be in our best interest. And so we choose to go against those thoughts. And we do what we believe is right for us to do. However, we have opened up the trapdoor to those realms of consciousness and, by so doing, have become a house divided.

And so we go ahead and do what we know, deep inside of us, is in our own best interest and we do it because we know we must do it. But we have tarried too long in those other realms of consciousness and, in so doing, those forms have risen great within us from the darkness of the deep. So the days pass and we do what we know we must do. The forms have not been worked with. They are *furious* they did not get their way and they take the energy from our being any way that they can drain it. And the next thing we know, our health is a little puny, because the energy necessary for the vital body has been drained by the forms—the thought forms that didn't get their way. And so we pay the price. Again and again and again, we pay the price.

My friends, we have merited this experience here in this school in keeping with the laws of our own evolution. Do not treat it so lightly. It is more valuable than all the gold this world has to offer. Your health is the only wealth you will ever have in eternity. Treat it so lightly and you guarantee the day your prayers will cry out without ending for its restoration and it will not come back to you so easily.

The human body requires a certain amount of pure energy flowing through what is known as the vital body for a harmonious flow of the chemicals within the human body that you may have health, following which is wealth and happiness.

Now, you can change your diets and you can do all kinds of health fad things. Your health is not dependent upon what is outside. Your health is totally dependent on what you are permitting your mind to do. You cannot tell yourself you are healthy and expect your health to be restored. The forms of creation you have given birth to many years ago—that is meaningless to them! You open the door to those realms in the instant you permit your mind to enter the illusion of the thought of I. That's what you open the door to.

The restoration of your health is totally dependent upon your effort to be free from the thought of I in order that the energy may flow through your vital body [and] not be dissipated and used up by the mental forms of creation.

All of us have had moments of experiences in our lives when we thought of something that interested us to such a degree that, all of a sudden, in those moments, we felt fantastic. And then, we leave that realm and return to the self and suddenly become aware of how miserable, once again, we are. Well, what happened in those moments of distraction? In those moments, we were no longer identified with—directing energy to—the mental forms of creation.

I assure you, for them, there is never enough. We gave them birth in realms of darkness and in realms of darkness they ever, ever seek the Light and the Light they never get. Their appetite is unbelievable: it cannot be filled. It is like a vacuum. Show me a person serving the realm of desire and I will show you a person that can never get enough—ever. That's what it offers.

Our choice is very simple. And the moment to make the choice is the moment of your awareness, the moment of now. When you wonder where you were and why you do this or that, all you have to do is say, "Just a minute. Just a minute. I am losing control. I must make more effort." When you are tempted, make the effort to be aware of who your tempter is. Do not be so deluded from the attachment to self that you think it is you. You only guarantee the regret after the temptation has passed. Be aware that through our own lack of effort are we tempted. Be aware that you do not have to serve those realms of consciousness.

For many, many, many, many years I have taught, and continue to teach, there's nothing wrong with desire. It is how man uses it. You see, you have a desire and you don't stop to say, "Now, desire, you be at peace and I will weigh out whether or not I choose to serve you in five minutes, five hours, five years, or fifty." And become aware of what happens in your mind. How strong is that thing you have created? Will it listen and consider you? Or does it enter and you are compulsed and cannot do what it dictates fast enough? If you, experiencing desire, cannot control it, be rest assured it absolutely and positively, from your lack of effort, is controlling you. Does it listen to you when you talk to it?

Does it back off and say, "I am your servant"? Or does it rise up and order you to do what it wants you to do when it wants you to do it or you go totally berserk and cannot serve it quick enough?

I tell you, my friends, desire is no longer divine if it does not have the soul faculties and the light of wisdom within it. And if it has the soul faculties and the light of wisdom within it, it has total consideration. It has the absolute principle of patience. And it knows and will not order you to do its bidding.

Thank you.

SEPTEMBER 16, 1982

CONSCIOUSNESS CLASS 226

Good evening, everyone.

Now, I know the last class we were discussing these various things on the mind and we had a little preview here, with some of the students, last evening on respect. And in keeping with our understanding, we grant to others, and can grant to others, of course, only what we grant to ourselves. So if we find that we do not grant to others respect, it reveals to us that we are not granting, in those particular areas, respect; although all of us, all of us have respect expressed in some area of consciousness. For example, we understand that respect—we respect that which we value. We respect that which we desire. We do not always have the respect after we get what we desire, but while we are chasing and struggling to attain our desires, we absolutely and positively show respect to the desire. We find ourselves showing ofttimes an overabundance of respect to our various desires, because we find ourselves often over-identified with them. We find our self bound by them. And we find our self, in some cases, obsessed and possessed by them.

Now, we understand that there is no intelligence that marks us here on Earth for so many days or years, but it is in keeping with laws that we establish. As one of my students reminded me this evening, we always get what we really want. But ofttimes when we get it, we don't see that that's what we asked for because what we see is the payment and are blinded, ofttimes, to the attainment.

If it was possible, which it is, if we made the effort to awaken within ourselves, we can be rest assured that we would be desiring a lot less, having a preview of what it was going to cost us. Having a preview of what a desire will cost us, we would very quickly put the reins on our mind and we would be much more selective with the things that we think that we desire, because we would see how much it will cost us in order to have them.

Why does it cost man such a dear price for the satisfaction of desire? Well, it is quite simple: it is in keeping with the demonstrable law that payment and attainment is the Law of Creation. And, of course, as long as we identify with self, we identify with a dual law. We are then controlled by a dual law and the payment, of course, has to be made.

Now, in all of these experiences, especially in leaving this earth realm, which we are all destined to do, these mountains of laws in our evolution that we bring with us to Earth, the ones we add to, and the few that we awaken to, they all serve their purpose in the final determination of how long we'll be on Earth. How healthy, how wealthy, how sad, or how glad we will be.

Let us not forget, for we have chosen to come to this school to, once again, gain control over the experiences in our life, but let us not forget that that control cannot be gained until we accept the first law of the universe: personal responsibility. When we accept that, when we really accept that there are no accidents in the universe, that everything that we are experiencing, or are about to experience or have experienced, are only effects—they never have been causes and they never will be causes. They are effects—effects of what we think and how we feel. So we know that we can think and we can feel in any moment how we want to feel and how we want to think. That demonstration is only possible with the total acceptance of natural law of the ability to respond personally to all personal experiences. Without that, we will always be the victim of so-called circumstances.

Now, in always getting what we really want, we take an objective look at it and we can see, "Well, the results of this experience are bringing to me what I have desired." Do not be blinded by the law known as the Law of Payment. Because to be blinded by the payment, you cannot see the fullness of the law that is being, and has been, established.

So we move each moment, because by moving in consciousness each moment, that is how we're going to stay free. Now if we do not move moment by moment, then we have to accept the opposite of freedom, the opposite of truth. It is only in the moment-by-moment conscious awareness can we ever be free, can we ever experience the effect of truth, which, of course, is freedom.

Now, in respect to self-desire, which, of course, we understand to be the functions, let us not forget that a function is nothing more nor less than an undeveloped soul faculty. And it is through our conscious awareness—to bring into balance in all of our motivation the soul faculty with the corresponding sense function. Now, when that balance is achieved, you will experience the fullness of life.

The fulfillment of desire is certainly different than the satisfaction of desire. It is as different as day and night. You can tell when you have fulfilled a desire and you can tell when you have satisfied a desire. When you've satisfied it, you often wonder why you did it and you have a multitude of experiences of regret. They gradually pass and you have this haunting feeling to try to fulfill the desire again, not realizing it didn't get fulfilled or you wouldn't still have the need. It did, however, it did get satisfied. So the choices are simple: the roller-coasters of the world of creation or a serene sailing on the sea of the illusion called time.

Every time we permit our minds to think in any way, we are feeding a law, a law unto our self. It is the purpose of these classes and this philosophy to help you to be aware of what laws you are establishing, for all laws return to the lawgiver. We are the giver of the laws that we have made. And we give them out to this world of creation and they return to us. And the returning of the laws that we have given to creation we, ofttimes, do not appreciate.

But we can change all of that because in everything, no matter how seeming bad it may be, in every struggle, in every experience, there is an essence that sustains it. And that essence you call God, the Divine Principle, Goodness, or whatever. But if you will pause in all of the experiences in life that you have, if you will just pause in consciousness, you will see the good that is in it. Now if you will make the effort of self-control—because it does take a control of the mind to continue to see the good that is in the seeming bad experience—you will establish, for you, the Law of Transmutation. And you will turn that around and that will become the greatest good in your life. That is very individual, of course, to each person. But we all have the capability, the possibility, of doing that with any and all experiences.

Unless we make more effort to encourage ourselves, more effort to see the good in our lives, then we can only experience what we tell our self what we don't want to experience.

We cannot ever find the way in anything as long as we insist on seeing the obstruction. So we find ourselves looking around at life, finding a mountain of obstructions. And it seems that we are prone to seeing the obstruction, because by seeing the obstruction we are able to justify to our mind that we are helpless. Therefore, what can we do? What could we do? We are helpless victims. That is what seeing the obstruction has to offer us. We are helpless. There is nothing we can do. We are victims of circumstances. Therefore, no effort needs to be made to change our thinking.

But the very patterns of mind and the created forms that continually dictate to us that we are helpless in these so-called circumstances and accidents and etc., those are the ones that we are serving. Now, of course, we don't have to continue to serve those thought patterns and those forms in these mental realms, but it's going to take, of course, effort to make the change. But we have made the first step by coming to this philosophy and sticking it out as long as we have. It does reveal, as the demonstration in life *is* the revelation in life, it does reveal, of course, that something within us is sufficiently strong in our evolution to at least bring us this far in our efforts to find a better way.

There's one thing about that which has been: we already know what it has to offer. There is no question in our mind. We've already walked the path. And so it's a matter of the moment by moment—to choose in the moment to see the good in whatever happens. That's how you're able to transmute the experience. That's how you're able to transform your life. If you would spend a simple seventy-two hours, just a short seventy-two hours to see the good in every thought you have, to see the good in every experience that you encounter, to see the good in every feeling that you have, you would see a change in your life for the better.

Now, people can talk to you and talk to you and talk to you. They can make great effort to encourage you. But, of course, they cannot, they cannot live for us. We have to have that desire to make a change for the better in our life. So if things get bad enough, the desire gets stronger. So, you see, it does serve a good purpose. Now some of us, it seems that our heads are like blocks of concrete and it takes God only knows what for that desire to make a change for the better to become strong in our consciousness. For each one, it takes what they need. And if we are patient, we will see for our self. We may not have the tolerance (by not having the understanding) why some people take so long to make changes in their thinking to bring about a better life for themselves.

Now, I'm going to—here, this is the eighth class—give you some time to ask questions on any of the philosophy that is important to you at this time, if you will just raise your hands. Yes, please.

There's two parts to the question. One is, What is a miracle? And how is it that we don't see more of them in our lives?

Thank you very much. Our understanding of what is termed or called a miracle is simply a lack of our understanding the law through which an experience (or miracle) takes place. In that respect, miracles—in that respect, miracles are happening every moment, for survival itself is the miracle of life. Because as we look at life and we see that somehow, looking at our own past, somehow we've survived this, somehow we have survived that, somehow we're still alive, in that respect, not understanding the law through which that has been made possible, that, of course, to our self, we can see is a miracle. Because we do not yet understand the law through which it has taken place. That's the only reason. But I assure you, what we call miracles—our lack of understanding those divine laws—they are taking place all the time.

Now, for example, you see, a person says, "Well, I have this health condition. The doctor says it's going to take this long a time for it to be cured." Well, now there are several factors involved in the healing process. Number one is the obstruction created by the human mind. Does the patient believe that particular doctor? And in that belief, is it sufficiently strong to override other beliefs that the patient has? Do you understand? Now, the doctor has based his belief on his experiences and on his own education and his own understanding. Therefore, doctor to doctor, there are differences and they vary. Now, so the patient is told, "Well, it's going to take so long a time—perhaps it'll take three months for this to be healed before you can do such and such." Now that enters the computer, our human mind, and if we have a—if it is in harmony with various desires and judgments that are already in control of us at the moment the doctor has spoken to us, then it becomes accepted on *that* level of consciousness. Now, there are eighty-one levels of consciousness and it does not become accepted by the other eighty unless that judgment, that belief, is in harmony with what the other levels want in their own selfish desires.

Now this is how all these experiences and things take place. So we find in life that some people are receptive to the Divine Healing Power in varying degrees. That is wholly dependent upon the judgments that are in their computer. And whether or not what they are being told is receptive. Now, sometimes a person, not understanding anything about divine or spiritual healing, not having any experience at all—in fact, the best student is the one who knows nothing. Because if they know everything, you have nothing to offer them. So what's the teacher doing? A waste of time, indeed. So we find, ofttimes, the less we know, the more wisdom we have. The reason for that is as we become more knowledgeable, we create within our mental realm of consciousness more judgments, more obstructions, and more difficulty.

In our study and hopeful application of these laws of life that are revealed, if there isn't a sincere daily effort made to open fully the soul faculty of honesty, then we find that the student, in time, has more and more problems. As each truth is revealed, the judgments of the mind use it to fulfill the various mental patterns that it is, in its evolution, attached to. Now it doesn't have to be that way. But it is that way unless there is sincerity, unless there is honesty with oneself.

So here we have healing. The doctor says it's going to take so long to heal. It enters the computer on the level of consciousness that the person is attached to and controlled by at the moment. Let us say that it is receptive to level number, say, 22, for example. And an hour, half hour, five minutes, two hours pass and they find themselves on level 30. To level 30, it's just barely harmonious and acceptable. And so we find the person starting to doubt whether or not that doctor knew what he was talking about. Because on that level, you understand, there's not as much receptivity or harmony for the particular judgment. And then the person starts to think and to question and to doubt.

And the most important thing of all—the one thing that establishes the law in the mental realm—the person begins to fear. King of the mind: the great force of fear. Now, unless the person, now trapped on that particular level—starting to doubt, question, and fear rises—moves to another level of consciousness in which they are more receptive, you see, through the law that like attracts like to the original level on which they accepted the doctor's statement, they will soon find that the levels that they are not consciously controlling will start to go to war! They'll start battling in the human consciousness.

And so, "Maybe he's right, but I question." And he goes someplace else, perhaps, depending how the levels rise up to gain control. Because the person, number one, is not consciously aware of the levels of consciousness [and] is not making the daily effort to control them. And you cannot control what you're not aware of. It's contrary to the natural law. And so the individual finds themselves in rather a state of confusion. And fear gets stronger. And finally they prove that the doctor was absolutely wrong! In fact, he didn't even know what he was talking about. Because that's how the human mind really works.

Now, it could work the other way. It could work in the positive way. They accepted what the doctor said. It was in harmony with the level at the time. It was in harmony with the levels later. And the next thing you know, the doctor was absolutely right.

Now, we understand that fear, the force of the human mind, is faith, negative faith. Because it offers to us—fear offers us the obstructions and the struggles of life. So faith in the human mind, known by most people as self-reliance, offers to us a life of fear. We are afraid of this, we are afraid of that. And we are afraid of things that haven't even happened. And by our fear of things that have not yet happened, we guarantee them—as man is a law unto himself—we guarantee them to happen to us. We are, in that respect, our own self-prophecy.

It doesn't have to be that way. We can choose another path. We can know beyond a shadow of any doubt that that is right for us is taking place and then make the constant effort to see it. If we cannot see that which we desire is taking place, if we cannot see it, then for us, in that realm of consciousness, it cannot be. We must learn to see that it is, not that it's going to be. Whatever it is, you see, when you enter a certain realm of consciousness, then you know beyond the shadow of any doubt that it is. Because for you it is.

It is this illusion of time that you must pass through and all of the obstructions in that illusion that your mind has already created. Now, a person may say, "Well, they speak their word and it happens. That's a seeming miracle." But it only happens because they've entered a realm of consciousness above and beyond the illusion and, therefore, have gained sufficient control for that which they desire, they speak forth and it takes place. But that takes an awakening of the human mind and how it works. And following the awakening of how it works, the effort to daily control it. Does that help with your question?

Yes.

Yes, the lady here, please.

In speaking of payment and attainment in creation and then, I also recall in parallel to that, that recently it was said that if we attain something without payment, we've been in the soul faculty—I believe they said. And that if we go back into self, the payment is extracted again. Would the same payment be extracted either way or would it be of another kind?

Thank you very much for your question in reference to payment and attainment. And the payment only exists in the world of opposites. Now, for example, the statement isn't that you're in the soul faculties. The statement is you're in the faculties and the functions—that they're in perfect balance. I believe if you will listen to that, you will find it is the balance of the faculties and the functions. Otherwise, you could not have that individual personal experience of your attainment.

Thank you.

You see. Because without the functions—you see, we must understand that functions, certainly, are not limited to a physical body. It's in the head, you know. Surely, we will all agree to that: that's where it takes place. It's not taking place in the foot. It's in our mind. And so, you see, the senses are not something that, when we take off our physical body of clay, that they go with it. They don't go with it at all. They go wherever we—our mental world—goes. There they are. Whether it's the mental world, the astral world, we still have an awareness of self. Yes.

Now, when there is a balance between the soul faculties, a perfect balance between the soul faculty and the corresponding sense function, then you are freed from identity with the Law of Creation, which is opposite and dual. Now, being free from a dual law, there is no payment, for there is no attainment. There just *is*. So if there just *is*, there is nothing that you are working to and therefore there is nothing that you are paying for. You are no longer identified with these pairs of opposites, for you have brought them all into perfect harmony and into perfect balance. You see?

So it is a matter of our choice of what we are identifying with. Now, if in an experience, you take a look and you see the obstruction, you are paying the price for the way. If you do not view the obstruction, you don't have the payment for the way, for you *are* the way. But if you insist in life on seeing the obstructions in life, then you have to be willing to pay the price of life: the price that you are obstruct—the price that you are making and extracting from life is what you choose to do. You choose to see the obstruction and, therefore, must pay the price. But we don't have to.

Thank you.

You're welcome. Yes, the lady back there, please.

Are there guidelines that one could use of turning off the mind?

The mind is an instrument that can be, and is designed to be, controlled. It cannot be turned off. There is no way to turn off the human mind. There is the possibility of entering a state of consciousness where there is one thought, one experience, and a moment of peace. But just to take a key and turn it off does not work. There are ways of controlling it, which are indispensable to the good of any individual. For without control of it, life is filled with a roller-coaster ride. It has its highs, only to guarantee its lows. Does that help with your question?

Yes, indeed.

The gentleman here, please.

Thank you for answering the first question. We know what this philosophy teaches on fear: when we get close to taking a victory, that fear will tend to rise and keep us from that particular attainment. But in case of illness, now, we make judgments—and the function of pride also has a good, a good effect because its ego cannot stand to listen to a dictate of a judgment made by an individual or a doctor when he says it's going to be—it'll take so long. Can you tell me what it takes to have the function of pride, the uneducated function, to, say, combat that attitude or make it more positive?

Yes. Well, pride certainly, in reference to your question, pride certainly serves or can serve and does serve, for many people at many times, it serves a wonderful purpose, you see. It's just like the human ego. The human ego serves a wonderful purpose. It gets us into trouble when we let it do its thing and we don't take conscious control of it. Because the human ego and pride doing its thing, it's going to do whatever the strongest patterns are that have been programmed into it. And ofttimes that does not serve us very well.

Now, one certainly can use the pride very well in reference to their health and etc. I mean, after all, I used a little of my own when I had surgery here the other class night. And I've had a few dental surgeries. I have a responsibility and I managed to face my responsibility, for me, very graciously, because my pride would not allow me to say, "Well, tonight's class I've given to some of the other directors these past few weeks," because I have great value for whatever responsibilities in life I incur. Because my own pride, my own upbringing demands that of me.

I don't have, but should have, of course, a little more tolerance to people who can so quickly and so easily shirk their responsibilities in life. But then, I have to also talk to my own mind and tell myself the truth, "Well, we all have different priorities in life. We all have different values in life. And because I expect respect for that which I value, of course, knowing the law, I must show as much respect as I can muster for those who have different values."

Now, in today's language they say—I've heard—different strokes for different folks, which is fine. However, we must consider whenever we make a choice in life, let us give it our very best effort as long as we choose to do whatever it is we're doing. And when we no longer want to give it our very best effort, then let us look around in this old realm of creation and choose something else to give our best effort to do. But whenever we have a job in life, we should learn to do it well or not at all. For it is better to do a few things in life very well than to do many things in life only partway. And the reason why, one of the most important reasons why, in doing anything in life, though it may be a few things, do them very, very well, because if you do not do them very, very well, you don't have healthy forms to live with in this eternity. But you have very sickly forms, diseased forms.

You see, it's like a woman having a baby. And from the moment of conception, she only goes two months and gets rid of it. Well, how long do you think that it will survive without the process of decay and stench? Well, now this is the way it is with the babies that we create with our thoughts. Thoughts are forms. When you make the conscious choice in anything, choose it wisely and leave it healthy by doing it in its formation—by forming it with your very best effort. Because if you do not, as the creator—for we are the creators—if you do not create your forms and put your best effort in—quality is not just a soul faculty, it is indispensable to good health. Indispensable to good health. Without the quality of consciousness, I guarantee you, health will not be the best.

Your thoughts, if you choose to have thoughts—and we all choose to have thoughts; our minds just keep on going on and on—choose them wisely, create them healthy by giving them, these babies you're creating, these forms, by giving them your very best effort. And don't walk away and leave them half created. Because they are not only unpleasant forms to see when you open your eyes to those realms, but they are discordant forms—half formed, a quarter formed, a third formed—but they are discordant and they are diseased.

So the gentleman has asked in reference to pride and viewing a health condition in a positive way. The positive way is to know and not permit the human mind to use the experience to satisfy suppressed desires. You see, my friends, suppressed desires in life, they set us up for our experiences. And this is why there are no accidents in the universe. I guarantee you there are no accidents. Nothing happens to us, to anything, neither does the leaf fall from the tree, by chance. It's in keeping with divine natural law. It does not fall by chance.

And so it is with our life. Our experiences are not by chance. They're in keeping with the laws that we are establishing. Let us be aware, fully aware and make great effort that it may be healthy. And the restoration of health is totally dependent and *wholly* dependent upon the soul faculty of honesty. And who are we to be honest with? Why, my good friends, the one we're most identified with. And I think everyone will agree that's known as self.

Be honest! You see, we set ourselves up constantly. Look, what happens to the human mind—say that we want to go on a little trip. Say that we want to get away. That we feel that we deserve—because we have worked so hard—that we deserve a vacation. We have a right to a vacation! The desire goes through the human computer and all these forms rise up to tell us, "Why, no, that's just not possible." And they give us all these dictates. Well, if the desire to have the vacation—think, my friends—if that desire is not educated or fulfilled, look out! You guarantee to set yourself up, for you are forgetting that desire is the divine expression. It has the great power of the Divinity itself. You have permitted yourself to be receptive to it and directing it into a certain form. The form that we are now speaking of is the form of vacation.

All right, now, so the vacation does not come. The mind justifies the many reasons why it can't have it. And time passes. The desire, with all its power, has not been released and expressed. It has not been educated. It has been pushed down into the computer, the deep recesses of our subconscious mind. It goes to work diligently to have its fulfillment and it does many things, ever working in those dark realms of consciousness, that we, someday, must cast the light of reason upon, to set us up that it may have, *regardless of the cost*, the vacation that we have desired. Think of that, my friends. It's doing that to us seven days a week, day in and day out, moment by moment by moment by moment.

But then, how do we work with this great power? If we will not make the conscious effort to be aware, if will not accept the possibility, if we will not enter the realms of consciousness through our own effort where all things are possible, we guarantee to set ourselves up. And when—you see? Say we ask for a vacation. We get the vacation because we're laid up in the hospital! It is a vacation from our usual routine. It may be longer than we had desired, but it is a vacation from the routine and the judgments that originally set us up to desire a vacation in the first place.

Try to understand how your mind works because many years are spent on the human mind. Because without an understanding of the human mind, it is almost a waste of time to discuss the eternal soul and the spiritual realms. We are identified with, and familiar with, the human mind to some extent. We can relate to our thoughts and how we feel. So we must awaken to how it really works.

Now, when you hear the teaching "We always get what we really want,"—believe me, just because we cannot see it at the moment, we always *do* get what we really do want.

Now, how is that going to help (that awareness) in the healing process? Why, it's the indispensable ingredient for the divine healing to take place and the seeming miracle to come about. Because, you see, what are we dealing with? We're dealing with judgments who made their law in our consciousness—that we needed this or we needed that or we needed a vacation, justified etc. So time passes. And circumstances, conditions, and seeming accidents seem to take place and we have a vacation, but it isn't the one that we desired. But it is a vacation, so the principle of the law is fulfilled and that's how it works.

So you want a healing? Then, it's got to be through honesty. Be aware. "OK, so I wanted to do this. And now I'm in a position to do it, but look at my payment. I don't appreciate it at all!" And then, through honesty, you trace through the consciousness and you find all of those dudes and you have a talk to them. And you accept the law that you alone have set into motion. And through that acceptance of personal responsibility, the healing, you become more receptive to. And the time of the restoration of health is shortened. And that's what healing is really all about.

Some are receptive; some are not. Some have few obstructions; some have mountains. Some have all these suppressed desires waiting to be fulfilled that are setting them up right around the clock.

Say, for example, that a person says, "Well, now I, I want to be home more often. I'm not home enough." And they have a job they work on five or six days a week. If they are not careful, if they are not honest, you may be rest assured, oh, they'll be home more often. Too bad. Somebody else got their job. But they are home. So you must take a look, my friends, what it's really like. It's like a woman—say she has two children. She says, "Oh, they're so cute. I wish I had another one." But she's already made a decision that two's enough. Well, the next thing you know, she's got a third one, and keep on going on and on and on.

There's a great deal about the human mind that we must make daily effort to understand. Through understanding, we will gain control over it and we're certainly going to benefit by it. Why, I spoke to one of my students just the other night who had difficulty staying awake. I said, "You know, you never have any difficulty staying awake; when I look into the universe and see one of those desires, why, you can be awake all night long. In fact, one occasion you have been! Because of that desire, you're wide awake. There's no problem with sleeping at all." So, don't you see, my friends, it's wherever we choose to put our thought. That's where it is.

And everyone has just as much will as I have. Some people say I have a lot of self-will or a lot of will. They don't tell me "self-will," but they say I've got a lot of will power. Well, I don't have anymore and I don't have any less than everyone else. It may seem that way because I choose to direct it consciously. But I never met a person that didn't have a lot of will power. I never met one that had more than myself, and I certainly never met one that had less. But they choose to direct it in different ways than, perhaps, I often choose to direct mine. But it doesn't mean that God shorted them of will power. No, not even the animals have been shorted of will power. Now, some people, they look at will power and they say, "Oh my God, that tenacity is unreal!" Well, it's expressing in the form of tenacity, but it's will power that is moving the form of tenacity. That's what it is. So we have plenty of will power—the power of our will. But it's not serving us well, because we're not making the conscious daily moment-by-moment effort to direct it. That's all.

Health is restored in keeping with the soul faculty of honesty, which opens up the doors of harmony, where health reigns supreme. I do hope that's helped with your questions.

Thank you. We'll have refreshments now.

SEPTEMBER 23, 1982

CONSCIOUSNESS CLASS 227

Good evening, class. Now this, if I recall here, is class number nine. Yes, we have two classes left to go; there are eleven classes. It seems that everyone is here that wishes to be here.

Now, we have discussed, of course, in these classes many different things: all the way from self-respect to getting what we want in life. The question is, of course, knowing what it is that we want. We also have discussed briefly, in different words, how we set ourselves up for various experiences. It behooves us to look at any experience in our life and see what is in the experience that we desired at some time to call it forth.

So often we have seeming disasters and seeming crises and seeming poor health and seeming something else and we, unfortunately, do not see that the experience that we set into motion and called forth is offering to us something that we have, at some time, desired. Because we do move from various levels of consciousness—and it is our purpose here to help us awaken to gain control over these levels by first understanding what these levels are, how they work, and then we're in a position to gain some degree of control over them.

It seems the number one problem that most of us seem to have, most of the time, is our supply in life. Now we all know that if we think we have little, we guarantee the law to have less. So if we think stingy, we experience stingy. And, of course, the opposite is also true: as we think abundantly, so we experience abundantly. But we also must use the faculty of discernment, for there are many things in life that we would not care to experience abundantly. Each year, long about Christmastime, there is a great abundance of what they call the common cold. And none of us would consciously desire to experience that abundantly. So we must use some degree, of course, of discernment.

When we say to ourselves that the law is demonstrable, that we always get what we really want, and then we have experiences that we think we don't want, we are not being honest with our self and becoming aware of the level of consciousness that we were in to set the experience into motion in the first place.

It has been greatly stressed in these classes—and always has been stressed in these classes—the Law of Personal Responsibility. Because we will always be the victim of what we call circumstances until we accept the Law of Personal Responsibility;

that when we deny that Law of Personal Responsibility, then, of course, we no longer become the captain of our ship nor the master of our destiny. So that is when we feel helpless and, ofttimes, hopeless. The moment we deny the demonstrable Law of Personal Responsibility, we become the victim, and the cause of all of our problems in life is beyond our control because it belongs (that cause) to someone else. It belongs, of course, to someone else because we made that so in our consciousness. We know we don't have to make that so. We know we make it so because of what we call patterns of long use or habit patterns.

Now I think we'll take a few moments here, for a while, during this class, and permit you to ask some of the questions that you have over the many things that have already been discussed. So if you will be so kind as to raise your hand, please, with your questions. Yes, please, the gentleman here.

How can we be more honest with ourselves?

It's an excellent question. How can man be more honest with himself? Well, we know that we cannot be honest with our self, or with anyone, until we first understand our self, because we cannot be honest with something that we do not understand. And so the first step to make is that effort to understand why we think the way we think and why we feel the way that we feel. If we do not feel good about our self, then we are not going to experience good in our life. And so we have to make, someday, that daily effort, *daily effort* to become aware of what type of thoughts and thought patterns that we have in our mind and, in becoming aware, to gradually, slowly but surely, to understand them. Once having brought some degree of understanding of them into our consciousness, then we can move to being honest with them.

If we will pause and think that whatever any human being says, does, thinks, or experiences, is, in potential, inside of our self—now, whether or not we choose to express the way someone else expresses is not what is important. What is important is that that potential lies within our self. By accepting that truth, we gradually, slowly but surely, begin to understand the levels of consciousness and in that understanding, we gain tolerance. And in that tolerance, we then become qualified to be honest with our self.

Now there is no way possible that we can be honest with our self without expressing the soul faculty of tolerance. It is not possible because you cannot be honest with something you cannot tolerate. How can you be honest with something you do not tolerate? Because, by the Law of Intolerance, you do not accept; you reject it. So, you see, my friends, first open up that soul faculty of duty, gratitude, and tolerance that you may have some degree of understanding and, in that understanding, demonstrate the faculty of honesty. Does that help with your question?

Yes. Thank you.

You're welcome. Yes, please, the lady here.

Is expressing your divinity one and the same with expressing through the eighty-one levels of consciousness?

Thank you very much for that most important question. Is expressing your divinity one and the same as expressing through eighty-one levels of consciousness? Indeed, it is. But we express through eighty-one levels of consciousness in what is called the divine expression by bringing the balance between the eighty-one levels of consciousness. There are forty soul faculties and forty sense functions. When they are brought into balance, then the Divinity, that number one, the eighty-first one, that expresses equally through all the functions and faculties in perfect balance, which is known to man as harmony and, therefore, is the perfect health, which is his birthright. Does that help with your question?

Yes, it does.

Yes. Yes, please, the lady in the back.

If, in the past, you have created a harmful thought form and you wish to lay that form to rest, is there something that you can focus on or use each day to try to offset the thought energy that has gone into that form?

Yes. Now, if you have created a thought form which has proven to be detrimental to you, is there a way of putting it to rest? Well, there most certainly is. First of all, by understanding that the form or thought, which is form, was created in a moment of error of ignorance—for no one consciously chooses a thought that they know, beyond a shadow of any doubt, is detrimental to them. No one would do that consciously. But we do, through lack of control of our mind, we do direct energy to thoughts that prove to be detrimental.

Now when the soul faculty of consideration is not balanced with the sense function of need, we have very serious problems in life. You see, when we permit our mind to think that we have a need, what happens in that moment—we are totally out of balance with the faculty of consideration. And in that imbalance, we establish a law of limit. By the very thought of need, we become the Law of Limit. And we do that by not bringing about in our consciousness an awareness of the soul faculty of consideration.

For example, say that a person says, "Well, I have a need for a pair of shoes," just for example. And they think about that and as they think about that, all of the thoughts representing the Law of Limit rise up in the consciousness. They do that because we are not considering the whole. Now when we think that we are in need, we not only establish the Law of Limit, but we also establish the Law of Denial. You see, my friends, denial and limit are inseparable. Whatever you deny, you limit; whatever you reject, you limit. And you pay the price of that limitation.

So often a person will feel that this person or that person has absolutely no consideration. But what we don't see is how they are controlled by the function of need. If you believe that you are in need, you may be rest assured you do not consider any other level of your consciousness and you certainly do not consider any other person. This, in turn, becomes known to man as pure selfishness. Show me a person in need and I will show you a person in selfishness, for their horizon is totally limited to one level of consciousness.

Now, to free our self from that, we start to think about something outside of that particular need that is in our consciousness. As we do that, our consciousness begins to expand, to encompass other experiences—present, past, and possibly future—and we free our self from that feeling that has certainly proven repeatedly to be detrimental to all people. Does that help with your question?

Thank you.

You're welcome.

Now we all know that the more we think of limit, the more limit we experience. The more we think of need, the more need that we have. But let us pause and think. We've already had the experiences of thinking, "Oh God, I need this. I need that. I'm short of this. I'm short of that." We've already had all of those experiences. We know how beautiful it works to think that we are in need and experience, yea, even more need. Now the law works whichever way we turn it. So why not make the effort in consciousness? We already know how beautifully and infallibly it works by keeping us in need and keeping us in limit. So why not use the same law, just simply redirect it? And see how beautiful it works, because the law works either in the negative and destructive way in consciousness, as well as in the positive and constructive way in consciousness. And we alone are the directors. So let's use the same law that's already proven to our mind how beautiful it works. Let's use the same law in the positive way. But that will take a little bit of conscious, daily effort on our part because we are so used to using that law in the negative way.

You see, my friends, the law, any law, is impartial. It has no personality. It just simply works. But it is up to us to choose which way we want that law to work for us. Now it certainly takes some degree of self-control, certainly takes some degree of self-control when you believe that you are struggling, when you believe that your health is poor, when you believe that you are in need, it certainly does take and does reveal to all of us individually and collectively how much control we have over the human mind.

The human mind, from our errors of past experiences, has become the obstruction in our way. We know we cannot see the way as long as we see the obstruction. So we try to move out of the mind and to see more clearly the path before us. And being out of the mind, look at the mind from an objective view and, slowly but surely, gain control over it. Because whatever in life we do not make the effort to control, we establish the law for it to control us. Now there's the choice in all of life: either you make the effort to control the thought or you lay down and let the thought control you.

If you tell a person who's upset that they are controlled by a thought in their mind, oh, they will agree, of course, because they know that it's their mind and it's their thought. They will justify twenty billion reasons why they have that thought and why they are having the experience that they have. But, my friends, you cannot help another to help themselves unless they are ready, willing, and able to do so.

Now ofttimes in life we ask for help. We always receive help because the law is absolutely impartial. We may not recognize the help that we have received. Sometimes we don't recognize it for a year or two later, but we always do receive in keeping with the Law of Giving. And in keeping with the Law of Giving, let us understand a little more clearly, perhaps, that most people, most people have great difficulty, great difficulty in receiving. I think we'd all agree to that. Stop and think of your desires and tell me if you have found any difficulty in receiving fulfillment of the desires that swim in your consciousness.

So we see that man has difficulty receiving. But then, does man have difficulty giving? We look and we see that one and that one and that one, they have problems asking. They have real problems asking. They have great difficulty communicating, because, you see, even as the Bible teaches, knock and the door shall open, ask and ye shall receive. If you do not ask, you do not give. For to speak is to give forth life-giving energy to the words and thoughts you form. So we find most people, having difficulty with communication—not talk. Talk is not only cheap, there's plenty of it. Communication, communication we have difficulty with. We have difficulty with communication because we have great difficulty with giving. We will not give forth our breath of life to open our mouth and ask. And that's where our problem in life is. We do not give forth; therefore, we do not receive.

Now, usually when things are what we judge really at a disaster for us, we may open our mouth and we may ask, but do we really ask? Do we ask or do we declare? You see, a person who asks (gives forth the breath of life) is in what is known in this philosophy as the divine will. And the divine will means total acceptance. So if we, in giving forth the breath of life, we speak, we ask, we can tell right away whether or not the divine will is flowing 2 percent, 10 percent, 20, 40, 50, 60, or 100 percent. Because what returns unto us, we can see what percent gets in. That, of course, is dependent upon what judgments and dictates we had before we spoke forth our breath of life.

Now if we ask and what we receive we are not comfortable with and we do not appreciate, it only reveals that it is, and was, not in harmony with the judgments we were serving at the moment of asking. So we receive. The judgments got furious because they had already dictated what we should be receiving and that's where one of our many, many, many problems are. We ask man, instead of God. We ask—you see, before we speak our word, let us pause and ask the question we're about to give the life-giving energy to, ask the question of that Divine Spirit within us. And then let the words come forth that they may reach the Divine Spirit that is flowing through someone else. Now that means we have got to be free from our judgments when we speak the word.

Say that a person wants help with this or they want help with that, and our minds dictate what that help is. Then why ever bother? If we already know what the help is, then we will chase the universe over to find that which will fit into those rigid judgments that we are serving.

Our purpose here is to make the effort, first, to become aware of what they are doing to us from lack of our own effort of daily working with them until they're finally educated. But if we're not going to do that, then we must pay the price of the limit and the need that they offer.

Now we've all have had experiences with certain thoughts in our mind. And we all know that when the thought—[when] we permit it to be in control of our mind, it has absolute zero interest for the rest of our life. It's not concerned about all the other things and experiences and responsibilities of our life. It's only interested in its particular thing, because we created it for that purpose. You see, a person ofttimes, you know—they get into desire and nothing else exists but the satisfaction of the desire. And the desire itself in our mind, it's not interested in anything else about our life—only in its own satisfaction. Now there's where the form really gets created. So it rises up, almost like an obsession, [and] takes control over us. We feed it the life-giving energy necessary for its continuity; [it] lays down and rests, rises up again and each time a little bit stronger. Now no one with the slightest light of reason would serve that type of a selfish master that is only considering and interested in one thing.

Now you may ask the rest of your questions, if you have any here. Yes, the lady there, please.

What has been said now is exactly what I have been going through. And I've been trying to rise above the level that has me in control and every time I try to be objective toward it, for a moment it works and then—this need I'm speaking of—something comes up and I'm required to attend to something that would keep me thinking about it instead of thinking away from it. Of course, I realize I attract that, but I don't know how to separate it at the time it's happening to keep it from growing.

Thank you very much. In reference to the seeming difficulty in gaining control over a thought form that we alone, of course, have created, as long as we permit our self to believe that we are the thought, we will forever be the victim of the thought. If we will make the effort to declare the truth in our consciousness frequently—that we are not the thought, but we are the power that sustains the thought—so that, slowly but surely, we can gain control over our mind and separate truth from creation.

Now we cannot serve two masters and have the fullness of life, for a house divided cannot stand. And so it is that we must someday awaken that we are not the thought. We are not creation. We are that which uses creation. Our problem in life is our false belief that we are creation. We are not creation. We have never been creation. We will never be creation. We are that which uses creation. We are *not* creation. And until we make that effort to separate truth, that which we are, from creation, that which is, then we cannot gain control over creation or over these thought forms that have proven repeatedly to be detrimental to us. Does that help with your question?

Yes. Thank you.

Yes, the lady here, please.

Since it seems like there's so many things to work upon, is it wise to concentrate on one problem you're having or to work on them all at once?

No. The lady is asking the question, Is it wise, when you have so many things to work on, to work on one thing or all of them at once? It is certainly wisdom that dictates one thing at a time and that done well. So choose whichever you prefer and work with it until you have gained control over it. Because by doing that, you will establish the law in your consciousness of your ability and will not continue to be the helpless victim of those realms of consciousness. Choose one at a time. Gain control over it and move on to the next, the next, and the next. And believe me, [in] those realms, as you slowly but surely gain control, the message will pass quickly, for they are very chummy in those realms of consciousness. Yes.

Yes, the lady here, please.

Could you explain creativity?

Now, by creativity, do you mean the process through which we are viewing and experiencing creation or do you mean the ability or talent of bringing forth and creating something in your consciousness?

I believe that's what I mean.

The latter?

The latter.

Yes. You see, all people are inspired. Now, there's not a human being that is not inspired. Therefore, we all have access to what man calls inspiration. Now from inspiration, as it enters the human mind, it becomes limited and restricted by what the human mind has already experienced, unless the person is fortunate enough to have control over the mind at the time the inspiration is flowing. Now if they are not able or have not had the experience of gaining control over their mind, then the inspiration becomes limited, distorted, and, unfortunately for the receiver, becomes mistaken for themselves. Now when that happens—the creativity, which, you understand, is not possible without inspiration—the person becomes reliant upon what they think is the human mind to accomplish what they choose to accomplish with their creative talents. When that happens, they soon experience great difficulties. Sometimes it looks beautiful and sometimes it's just terrible. That is because the human mind has taken claim to that which it can never claim. Now if a person is spending some time each day to gain control over their thoughts so that they may experience the power of concentration, then they will be free from that interference that's created by the human mind.

Now, I hope that's helped with your question. Yes. *[After a short pause, the Teacher continues.]* Well, we have a wonderful dinner tonight. We may have a short class if—I don't know where everyone is this evening. Do you?

No.

Any more questions? Yes, the lady here, please.

When a person is working on educating a level of consciousness . . .

You go right ahead.

And they realize when the defenses rise for the level to protect itself that it is not them, but they allow it to express and to feel it in the process of trying to work with it, is that wise? Or is it better just to redirect the energy to another area, rather than to allow it to express, even though, inside of you, you are trying to work with it?

Well, I think we should ask our self the question, What inside of us, if anything, has a need to experience the level that has already proven itself to be detrimental to us? Now, if we have a need, we feel there is a need inside of us to have these horrible feelings of a detrimental level expressing itself through us and we find that we have some kind of masochistic tendency—that we have a need to suffer—then, of course, in that respect, for the individual, of their conscious choice to suffer, yes, it would be better for them to let it express through themselves. But if you already know how detrimental the level is and you already know what it feels like and you understand that you don't have a need to suffer like that, then it is in your best interest to simply redirect the energy. Because that that you give attention to, you give and direct energy to.

So if a level, rising up and expressing through you, has proven itself to be detrimental, why make it stronger? It is not in one's best interest to make it stronger by placing more attention upon it. Now if we a find that we somehow have some kind of a need to have those things express through us, though we're aware of what's happening, then it would behoove us to be honest with our self and ask our self if that's the only way we're able to find to get attention or energy directed towards us.

You see, everything, every person, every flower, every blade of grass, every animal, every bird, every human needs energy. Without energy, they're not on this planet. Therefore, every blade of grass, every leaf, every flower, every dog, every cat, every bird, every human needs attention. They must have attention or they do not exist on this planet. Now this is where the real problems really are.

Without energy, we do not survive. The law through which energy flows is the Law of Attention. Therefore, we must have attention because we must have energy or we don't survive. Now our minds have found many devious ways of getting energy through the demonstrable Law of Attention. But those devious ways have proven to be so detrimental. A person will go through a course of a day and feel very low on energy—"Got to do something. Need some energy." A thought goes into the computer. The computer comes up and offers to you the experiences through which you have gained energy before. Now remember, the law is established: you have a need of energy. Now you will do, if you are controlled by the mind, you will do whatever is necessary to get that energy. It doesn't matter whether you destroy yourself or someone around you. It doesn't matter at all. Your basic motive is energy and it flows through attention.

Our purpose in these classes is to help you to find more constructive, beneficial ways of receiving your energy.

Because we ground our self out from self-thought, we find our self in serious problems from the lack of energy. And that is something we all need to work on. We can receive all kinds of energy by doing a good job in life. But if our mind and our experience have proven to us that when we foul up and we become a you know what, we get more energy and, then, when we find we need energy, that's what we do: we foul up and we do all kinds of things in order that we may have more energy, as the living demonstration is on my right here. *[The student on the Teacher's right had fallen asleep.]* Do you understand? Does that help with your question?

Yes.

Fine. Now some people have to snore to get energy. Some people have to just sleep to get energy. Some people have to do terrible lousy jobs to get energy. Some people have to go contrary to rules and regulations to get energy. Children do all kinds of things to get energy. Yes, the gentleman in the back, please.

Yes. When one places his focus and attention on the Divine, knowing full well that everything will be taken care of in creation, but one is tempted or distracted by creation, by forms, by thought back into physical reality, how—and sometimes it seems to be all encompassing and smothering that you can no longer see the light. What can we do or how can we snap out of that to bring our attention back to where it should be?

Thank you very much for that most important question. In being almost—it's almost like a possession, creation can be. Because when you understand, my friends, that it is Mother Nature, nature—creation is the magnetic field in which we live. We are in it, but we must never allow our self to become a part of it. It's when we become a part of it that we become controlled by it.

Now, it is a magnetic field. Its nature is to gather and garner. And we enter that magnetic field and creation from the lack of conscious awareness of where we are at any given moment. So we know that from the lack of conscious awareness we enter that magnetic field; we become a part of creation, instead of being the motivating power through creation. When we become trapped by it, the only way I know to get freed from it is to affirm the truth that you are in it and not a part of it. And through that constant affirmation—that you are in it and not a part of it—you will, slowly but surely, gradually wrench yourself free from the magnetic force of creation.

You see, the Spirit, the Divine Principle is an electric vibration in comparison to the receptive vibration of Mother Nature or creation. And one is power and the other is force. Nature is force. All thought is force. All emotion is force. It has great magnetic hold, but it does not have endurance. It does not have endurance.

You see, you will find that nature—in the process of form, there is great pain. In the process of disintegration, there is great pain. What you understand as pain only exists in the magnetic realm of consciousness. It does not exist in the formless free Spirit. Duality, form, only exists in a magnetic field. It strives to attract its kind. So if you have one positive thought, it will attract all other positive thoughts into your life in that particular area. If you have one negative or magnetic thought, it will attract all of its kind.

You see, we think many thoughts. Some thoughts—we have a feeling for a thought or we don't, would you not agree? Well, remember, the thought that you have a feeling for, the thought that you have an emotion for was given birth in your magnetic field. It will bring you pleasure and guaranteed to bring you pain. For all thoughts that you have emotion for are magnetic and they will offer pain. They will tempt you with pleasure, and you will pay the price of pain. Man should seek the fullness of life, for only a fool seeks the pleasure of life. Because, I am sure, if we knew the pain that follows all pleasure, we would very soon stop seeking pleasure. Because none of us seem to enjoy the pain. Does that help with your question?

Yes. Yes.

Yes, the lady over here, please.

Is that similar—I think my understanding was in one of the classes about desire and you had said if we really saw the payment of desire, we would not desire things. So would that mean that to not desire, which comes from the soul, you would have to be on the eighty-first level of consciousness moment to moment, all the time?

No, no, no. Desire is the expression of the Divinity. It is when man—when the desire enters the human mind, it comes under the Law of Payment and Attainment because we make it so with our own judgments.

You see, say that a person is thirsty. They desire to quench the thirst, do you understand?

Yes.

Now that is a free, clean desire. It enters the mind. All it is, is we're thirsty. We just want something to quench the thirst. And then the mind goes to work and it says, "Water? I don't want a glass of water. No. A soda? Perhaps a soda. No, a milkshake instead!" And it goes through all of this. That's when you enter the realm, the magnetic field, and that's when you pay a terrible price.

You see, it's like a person having a desire: they want to get married. And they take a look around and they say well, they want to marry a woman. And then that's only a split [second] thought—that just lasts a split second. She's got to be blonde-haired, blue-eyed, maybe green eyes, no, maybe gray eyes. And she's got to be so tall, so broad, so wide, so much money in the bank, so much this, so much that. And that's where all the payment is. The desire is divine. It is the expression of the

Divinity. But it leaves principle; to enter form, it gains personality. Now remember, principle is principle until it enters form. Then it becomes personal, personality. Does that help with your question?

Yes. Thank you.

You're welcome. Yes, the gentleman here, please.

What is the true cause of our resistance to communication?

When in our life, we have asked and have not received in keeping with the judgments preceding the request, and those experiences have been repeated for us many, many, many times, rather than suffer the hurt which is in those experiences, we make a decision: we just won't ask anymore. Therefore, we find people who, on certain matters, they will not communicate no matter what. Because what is at stake, what they are defending is a level of consciousness that has been deeply hurt in their early experiences in life. Does that help with your question?

Yes.

Because that's what they're defending. You see, the truth, which is within us, that doesn't need defense. It's the falsehood, it's the forms that need defending. It's not the truth. Yes, the lady here, please.

So when is it a good idea to be in a relationship?

What relationship?

Well, like, let's say—you were talking about—like, if you have—you have a desire to be in a relationship with somebody. But it sounds like it's fraught with, you know, a lot trouble. So I'm wondering when is it good to approach . . .

Well, now that's an excellent question. First of all, a person must say to themselves they have a desire to be in a relationship, but what do they mean by "relationship"? I mean, what do they really mean? You see, a person must awaken inside themselves and say to themselves, "I want a relationship. What do I mean, 'I want a relationship?' What is it? What do I mean by that? What does it mean to me?" Then you look at it and say, "Oh, it means someone to go to the movies with. Oh, it means someone to sit down and to eat with, because I'm tired of eating by myself. Oh, it means this; it means that." And you have to go down your list.

Because if you don't, one of those on the list—or maybe more—will attract a person to you and you call that a relationship. So in certain ways the relationship is just fantastic, but in all those other ways, it totally is a disaster. Because, you see, the person in the desire for the relationship was not honest with themselves. They didn't make their list out and say, "Subject matter: Relationship," and go down the list. *[Many students laugh.]*

See, that's the thing to do. That's reasonable. That's the business of living. You just go down the list. "I want the person to do this. I don't want them to do that. I want them to be here when I want this." And on down the list. And then you submit that to someone that you are attracted to and either they will be in accord or their desire is so blinding, they'll agree automatically—and you'll soon find out later—or they won't. Now that's honesty. Don't you see? And you put down all the things you can't tolerate, because maybe they pick their teeth and you can't stand a person that picks their teeth. You see, that, you see, now that's—honesty will lead you through. Now, I admit, it will take a little while, but it could save you years of disaster. Perhaps you don't like a person that snores. Well, you have to put that on the list. Do you see what I mean? Then, you come to terms whether or not, in your desire for a relationship, there's anyone on earth, or in heaven, that can fit in, you see? I mean percentage-wise.

Say that you have a little over a thousand things that they would have to fit in to. Well, if they fit in to, maybe, eight hundred, are you willing to have tolerance for the other two hundred? Does that help with your question?

Yes.

Don't you think you would feel much better, rather than to find out the hard way later on?

Oh, yes.

I think, now if a person in a relationship, marriage, or anything else, if they would be honest with themselves and take their inventory, you know, of what it is they really want and what they're willing to negotiate and what they're not willing to negotiate—one should get that taken care of up front before they step into any kind of relationship. Because, don't you see, my friends, you will see where *you* are and won't be deluded and think, "Oh, it's where they are that's the problem." Because you've already done your inventory. Then you really know where you are, being honest with yourself. And then they know where you're coming from. And either they fit in or they don't fit in. So why even make the first date if they don't fit in?

But unless you have some expanding tolerance, you may find difficulty in having anybody fit in, you see. Because everyone carries these packages around with them.

And another thing: to a human being what they desire as a relationship one day may mean something entirely different to the mind the next day. And they're not even aware. Say that a person, they want to see a movie. And they're out sitting in the movie house by themselves and they say, "Oh God, now I wish I had a relationship." So at that moment they desire a relationship. Then, the next day, they're doing something else and they say, "Oh, here I am all by myself having to carry this heavy load. Now, if only—I wish I had a relationship." Well, what is it they want? They want someone to carry the groceries. They want someone to take them to the movies. They want someone to sit across while they eat and maybe they even want them to cook for them. We must be honest with our self to find out what it is that we mean by the word *relationship*.

When you, when you have a desire for something, don't just go off blind trying to fulfill it because you won't fulfill it at all. You'll temporarily satisfy it and you'll always be followed by regret. Don't you see, the reason that you have desire and regret is because in your desire, to your mind, it means different things to different levels of consciousness. So you have a desire to do something or be with a person or etc. or a relationship and, on that level, that's what it means and that's what you're aware of. And two days later, your desire for a relationship means something entirely different because you're now on a different level of consciousness. So it is a disaster for a person just to have a desire and not become aware what in the world that desire means to their mind. Because it means one thing at one moment, only to mean something else at another moment because you are on different levels of consciousness. There is no harmony, peace, or abundant good until we gain control. Through an awakening of our levels of consciousness, we gain control over them. Then when you say the word *relationship*, you've got the whole list and you know exactly what it means to you. So there are no surprises. Does that help with your question?

Yes.

Thank you. We have time for one more. Yes, please.

I would like to ask how to keep it in principle, then if we're making that list.

Excellent question. Certainly, certainly, indeed it does, because the moment principle enters form, it's now personality. Now when you have a desire for a relationship, that does involve a person, doesn't it?

Right.

A form. So it's already entered personality, you see. In that moment, in the moment that the desire, which is principle, the moment it enters the mental realm, it has a form. And the moment it has a form, it has personality. So, you see, in the very desire, when the mind got it—that's why we give it back to God, the desire that we stole. It's the mind. When the mind gets it, it has form. Before the mind gets it, it doesn't have any form. It's the principle itself. Yes?

Then you're saying—it seems like a paradox. Then don't have a list, because that would be personality. It wouldn't be principle of the law that...

No, but you need a list, because you live in a mental world.

Oh.

Now as long as you insist on identifying with the thought of I, then it behooves you to have a list to know what that offers you, what it means to you. Now the next stage is the evolving up out of that realm. But as long as we are going to identify—I don't know, one of my students said years ago their most favorite subject is the thought of I. You know, you talk about a person and they feel great. And we're very interested in the thought of I. So we have to wait until, in time, we evolve out of this thought-of-I business.

But while we're in the thought of I and we have the desire, the principle enters the mental realm and it immediately takes form. And because it takes form, you've got to deal with form. So it behooves you to make your list out and see if you can find anyone that'll agree with it. I'm sure if you're willing to negotiate over half of it—60 some percent of it—you'll find someone who's—but, you see, it would be foolhardy for you to make out the list and not have them make out their list. Because you should know where they're coming in from. Does that help with your question?

Thank you.

Yes. All right. Yes.

Is there sexuality in spirit?

Well, it depends on what you mean by that.

OK. If there are male and female in spirit.

Yes, but it depends on what you mean by that. Do you mean a thought in the mind or do you mean a physical act?

Well—sexuality is a thought in the mind?

It most certainly is.

OK.

And without the thought, there isn't any. It doesn't exist. And I guarantee you, if it wasn't a thought in the mind, we wouldn't have so many of the things that we see in this world. Without the thought, it does not exist. But, you see, you should go beyond, beyond that. If that is the way we have limited experiencing God, then if we don't always have it, then we have real problems.

You see, it's all these different things. It's not the thing itself. It's what we have, in our ignorance, created, that we, by—what is happening is, we've made all these judgments. And if it doesn't fit in with the judgments (the experience) then we don't feel good. So we say, "Well, that was a bum experience. I don't know why I wasted my time, energy, and money," and on down the list. But what we are really doing—because we are identified with the thought of I—we are satisfying those different judgments in our mind. We don't have to do that, but that's what we're doing. Yes.

OK, but we are taught or lead to believe that it takes a man and a woman to conceive.

No, it does not take a man and a woman to conceive. It doesn't take a woman; it doesn't take a man. It simply takes the thought, for that's where conception is. You are conceiving constantly. You're giving birth to this thought, to that thought, to all kinds of thoughts. Conception is conception. Do you understand that?

Oh, yes, I accept. I mean—

No, no, no, I don't want anyone to accept anything they don't make the effort to understand. We are conceiving—do you mean to tell me that it takes another person for you to conceive a thought about something?

No.

Ah! Therefore, it is our delusion and our belief that it takes someone else to do anything. Now what I'm interested in is, if we permit our mind to dictate that it takes such and such or someone else for us to experience what we choose to experience, then we are dependent upon circumstances seemingly beyond our control. Of course, we attract the circumstances, because like attracts like and becomes the Law of Attachment.

Does the ear of corn need something else to conceive?

No, sir.

Well, it most certainly does not. I never saw a female ear of corn. I never even saw a male ear of corn. And I wonder if anybody else saw a male and a separate female ear of corn. It's self-producing, like the race used to be. But then that's another discussion.

Thank you very much. Have a nice refreshment.

SEPTEMBER 30, 1982

CONSCIOUSNESS CLASS 228

Good evening, class. This evening, our tenth class—we have one more for this semester. Now several of the students have asked if there will be another semester. I was informed this morning that there will be. I was not, however, given the exact date. I doubt that it will be the remainder of this year because of the holidays and the bazaar and the other work that has to be done.

Now you'll find that, as you spend the time, the effort, the energy, and the years to study on any spiritual path, that ofttimes a person seems to become quite discouraged with what they think, or don't think, is their growth. And one should pause and think, because the teachings in life that one receives are reflections of their own growth and efforts in life. And that law, of course, is demonstrable in anything and demonstrable in everything. So that kind of shoots the bottom out of the justification of being discouraged, I would think, in reference to one's spiritual growth.

We must try to understand that the mind is mental substance and, therefore, does not have the capability of understanding that which is spiritual. So if we are questioning our mind for spiritual matters, then we can expect both the yeses and the noes, for that's what the mental world has to offer.

If we will take a few moments each day—because each day is what's necessary—to make some effort to apply at least one of the many teachings that have already been given. Long ago it was stated that this philosophy is taught in bits and pieces. It's like a great puzzle and the pieces all fit to together if you work on the puzzle long enough. We receive in bits and pieces because that's what we allow our self. None of us are completely receptive to anything at any given moment because that would be contrary to our identification with varying levels of consciousness.

And just a few days ago I revealed to a few of my students one of our wonderful teachings that is so demonstrable, as they all are, and that is: presumption, the Law of Descent. Now we've all heard that presumption is the Law of Descent. But I assure you there were very few—only those that it was revealed to the other day—[that realized] that presumption is the Law of Descent and the birth of disaster.

Now if we will be honest with our self, we can take a look at all disasters in our life and we can see that they were born in the level of consciousness known as presumption. Now many people think that the only reason that a person presumes anything is because they're lazy. But we must go far beyond that to see why we presume things. In our consciousness, there's these various levels that are constantly demanding their fulfillment.

And if we permit our self to be over-identified with our self, then, of course, we are victimized by these multitudes of desires and demands to do things. And so as we are over-identified with that realm of consciousness and receptive to the many contrary demands from the different levels, we presume many things in order that we may continue to serve the demands of these different levels that we, unfortunately, believe that we are.

It doesn't matter in life what you believe in. It does matter in life that in the believing process, you become it. And so we have become the struggle, because we have, of course, identified with the struggle. We have become the discouragements, because we identify with them. And it seems to be difficult for most people to gain sufficient control over their mind, through the power of concentration, to consciously choose what they will identify with. Because in the conscious choice of what you will identify with—a *conscious* choice—you have the potential of the light of reason.

We understand and have taught before that the light of reason and all soul faculties flow through the conscious mind; that all functions express and flow through the subconscious mind. But when we permit our self to think that we are the thought which rises from the depths of our subconscious mind, by permitting that error in our thinking, then we become the error itself.

Now we try, we try to make a change. Even though we know consciously that it is in our best interest, even though we *know* that we must make the change—we know it deep inside of our being—and yet when it comes to make the change, we either get a pretty good start and flake out before we get to the finish line or we get a very slow start and flake out or it seems that we keep viewing it and don't even get started. And we have to ask our self what inside of our self does that to us. Here, we consciously know what we want to do. We consciously know what we *have* to do. And yet, something inside of us does not permit us to do it. Now looking at that level of consciousness clearly, honestly, and objectively, it reveals to us that we are serving something that is not in our best interest. And yet, we cannot seem to break the bond.

We will not be able to break the bond until we separate truth from creation, until we consciously make the effort to declare in our consciousness that we are not the thought, but are the power that moves the thought. Unless we do that frequently, we will continue to be controlled by the magnetic forms of patterns of the past, residing in the depths of our own subconscious mind. There is no other way to be freed from them except through that conscious, frequent effort.

Hardly a day goes by that there isn't some experience that we seemingly do not appreciate. And time and time again, we permit our mind to tell us that the cause and the fault was beyond our control; that it was something else—or someone else—that did it to us. It is in that type of thinking that we continue to be controlled by patterns and forms that are not in our best interest. It is those things that hold us. And their only hold upon us is our identification with the thought, which is the form: that it is us.

Now when you feel not too well, if you permit your mind to think that you do not feel well, then you direct energy to the form that has awakened within your consciousness that is telling you that you don't feel well. And by your attention and energy being directed to the form, you may be rest assured you will feel worse. That is, of course, the law that has been revealed about obstructions: the obstructions are the thoughts that we continue to direct energy to.

The moment that we permit our mind to deny our ability to respond to any thought, any feeling, and any experience in life, the moment that we permit our mind to deny our divinity of the ability to respond intelligently and reasonably to any experience, then we are bound and controlled by what has been. Now we have taught for many, many years, that *is* personal responsibility. Until we accept that in all areas of our life, we cannot move farther upon the path of light, truth, and freedom.

The greatest benefit in this particular school to any student is not only the teaching, but the application that exposure frees the soul. The evolution and freedom of any individual anywhere at any time is revealed in the reaction or the action to the light of reason known as exposure. You see, that is what exposure, that frees the soul, really is. It is the light of reason.

Now the light of reason is not subject to anyone's particular judgment. The light of reason is exactly what it says: it is the light of reason. And the light of reason will direct the responsibility of any experience at any time in anyone's life back to the individual who has the experience. That is why exposure, freeing the soul, the light, which is the light of reason, is the greatest benefit to any person that this organization has to offer.

Because you have all experienced—and I'm sure will continue—that out in the world in what they call the mundane jungle, it is a very rare person who cares enough to make the effort to reveal to you the truth. They have other interests concerning you. Therefore, it is rare that they will ever take the chance of your not liking them. You must remember, my friends, any mind, anywhere, that has a need for people to like them has a desire to get something from the person that they want to like them. Now when we face that, perhaps we'll start to be free from the insatiable need of people to like us. Because in the need for people to like us, we sell cheaply the light of truth, the light of honesty, and the light of freedom.

If we will, in our thinking, tell our self whatever we think we need is not dependent upon what we think some person has or has not—because in making the effort to tell our self that truth, we will, slowly but surely, move to the source that can supply it, and will supply it, without this terrible price tag in creation. In the process, of course, I can assure you we will all learn the wisdom of patience and the freedom from dictating how things shall be.

So when we react to the light of reason, we should be grateful, in that moment that we pause, that we see clearly that we have permitted our mind to believe that we are the thing that is reacting. Our basic teaching is truth needs no defense. That that is does not need to be defended, but that that is not needs all the defense that your emotions can possibly muster. And so one of the first things one experiences in the light of reason—the exposure that frees the soul—one of the first things that you experience is what is called justification, excuses, which is a defense, a defense of that which, through your error of identification with a thought pattern, a form, is controlling you at the moment.

Now we would not have this great need to defend our thoughts and acts if we were not so identified with them. It seems so very difficult for us to simply admit the truth. If we did something or didn't do something, if we took care of our responsibilities or did not take care of our responsibilities in life, what is the great, big deal that we must justify our reasons for not doing it? Because, you see, my friends, you cannot justify reason. You can only justify falsehood. There is no possible way that you can justify truth and reason and the soul faculties. You can only justify the sense functions.

When that effort is made daily, there will be no question where you are in consciousness. There will no longer be any question how much you have grown or have not grown, because you yourself will know, day by day, where you are, how far you have come over the years and possibly, with continued effort, how far you'll be ten years from this day. So through that daily practice, you'll know right where you are in evolution.

Now we are all here on Earth and we all got here in keeping with the laws we long ago established and we will continue on. Many are called and few are chosen. But let us never forget we choose our self. There isn't someone else that chooses for us. It's like when a person asks a question and they're waiting for support for the judgment they already have. I am asked many questions and many people are not pleased, because it wasn't a question in the first place. It was a seeking of support for a judgment that one had already made. And because ofttimes what I have to say in answer is not supportive of the judgment that is brought to me, many people, many times, are not happy.

But that's our problem in life: we seem to have spent so many years going around the world trying to make someone happy because we were trying to get something. And certainly, it is a merry-go-round of experience. When we no longer have the need to get something, we will no longer sell out our divinity. When that day happens, that moment, then we will surely do what we know we must do and we will not be so concerned about what people do with it or don't do with it.

We've spoken before on how we loan many things in life and the loan is always revealed by our constant attachment to that which we have supposedly given. But as we are concerned, we only reveal to our self we never gave it at all. We loaned it and all those strings are tied to us. Let us take an honest view at the price tag of selling out because we want someone to like us, because, in truth, we want something from them. This is this great need to have other people like you. Because if we're honest with our self, we will very quickly see there's something we judge that they have that we want. And we don't know just when we're going to get it. But as long as we want it, we will surely, quickly sell out to the fickle minds of this old Earth planet.

It's a very expensive way to live. It's also a very painful way to live, because, through constant practice with that level of consciousness, you reach the day in evolution when you really don't know who you are and you certainly don't know why you're here on Earth, let alone how you got here or where you're really going. And, slowly but surely, nothing really seems to matter.

There's no light in the eyes that reflect the soul, for there's no enthusiasm left. Nothing seems to bring us cheer. The sky seems filled with gray clouds. The sun seems to have gone out for us and we begin, then, to exist. So we move like machines to our job and back again and we eat and we sleep, but nothing seems to really have any value. For we spent so many years trying to please others, because there was so much we wanted and we judged that they had it or may have it.

I show you where the end result is: existence, not life. Oh, we still have the breath to breathe, but there's no joy. There is no real peace, for there's no truth, for there is no personal responsibility left for us. Because that's the price that we have extracted from life and, having done that, we simply exist. This is why, once having reached that stage in evolution, it is so very difficult to find anything to enthuse us. It's very difficult to find anything that brings a lasting feeling of joy, for we say to our self, "If life is like this, then what's the sense of living?"

But the truth of the matter is, life is not like that. Existence is like that. And there's a vast difference between life (living) and existence (simple survival). Now we all know, even though sometimes we reach that state of consciousness, we still know that there is something better. The only problem with knowing that, we still look outside to find it. And then, we do not find it. Because it isn't outside. It never was outside. It never will be outside.

And when I say that life is ever as we make it and always as we take it, that's not just a pleasant saying. That is a demonstrable truth. That is a law that works for you, is waiting to work for you, moment by moment by moment.

You can be wherever you want to be once you decide to make the effort to control your mind. But you cannot be where you want to be when you want to be until you learn to control the mind, which establishes the laws in the world that you identify with and believe that you are. So as long as we identify with self, with mind, with a mental world, then let's gain control over it. Let's gain control over it and use it wisely and stop letting it be the control of our life.

When you think you feel the worst, when you think your struggle is the greatest, that's when the opportunity for you is the greatest. Because in that moment, you can see clearly, very clearly, the law. It's right in front of you. You can take control of it. You can direct it and you can bring about for you whatever change is necessary.

Now many teachers have taught that a house divided cannot stand. And yet we desire to make changes and make them not. Let us be honest with our self and let us take a good look at our desires, that we all have, to bring about certain changes in our life in certain ways. Now—and we find such difficulty we do not make the change we desire. It is because we are transgressing the natural law of life. Sometimes you will find a person who desires to make a change and as long as there is someone close by to constantly repeat the laws necessary to bring about the change, the change for them happens. But they do not grow as strong or as healthy or as well spiritually as if they would make that effort of repetition, the continuity of repetition.

The breath of life reveals to all of us the continuity of repetition—continuously repeating again and again and again and again. We quit before the victory because we transgress the Law of Continuity, the repetition that is necessary to take us through the gate of victory in anything in life that we desire. That's sad, but it's very, very true. What we do not see is that the great struggle, the patterns that we are serving were born under the Law of Continuity, repetition. And so to give birth and have a strong law to rise to a greater change and a broader horizon, we must use the same law, for the way out of a thing is the way that we got into the thing. And the way that we got into the patterns of yesterday is through the Law of Repetition, the Law of Continuity. And only through your conscious choice and then your continuous effort and constant repetition will you move on to the next step.

Now in our life's experiences we see, time and again, certain disasters. In keeping with the Law of Presumption, we gave birth to disaster. But they're also—disasters are telling us something else. They're not only knocking at the door of our conscience, they broke the door down! And they're now called disaster. They had knocked for a long time and nobody answered. We did not answer our conscience. We didn't listen. We paid no attention. And so finally, they beat on the door and broke it down and now we call that disaster, all right?

And what does disaster tell us in our life? Like it or not, we've got to make a change in our thinking! We've got to make a change in the way we think and the way we do things. We just have to or continue to experience disaster upon disaster upon disaster. So our choice is very simple: make the necessary changes or guarantee the continuity of the Law of Disaster. That is our choice. How fortunate we are not left without choice. We don't need to go see anyone about what changes we need to make. The disasters that broke down our door of our conscience, they've told us loud and clear: "This is the experience that you have merited in keeping with the way that you insist on thinking and acting in life."

Now none of us like to hear the benefits of struggle and disaster, but they are there, for from the disasters and the great struggles, sooner or later we force our self to make some changes in our self.

Now remember, friends, the more we love our self, the more difficult it is for us to make a change, because we so firmly believe and so love that which we think we are, but which we are not. So people—no matter who we are, the more difficult it is for you to bring about changes in consciousness to bring you a boarder horizon, a freer life, a more abundant life, it's totally dependent on what you've done with the power of the universe, known as love, the cement that holds it all together. If you have and are a channel through which it may flow to return to the Source to flow again, then changes in your consciousness shall not be difficult. But if you have stolen that great power and believe it is all yours by directing it to the obstruction, creating a dam to the river of life—the dam of self—then the changes shall be extremely difficult for you and they shall come about only through what the human mind calls unfortunate circumstances and, of course, don't forget, with that falsehood, "beyond my control."

We know—at least we have been taught here that there are no accidents in the universe, for an accident is a circumstance, an experience beyond your control. And the moment that we permit our mind to tell us that anything, anyplace, at any time is beyond our control, that's the moment we lose hope and we lose, completely in that moment, the light of reason.

We like to think we are the captain of our ships. We like to think that we are the masters of our destiny. I assure you, my friends, no one is the captain of their ship as long as they permit their mind to think for one second, one small second, that any experience that they encounter is circumstances beyond their control, called by man, "accident." From the common cold to cancer, there are no accidents. Because accidents (circumstances beyond one's control) are contrary to the demonstrable law that you *are*. And because you are, in consciousness, the light and the truth, all things are subject to it. All things, all thought, which is form, is subject to the source that sustains them.

The bondage and the slavery that we have, through our error, permitted our self to enter is that the thought tells us that we are it. We no longer tell the thought, "You are a vehicle of form that I have created by my mind in a world of mental substance. And because I and I alone have created you, you are subject to my will." That *is* the truth.

And so when you know you must change for your own good and when you know it deep in your being and when the thought that you believe is you rises up in your consciousness and tells you no, you must learn to cast the light of truth upon it and tell it what it really is: a thought form that you created, subject to your will, and order it to do your bidding or forever be the slave of all creation.

Thank you.

OCTOBER 7, 1982

CONSCIOUSNESS CLASS 229

This, of course, everybody knows, is the final class of this semester. Now there's so many things to discuss and to make the effort to be aware of, but tonight experiences have helped us and guided us to understand something about laws.

Now, rules and regulations, whether they're in Serenity, they're in some other organization, or they're in society, are only effects. They are given birth by transgressions. So we find in society a mountain of laws, rules, and regulations; traffic laws, all kinds of laws that we have to abide by. Now how does this affect our personal life? Well, as far as traffic laws are concerned—regulations governing the flow of traffic throughout our land and throughout the world—it's quite simple: it affects us every time that we walk across the street, because there's such a law and regulation as jaywalking. It affects us every time we get into our car and drive anywhere at all.

How does it affect us with our health, with our finances, with our happiness, and everything else? Quite simply. Because laws, mental laws, man's laws—because no one can say a red traffic light is God's law. That's man's law. All those laws, all those rules and regulations were given birth because someone did not abide by the law, the divine Law of Total Consideration.

Now surely we all remember from our teachings what total consideration is. Is there anyone who does not understand it's divine love? And is there someone missing? Because it is the living demonstration that total consideration was not used here this evening to start your final class. Now—and we were just discussing this because, as you know, one of our students just entered, contrary to our rule and regulation of the time the class shall start. So we see by the living demonstration that total consideration or divine love is not being expressed.

And because total consideration, divine love, God's law, the infinite law, is transgressed—it is transgressed because man is not considering totally, in the sense that this total consideration flowing through us has been limited to specific areas of our consciousness. Now when that happens, you give birth to obstructions, known as regulations, laws, or limits.

Now none of us want to experience limits or obstructions to our personal desires. And we find ourselves very frustrated because we see in our daily experiences that there are obstructions to the things that we desire. There are obstructions to the things we want to do. And, slowly but surely, we become very weary of experiencing those obstructions on our path. And that weariness is known to us, to our mind, as struggle. And we don't like to have to constantly struggle. Now I'm trying to show you the cause of your struggle, the cause of the obstructions in life to the things that you desire.

I have spoken to a few students several times about presumption, the Law of Descent. Now presumption, the Law of Descent, means just what it says: a descent—not an ascent—but a descent into darkness. Presumption, the Law of Descent is the birth of disaster. So we find in our daily activities that this isn't going smoothly. It is not going harmoniously. Things are not flowing for us harmoniously. And we have all kinds of problems. And we wake up in the morning and there's one problem right after the other. We hardly crawl out of bed before there's a problem. We hardly get dressed before we find the struggle of life.

I assure you that that is not the design of life, but that is what we have made of life, because we have taken this divine love, this great power, this intelligent energy, we have taken it and we have restricted it and limited it to very narrow patterns of our mind that we absolutely refuse to change. And because we are so tenacious—and we're all equally tenacious. It's all a matter of direction. We all have and experience divine love. It's a matter of direction. It's a matter whether we want to broaden it or keep it limited into the patterns that we have so rigidly established in our life.

I've said before, and I say again, life is beautiful when *you* are no longer attached to the way that your ego, the uneducated part, dictates that it shall be. Now, when you are no longer attached to the dictate of how life, for you, should be, then you will awaken to how beautiful life truly is. Now when you take all this great Energy, called God, and you restrict it to certain areas, what you have done, my friends, is totally burned out, literally burned out the benefit that can return unto you.

Now there are times in your life when you try to get something accomplished. And you try and you try and you try and all you ever experience is obstruction upon obstruction upon obstruction upon obstruction. It just doesn't seem ever to work out. Be grateful with those experiences because they are telling you in no uncertain terms that, sooner or later, you will have to change the way you think. Because if you don't, there won't be much of you left. The experiences are telling you, those experiences, they're telling you to broaden your horizons, to accept something greater than what your mind has already offered to you.

Now the question is, How many years, how many trillions of experiences will it take for us to accept that there is a better way? If you are happy and if you are pleased with the experiences that you already had, then, for you, it is evident and, for you, it is obvious, there is no need in any way, shape, or form to make any changes in your thinking. However, if life has revealed to you a desire for something better than what you have already experienced and continue to experience, then it's time. The time has come. Reason is knocking at the door of your conscience and the time has come to accept the possibility of making changes in the way that you think. For it's the way you think, in the sense of directing the intelligent energy to these various patterns and realms of consciousness, that is causing all the obstructions, all of the limits in your life.

Now, you tell a person to change their attitude in order that they may experience a greater flow and depending on the student's effort, years of study of application of divine, natural, demonstrable spiritual laws, they'll tell you one word: "But." And that's where the problems are. The problems are all the "buts," because they reveal immediately to the listening ear the defense of a level that is absolutely unwilling to change in any way, shape, or form. And this is why we have this beautiful teaching revealed to us many years ago: O suffer senses not in vain for freedom of your soul is gain. The suffering of the senses is very obvious. It is our unwillingness to broaden our horizon. It is our own unwillingness to make any changes.

Now, why are we unwilling to make the changes that will bring us a more abundant life, a healthier life, a better life, with all of the good that is our birthright? What inside of us—how does it work?—that we absolutely will not make those changes? My friends, when you believe you are the thought that's in your mind and in that belief you become it, for you the path is only one of suffering and struggle. A few moments of breath— a few moments of fresh air, but in keeping with your belief is your attachment to those attitudes of mind and to those ways of thinking, to those patterns of thinking, and therefore you cannot wrench yourself free. Now, because you are not the thought, but you are greater than the thought, then pause to think. It is always possible (when you are ready) to make the change.

Why do we have so many problems and difficulties in the jobs that we merit in life? Think, my friends, because we think we are doing the job and because we believe that we are the thought that we think, all of the limits, the patterns of mind of the past, all of the experiences of yesteryear control us while we're doing our jobs. Because we made them *our* jobs. Now when you say that this is my job and that is not my job or these are our jobs, then what you're really saying and what you are really doing is quite simple. It's not a matter of accepting the responsibility for what you have merited—that's something entirely different. The phrase that is used that I have heard for many years is, "That's not my job. *This* is my job." What the mind is telling you is quite simple: "This is mine! Therefore I will do it my way." And that's when all the problems begin.

Because "This is mine,"—whether you call it a job or a million dollars, it doesn't—there's no difference to the principle of that law. "This is mine. That is yours. And because it is mine, I have total control over this and I will do it my way even though my way is contrary to the job that I have been given. I will do it my way because it is my job." This is how our minds think and create all of these problems in our life.

Now, we say, well, we go on our job and we are paid for the work that we do. And we do it the way the boss, the employer wants it done. Oh, that's not true, my friends. We *think* we do it the way the boss or the employer wants it done and in a sense and on the surface that is, usually, what we do: sufficient cover-up not to get fired. But because we believe it is our job, we have these experiences called, "Oh, it's an accident." "I forgot." "It just slipped through my hands." And go on down the list. It's called rejection, retaliation, revenge. And that's what our belief that we are the thought in our mind has to offer for us in our life.

Now, you go to communicate with someone else about a particular job and then the problems really get multiplied. For you have this particular job and you know how—and have accepted—it is to be done. And now you go to train someone else. At the very thought that they have—that they are now going to get that and it is now going to be theirs, their entire army of "their way" rises up. And you find that there wasn't clear communication in the instruction that you received when you got your job. Now think about that, friends. And it's not limited to just going to work on a job. It's every time you receive an instruction, every time you receive any guidance or any communication from anyone at any time; unless you begin to take control over your mind, that's what life has to offer you: struggle, frustration, disaster.

I don't know of anyone with any intelligence, once awakening to what they are permitting their mind to do to them, would insist on remaining attached to it. Now we may stop to think, "It's all I have." Well, as long as we think it's all we have, that's all we will ever get. Now I remember the years when one of my students kept saying, "Well, I just don't understand. I don't understand. I don't understand." I said, "If you don't stop saying that you don't understand, you never will understand. For you establish the law where it is not possible for you to understand and you will remain stupid."

Now let us think, in this final class of this semester, what it is we really want to do. If there is something that you want to do, don't permit your mind to tell you that what you want to do is dependent upon what someone else does. For example, say you want to build a house. If you permit your mind to tell you that you want to build a house but the bank's not making any loans, then, for you, that's all you'll ever get.

So, you see, my friends, if you don't apply what you have been given, in keeping with the very law that you are learning, you can reap no benefit from it, for you have done nothing with it. You see, that that is not used decays. So if you receive the way and do not move, then, for you, it has done nothing and will do nothing until you choose to make the move. Now, hopefully we understand a little bit, perhaps, about laws—man's laws, the mental laws, society's laws, the laws of our personal life, how we're setting them into motion, the true cause of limiting God's love, total consideration, to one or two or three or five little areas of consciousness.

You see, my friends, the only time we can have a "my way" is when we believe we are the thought that's in our mind. And when I speak to you about God's way, that's the broadest of all horizons. For God's way in consciousness, in your consciousness, to which you are identified with, there is no limit, there is no obstruction.

We all have will. Therefore, because we always have will, we always have a way. Because that is the Law of Way, the lord of the universe—to man's mind, will power. You need will power in order to fully serve your eternal soul. You need an ego in order to fully serve the purpose of your journey through eternity. But the ego, which you need, which is designed to serve your soul, needs education. And what do I mean by education? It's very simple: by directing God's love, the divine intelligent energy to a limited few patterns of mind, based upon experiences of the past, darkens the human ego. Now, education of the ego is a retraining of those dark areas of our ego. And that education process takes place when we permit, through total consideration, divine love, the light of reason, a soul faculty, to bring understanding into our consciousness in the areas that are so dark.

And anytime you take God's love and this great power and you direct it into patterns of mind of things that have passed and the way you used to do things, then you've got a struggle and you've got problems in your life. And they will not end until you choose to make the change that is necessary for you. Because, don't you see, my friends, you've taken total consideration and it's limited here, so all of this over here is nonexistent to you. And therefore the light of reason is shining over that that, to you, you do not identify with and, therefore, cannot improve your life.

Now, as we have taught to keep faith with reason, she will transfigure thee because reason, this great power and this great light, must be cast over all areas of our consciousness. Because without that, we'll keep banging our head against the wall trying to do something with laws and forms that we established years ago that will not serve us well. And we will knock, but the door will not open. And who is it that experiences knocking at the door of opportunity and it does not open? I tell you any person unwilling to accept change, unwilling to accept the possibility, is a person who knocks at the door of opportunity and that door absolutely will not open. Because we will only allow it to open the way that we're used to it opening. And until that door is the way we're used to doing something and getting something, that door, for us, will not open.

I'm only trying to save you the struggle, the time, and the effort and the energy banging at doors of opportunity that just will not open, my friends. There's no way that they will open as long as you insist and are not willing to give up what has already proven to you to be detrimental, to be disastrous in your life.

Now, all of us, hearing these wonderful classes—would you like to be excused a moment?

Yes.

You go right ahead.

Thank you.

Certainly—hearing these classes, hopefully playing the recorded tapes, in order that you may, slowly but surely, permit a little light into your consciousness. You see, my friends, it takes an unbelievable amount of repetition to bring about the smallest change in your life. It takes a phenomenal amount of effort, because it takes a phenomenal amount of energy, because so many years have passed that you have directed so much energy into patterns of mind, attitudes, forms created that served well maybe twenty or thirty years ago. But things are never the same. Creation is in a constant state of change. He or she who is unwilling to awaken in the morning accepting the possibility of change in their life is going contrary to the Law of Creation and, in going contrary to the Law of Creation, shall have nothing but struggle in life. For the Law of Creation reveals unto us change is a constant process in all form.

Now if we choose, which we seem to choose moment by moment, to identify with creation and we insist on not changing, then creation shall extract her price from us and we shall be the one left without. For that is the law and that is demonstrable. You cannot identify with the principle of anything, including the principle of creation, whose laws clearly reveal and demonstrate to you, change, evolution and try to stem the tide and not change your thinking. For you will start the destruction process and it shall not end as long as you identify with form or creation.

So it isn't a matter of liking or not liking to change. It is inevitable. It is only a matter of how long you will procrastinate and how willing—and how much a price and how much struggle and how much pain you are willing to pay for. For no one can deny their identification with and attachment—at least at times—to what we know as creation.

Now when you choose no longer to identify with creation, when you, through the powers of concentration, rise up and free yourself from form, while still flowing through form, known as objective—objectivity, then, my friends, you will not suffer. Not being identified with, you cannot suffer from. But because we insist on being identified with creation and because we flatly refuse to change our thinking, which is an inseparable part of creation, we suffer and the pain gets greater, I assure you.

And we go out in the universe looking for vacations in anything to give us a break. A break from what? A break from our own thinking that we refuse to change and that is in the process of its own destruction. I'm sure you will all agree that is not the way to be happy, let alone to be free.

Now this little, humble school here offers you the greatest opportunity you will ever find on this planet Earth. It offers you the soul faculty of care, consideration, responsibility, understanding, reason, and all the other soul faculties. And it offers you the most important one—one of the most important—it's not the most important, but one of the most important—the dignity, the dignity of discipline. Now we all truly want more discipline, not just because we want more dignity. No, no, no, no, no. But because we all want more control. Now show me a person with no discipline, I will show you a person, helpless, pathetic, with no control. So we're all crying out, even though our motives may be different—some, hopefully, the spiritual motivation of the dignity of discipline, the benefit of improving one's character.

But let us be honest with our self: we all want discipline because we all want control. Now we want to control our jobs. We want to control our money. We want to control our health. We want to control our sex. We want to control our food. We want to control everything that our senses experience. Therefore, we really do want discipline, because we know we are not able to control the things we want to control and we do want to control. We want to control our bank accounts and our income and on down the list. We want to control those things. But because we're not making the effort to discipline ourselves, we cannot control what we do not discipline. And that control, of course, is right up here in our thought.

Now, we don't want to be emotionally upset. We don't want to be hurt and feel rejected. We don't want to be ill. We don't want all those things, but they are effects of our lack of discipline. That's all they are. They're effects of our lack of discipline. We don't want to feel miserable. We don't want to be in the emotional forces, but we don't have enough discipline and therefore we cannot control those things.

I have found in my experiences of many years that, sooner or later, my students, over the years, those who are present, those who have gone, have always been grateful, in hindsight, for whatever discipline that I have shared with them. And you've got to remember, my friends, when we receive discipline, we never like it. We don't like it because we awaken within our consciousness that we have no control. And none of us want to be left without self-control.

Now, perhaps we'll understand a little bit better that freedom is not self-control, it is the effect of self-control.

Thank you very much and enjoy a nice prime rib dinner. Thank you.

OCTOBER 14, 1982

CONSCIOUSNESS CLASS 230

Class, most all of you have been in our classes before, but this particular course, this semester, has been dedicated to personal growth. Now personal growth means many different things, of course, to our mind. But without change—changes in consciousness—there is no possibility of growth, which is, of course, the effect of changes.

Now we find in our experiences in life, it seems ofttimes with great difficulty we make changes. We must remember that a change that we make in our consciousness is a struggle and a difficulty for the levels of consciousness that are in control and, therefore, view the change that we tempt to make as an annihilation of their very existence. All experiences we already are aware of are effects of certain types of thinking that takes place in our mind.

The continuity of any experience is always dependent upon the value priority that we have at any given moment. For example, we have many experiences that we find distasteful. And we ofttimes delude our self because we blame the cause of the experience on something that is beyond our control. Because we blame the cause of experiences that we find distasteful to us to something that is beyond our control—that is, by blaming outside for the experience—we have great difficulty in making the changes that are necessary for us.

Now all of these experiences that we have become an important ingredient in the change in our consciousness. So whether or not we like change will in no way stop the changes from coming.

Now these classes are designed to help us to see more clearly the repetition of experiences in our life. We go through life; through the laws of association, we attract to ourselves the necessary experiences for our own growth. Now if we view those experiences that we encounter as necessary for our own growth and our own freedom—because that is what the final effect of the experiences are in truth—then we will not mistake the particular experience as our final journey in life.

Now, as we have in the past—always had a time for questions on the philosophy—we will also continue on with those type of classes.

We have spent many years in explaining to students how the human mind works, how the consciousness of our being that is magnetic is the very thing that has what is known as fear. Whatever experience we have in life, we fear its continuity. And because we fear it, we guarantee its continuity. For example, we have an experience that is distasteful and we fear that the experience will repeat itself. We do that because we deny the truth in the experience: that it is caused and created by our own consciousness, which, by the very law, we have control over at any moment that we choose to have control over it. It is through the denial that we have the destiny and the continuity of the experiences that we judge to be distasteful.

Now, for example, we have experiences that we judge are beneficial. Many experiences in our life we feel are beneficial. And stop and think what we do with that type of thinking. We feel the experience is beneficial and, as time passes, we begin to find the negative aspect of the experience that we judged at one time in our life was beneficial. In other words, we diligently work to find something wrong with what we judge to be good, because it is the very nature and design of the human mind to bring about the changes necessary for our own growth.

I'm going to take a few minutes here in the beginning of this class to let you ask a few questions, because it's important that you ask questions that you feel are important to you. Because a question that is important to you, though you may think may not be important to someone else, is still important for your own growth. So if you have any questions, in the few minutes that we have at this time, you just, please, raise your hands. *[After a short pause, the Teacher continues.]* Like any class in any school, the first hand is always the most difficult, isn't it? Yes.

Are we to suppose that we should not view an experience as beneficial or not beneficial if—with the description you have given?

In reference to the question, Should we view an experience not as beneficial or as beneficial? Because we have identified with what we know as creation, because we have identified with creation, we, therefore, are governed by the Law of Creation, which is the Law of Duality. Therefore, as long as we have identified with creation, in other words, as long as we entertain the thought of I instead of the I which we are, then it is not only necessary, but it is inevitable that we view an experience positive or negative. In order to view experience neither as positive nor as negative we cannot view it from a personal level of consciousness, because it's contrary to the Law of Identity with the duality of creation. Does that help with your question?

Yes. Thank you.

To enter a realm of objectivity, to be objective in everything or anything you view or sense, requires the Law of Disassociation in order to enter a realm of objectivity where you do not react. You see, it is the reacting mind, it is the magnetic mind where experiences—all experiences—take place.

Now the spirit that we are, that which we are—not that which we think we are, but that which we are—does not grow. That doesn't grow. The truth *is*. You can't change it. It just *is*. So because we are truth—that which we are—there is no change and there is no growth. The change and growth is ever subject to and dependent upon identification with the Law of Duality. This is why we teach only through the separation of truth from creation does man ever experience freedom. That help with your question?

Yes.

Certainly. Yes.

If we disassociate, are we just free from the effect of the duality of creation or are we actually free from the dual law itself?

When one disassociates, one is freed from the identification with the dual law and, therefore, does not experience the effects thereof.

Thank you.

You're welcome. Yes.

Yes. What causes one to segment their experiences through life in such a way as to almost forget different areas until one has to piece together a whole picture and realize that they hadn't even remembered those good points about themselves?

Thank you. In reference to forgetting or seeming to forget experiences in life, we must try to understand that nothing, in truth, is forgotten. Everything that we experience in life is recorded in what is known as the memory par excellence, which is ever available to our view.

Now we seem to forget what, at any given moment, we do not have value for. For example, we are in a constant process of making choices. Now this process goes on constantly. Rarely are we aware of the choices that are being made by the human mind moment by moment. Try to understand that the nature of the human mind is to preserve and to protect that which it believes it has. Consequently, man experiences a fear more often than he consciously realizes. The reacting mind—a reacting to experiences that one encounters—is totally, wholly, and completely dependent upon fear, which serves the reacting mind in the sense of preserving and protecting what it thinks it already has. Does that help with your question?

Thank you.

You're welcome. Yes, the gentleman here, please.

A moment ago, am I correct that I heard you say that we are truth and truth doesn't grow?

Growth is dependent upon change. And truth does not change. Therefore, truth does not grow. Identity changes or grows and, in so doing, becomes more receptive to more light or truth. Truth itself cannot change and be truth. Our identification or form is what changes, is what evolves, is what grows, is what expands. Our consciousness expands, not truth.

Thank you.

You're welcome. The lady in the back, please.

As these fears come up, how—what can you apply at that moment so you don't lose control—like a very large fear?

Yes. Well, if we understand—for example, when these fears come up and especially a very large fear, when we understand that a large fear is protecting a large amount of what we judge we have and find our security in—so often we think of security as a roof over our head, clothes on our back, and food in our mouth. Security goes far beyond those limits. Our minds are working to feel secure in that and those experiences that it has already had that it judges brought to them feelings of goodness. Therefore, when we have experiences and they are recorded within our mind and we judge that we experienced a good feeling from those particular experiences, then our mind works to preserve and to protect that which, in truth, has passed.

When we understand that a past event is only past to the priorities of the conscious mind at any given moment, then we can see clearly how diligently we work to protect what we think we have. For example, if you tell a person that they should make a change in reference to the way they thought twenty years ago about a certain person, if the person is preserving in their consciousness the experience as it was twenty years ago, then that person will experience what you call fear, which is the mind's way of protecting what it thinks it has, because it has it in its own mind, not outside.

So here, we go through life—remember that it is our conscious mind that is electrical. It is our conscious mind where the faculty of reason flows. And it is our subconscious mind that is magnetic. It is our subconscious mind that fears and works to preserve and to protect, because it is our subconscious mind where all these experiences are stored. Does that help with your question?

Oh, you want to know how you overcome that fear?

Yes.

Well, first of all, the fear only exists and can only be experienced through the identity or the directed energy, through attention, to what we call the self. Therefore, if one makes the effort to redirect the energy through the channel of attention to something that is not related to the experience, one soon finds that the fear has disappeared.

You see, we are the ones who either act or we react in life. Now we act or we react in keeping with our efforts to gain control over this Law of Identity. Remember that we are formless free spirit. The law is what we choose: we choose the Law of Identity. The Law of Identity exists. It is ever subject to our choice. You choose at any moment to identify with a person, place, or thing. Is that not correct?

Yes.

But we alone make that choice. Now when we say that we met someone on the street and we did not choose to meet that person and have that experience, we are speaking a half-truth. Ofttimes we did not consciously—with conscious awareness—choose to meet that particular person and have that particular type of experience. But then, we are not awakened to our reacting mind, who set—which set the law into motion and attracted that into our universe, which, in truth, can, through the light of reason, serve as a wonderful growth process. Does that help with your question?

Yes. Thank you.

Good. Remember, friends, if we do not first study and apply the laws that govern a mental world, then we are not in a reasonable position to deal with the laws that govern a spiritual world. Because we are more familiar with a mental and material world, we must begin with what we are most familiar with.

Now the magic wand or magic staff that—many times, over the years, a person has asked, Is there something you can just do? The only magic—if you can call it magic staff or magic wand—that I have ever been aware of could be the magic wand of effort. But then, a person ofttimes makes great effort, but not understanding the laws that govern any particular situation, the effort, in that respect, does not bring about the desired results.

Now whatever it is in life that we choose, we must remember, when we choose it, we establish the law that governs it.

Now you take a person that gets married. They make a choice to get married to a certain person. In making that choice, they establish the law for themselves that is governing the person that they marry. Now many times the marriage will work out, as the two people involved make these necessary changes. But, you see, these laws are what *we* choose and what *we* set into motion. Ofttimes in a marriage or a relationship, people are very, very stubborn. They don't want to make the changes that are necessary. But then, they have to pay the price of not wanting to make the changes that are necessary, which establishes another law.

Now, you know, we can sit and we can close our eyes, but can we sit and still our mind? That must be the question we should ask our self in this course on personal growth. If you can sit and still your mind as quickly as you can sit and close your eyes, then you are well on the way of moving in consciousness from a world of creation to a world of light and truth. Some of you, I'm aware, are able to still your mind for a moment. Because it is only when you gain control over your mind that you can become receptive to vibrations of consciousness that are not governed by mental substance. And that which is not governed by mental substance is not subject to nor victim of mental substance.

That's very important—to work to make that step in consciousness, because think what it offers—and is inevitable on our path in evolution. It means to us, and offers to us, the ability, which is our divine right in evolution, to look at all form and see it for what it is: to see it as a beginning and a guaranteed ending; to see it as a vehicle serving the Light that we are and serving it for who knows how long or how short a time. So when we still our mind, we can enter that realm of consciousness and, by so doing, are we freed from fear, frustration, from dictate, from disappointment. Because then, we see creation for what creation has been designed for. And creation is designed, as we all know, I'm sure, as a vehicle of service to the formless free

Spirit that is. Now we're formless and free and aware of that truth when our mind is still. Though it may be a split second, a very short moment, it is worth entering at least once a day. Because there, no worry, no concern, nothing of mental substance can exist.

Any more questions? The lady that's falling asleep. Perhaps it's too warm in here. All right. Yes, that question will awaken you.

Good. When you know what you want do, what you have to do, and you do it, but the mind battles it, even though it is what the mind has judged it wants to do, how can you—why does it . . . It seems to be fulfilling its own judgments while fulfilling your purpose, but it pulls away from wanting to do it and makes the effort very difficult. Is there anything that we can do in trying to still our mind so that it's not so difficult?

Well, in reference to the question that one knows what they want to do and then the statement that one has to do, now that implies that what we think we want to do, we are doing under duress.

First of all, if we say we want to do something and we follow that desire of wanting to do something with the statement that we have to do, that reveals that the payment for what we want is not what we want. In other words, we want what we want freed from the payment to attain it.

Now when we look at it in that light, then we can see that ofttimes in life desires bombard our consciousness like hailstorms and we want them all fulfilled. But because there are so many and because they are so great, through our experiences in life we become aware that the payments for their fulfillment are heavier than the mass of desires that are bombarding our consciousness, our mind, in its own self-preservation, tries to find a shortcut. And that shortcut is known, to our mind, as to find a way to get something without having to pay the price that everyone pays.

Now the financial world learned that lesson eons ago and every once in a while you'll see a sign up somewhere that says "Sale, Special Sale." And you'll see the department stores absolutely jammed with people because they learned long, long ago that there is a part of the human mind that wants a shortcut. There is a part of the human mind that's ever trying to get something, well, to put it bluntly, for nothing or—better still—for those with the light of reason, a little bit of light of reason, for almost nothing, you see. And so the world of discount has become a very popular world, because that's a part of the human mind, you see. That's a part of the human mind: to find a shortcut. There are no shortcuts in the sense if you mean by "shortcut," less payment and bigger desire. You see, the payment is ever equal in proportion to the desire. So if you have a $5 desire, you have a $5 payment equal in energy, for dollars or money is the effect of directed energy. That's all that it is: it is the effect. Does that help with your question?

Yes.

So one works on the education process of their desires, knowing they all have a price tag. And then one can intelligently choose just how much a price they're willing to pay. And they'll soon find the desires get less and so does the payment.

Now I realize that there, of course, has always been—there still is—much interest in this other world around and about us. And I think it's very important, at this time, that perhaps we have a few moments discussion on the Spirit that is ever present. So often some of us have experiences and sensing of what we know in this philosophy as vibration. And we become aware of a presence or a thought of a person, become aware of, sometimes, things yet to happen and, more important, an awakening to what is our real work or job here in this particular incarnation.

Some of you have, over the years, been aware of certain talents that you have, ofttimes. And usually they are not what the mind would choose. But everyone here on the planet Earth has come here for a particular job that they have to do. There are no exceptions to that law. In evolutionary incarnation, the soul journeys and spends time and experience on various planets. And each soul that enters Earth has come to do a specific job that only they can do. Therefore, it behooves a person to become aware of the work they have to do, because if, in their evolution, they do not become aware of their particular job that they have to do on any particular planet, when they leave the vehicle composed of the matter of that particular planet, their form must, and does, remain in the sphere of that planet until the job they went to that planet [for] is completed.

Now then, of course, the question arises, "Well, what is my job?" You see, there's a part of us that knows what our job is. It knows it deep inside of us. Sometimes a person will say, "Well, I've always wanted to do such and such." Because, you see, that awareness, you came to Earth with. It's always been with you. But it is the human mind, which has gathered and garnered various experiences, that keeps a person from doing the job that they have to do.

Now there is, of course, no personal growth without doing the job that one has earned in eternity to do. Some people, they're artists and they have that work to do. And ofttimes they do that work, but not just the way that their mind dictates. Therefore, they do some of the work they have to do—some, which is better than none at all.

Now ofttimes a person has a menial task in life or it seems that their job, through which they earn their living, is a menial task. And they don't see that there is opportunity, wherever they are, to do the job they came to the planet to do. We are never left without opportunity to do our job. It is only our mind that tells us that circumstances and conditions are not the way that are satisfactory to our mind. Therefore, we cannot do what we know we should be doing. We cannot do it the way our mind dictates we can do it, but we can do it. And it is not our mind, you see—if it was our mind that had the full awareness of the job we came to Earth to do, then we could listen to our mind and get our job done. But time and again, we see that our mind is the obstruction to doing the job we've come to the planet to do.

Now some people, they know inside of themselves that they have a job to do, to serve the Light or God or whatever you want to call it. But then their mind says, "Well, I can't do it the way I want to do it." But, you know, when we can't do something the way that our mind wants us to do it, then our spirit is serving very, very well.

Now in this course on personal growth—and before we complete this particular semester—each student present will become aware of the principle of the work they've come to the planet to do. I'm not going to sit here and tell you, but I am going to help you in all ways possible to awaken to that truth that is already inside of you, because you came with it.

One must not permit their mind to say that it is so late to get started. That's like a person that wakes up in the morning, they look at the clock and say, "Oh, I'm going to be five minutes late for work. I just better go back to sleep." And so they show up five hours late. That's not an intelligent type of thinking.

So during this coming week, it is important for you—individually and collectively—to think and let your mind be still, so that you may find that which you know you must do in order to fulfill the purpose of your journey here on Earth.

Now many times in my experiences with people, they have been aware of what they know they have to do. They have been aware of that. They certainly have been aware of it. And the human mind comes up with a mountain of justification to keep them from doing it. Try to understand that it is the nature of our mind to preserve and to protect what it already has. Therefore, the human mind is serving its purpose for that which it has been designed. Therefore, when you awaken to this spiritual light within you and begin to work on what you have come to

Earth to work on, you must face a human mind that is designed to keep the status quo.

But remember, all that you have learned to this point in your Earth journey, all of that is limited to your entrance to Earth. Now that awareness of before you came here and where you are going is beyond the limits of a mental world. Because, you see, as you open a door, you close a window. As you open a window, you close a door. Because that is what identity offers.

Now if you didn't have identity, then you would not be able to function in the form that you have presently earned in evolution. Now if you don't identify with your job, you soon find you don't have a livelihood. So identity is something that serves a useful purpose, as long as we remember that we are not that which we identify with. It is when we forget and we believe that we are that which we identify with that we begin to have problems. Does that help with your question there?

Yes, sir.

All right. Are there any other questions here? Yes.

Yes. I would like for you to explain if it's—well, why you—when we close a door, we open a window whether or not to close a door or close a window? Why is it that?

Well, what does it mean? Well, you see, a door is something that is designed for one to pass through, isn't it? That is the purpose of the design of a door. And a window is designed for one to view through. Would you not agree? To look through, to see.

So as we close a door—we pass through a door and it's closed. We open a window. You see, when we let go of that which has passed, we enter that which is. Now we cannot enter that which is until we let go of that which has been. And so here we have our attention either on what is or we have our attention on what has been.

Now in all of our experiences in life we are constantly faced with this process: the closing of a door for the opening of a window. And so, as the other student said, in moving harmoniously through these many experiences of life, it is ever dependent upon the degree of control that we have in closing the door that we've already passed through.

If our minds were able to view all of the incarnations, throughout all the eons of time, then we would not be able to identify with the one particular incarnation and the work that we have to do at this particular time. So it is in the divine design—that law—that the window opens after the door closes. Does that help with your question?

For example, if a man is married four times and in his fourth marriage he's constantly thinking of his first, then is he free to experience the changes, the growth process, or is he just rehashing what has already been only under the delusion that it is someone else? You see, we are, in life, by this magnetic law, repeatedly attracted to that and to those who, in our past, we have judged have been the instruments through which some good has come into our life. Does that help with your question?

Yes.

And so we look at people, places, and things with a very slanted view unless we are still in our consciousness that we may see what *is* and not have it shadowed by what has been. I think we call that the ribbon of comparison. Did you ever meet a person, place, or thing that your mind did not compare it, through the Law of Association, to what has already been? When you met your wife, did you not, within your consciousness, compare her to what had been before?

I did.

Well, so does everyone else. But it takes an honest man to admit it. I hope that's helped with your question.

Thank you.

Yes.

In speaking of that which we come to Earth to do, are we speaking of our soul talent or something to make us grow?

Well, it is our soul talent through which we do grow.

I see.

Because our soul talent, as I've said before, is not a gift that's parceled out to certain people. It is an effect of eons of evolution in working in a particular area until it has become perfected and through that perfection, our soul is able to express itself. Therefore, it is called a soul talent. You see, when a person becomes proficient at any particular work in life, one says it's automatic. It's just automatic because they have done it so many times. Well, in evolution when you have a job that you've done so many eons and eons of times without number, then you no longer use the mental substance in a conscious awareness: "And let me see, I move this like this." You move that like that through a law that you have established. Therefore, a person says to that person, "It is natural. Playing the piano is just absolutely natural." They don't even have to make any effort.

But what they don't see is the eons and the untold trillions of times the person has already done that in evolution. So you have people that come to Earth and they're great musicians at five years old. Because they don't see beyond the five years. They don't see the evolution. Therefore, the soul is free to flow through an unobstructed vehicle. And we say that person in that particular talent is a genius. But it is the soul, you see, expressing freely. Does that help with your question?

Yes. Thank you.

Yes. I always like to take a look to see whether the question marks are vertical or horizontal, as I look at my students. You know what a horizontal question mark over a person's consciousness is? It is one that wants to express itself, but is limited by pride. Now we all know what pride is. I think we all know, don't we? Pride is man's belief in his own perfection and, like brass, is in constant need of polishing.

You know, pride is not a bad thing. It depends on what we do with it. When we know that pride is something that we can use in a constructive way, that it can be beneficial, when we know that it is something we use, like a fork to eat our dinner or our breakfast, and that it is not us, then we have no problem in using it for the purpose of its design. It is a tool to be used for the greater good of the individual who is using it. However, you see, there is great truth in this: pride is man's belief in his own perfection. Because that which is man—by man, I mean humanity—that which *is* man *is* perfect. But that which is man which is perfect is not subject to nor dependent upon belief. The problem is the belief, you see. Man believes he is perfect and that's pride. But that which is man *is* perfect and therefore there's no belief. It just is. There's all the difference in the world.

So all philosophies have taught the great sin of pride. Well, look what pride does to us. Because we believe we are the pride, that's where the problem is. That's when we take a slight for an injury. It's like a thought. If we believe we are the thought, then we've got problems because we have so many diverse and contrary thoughts. If we believe we are the desire, we have problems. That's where the problems are. If, in our evolution, we are at a state of our growth where we must believe, we feel that we must believe, then at least, with our beliefs, it would behoove us to believe in something worthwhile, something that is beneficial to us, instead of believing in such things as pride that cost us so dearly. Because we ofttimes do things under the guise of pride that are totally contrary to the light of reason that we have inside of our self. And then, because we ofttimes do those things, we experience those of realms of regret.

Whoever regrets the past only is in a dream world wishing they had done differently. That which is gone is gone. So, you see, it depends on us. If we want to live in a dream world and say, "I regret what I did yesterday or last year or the year before"— we can't do anything about that which has passed except use it as a device to enjoy the pity of self. That's the only thing we can use it for. I mean, if it rained last week, it rained last week. Are we going to regret that it rained last week because it's already passed? But we can use it to feel sorry for our self.

Now that brings up the subject of energy, which is very important to all of us because we all use energy and without energy we aren't even beings, you see. We have no vehicles to move around in. So energy is very important. Now, you look at a little child and if it is spending much of its thinking about itself, you will find it gets into a lot of problems, so that it can get a lot of attention. So that it can have the energy that it needs because what it's receptive to, it's wasting. Now we take that example from a little baby and little children.

Ah, but let's move on and see that the little baby and the little child did not change. Now that's one thing we can understand: that in what we call our emotional world, that little baby, it did not grow. Oh no, no, no, no, no. This is why, when a person is emotional, they are not reasonable. This is why, when a person is emotional, they will sacrifice the very things that are so beneficial to them. And they know it. But in a state of emotion, they'll sacrifice the whole thing. They'll throw the baby out with the bathwater. That only proves to us, in a most demonstrable way, that the little baby does not grow in the magnetic world of our consciousness. And it still acts and reacts as it did thirty, forty years ago, however old we seem to be.

So the older that we get—some people say that wisdom comes with age. I assure you it's not dependent upon age, but it does seem to come along as we get older because, through many experiences, our mind says to us, "It's not worth getting upset over that." And it isn't worth being hurt over that or that or something else. Therefore, as we get older, we, slowly but surely, begin to accept that there has to be a better way. "I've already been through that so many times. It just isn't worth it." And you move on to something else. So in that sense, we are getting gradually, slowly but surely, free from those realms. But remember, if you want to awaken the emotional world, just look up at your pride and, I guarantee you, if anyone scratches it in any way that you judge is detrimental to it, all the emotional realm will come up to protect you. That help with your question?

But as I said a moment ago, let's use pride wisely. I have not met anyone that is absent of it, including myself. But we can, through our own awareness and acceptance, use it in constructive and beneficial ways.

Now this week, for your homework, there is one thing: to write down on a piece of paper what it is you really and truly feel you want to do. Now after you write that down, you write down how long you felt or thought that way. And then, of course, there are those five or six other things you've always wanted to do. Don't forget to write those down. But write them down on a piece of paper in your own priorities. As the number one thing you always wanted to do, the number two—Now don't worry, you won't have to show it to me or anyone else. But it is important that you write it down, because it is important that you experience within your consciousness what happens with you when you do write it down. That's what's important for that is your own personal growth and awakening.

Now you will find, I can assure you, that you will—some of you—will adjust one, two, three, four, five. You will adjust which one shall be number one. But in that process, you will become aware of what your mind is doing, has always done, to what you really want to do.

Now when you write that down, do not concern yourself with the mountain of justifications why you've never done it or got started and stopped. You're not interested in that. We're already aware that that exists in the human consciousness. What is important is to permit that inner being to rise up, you see.

It's like a person who is an artist. So they're used to painting on a certain media, you see, canvas or china or wood or this or that or steel or you name it or glass. But what happens with the feeling, you see? Is it a feeling of the soul and the spirit? Or is it a sensation of the mind? Now try to understand: our heart feels; our mind senses. And so we should distinguish between what we *sense* and what we *feel*. There is a vast difference between a feeling and a sensation. Remember, sensation is indispensable to need and need reveals denial. A person can feel, and feel very well or feel any way they choose to feel and it's not dependent upon anything outside. But sensation is ever dependent upon external stimulus. So you want to distinguish between feeling and sensation.

Well, it seems to me—what time do you have? Have sixty minutes passed?

Yes.

Ah. Well, I want to be sure that you have your tapes. That's very important. Are there any questions now before we conclude this evening's class?

Well, you know—I think you can shut it off now. *[The Teacher refers to shutting off the tape recorder.]* Is it going to fit onto a C-60? *[A C-60 refers to a sixty-minute audio cassette tape and a C-90 refers to a ninety-minute audio cassette.]*

No.

Well, we might as well leave it on, then, if it's got to go on a C-90. We'll leave it on.

Now we all know, I know, whenever we go to any class, we have certain thoughts what the class is going be about or be like. I can assure you from my years of experience, they're never what we thought they were going to be. They're never what I think they're going to be and, I can assure you from hundreds and hundreds of students over the many years, they never seem to be what my students think they're going to be. But what is important is what we do with what we receive. Because in life, we must remember, we receive in keeping with the law we have established. So if we are receiving, which is demonstrably true, in keeping with the law that we have established, then it only stands to reason that when we receive it, we should do something with it. Wouldn't you agree?

Yes.

I think so. I think in any study in life that, when we make the effort to do something with what we receive, then we fulfill the law that it may return ever in a more beneficial way. If we do a good job inside, there will never be a concern about anything outside. Because everything outside, through the Law of Attraction, can only be as good as the job that we're doing inside.

You know, it is a wonderful opportunity for all of us to meet people in our lives who are contrary to what we desire, who are stubborn. Because in their stubbornness, they are instruments through which we can educate our own stubbornness. Because, you see, they become instruments for our growth when we see, so often in life, what they're willing to sacrifice and how, sometimes, stupid some people may appear because of the tenacity of their stubbornness and unwillingness to make changes within their consciousness. So each and every person that enters our life is an instrument through which the divine Light is ever evolving our being. So we look especially at the ones that we judge that cause us so much grief, for they are the instruments through which our greatest help has come.

Now try to remember in thanking, in giving thanks or gratitude, do not be deceived by the form and not perceive the law that is working for you, because the stone the builder rejects becomes the cornerstone. We must not fall into the trap of seeing the form at the sacrifice and the loss of the law that is involved.

So all of us, of course, can benefit through the guaranteed success of tolerance, for it is through tolerance that we experience success in life. Because no matter what we think—sometimes things seem to go very smoothly and work very successfully. Didn't have to have any tolerance at all. What we are saying is,

"Those levels of consciousness that can't tolerate this particular situation, they weren't even in control of my mind at this time. Therefore, I didn't have to have any tolerance at all." But just wait down the road when that level rises up and you'll see how much tolerance that it takes. So without tolerance, there's no success. Whether the path is a spiritual, mental, or material one, it requires tolerance. And the tolerance is inside oneself.

For example, someone doesn't like someone and that someone seems to be frequently around their universe. Well, that person is an instrument through which they are growing in the faculty of tolerance, which is indispensable and absolutely necessary for their own success. If life was as easy as our mind sometimes likes to want it to be, then we would not be able to weather the storms that we insist on setting into motion.

Thank you very much. And we'll see you next Thursday. And please don't forget to write down your list. Because only in that process will your mind become aware of these things that have been in your life for so very long. But when you do write them down, be by yourself where you can be peaceful. And you will be surprised. Surprised that you finally put it on paper, perhaps. Not surprised at what you've always wanted to do. And remember, what you always wanted to do is not dependent on someone or something outside because your spirit is not dependent. Your soul talent is not dependent. And it never was and never will be. It is not dependent.

Say, for example, you want to be a singer. Well, a person, then, is a singer. But they don't stop at the principle of singing, you see. You see, the soul talent would reveal this: "I feel so good when I sing. I always wanted to be a singer." But the mind takes that and says, "I have to do this, that, that, that, and that." That has nothing to do with your soul talent, absolutely nothing. That is mental justification and obstruction.

So when you write down the things you've always wanted to do, put them down and do not permit that mental world to cloud them. You must get into a state of consciousness that what you always wanted to do, you are doing. That's when you write it down.

Thank you very much.

JANUARY 19, 1984

CONSCIOUSNESS CLASS 231

All right, we'll continue on with our classes this evening.

You were given, last week, a little homework to do. The basic purpose, of course, of that is for you to have a little awakening inside of yourselves. I am well aware that some of you had a few experiences, emotionally, in reference to your homework, but then that helps us to become aware of our own levels of consciousness and obstructions.

Now the most important thing, I think, that we should realize is that you cannot educate a talent, a natural soul talent. You may educate the obstruction to the talent, but not the talent itself. Because, you see, the expression of inspiration is the talent of the soul. Now if you understand what natural or soul talent really is, then you'll understand that it is only the obstruction to the talent that needs evolution, refinement, or education. A person has a natural talent to sing. Well, they have to use the mind, the vehicle of the mind in order to express in a mental and a physical, material world. So it is the mind, the mental vehicle, that needs the educating or the refining.

Now what is a natural talent? A soul talent, as I explained last week, is what you, in your evolution, have already earned or perfected. We also discussed pride. And this evening, we will continue on with our classes in reference to what we find our security in.

Now through the Law of Identity, through this process of identifying, we enter this world a formless free spirit encased in what is called a soul, an individualized soul. And we understand the process of individualization is the process of identity. For example, you cannot have an individual (that is something that is whole and complete within itself) until you have the Law of Identity. For they are basically one and the same. You identify with something; you limit that which you identify with. For example, [if] you identify with a particular job or work that you're doing in life, then you are limiting yourself to that which you have identified with.

Now, the individualized soul is the effect of the divine, formless Spirit which identifies in a spiritual realm and, through that Law of Identity, separates itself from what is referred to as the Allsoul—separate only in its own identification. Now, if that doesn't make sense to you, then you raise your hand so we can have a more thorough discussion upon it.

However, our daily activities and our daily thoughts and our daily experiences are effects of this Law of Identity. Now, when we identify with anything, we limit through the process of judgment. Because when we identify, when we concentrate our energies in any particular avenue of expression, we limit, we limit our being to that particular avenue of expression. And so we find from that process we have what we call belief.

As we discussed last week, pride is man's belief in his own perfection. It is not the perfection that is the problem. That which we are is perfect. That which we believe we are is not. Because it is belief, the identifying with a thing, that is the limit of the thing, of which the foundation is judgment. We identify, we limit, and therefore we experience what is known as judgment.

Now each judgment that the mind makes becomes the security and the stability of our mental world. For example, when we identify with our self, with what we believe we are, we identify with what we believe we are and therefore our mind works to defend what we believe. It is falsehood that requires and is indispensable to defend. Truth has no need. And because truth has no need, there is no defense. You cannot defend truth; you can only defend belief. So when you find yourself working and striving with your mind to defend anything, try to remember, it is the belief that you are defending. It is not truth.

Now, a person may say that, "This is the truth to me. Therefore, someone is trying to destroy what is my truth." Well, they cannot destroy what is your truth if it is truth. You can destroy, from your belief, what you identify with. You can destroy that within your consciousness and that happens all the time. This is why you find in many religions—most religions—this great need to proselytize because there is such an insecurity in the belief; there is the need to gain support for the belief. Now consequently from those experiences, a person, slowly but surely, gradually frees themselves from this bondage of belief.

Now we've had classes on awareness belief become, which are steps of evolution. We believe what we are aware of. We do not believe what we are not aware of. Now we have faith, we have faith in what we are not aware of, but we can only believe what we are aware of in our consciousness. Therefore, man believes in many things, for belief is limited to form or things. Faith is not limited to forms or things; belief is. They're entirely two different realms of consciousness. One is the servant of a mental world; it's called belief. The other is the servant of the divine eternal Light; that's known as faith. So we separate truth (faith) from creation (belief).

Now in our daily activities we are constantly faced with that which has been. Those are necessary experiences for our own growth and freedom. By facing what has been, we are granted the opportunity to choose to live in the shadows of that which has passed or to grow in the Light of that which is.

That which has passed is the night of our life. That which is to be is the twilight of our life. And that which is now, that which *is*, is the noon or the light of our life. So we are constantly, in our consciousness, facing stumbling in the dark, groping along like a sleepwalker in the twilight, or walking in the reality of the Light of what is moment by moment. The Light that we are is moment by moment. It is not something that is going to be. It is not something that has been. The Light, the light of reason, the light of truth is what is moment by moment. For our consciousness, which is the stream of life, our consciousness is moving. And because it is moving, the light of truth is moment by moment by moment.

If you study something, no matter what it is you study, and you believe that you have it, you are in the darkness and not in the light. If you believe you are going to get it, you are in the twilight, not in the light. Because to *be* is not to have been and it's not something that's going to be. Because we *be*, because truth is a constant, continuous flow of the Light itself—that's what truth is: a continuous flow of the Light. We understand that to be the stream of consciousness of life. So in all of your activities in life, if you will make the effort to remember, this is the moment, this moment that you are, moment by moment, what has been cannot affect your life unless you choose it to affect your life. If you choose what has been to affect what is, then you cannot have freedom because you are not expressing the truth that you are. If you live in the hopes of a better tomorrow, then you cannot have freedom, for you are bound in the twilight zone, the dream world of consciousness.

Some time ago we stated that life is but a dream. Now, are we the dream or the dreamer? If we, moment by moment, are consciously aware, then we are the dreamer and not the dream. When we permit the consciousness to go back to what has been, we are the dream. When we permit the consciousness to go forward to what may be, we are the dream. It is only when we, moment by moment, take charge of our consciousness that we become the dreamer, the creators that we are designed to be.

Long, long ago I taught that God is not a creator. The belief that God is the creator places man in his consciousness as a victim of circumstance. Therefore, the mind has the grand cop-out: it can then say, "I am the way that I am because I am created this way. My experiences in life are a struggle for me because I was born into certain circumstances. My God brought this about." That type of thinking keeps a person in mental bondage because it keeps them from facing the very thing that will free us in the moment. It keeps us from personal responsibility.

Whatever we experience in life, we can change. Not what is out there, but we can, at any moment, change what is in. We can change the image that we hold of the experience. Now because all of life is subject to the images that we hold within our consciousness and because it *is* our consciousness, we can change those images. To tempt to change what someone else thinks, what someone else does is to place oneself in difficult, to say the least, circumstances. We are what we choose to be. And we choose to be the good that we are when we pause to think. Now when we pause to think, our identification with the images that exist within our consciousness is no longer directed to the night. It is no longer directed to the twilight zone of our tomorrows. But it is held firm in consciousness and then we become truly the captains of our ship. That's when we are masters of our destiny.

So the great step in evolution is to take control of the mind: to use it for what it has been designed to be used for, as an instrument through which our soul may express itself more fully and more freely. When we understand that we are, in truth, whole and complete—God did not make half humans. God did not make half animals, for God did not make all the things that we see. The laws of life, the laws of creation, the negative and positive poles of the universe came together under the intelligence of divine guidance and divine direction. But God, the God that is, did not make these things. Now when we understand that God did not make these things, when we understand that creation is subject to a law infallible, known as the Law of Duality, when we no longer identify with limit, which is judgment, then we no longer have the belief that we are incomplete. We no longer have the *belief* in perfection, for that is when we *be* the perfection that we are.

And so we find that all people, including animals, have what is known as pride. For we look at the animal and rarely do we consider that the animal believes. The animal believes that you're going to feed them if that has been the pattern that you have educated the animal's mind to. The animal believes you're going to take him for a walk. The animal believes that you're going to get up at a certain time and do certain routines. The animal believes that you'll return home. The animal believes those things in keeping with what the animal has been programmed to.

Now we step up the ladder, it seems, supposedly, and we look at the human. The human believes that a certain person is going to do a certain thing in keeping with the pattern that has been established. Now when the person does not do the thing that the other person believes they're going to do, then they get emotional and they get upset. Well, the animal gets emotional and the animal gets upset when the animal's master does not feed him, does not take him for a walk, and does not do the things that the animal believes that the master is going to do. Now let us pause and think. When we get upset because someone doesn't do what we believe they're going to do, then we must face the demonstrable truth that that person in that moment is our master, just as we are the master of the dog or the cat. That person is now our master and that person, in our consciousness, has us on their leash.

Think about that for a few moments.

Now we've discussed this in other ways. We've discussed how we lose our happiness, our joy, our peace, and our freedom. But we are doing emotionally, in those has-beens—that which has passed—we are doing what we see the animal do. It is more refined. It is much more subtle, but we are still doing it. For when we live in the past or when we live in the future, we are controlled by the emotions of our mind. And so we look at the animal and we believe we are more evolved. And when we use the light of reason that flows through us, in that respect, we demonstrate a more refined state of evolution.

But how often, the question must be asked, how often do we act? Demonstration upon demonstration reveals that we do not act: we react. When your consciousness is in the past or your consciousness is in the future, there is no acting; there is only reacting. And that's when we become what we call the victim of circumstances. You cannot act when your consciousness is past or future. Past or future—the consciousness reacts. You can only act when your consciousness is in the present. Now we think that we are acting over something that happened last week—that we are pausing and making an intelligent choice. If that which has happened last week is in control of our consciousness at the moment, we are reacting and emotion is involved in it.

We'll pause for a few moments to see if you have any questions at this time. Yes.

It's said that the stone the builder rejects becomes a cornerstone. Can you expand on that, please?

Well, yes, the stone the builder rejected became the cornerstone. You see, in order to reject something in the consciousness, you have to express what is known as judgment. In order to express what is known as judgment, you have to be controlled by what has been. You see, judgment is wholly, totally, and completely dependent upon what has already passed through the consciousness of an individual. It is a shadow.

All right, now, we reject. You see, what this teaching is saying—the stone the builder rejected became the cornerstone. Well, what we reject in life—remember this—what we reject in life, we become dependent upon. Now think of that for a moment. We reject many things in life and we become dependent on many things in life. Now in order to reject something, you have to, number one, have made a judgment. You understand that? Because you can't reject what is not judged and the judgment is dependent on what you've already experienced. So a choice is made by what has been to reject what has entered your universe by the very Law of Attraction.

Now the law clearly demonstrates that like attracts like and becomes the Law of Attachment. So an experience enters your life and you reject it. In other words, you tell the law, the infallible law, that you don't want what you have brought into your life. To do that is to serve the realm of consciousness known as adversity. This philosophy teaches that our adversities become our attachments. And if we look through our life, if we glance over at what has been, we can clearly see that, time and time again, we have become attached to what, at one time in our life, we were adverse to. So adversity and attachment clearly reveal to us their total dependence upon judgments, their total dependence upon limit. Does that help with your question?

Yes. Thank you.

And so the stone, the stone the builder rejects becomes the cornerstone because the adversity contained within the rejection becomes the attachment.

Thank you.

Yes, please.

I'd like to hear some—the question in my mind is trust. And there is—it's a very big question in my mind. Maybe as to how far to trust or it's something I don't really understand.

Well, in reference to the word *trust*, the distance implied in the question—How far to trust?—the distance implied reveals the trust is dependent upon experiences that have passed.

In reference to trust, we should consider that when we feel the need to trust, we must consider that we have denied and, therefore, are experiencing a dependence. See, one does not trust what they do not feel secure in depending upon. Therefore, we experience, in our life at varying times in our evolution, a need, which—we understand, all need is the effect of denial. For man cannot need until man judges he has naught. Man cannot have naught until he has denied that he has. Consequently, we move from judgment, denial, to need. And here we are at this moment at trust.

Now do you understand and feel comfortable with the explanation of the word *trust*? Do you experience trust prior to experiencing need? That's the question. Have you experienced trust without experiencing need?

I'm not sure.

Well, when—perhaps it would help you best to understand—what do you feel the word *trust* means to you?

It means...

That which is reliable?

That which is reliable and...

Dependable?

Yes. The lack of suspicion.

The lack of suspicion.

The opposite.

The opposite of suspicion.

Yes.

Well, in this philosophy the opposite of suspicion is not trust. It's known as credulity. But anyway, the opposite of suspicion. In the experiencing of suspicion do—well, I best put it this way: one who experiences suspicion, experiences, as you say, "A lack of trust." Is that correct?

Yes.

And one experiences suspicion based upon experiences that have passed. Would you not agree?

Yes.

Therefore, one sees clearly that the experiencing of suspicion is dependent upon the review and dependence of what has been. Would you not agree?

Yes.

Now this is what—and I'm glad you brought the question up on trust—this is what tonight's class, at this time, is all about. To depend on what has been places a person in a very delicate position in consciousness. For to depend on what has been offers to the human consciousness, of course, suspicion. And because it offers suspicion, it also offers need. And because it offers need, it also offers the possibility of trust. Now that's a mental world. And it's a round-robin for most all people.

Therefore, as I have stated many times, like things. Learn to like creation. Don't ever love it. Love God. Like creation. And you can trust that life will not fail you. Does that help with your question?

Yes.

You see, it's when we love limit—you see, it's like when you say, "I love this glass." When the glass breaks, are you brokenhearted? You like the glass. You like the table. You like people. If you say that you love people, if you mean by that statement that you love the formless, free Spirit, intelligent energy flowing through the form, then you have no worry or concern about trust or suspicion. However, if you love what the consciousness says to your mind in the realm of belief (that they will bring to you, some magical way, the goodness of life), then there is nothing but problems.

You see, ofttimes we mistake, unfortunately, God's work and God's expression because we see the form through which God is flowing and, by seeing the form, cannot experience the

God. Now if we, in our consciousness, take control and enter the present eternal moment where we are free, then we are not blinded by the form through which God, at any moment, could be flowing. Does that help with your question?

Yes.

Thank you. Are there any other questions at this time? Are there any questions on staying awake? I don't really think, myself, the classes are this long that we get sleepy. I think perhaps we maybe sleepy from other experiences. But I don't really think we're sleepy from this few minutes of class. Yes.

When we become aware of something in which we have become secure on in creation, how can we best work with that weakness?

I see. Your question is, When we become aware of our dependence upon something for our experience and feeling of security, how can we strengthen the weakness and, therefore, be free from the dependence? Is that the question?

Yes.

I see. First of all, the first step is already made. It's called awareness, awareness that we are dependent. Right?

Yes.

All right. Now the next step is the most important step because, from the awareness, what is offered to the consciousness is the belief. The belief that we need the thing, whatever it is, for the feeling of security. So that's the critical step because in the question is already implied that the weakness already exists, which means a repetition of the experience within the consciousness. Correct?

Correct.

Fine. So one is now aware that they want to be free from the dependence upon that which they cannot control. And because they cannot control it, therefore they are the victim of it. And that's known, to the human consciousness, as weakness. Correct?

Correct.

All right. Because we all feel this weakness when we become aware that we are dependent upon something beyond our control for feeling secure. In other words, we are no longer captain of our ship. We are no longer master of destiny, but we are subject to the fickle minds of something else. Correct?

Correct.

Fine. Well, then one begins to broaden their horizons. For the dependence that one experiences is the effect of the mind's judgment that through a certain thing they feel good. Correct?

Correct.

Isn't that what you're discussing? I think this is what we all understand. That tells the consciousness, tells our mind that there is a false belief in our consciousness that has judged we cannot experience God or goodness unless certain things happen. You understand that?

Yes.

So it's a process of talking with the judgment that is within the consciousness. And, slowly but surely, we wrench our way free.

Now the struggle in freeing our self from a dependence which we have become aware of is dependent on how much over-identification there is with the self. Now if we are greatly over-identified with our self, then we have to work very hard to free our self from the over-identification. Now that over-identification, the degree and extent thereof, comes under the vibration of self-love. You see, man is, humanity is, all form is the Light, the Love, and the Life. That is the triangle of truth.

The teaching [is], given back in 1968, "Love all life and know the Light." But the question then must be asked, What is life? Is life the form of the flower? Is life the form of the plant? Is life the form of a human being? Is life the form of an ant or angel? Well, it's not the form of any. It is the very intelligent energy flowing through it. That's life. You see, life *is*. There is no beginning or ending to life. There is beginning and ending to the vehicle through which life is expressing. There's a beginning and an ending to creation. There's a beginning and an ending to the creation, the forms of the human consciousness. That's the beginning and ending. The beginnings and endings are form. The beginnings and endings are not life. Our life did not begin on the planet Earth. Our life doesn't end on the planet Earth.

You see, my friends, we, in our belief and through our senses, which we experience—now we experience through our senses for we have identified with self. When we no longer identify with self, then we experience through other rates of vibration that are not dependent upon our physical senses. So when we understand that Life *is*, Light *is*, and Love *is*, that Life, Love, and Light are not dependent—that which is whole and complete cannot be dependent. Therefore we are Light, we are Life, we are Love. And to be dependent is to reveal that we have descended from the eternal moment into a shadow, past or future. So it is in the consciousness, descending into the past or into the future, that is where we lose, temporarily—whatever moments we choose to be there—that's where we lose the Light, and we enter the lesser light. The lesser light is the light of sensation.

You see, ofttimes we mistake sensation for joy. Ofttimes we mistake sensation for fulfillment. You cannot fill that which is full. You can only fill that which you believe has room to be filled. And dependent upon your belief, depends on how empty it is at any given moment. So we see clearly that all of life, as our reality of life is, is dependent upon our identification. [If] we permit our consciousness to identify with limit, then we're going to experience what limit has to offer. Limit has to offer to us all that has been in this short earthly span and all we hope to be. That's not life. That's only an expression of the vehicle through which life, the consciousness, is moving.

Therefore, when a person thinks humble, yet well, of themselves, you see, then they begin to free themselves from that which has been and from dependence. For we depend only on that which our consciousness has denied.

When we move from belief to reality, to this eternal being that we are in this instant, in this moment, we no longer experience the need because we no longer experience the denial because we are no longer in the realms where judgment exists. Does that help with your question?

Yes. Thank you.

You see, the question one must ask their consciousness: "Do I in this moment feel or experience this need or lack to my being?" That's the question. Have you asked the question? Ask yourself the question. Because, you see, a person moves in consciousness through what they view, through what they sense, through what they hear, as long as they identify with self. So we walk down the street and someone passes by. In our consciousness, there's a similarity to an image that we hold within the consciousness, of the past. And all of a sudden, we experience need. But is that conscious control of life?

That's like a person that decides, "Well, today I feel that I'm going to cut down here. I'm getting a little bit heavy and I want to cut down here." And they go out to the restaurant and they look around. And all of a sudden they see something—that they have a has-been within their consciousness. That has-been experience rises up and you can forget that day that they were going to, kind of, trim down that day. Totally forget it, dependent, of course, upon the identification with self.

But we're here to learn the ways in which to free our self. Because it is only in that freedom that we can experience what we truly are and stop experiencing, by changing identification, with what we thought we were. Because we're constantly changing what we think we are.

We have a relationship or association or a marriage or this or that, and depending on how the person acts at any given moment, we feel a certain way. Well, no one can ever state that

that's freedom. It is not possible, no. Now some people, they have relationships and they take a look. They look at it more intelligently. They do not place that relationship as their God. That that controls us is our god. And so, many are the false gods with clay feet.

But we are here to be freed from the gods of clay feet. What are clay feet? Why, of course, they're crumbling understanding. You know, we go through these experiences and we understand this is going to be this way or that's going be that way. And one day we wake up and that's all crumbled. Well, our understanding was based upon what we decided was our need, what we decided how our need was going to be filled. Had we decided there was no need, the experience would not be.

Experience is necessary as long as we choose to identify with creation. Our philosophy teaches the way to be in creation—because we are within this temple; this is creation—to be in creation, never a part of creation; to be with a person, place, or thing, never a part of a person, place, or thing. That that has an effect upon you, you are a part of. When you can be with a person, place, or thing and it has no effect upon you unless you consciously choose it to have [an] effect upon you, then you are not a part of it. But we are ever a part of that which has an effect upon us without our conscious choice and decision for it to have an effect upon us.

When we consciously choose that a person is going to have a certain effect upon us, then we say, "I have chosen to have this experience of this effect of this person upon me for ten minutes." When the ten minutes are up, you no longer have the effect. That's freedom. But when you are affected by a person, place, or thing and you cannot consciously choose to end within your consciousness this effect, then that is bondage because you no longer are in control of your own destiny.

You see, there is not something outside that has dictated our destiny. Everything that is dictating our destiny, that ever has and ever will, is within the consciousness, for that's where God is. For if God is not within the consciousness, then God does not exist outside the consciousness.

So we begin with what we have. We have our own little house, our own little realm and that's where our God is. Now when we choose the Life, in reference to our own soul's eons of evolution, when we consciously make those choices, then we are in control of our destiny. You see, it is not only our divine birthright, but it is our divine responsibility to be in control of that which, by the very laws of evolution, we have been granted control of. We have been granted, by the laws of evolution, control of the house of clay in which our true being is expressing itself. It is not only our divine right, it is our divine responsibility. But that takes a conscious effort moment by moment to be aware of our thoughts to gain control over our emotions.

Now we all know—most of us—I'm sure, that emotions, of course, are the servants of our pride. What is threatened when we express these emotions that we have? What is threatened? Our eternal being? Our soul? That's not threatened. You cannot threaten that which is. You cannot threaten that which does not begin and, therefore, does not end. The only thing that can be threatened is belief. And belief is creation, form, and limit. Did that help with your question?

Yes. Thank you.

Yes. We have time for a few more questions.

We've been taught that our denial—our destinies—our denials are our destinies.

Our denials *are* our destinies.

OK. In reference to what you were talking about, about creating our own destiny consciously and our soul talents, can we—what would be the correlation between the two if denial is our destiny?

Denial is our destiny. You see, now look at it—as the statement clearly says, our denials are our destinies. When you deny something, do you not experience need thereof? Do you not, through identification with self, follow the need to its hopeful fulfillment? In that respect, in the mental world, our denials are our destiny.

Now there's a vast difference between our denials are our destiny through our own identification with self and the purpose and the responsibility of our being. When you spend twenty-six centuries evolving some particular avenue of expression, do you not think there is a responsibility for its continuity in service to the Light which sustains it, whether you're a carpenter, a dressmaker, a designer or anything else? When you awaken to a soul talent—the soul talent is the purpose of being on the planet that one is expressing on. That was our class last evening. So in that respect, that's a destiny, but it's not the destiny of denial. Only in the sense that the mental world has denied its existence or its possibility.

You see, when the statement is made, "To God all things are possible," then the question must be asked, "Well, where is this God to which all things are possible? For I want the fulfillment of the possibility immediately." Well, to have that, we've got go through a miraculous—whatever they call it—rebirth or something within consciousness and totally eliminate all those magnetic fields that pull us to what has been.

We all know, to be attracted to what has been requires emotion. Because, you see, we are attracted to the past in keeping with the emotions that we permit our self to experience. The philosophy does not teach to be without emotion. That's ridiculous. You have a responsibility, as an emotional being, to use them wisely. One can express their emotions in many ways. Emotions can be expressed and freed from dependence upon anything outside.

You see, you look at the sky. Through belief, you say to yourself, "It's up there so many, many, many miles away. It's just infinite, etc." All right. Now someone else says, "It's not quite as far." Or you look at a cloud and you say how beautiful that is and you feel good and you express within your consciousness some emotion over the cloud. That exists in your consciousness. It is your view of the cloud. Your view of the cloud is subject to your identification with self and what you have to offer at the moment you are viewing the cloud. Therefore, we see the world and everything in it ever subject to whatever past experiences are in control at the moment.

Now we don't have to see the world that way. We have, by our laws of evolution, the divine choice to see the world the way it is, not the way we believe it is. If you listen to some people, then you see the world on the verge of total annihilation and disaster and it's about to be blown up at any moment. And you get to express all your emotions involved in those judgments. Now if you want to consciously choose to have that emotional experience, that's one thing. And you choose it for whatever time you want to choose to have that experience. And when you have decided that the time is up for that emotional experience and you set it aside on the shelf, then you're free. However, if you permit yourself to get involved in that emotional uproar and you're not able to shut it off in consciousness when you choose to do so, you are not free—just the opposite. Something else is in control.

And that is contrary to your responsibility and your birthright. Because even in the—all the religions of the past have taught very clearly: and God has given you charge over all creation. Well, God has given us charge over all creation. God has—we have earned that responsibility, you see. Because we understand that God is not a giver. If God was a giver, then God's a taker. So it's in a constant process of giving and taking. We don't know when he is going to take when it's something that we want him to give. And now that kind of thinking has caused a lot of problems in life: that God gives to one and he takes from another one and that kind of foolishness. Because that puts responsibility out there, beyond one's control and in so doing, one cannot be free that way.

So when we stop and we pause and we think, "This is the way that I choose to feel at this time," then you have, available to you within your consciousness, all of the has-beens that will grant unto you that feeling, because they were created for that specific feeling at any time you choose to experience that feeling. You want to feel good? You have experiences in the past; you pull them forward consciously and so you feel good for that length of time. However, remember to be consciously aware of what you are doing. You don't have to be dependent on what has been to feel good. You can feel good at any moment by conscious choice.

Are there any other questions before class concludes? And it kind of looks like we're getting close to time, doesn't it? Somebody asked me about time last time and I said, "Well, of course we can get it on a sixty." *[The Teacher refers to a sixty-minute audio cassette tape.]* Any other questions? Yes, one more question. We'll just make it.

When we were asked to put down the five things that we have—

Absolutely.

Does that indicate that we might have that many soul talents or just something that is real on earth?

Talent, soul talent is not necessarily limited to one particular thing. It could be twenty. Because, you see, you want to consider you're not talking about fifty or sixty years. You're talking about eons of evolution.

And so next class, we're going to discuss our eons of evolution. Thank you.

JANUARY 26, 1984

CONSCIOUSNESS CLASS 232

Good evening, everyone. As we stated last week, this evening's class: "Eons of Evolution."

When we understand that the identification and uniqueness of the part is dependent upon the denial of the whole, then we'll understand that the power of our spirit is faith and the force of our mind is belief. Now we believe that we are, and because we believe that we are, we follow the path of creation. We believe that we are thinking. Therefore, we believe we are the thought. And because we believe we are the thinker and believe we are the thought, we establish the Law of Experience.

When we follow the path of creation, we find our self moving through so-called time and space with a constant experience of need. That is the force of the human mind. And through this process, we slowly, gradually broaden our horizons by expanding our beliefs.

As we follow the path of the spirit, that which we are (not that which we are becoming)—in identification or denial of the whole, we are in a constant state of becoming. When we are in the path of the spirit which we are—not that which we think we are—then we are the fullness moment by moment. There is no hope of what is to be, for all that is, is what we experience in the moment of the awakening to the wholeness which we are.

The expansion of our beliefs, slowly but surely, brings us to the awakening or the return to the consciousness of the Light that we have always been, therefore, will always be, because we *are*.

Now I realize that it is—we make it so—difficult to have faith, to express our faith when we are identifying or denying that which we are. For example, we encounter various experiences and situations in our life in keeping with beliefs or laws which we have established and, therefore, find great difficulty in having faith in the outcome that we hope for. Because we think of what the outcome should be reveals to us that we are still identified. Therefore, we are still experiencing and expressing belief. Consequently, we are still denying that which we are.

To move in evolution from what we are to what we think we are, is where we are at this time in our evolution. We believe many things; therefore, we experience many things; therefore, we are dependent upon many things. To disassociate from belief is to gain control over the mind and the force which the human mind offers. For without belief, there is no fear. Fear cannot exist without belief. Without belief, there is no judgment, for judgment cannot exist for there is no denial.

In keeping with that teaching, some time ago we gave to you what is called total acceptance. Total acceptance being the will of God. The will of a thing is the movement and direction of a thing. And so the will of God is the movement or direction of goodness. To experience the goodness, the movement of goodness and direction, to experience that, then we must entertain the possibility of what is termed total acceptance.

What we accept, we are freed from being controlled by. Now stop and think about that for a few moments. The acceptance is something that is taking place within our consciousness. We have the power within us to accept the right of expression of all things in the universe. The acceptance of the right of expression does not place a person as a victim of the expression of that which they accept the right of; it does directly the opposite. It frees us from control within our consciousness of that which we *believe* is not beneficial to us. For example, we entertain the type of thinking that someone is doing such and such. It is not acceptable within our consciousness. When we permit our mind to think that way, we, in that moment, become the victim of that very expression within our own consciousness. It's commonly referred to as intolerance.

Whenever we feel or believe—because we must believe in order to feel—that we cannot tolerate something, it is in that belief that we become the victim of it within our own consciousness. For we have entered that realm of force and in so doing, we have denied and, therefore, separated our self from the whole, from that which we are, and have placed our self upon the path of becoming.

We understand that truth *is*. Truth does not become. It is man's mental awareness that is in a constant process of becoming. And it is that belief and that force that keeps us from the experience of the whole of goodness, that which we truly are. For in becoming is the process of constant denial.

To be what you desire to be is to deny what you believe that you are. Therefore, man is in a constant process of denial and hope to be. Through that process of denial and hope to be, man is not in the present, where truth *is*. So we pause, and we think we pause. But we do not pause, because our consciousness is moving through the process, the mental process of becoming.

We awaken in the morning and we *believe* it will be, for us, a good day. We *believe* that such and such will happen. And our consciousness works diligently to bring that about. But in this process, this mental force known as belief, it comes up against the many obstructions of beliefs that have been.

You see, in a world of belief, that which has been ever is for us. For we, in our belief, have made it so. And so yesterday (the shadow) is ever in front of our tomorrow because we are not in the moment of our consciousness known as the present.

Now I do think that if you will pause and you will study and apply what has been said, you will begin to move from the ever need of tomorrow, the ever regret of yesterday, to the moment in which you be.

I've spoken before on that which has been is a shadow and that which is to be is a shadow and only that which is, is the

Light that we are. But it is a constant process to awaken, for the world of belief is a world of sleep and satisfaction. We sleep because we believe. And because we believe, we need. And because we need, we deny. And so we find our self requiring, we think, varying hours of sleep. When what is truly—what our soul is ever guiding us to is rest. Rest is when the consciousness is still. That is the only time that we are rejuvenated. We can rest for five minutes, nine minutes, or for many minutes.

But sleep is an active process, a very active process. A person goes to sleep—what they call sleep—and they enter that realm of belief, for they enter that realm, that mental realm of satisfaction. And so, the many forms of what has been within the consciousness, they rise up. They are very active. And they gain energy while we are in a state of unconsciousness. Now by a state of unconsciousness I mean that our faculty of reason, which flows through our conscious mind, is not guardian at the threshold.

And so I have spoken before in classes about the importance of taking control of your mind before you lose consciousness. For you have, at that critical time, a choice to make: you may choose those forms which you want to be guardian of the threshold of the mental realm of belief and force, to place them on duty while you are in a state of unconsciousness in respect to your light of reason or those forms which feel, through their belief, that they are in need of sustenance or energy, [and they] drain the vitality of your being during this state known as sleep.

So it is important before you go to sleep, as it is important when you first awaken, [to be aware of] what your thoughts are, for that reveals the beliefs that are in control at that moment. To consciously choose the forms of belief is the first step in becoming freed from the mental world of creation, the world of force, the world of belief.

Faith, the spiritual light that we are, places us in the wholeness of our being. That is the power of our spirit. That is what we are. We think we are many things in our life and in that thinking, for a time, for only a time, we believe and therefore, for us, *for us* it is true. For truth is individually perceived and is ever subject within the consciousness of each and every individual [to] how much control they have over the mental world in which their eternal being is moving and expressing.

Now we'll pause for just a few moments to see if there are any questions in reference to this evening's discussion on eons of evolution. If there is, please raise your hand. If you've found it confusing, please raise your hand. Yes.

Is a prayer, on going to sleep, a prayer of acceptance of waking-up in good health and feeling good a way?

Well, in reference to the question, Is a prayer of being in good health upon awakening the way? Well, it is, of course, a way—a way ever dependent on the evolution of the individual.

Now, first of all, in order to think that we are not in good health, we, of course, accept, from our demonstration, that we temporarily are identifying with a mental world or belief. Therefore, in that world of ours, we have available to us shadows or experiences of the past in which we believe that we were in perfect health. Do you understand that?

Yes.

If we are going to permit our self to identify—and that is what we do: we permit our self to identify—then we must work with that which the realm of identity has offered to us from our own beliefs. So if a person, upon going to sleep, accepts that they will awaken feeling good, in good health and etc., then, of course, that, for them, is beneficial. But we also must realize that the form of belief of good health, in respect to identification, is subject to whatever forms are within the consciousness that may, at that particular time, be stronger. For example, a person is having a experience of, say, a cold or something, whatever they want to call it or a bug or something. And they're feeling rather puny. The senses are alerting our consciousness that we are not feeling very well. Do you understand that?

Yes.

All right. And sometimes the alert is more like an alarm that doesn't go off. It doesn't stop ringing. That reveals to us that that is a very strong form in our consciousness. Do you understand?

Yes.

All right. Now if you have a belief which is greater than that that is ringing within the consciousness, then, of course, it is beneficial. But there is something much greater than the belief in the prayer of good health. There is the power of the Spirit and that is called faith.

Now belief is dependent and faith is not. Belief is dependent upon what has been. Faith is not dependent on anything, for it is a flow in the consciousness in the moment that the mind is still. Therefore, it would, of course, be more beneficial indeed to use faith, instead of belief. That help with your question?

Yes. Thank you.

Yes. The lady in the back, please.

Living in a world of faith and spirit, how do we create them? What's the connection between living in spirit and creating in this world?

Thank you. What is the difference between living in spirit and creating in this world? First of all, we are spirit. That is what we are. We are spirit, formless and free. The entrance of the formless, free spirit into a world of creation is the path of identification. Now we believe we are unique; that belief is subject to and dependent upon identification.

Now take a look at identification, belief, and uniqueness. Identification, uniqueness, and belief is dependent upon comparison. We believe we are unique as we look out with our senses over creation. We see that many people may be similar, but we are unique, for they are different. We have awakened within our consciousness the function of comparison. Comparison is dependent upon judgment and judgment is dependent upon denial. As I stated in the beginning of the class, the identification and uniqueness of the part, you see, the identification and the uniqueness of the part is subject to and dependent upon the denial of the whole. Therefore, we believe we are unique and in that belief we are separate. And in that belief we are the victim of creation. Does that help with question? If not, please continue.

So if we're living in faith and spirit all the time, we wouldn't be here then, right? We wouldn't need to be here or—

There is no need in faith and spirit; that is true. Faith is the power of spirit. It is not the spirit that needs. Through the process of identification, denial is established. It is in denial that we experience need. Now faith is the bridge that moves us from creation to truth. Faith is that bridge that moves us from this individualization, this part, this separation. You see, faith moves us to the wholeness, that which we are. Belief keeps us separate from it.

So working on different talents that we have, it came from denial that we are not—it takes eons of time to develop—to perfect certain things because we live in a world of belief or—

Because we live in a world of belief. Without belief, you don't have identity. Identity, separation, belief, judgment, comparison, they are the sleep of satisfaction. They are what creation offers. That is what they are. They are limit. They are uniqueness.

So there's nothing to learn if you're living in faith and spirit.

Spirit, Intelligent Spirit *is* what we know as God. Infinite, intelligent Spirit, that is God. God cannot learn. Only mental substance, only identification can learn. Knowledge is the domain of a mental world. Knowledge knows much; wisdom knows better. So it is not our spirit that learns. It is form, creation, individualization, that is what learns. That is what changes. That is what is refined and evolved. Does that help with your question?

Yes. Thank you.

Yes. You see, it's like, with a talent, the talent *is*. The expression of the talent is subject to the identification in which the talent is striving to express itself. A person says, "I sing real good sometimes. And sometimes I don't sing so good." Well, that is an expression of the person believing that they are the singing, that *they* are—not this intelligent being which they, in truth, are, but what they *believe* they are. And they believe they are the thought because they believe they are the thinker. Yes. Does that help with your question?

Yes. Thank you.

This is what needs the training, which, in truth, is the expansion in consciousness. That is a process that is taking place through what is known as the karmic wheel of cause and effect. The karmic wheel of cause and effect is not what you are; it is what you think you are, but never what you are. It cannot be what you are. It can only be what you think you are. Because what you think you are is subject to the Law of Belief and that is changing or evolving. Yes, a question here, please.

How do we generate the power of faith?

The power of faith is not a subject of, or controlled by, the mental world or the minds of men. It is experienced when the mind is controlled and, therefore, perfectly still. Now the mind can be stilled and is stilled by the power of will. So man wills his mind to be still, for the will is the lord of our universe. That is something that we can do.

Now there is the divine will, which is that great power. Then there is the mental will. Mental will is ever interested in form because mental will *is* form. Through a process known as disassociation, which has been given some time ago—a special class on disassociation—we enter the realms of faith. That's when we are. Now everyone has experienced moments in their life, they have experienced moments when they know they're free. It may be a fleeting moment, but everyone has had the experience of freedom. That is the moment in which they crossed the bridge of faith within their consciousness and entered the spirit which they truly are. Does that help with your question?

Yes, sir.

Through disassociation—you see, we must first disassociate in order to free our self from the denial which is known as identification. Because it is through identification that we deny and become the part. We temporarily, in that sense, lose what we are to become what we think we are. And that takes place, you see, when we think, "Ah, I am different. I am unique. There are other humans on the planet, but there is no one like me." Now that's creation. That's the variety of creation. That is what the mental world offers. Now I am not saying that when the senses view and they see that everything is different, that one cannot convince themselves they are unique, for no one looks, acts, and thinks exactly as they do. But that is a world of change. That is a world of limit. That is a world of form. And that is not what we are. We are only that the moment that we believe. And when we stop belief, that's the moment we cross the bridge of faith and we be. That means that there is no past. That means that there is no future. That means there only *is*. That's truth. Does that help with your question? Go ahead. Yes.

Will daily meditation assist us in this technique?

Daily meditation absolutely and positively *can* assist in that awakening because daily meditation offers to the human mind the opportunity to gain control over the consciousness. To gain control over the consciousness, it is necessary to still the mind. You see, when we experience opportunities, so to speak, of expressing our emotions, that's when the opportunity is truly golden to take control over the mind. Because, you see, that's when we can pause and speak the truth: "This is an experience within my consciousness. It has a beginning and, by the Law of Beginning, it has an ending. I alone, within my consciousness, can choose to end it soon or take months or years to end it." You see, because it is taking place within our consciousness and we take control over our consciousness—no matter what the experience—we can choose to end it at the moment of our choice.

Now the effect of that is freedom. That is freedom from control. And through a process of daily meditation, we can, slowly but surely, gain control over our mind. To gain control over our mind is to use this force known as belief in an intelligent and, therefore, constructive way for our greater good. If we are having an experience—which, of course, all experience takes place within our consciousness—and we cannot tell our consciousness, "I choose now not to continue with this experience," and if that experience in our consciousness does not end at the moment of our choice, then we know we are controlled by creation. And we are controlled by creation through over-identification. [Through] over-identification with creation, we become the victims of creation.

When the human mind—you can push the button as you do on your television receiver and the channel is shut off or you can turn the knob and change the channel, that is when the human mind serves a good purpose for the eternal being that we are. Now that is something that we work on daily. We don't like the channel that's being broadcast within our consciousness? We turn the knob and choose a different channel. That is our divine right of choice. The human mind is designed as a vehicle or servant of the true being that we are. And when the human mind forgets that it is our servant, it very quickly becomes our master. Does that help with the question?

Yes. Very much. Thank you.

You see, we should, at any given moment of our choice, say, "I choose not this experience within my consciousness. The power within me, that which I am, is expressed through my faith. That is my bridge to freedom." Faith is our bridge to freedom. Yes, we have time for another question.

In expression, can we be in both belief and faith at the same time—

No.

But in different areas?

Not at the same time, no. No one serves two masters and ever is freed. You see, we move in consciousness from belief and moments of faith. Oh, yes. But we, in consciousness, are not both places at the same time. Does that help with your question?

Yes.

Yes. The lady here, please.

What would be a constructive way of using belief?

A constructive way of using belief is, of course, dependent upon our identification with creation. The more identified with creation that we are, then the more beliefs that we experience and laws we establish. So constructive ways of using belief in the sense of being in creation and never a part of creation, being with a person, place, or thing and never a part of a person, place, or thing—constructive ways of using belief is, as long we're going to identify with creation, believe in the goodness that we are, believe in the goodness that others are and in that process, we will experience the goodness. For whoever sees the goodness in another first sees that goodness within themselves and, consequently, that indeed will be instrumental in refining or evolving the forms of creation. And that way it would be a most wise and constructive use of the force of belief.

For example, in this world of creation at this time, we see the great force of fear throughout the world—the belief, you see, the *belief* in a holocaust, the belief in the annihilation of the planet. We, within our consciousness, can do great good, through our own belief by believing in the intelligent Power that is greater than all of the thoughts of the human mind. Because that which sustains a thing is greater than the thing. And so the power of the Divine Spirit is far greater than all the fear of a total disaster of the planet Earth or the universe. Now that's one of the many ways in which we can use belief constructively.

We believe it. Therefore when the opposite comes to us in keeping with the law that likes attracts likes, it can strengthen our belief! You see, a person has an experience and then they look out there and say, "Oh, that person and etc.," and they have a bad experience with that person. But, you see, the darkness is in the denial of the law that like attracts like and becomes the Law of Attachment. The person is called out of the universe to enter this person's universe in keeping with their beliefs, for the law does not fail. The mental laws do not fail. The divine laws do not fail. Law never faileth. For law to fail, it would not be law. Did that help with your question?

Yes.

Thank you. Believe it or not, time is up. Thank you very much.

FEBRUARY 2, 1984

CONSCIOUSNESS CLASS 233

Good evening, class.

This evening we'll continue on with our classes in reference to the power of faith, the force of belief: the wisdom and the benefit, of course, of power, when we understand what it truly is, in comparison to belief.

Whatever we choose to believe in life, we must first understand that all belief is form and, by the nature of form, is limit. And all limit contains within it the necessary ingredient known as resistance. So whatever we choose to believe in our day-to-day activities and our living, we must first understand that within the belief is a resistance: a resistance to that which is not harmonious with it. For example, we *believe* we're going to do something and at the moment of entertaining the belief of what we are going to do, within our consciousness is the process of resisting that which is not in harmony with it. And so we find in our lives that we have, in many endeavors, an excellent start and a very poor finish. It is because we are using belief instead of faith.

Now as we discussed in our last class in reference to total acceptance being the will of the Divinity or divine will, the will of God, when we use, in our consciousness, a total acceptance in anything we choose to involve our self, we are using, in that process, the power of faith, compared to the formation of belief, which contains limit through judgment. For we must first understand that we believe or believe not ever in keeping with the judgments we have made in life, which are, of course, dependent upon the experiences in our life that we have already had. So a person goes about believing many things and in so doing, a person goes about life doubting many things.

The path of nonresistance is, in truth, the path of wisdom and it *is* the Light and it *is* the Power itself. Now a person says, "Well, if I don't stand up for this, if I don't stand up for that," but what do we mean when we say that? Where are we standing up? We usually mean that we are defending something that we believe in, that we judge someone else is attacking and therefore we fear because it is the nature of the human mind to protect whatever it judges it possesses.

The mind makes the judgment [that] whatever thought that enters it, *it* possesses as long as it chooses to possess it. That, of course, is a fallacy, because the human mind is sustained by a power that, once the power is removed, the human mind no longer is. So if we will apply this very basic simple law in the power of faith—how does one use the power of faith when they want to make changes? What usually happens, when we *think*, when we *think* that we accept, that guarantees, in that process, that we do not accept. When we think that we have made certain changes, the next step in that thinking process is that we believe we have made certain changes. Then time marches on and we soon find out the change we thought we had made, we believed and were sure that we had made, was not made at all. Therefore that is not the path of freedom. That is the constant path of what we call creation.

It takes constant effort, constant effort, because constant effort we are using all the time. We are using effort, energy to see, to hear, to sense, to walk, to work. And all of those things take effort.

In these classes of personal growth, it is an awakening to choose consciously, to consciously choose where you want to direct your energy at any given moment. Some time ago I spoke to you on asking yourself the question, "Why this and why now?" For there are no accidents in the universe. Nothing happens by chance. Everything takes place by immutable, inevitable law. The only thing that one can rely on, with any security, is the law. For the law does not fail. And the Law of Life is the Light of Life. There's no difference between the Light, the Love, the Life, for all of it is the Law.

We, in our efforts to awaken to that light within us, must pass through creation. Now we are already in the process of passing through creation and there are moments when we are not identified with limit. There are moments when we are not identified with struggle. And it is in those moments that we are vehicles through which the power, the light, what we call faith, is moving.

It is our purpose in sharing with you this philosophy and understanding that you may, number one, consciously enter those realms of consciousness in which you may personally experience that freedom and that power—that which you truly are and not that which we think we are. The statement, "I am Spirit formless and free," that *is* what we are. "Whatever I think that will I be." That is what we become; through placing our attention upon limit, we become limit.

Now a person, for example, would like to have an improvement in their life, in certain areas of their life. And so they say,

"Well, I will demonstrate my faith." When that thought moves in the consciousness, what is known as belief takes over. Now how does belief take over? It takes over because we have established the Law of Separation through identity.

It is, of course, difficult at times to be freed from creation. But one of the simple things that a person can easily do—we all experience desire in the course of a day. We desire to eat. We desire to drink. We desire to work. We desire not to work. We desire to sit down. We desire to lay down. We desire to stand up. We desire to run. We desire to walk. So we are constantly expressing the Divinity. But is it us that is constantly expressing the Divinity or is it something that has been? We find, usually, in fact, most all the time, it's something that has been which we believe that we are.

Now, you have an experience in life and you judge from the experience that you feel very good. To feel good is to know God. And there's nothing wrong with that. There may be plenty wrong in how you judge that you will feel good or know God. And so you have an experience in life in which you judge that you feel good. Therefore you want to repeat that experience because feeling good is a necessity; it is not a luxury. Feeling good or knowing God *is* an absolute necessity of life. That is a part of life. It's indispensable to life. And so the human consciousness constantly strives to know God or to feel good, which is one and the same.

And so a person has his experience. And they feel good and they work to repeat the experience. Then the time comes, usually, that that good feeling is not the same; it doesn't feel as good. What has happened? Their consciousness—they've made a change in their consciousness. Other variables, other factors, they've permitted to enter into that initial or original experience. And consequently, they make the judgment: "It's not as good as it used to be." It's like you take one spoon—say that you like ice cream and you have one spoonful; it tastes good. Say that you eat a gallon of it. It doesn't taste so good. So, you see, it's all taking place within the human mind.

Then a person goes on in life and their mind—they stop and they think there's a need of knowing God or feeling good. And they go through their mind, through their computer and there are all these experiences. And they work to recapture one of those experiences. But are they doing that consciously or are one of those experiences, which now exist in a mental world? For nothing is ever lost. You see, that which is created by our mind in a mental world, expressed by our mind, is in mental substance. It is recorded indelibly in mental substance. Now that recording of an experience is a form, as all thought is form. Those forms exist. They're known as the shadows of the past.

Now, ofttimes they will come into a person's consciousness and they will demand that a person do a certain thing that they used to do. If the person believes, if they believe they are the limit, if they believe they are the bone and the flesh (the vehicle through which their eternal being is expressing) if they believe that, then they are controlled by creation, controlled by all form, controlled by what has been or what may be. Now that's belief. That's resistance. That is force. It accomplishes much, but it binds, for all limit is bondage.

A person, from years of experiencing limit or bondage, struggling to be freed from it, slowly but surely begins to awaken. And that is why, when we look about the world, we ofttimes question why is there so much suffering. What could this person or that person have done to suffer so badly? But we are not looking objectively at the evolution. We are not looking with our soul. Therefore we cannot see their soul. We look with our shell and therefore we see their shell. We see that which begins and, by seeing that which begins, we can only see that which ends. That is not what we are. It never was what we are and it never will be what we are.

So in this semester, the daily homework that we should all be doing is take a conscious awareness of our thoughts, a conscious awareness of our feelings.

Earlier this evening, I spoke to the duet. And I have spoken to the choir before. But this evening, I heard them sing those two beautiful songs the first time. Was it "Beyond the Sunset"? Was it?

Yes.

"Beyond the Sunset" and "Santa Lucia"?

Yes.

Yes. I listened to it out there and I didn't feel anything. It didn't register feeling in the expression of the words. And so I went in and I spoke to the ladies and I said, "I want you to sing those two songs again. But before you do, I want you to think of the boyfriend that you've lost." And so they started to sing and I told them that was the wrong boyfriend: to pick another one. They paused a moment and they started again. And the song was filled with feeling, you see.

Now why was it filled with feeling? How did this feeling come up? It wasn't something that their mind consciously strained and made this effort. These feelings rose up. Now this is the benefit, you see. You see, past experience is known in this philosophy as has-beens, shadows of events that have already passed; they have no life in truth, only that which we give them through attention, which is the vehicle through which energy flows through our being to them. They can be used constructively. If there is not feeling in a song, there's some has-been, there is some experience within our life in which we can consciously bring into the fore, into the conscious moment and reexperience those feelings and use them to bring the fullness into a song. Is that not correct?

Yes.

Did you not notice the difference in the feeling?

Yes.

You see, one thing comes from the head and the other comes from the heart. And so we must learn to put our heart in whatever we do. And we must learn to use that which has passed—that's ever available to us—to consciously use it for the benefit of the moment. For whoever benefits themselves is therefore, in keeping with the law, is therefore qualified to be an instrument through which another is benefited. For as the teaching is, of old, "O, physician heal thyself." And so it is we grant to another what we first grant to our self. We grant unto our self first the goodness of life, ever in keeping with personal responsibility. And then we qualify our self to be the instrument through which that may be shared with those, in keeping with the laws established, [who] may benefit therefrom.

Whether or not it is putting feeling into a song and using a has-been to accomplish that good, there is no question that good comes from it. Now that's using past events wisely, if, in so doing, when you have finished with the purpose of using a has-been or past event, you close the door as you opened the door—you understand? Because if you don't, then those feelings of past experiences, they start to spread all over. And you don't know what's going to happen and usually it's quite destructive.

Now we're going to take a few moments for you to have or to speak forth any questions that you have in reference to the classes or any questions you may have in reference to your own personal growth. Please raise your hand. Yes, the lady there, please.

How does one, in reference to success, if one is doing something a certain way, how does one do something in a diff—in a better way to become successful? If someone isn't getting anywhere in the methods they are using to be successful, how do they...

Make the change?

Yes.

Well, first of all, if the law or the experience is revealing that our efforts are not producing what we feel they should be producing, then it reveals to us there is a need to make the change in our method.

Yes.

That's what you're speaking of, yes. First of all, working in that mental realm, one must ask themselves the question, "In this particular area of endeavor in my life, do I have, existing in my past experiences, a pattern of success?" That's the first question. So I ask that question of you. Do you have, in that particular area of endeavor, a time in your life when there was success?

Yes.

Ah! Now, therefore you have, within the consciousness available to you, forms of success in that particular area. You follow me so far?

Yes.

As you were the one, this very evening, who was able to call up has-been experiences and put feeling into a song—correct?

Yes.

You can do the same thing with forms that were successful in a particular area in which you, once again, choose to be successful. Do you understand that?

Yes.

Therefore, working in a mental realm, you use them as workers consciously, instead of being used by them.

So how does one—

For example, that tells me—you see, when you go to the law involved—you're trying to have success in a particular area. You have not had success this time, correct?

Right.

However, you have had in your life a time when there was success. Is that correct?

Yes.

Fine. However, the experience reveals that you've also had another time in your life when it was not successful. Is that not correct?

Yes.

Well, now I want you to follow me very clearly because, you see, what you have—you have an army here in a certain area of endeavor that is successful. A successful army. Then you have another army over here that is not successful. Now presently you are trying, once again, to, say, open up a door. Do you understand?

Yes.

Well, that reveals, because you have not had success, you've got the wrong army working for you.

Yes.

Now you don't want that army.

No.

Because you want success. Is that not correct? So you must consciously become aware of the type of thinking that's been taking place within your consciousness. For that type of thinking reveals that the failure has-beens are in control at this particular time. Do you follow me so far?

Yes.

You must consciously, then, choose those has-beens of success. In other words, you must become aware of your thought patterns, your emotions, your feelings, and your attitude of mind, for it is proving not to be successful at this time. Do you understand that?

Yes.

That's a mental world. But you can use it in a successful way because successful forms exist there for you within the consciousness. You see, that is what creation has to offer. And while you're in it, you work with it intelligently—while you're making the evolutionary steps to pass through creation to enter the realm of light and spirit, to enter where the power of faith moves all mountains. How does the power of faith, how does faith move a mountain? Because, don't you see, there is no resistance in faith. It is all. You see, faith, in the moving of the mountain, *is* the mountain, you see. There's nothing resisting it because it is it! That's the difference with faith and belief.

Now if a man believes—you see, it's like will power. So often a person says, "It's taking all my will power." Will power, the power of will, is not a strain. It's a very passive experience. Moving the mountain is not a struggle of great will of the human mind. That's belief. That's the step below. That's resistance. That which we accept in consciousness we establish the law to control and that which we resist in consciousness we become controlled by. Therefore, our adversities—our resistance—become our own attachments. And so if you look at it (life itself) and you accept—those who accept are never the victims. They are the victors.

All creation has been placed before the eternal being that we are. It is subject to the guidance of that which we truly are. But through our own resistance, we are controlled by it and being controlled by it, from over-identification with it, we believe that we are it. We believe we are the thought in the moment the thought is passing through our consciousness. Yet, after it has passed through our consciousness, we know that we are not that. For now there is a different thought. And so truth is constantly revealing itself to us. We are not the emotion that just passed. We are only it as long as we believe it. And we don't believe some of those things very long at all.

And so there, *there* is what we face: we face the total acceptance, which is the divine will and, from that, control over creation within our sphere and zone of action, or we face resistance. We face the constant struggle of force through belief, and we face being the victim of that which is temporal. And so it is certainly not wisdom to place that which we are—eternal, eternity, infinity itself; that is what we are—to place that as the servant of temporal creation. No matter what the feeling and no matter what the thought, it has a coming and a guaranteed going. There is no reliability, there is no security in creation. There is constant change. There is constant temptation. There is no security. There is no freedom.

Our purpose—the purpose of the Divine Spirit entering form or creation—is to evolve, to refine and to evolve form. That is our purpose in our evolution. We are responsible and [have] charge over all creation, that is, all creation in our consciousness. We have that responsibility because we have—we *are* the power that sustains it. And we're not very responsible when we permit our forms, our thoughts to deceive us that we believe that we are them. Does that help with your question?

Yes. Yes, the lady in the back please.

In the realm of desire, if you're noticing that there's this need to express a particular desire, but you—there's the need, but then you don't want to fulfill it, how do you get out of that confusion?

Well, first of all, in reference to the realm of desire, there are many avenues of expression, for desire is the divine expression. Well, in reference to your question, there is the implication that the fulfillment of the divine expression, you have chosen to limit to [a] particular form. Is that correct?

Yes.

Well, that's where the problem exists. You see, here is this Divinity, the divine expression and here we are and we have judged that this expression shall take place only in this particular way—very limited. Is that correct?

Yes.

That's where the problem is. The problem is quite simple: the broadening of one's horizons, the expanding of one's consciousness. But only we can do that. That is entirely up to us. If we tell our self that we feel good only when we do such and such, then we must pay the price of doing such and such because that is our own self-deception. You see, it reveals to us that we value our judgments more than we do the divine expression itself.

You see, the divine expression called desire doesn't tell us that we only feel good through this expression, that expression, or that expression. It doesn't tell a person they only feel good when they have chocolate cake. Does it? After all, there's some people, they have vanilla cake and feel just as good, if not better. So, you see, this is something that we are doing. *We are the limit. We* have made the judgment. Now when we believe that we are the judgment, then we have great problems in expanding our consciousness and broadening our horizons, for we have placed creation superior to that which we are by believing we are that which we have created. And so the place to work, quite simply, is to work on the judgments that we alone have made.

You see, in keeping with the teachings of old, "Judge not that ye be not judged,"—don't you understand?—when we judge, you have the experience of being judged. There is something within the consciousness that's judging you. They're telling you that you can only have this fulfillment in this or that particular way. So because we judge, we are being judged. They don't come up to our consciousness and say, "I'm judging you now." No, they limit you in keeping with your establishment of the Law of Judgment. For the Law of Judgment is the Law of Resistance. It is the Law of Limit. It is placing form over the formless and the free. Does that help with your question?

Yes. And somehow it feels like the frustration . . .

That's the payment of the judgment. You see, a person—what does frustration mean to a person? What does it mean to you? If you say, "I'm frustrated," what does it mean to you?

Well, it means that that I'm . . .

Battling a desire?

Yes, I'm confused. Yes, I don't know how to unravel it. It's like it's before me and it seems to be too complex for me to—yes, battling a desire.

Well, one often experiences what they term frustration from resisting desire. Would you not agree with that?

Yes.

All right. This philosophy teaches to educate and never suppress desire. For it takes energy to suppress and that is directing energy to the very thing that we don't want to do. And we make it stronger and stronger and stronger within our consciousness. And in keeping with our belief that it is us, it someday consumes us. So suppression of desire, the divine expression, is not the path of wisdom.

Educating desire is the path of wisdom. The education of desire is to face honestly and clearly the cause of the limit, known as judgment, that we have placed in front of the divine expression and how we will permit it to be fulfilled. Do you understand? All right. So the Divine, the Divinity, the Divine expression has no dictate. It contains no judgment. It contains no dictate that you can only experience the fulfillment of itself through this or that or that or that limited avenue of expression. The place to work, my good student, is in the consciousness where the judges reign: within. Does that help you with your question?

Yes. Thank you.

Now that takes an honesty with oneself and a freedom from identifying with the judgment, in the sense we believe that it is us.

Are there any other questions this evening? Yes, the lady here has been waiting. Yes.

Yes. When you were speaking before about calling forth a successful has-been in order to gain success in an area in your life, how would one use faith, instead of having to call—isn't it using belief, calling?

Why, of course. I already explained, I feel—I know I did at the time: that if you're working in a mental realm—now, you see, you must remember that man is a law unto himself in keeping with the law he alone establishes. When we identify with self, then we're in a mental realm. We're in a mental world. And that works in a mental world. That is what you have available for you in a mental world: you have has-beens that are successful in a particular area of your endeavor; you have has-beens that are a failure. And, you see, when you become aware of those sets of has-beens and what caused them, you can use them intelligently.

The next step is faith. So how do you use faith? You see, faith is not something that you pause and you think, "I have faith that it's going to be a good day tomorrow." When we say that, we have already established the Law of Belief. That's not faith. You see, faith does not contain concern. Faith doesn't contain that. It's belief; belief has concern because belief is limit and that—and it's resistance. It's force. It requires defense.

You see, faith is truth. It has no need. It has no defense. It *is*. It just *is*. You see, if a person says to themselves, "It's a good day." It is a good day for them. They don't *think* it's going to be a good day. They don't have *faith* that something's going to work out for them. It already *is*. For them, it *is*. But that takes control of the human mind. And that which controls the human mind, that controls our mind, that which is the very thing that sustains all these forms and thoughts and attitudes, that's far greater than the forms themselves, because without that, they do not exist. They only live as long as that is flowing through us. So you don't have *faith* that a job is going to work out. It's working out. There are no dictates. It just is. That's the difference between belief (what you hope to be) and what is. Does that help with your question?

Thank you.

You see? But if you're working through—but remember, one does not enter the realms of faith and truth as long as they think they are the form they're expressing through. We can easily tell how identified we are with this creation: let something happen to it and we'll see how much attention we give it. And that'll tell us how identified with it we are. The lady over here, please.

Along the same lines as—going a little bit further, if one uses visualization and acceptance—visualization of the success—are you in the moment of now during that visualization?

No. No, in the process of visualization of success, you're under the laws of belief; you're identified with the mental world. That's one of the steps of growth of evolution. Belief serves its purpose, but all belief is under the Law of Duality. For every belief that you permit within your consciousness, you have a doubt. And for every doubt, you have a fear, because that's the way the mind works. [That is] its own defense.

Well, if you have used visualization and you learn what you've just taught us, how can you move from that to change it?

The only movement is just be. You don't *think* or *believe* that something good is going to happen. Something good *is*. You—we move from form, past and future, to formless that just is. You see, that that is formless—you see, there isn't a tomorrow and there isn't a yesterday. There just *is*, moment by moment by moment. Yes.

Thank you.

You're welcome. Are there any other questions this evening? Yes, the lady over here, please. Yes.

If a person is able to disassociate from the Law of Cause and Effect, does that bring that effect they disassociated from as the end of the law and a new law begins? Or is the Law of Cause and Effect a continuum, without beginning and ending as long as you're identified with creation?

You just gave your own answer. In disassociation from what you call the Law of Cause and Effect, there is no disassociation as long as you identify. And we identify by saying, in our mind, "I disassociate with that." In that moment, we have identified with it. Therefore there is no disassociation, you see. And we do not have objectivity in that respect.

Can there be momentaril—momentary disassociation?

Oh, certainly, because there's momentarily—there are moments in which we are not identified with what we *think* is self, you see.

You see, people fear what they call death. Why do they fear death? Because they believe they are that which is disintegrating. That's why they fear. Fear is the defense mechanism. Don't you see? What is there to fear if there is no belief through self-identification? There's nothing to fear. That only exists through identification.

Look, if a person becomes over-identified with the self and their hair starts to turn gray, they have several emotional problems. Even though millions of people all over the universe, their hair turns gray, there's problems. If they start to become wrinkled, there's problems. If there's a little difficulty in walking, there's problems. There's all types of problems. That's dependent on how much over-identification there is with the limit or the suit that we are wearing. What if we entertained the thought that we will awaken in the morning and we will not be the same form? What would happen? What takes place within our consciousness and our emotions? That shows us how attached we are. And that attachment reveals to us our own bondage. Does that help with your question?

Yes. The lady back there, please.

If one is beginning to perceive that you—that one—that you're being—that you're controlled by others—

Do you mean by others, forms within your consciousness?

Ah, well—right, it's within yourself. But you perceive that others around you can control you by whatever they do or don't do. So what is the next—what's the next step in dealing with that in your life?

Thank you. First of all, to permit the human consciousness to believe that someone else is controlling them is to deny the law, the demonstrable Law of Personal Responsibility. So we must first work with that denial, for our denials become our destinies. Therefore we must cast the light of reason upon our denials and in so doing, we awaken within our consciousness: "I have a thought within my mind that tells me that another human being is controlling my life. Upon what foundation do I base this thought?" Then, slowly but surely, you begin to pull the carpet out from under that deception, because you will find, within your own mind, that you have made judgments that dictate that another person must do certain things in order for you to feel and to be the way that you judge that you want to be. So you face this final step, this denial, and you see that you have placed yourself in this error: the victim within your own consciousness of what a person beyond your control does, thinks, or doesn't think. Do you understand?

Yes.

And so the thing is to regain, within your own consciousness, your divine right to your own divinity. And as you cast the light of reason over all of those things, you will, slowly but surely, free yourself from those errors, those judgments within your consciousness that have told your consciousness that you are dependent on something or someone that is beyond your control. Does that help you?

Thank you.

You're welcome. Yes, the lady here, please.

In reference to resistance, if one isn't—if one is resisting where one is physically staying and doesn't accept where they're staying, then does that set up a law for no movement for no new doors opening up?

Why, certainly. Certainly.

And then concern comes in?

Why, certainly. That's directing energy to the obstruction.

So resistance is the key to concern.

Absolutely. Show me a person in concern, I'll show you one that is not freed from resistance. Did you ever see concern where resistance didn't exist? If you are concerned about something, you are resisting something. Is that not correct?

Yes. Now I see. Thank you.

And now, perhaps you may understand why we teach that self-concern, self-pity is the most destructive force in the universe that we can experience. Show me a person discouraged and I'll show you one on the way down. Show me a person encouraged and I'll show you one on the way up. But the choice is made by each and every individual, moment by moment. The path of nonresistance is the path of peace. And the path of peace is the path of power. And that's where truth and freedom truly live.

The gentleman over here, please.

Could you speak on the difference between belief and faith in regard to the five steps of creation?

Well, the five steps of creation are totally dependent upon belief, for that's what creation is.

But it seems that the other steps are not part of creation.

Well, now you speak the steps of creation.

Love, belief.

Two types of love, you know—divine or conjugal.

Desire.

Yes, the divine expression. Without creation, it doesn't express, does it? Yes?

Will.

Yes, two types of will, you know.

Yes.

Divine and man in action. What is in action? Is it movement or non-movement? What are the final steps of creation that you have been given?

The final steps?

Yes. Some of you have had the steps of creation. Perhaps you know. *[The Teacher addresses a different student.]*

The last one, I understood it to be creation.

So, you see, in that particular class—and several before it—we were speaking of the planet of Earth. We're speaking of the power of faith. We were speaking, at that time, in reference to the lessons you have to learn and why you entered this planet, this planet of faith. Here is where you learn faith, on this planet. This is the fifth planet in your solar system. Are there any other questions, now, before we conclude class this evening, for time marches on very quickly? Yes.

I'd like to ask why it seems that more energy is dissipated speaking to one on the telephone as opposed to in person?

Well, it is really quite simple. When you are exposed to a person physically and right in front of them, it is not only a matter that you may look them in the eyes, which we have already given classes on the looking glass of the eternal being, but you are exposed to their aura and they are exposed to your aura. Now when you speak over a telephone line or some other means of communication, it is a very rare person whose aura that extends that distance. Now whatever comes within your aura is subject to the dictates of your consciousness. Therefore it is in the best interest of a person, if they have something important to say to an individual, to face them where they can sit down, or stand, look at them and communicate.

Too much, also, in another way of speaking, too much is hidden not only from view, but from the consciousness over telephones and other means of communication. It is always best to face a person and look at them, because you then have two auras. And those auras will come together in the establishing of the contact of communication. One of them will be superior. They may stay superior or they may be inferior. That is, do the influencing or being influenced by; that depends on the evolution of the individual and the degree of self-control they have over their own forms. Does that help with your question?

Yes. Thank you.

You're welcome. The lady there, please.

I've heard somewhere that the astral body is—goes with us around the outside of the aura. Is that, is that some—

Ah, well, I know for a truth that you did not hear it in this philosophy.

No, I didn't.

Because it's not a part of this philosophy. No, it is not.

I think I read it somewhere. Thank you.

Ah, yes, I wouldn't doubt that. Yes, the lady there, please.

So when you were saying earlier about a singer should turn their feelings off when—after they have sung. What does that feel like?

What does it feel like? It feels like before you started. For example, when you have a job to do—see, I'm a firm, firm teacher to prepare oneself—to be prepared. One prepares themselves. How do they prepare themselves? They prepare their consciousness. You have a job to do? You go to work within your consciousness on those forms you're going to work [with] in creation. You go to work on those forms that will be beneficial to the work that you have to do.

Now if I was to sing, I would take a look at the words and the music and I would see, "There's a lot of feeling here. Certain types of sadness—there's a joyous feeling here. There's a lonely feeling here." And I would look over the sheet music (the music and the words) because if it's properly composed, the music will reflect the feeling of the words. And then the singer does their part. And so I would look over that song and that music and I would prepare myself within my consciousness: "This is the feeling I need for this section here. Now I must change my feeling for this section. Then I get a different feeling over here. Then I go back to this feeling over here." And you become aware of what scenes within the consciousness, what forms are necessary to paint your picture.

You see, singing a song is painting a picture. It's done with a different media, that's all. It's not a brush and paint, but it's painting a picture. And so a singer must learn how to paint a beautiful picture in keeping with the composition of the music and the words that have been written. And that work should be done before they even think of opening up their mouth for the words to come out. That way, those feelings are expressed at the appropriate times and then the song is beautiful in keeping with the composition. The feeling, you see, must be there, for if it is not there, the power of the word is not there. You see, if the heart is not in the word, then it is hollow and it is empty. And one must learn how to put the heart into the work that they have to do by the control of their mind. Does that help with your question?

So would that have anything to do with the force of letting it happen? What would cause the forcing of—

The forcing is a mental activity. When you let it happen, then all of these forms within the consciousness, they are moving within the consciousness in keeping with where those feelings are supposed to be in the song itself. Do you understand?

Say that again.

Well, I have it on tape.

OK. Great.

So I know you're going to hear it again.

And our time is up. Thank you very much. Thank you.

FEBRUARY 9, 1984

CONSCIOUSNESS CLASS 234

Now you've had a great deal to think about and to consider these past few weeks of class. And it's very important that through your interest and your questioning you reveal to yourself your understanding. Because we study many things in life and, of course, we study them ever in keeping with the perspective of it that we have at any given time. And it's very important in your own personal growth that you question your own understanding of anything that you are interested in at any time.

For example, a person will study a specific law of life and in keeping with their understanding of that moment, they will attempt to apply that particular law, expecting, of course, beneficial results. However, through a lack of understanding the law they're attempting to apply, they are, in truth, applying a different law. And therefore the results of the experiences (the effects that they have) are not in keeping with the judgment that was made in their efforts to establish the law that they chose to establish for a specific purpose of benefit in their life. That, of course, creates a problem. And a student often asks, after the return of the law, Why did such and such and such work out a certain way? Well, if we first understand the law that we are applying, there will be, of course, for us, no question in reference to what the results are going to be. Because if that were not true, then man cannot be captain of his ship and cannot be master of his destiny. That would be contrary to that demonstrable law that we alone are the law unto our self.

So we're going to take a few moments here this evening for you to think and to consider the laws that you attempt to apply and the results, especially if you feel they have not been in keeping with what you judged the law was that you had established. So we'll let you, the brave ones, raise their hands first. Yes, please.

Success.

One is successful in ways that they do not recognize success. Now, for example, one time I recall discussing in a class with a particular student who was having phenomenal success, but they could not see it. They were successful in being a failure. Now that may seem strange, but it takes effort and the continuity of effort to fail in anything. And a person who puts that much effort in is establishing a law; they are establishing a law to be successful to fail in a particular endeavor.

Now why do some people do things like that? Why do some people seem to be excellent starters and very poor finishers in whatever they get involved in?

First of all, in understanding these eighty-one levels of consciousness, we begin to gain some insight that these levels of consciousness—until the light of reason is cast over the human mind, known as the education (not the annihilation) of the human ego—these levels of consciousness, those forty functions, are rarely, if ever, harmonious with each other. So a person may be expressing through a particular level and on that level of consciousness they choose to have success with a personal endeavor of theirs. However, because they have not yet demonstrated a sufficient degree of self-control to remain on that particular level of consciousness where they chose to be successful in a certain endeavor, time passes and they move, without their conscious awareness, they move to another level of consciousness where success in that particular project is far from a priority.

So we find people starting and not finishing or starting and barely finishing. And then we look and say that person just doesn't seem to have it. Well, everyone has what it takes to complete and be successful in anything that they choose to involve themselves in. An awakening of the level where the priority is and our effort to maintain a degree of control to remain on that level is what is absolutely necessary. Does that help with your question?

Yes. Thank you.

You're welcome. Yes, please.

In applying self-control.

What is the question in reference to applying?

Compulsion—lack of control and compulsion.

Compulsion. Well, now first all, what do you feel that you mean by the word *compulsion*? Do you feel that that means to you an influence, a force that is beyond your control?

Only at the moment.

Yes, I see. In other words, an influence in your consciousness that at the moment of its registration you feel helpless. In other words, it has—you feel helpless to resist it. Is that the statement?

First of all, in order to have a feeling of helplessness in anything, we must first deny the Law of Personal Responsibility. Because it is necessary to deny the Law of Personal Responsibility in order to transfer the responsibility and the authority to another person, place, or thing. We look at that [and] recognize it for what it is: a transference, by our own choice, of authority and responsibility over our life to someone or something else.

Now, first recognizing the actual process that took place within the consciousness is the first step in gaining control over it, because it is not possible to control anything that one is not first aware of. Now a person, for example, is aware of the basic mechanism of an automobile. They put a key in the ignition. They turn it. They step on the gas. They have a brake. They have a steering wheel, etc., etc. So by having a basic awareness of the vehicle, you then place yourself or qualify yourself to control it. So there is no difference between a mundane material object [and] an object in a mental world of consciousness. For the automobile first exists in the mental world of consciousness and that's where the control first takes place, before the physical hands and feet ever manipulate the vehicle. Does that help with your question?

Yes. Thank you.

You're welcome. *[After a short pause, the Teacher continues.]* Why, I have a question, if one of my students doesn't want to ask, but I'll answer this one.

System and order.

Well, first of all, system and order is something, I think, that we should think about. What does it mean to us? Now the flower has system and order. All form has system and order, for all form has authority. That that has authority is governed and controlled. It's the design and it's the purpose of design. Whatever is form is limit. Whatever is limit is movement. And whatever is movement is ever subject to control.

So system and order in a person's life is in a constant process of changing. We apply a certain system and a certain order to brushing our teeth. We apply a certain system, a certain order to the way we dress. We apply a certain system and a certain order to how we're going to do our jobs in life and to eat and all of these mundane things. And when we find this, what we call, system and order, which, for us, we understand to be established patterns—when something obstructs the flow or the movement of what we call system and order, we have problems or we react. Would you not agree?

We have a reaction, mentally, emotionally, psychologically. We react because it is our nature to protect and to defend. So we are in a constant process of protecting and defending whatever we judge at any moment is a threat to us.

Therefore you find great difficulty amongst people: when they become more familiar with each other, they become, slowly but surely, awakened that there are ever-increasing differences of system and order between them. Unless there is an adjustment within the consciousness of the person who believes that their system and order is the right way—and it is the right way because it has protected them over the X number of years of their life—unless there is some type of reason flowing through communication, then you have two people, or more, going along different paths, because survival is the basic instinct of the human being, the animal form. Did you have some other area in which you wish to understand system and order?

No. Thank you.

You're welcome. The lady there, please.

It seems to me that all form, including people that we see, are really only thoughts. Is that correct?

Well, if you ponder perhaps that the universe is the law's meditation; that man is an idea of it, as mind is one in substance with the idea—and the whole idea—so man and the law and the universe are one and the same.

So you can look at anything and, of course, as you look, what are you viewing? Are you viewing an object out there? You are viewing rates of vibrations that are registering in the consciousness as an image. The form exists within your consciousness. Now that's the only place it exists for everyone. However, belief, that glue of creation, it causes us to think that the object is out there. It is only out there as long as we believe it. But that shows you how strong we believe.

Now say that throughout history, throughout ages, people pass through objects and etc. Why, of course, there's a change of vibration within the consciousness and this form within the consciousness, held together by belief, returns within the consciousness to the source from which it is composed. Therefore, for that person at that moment, it does not exist. Does that help with your question?

Thank you.

Yes.

So when they work on passing through things, they're working on the object to rid the object from their consciousness rather than their own physical being, for it—

Well—

To also dissolve the belief in the physical?

Well—no. First of all, the object exists—an image in consciousness. It is kept there, as I explained, the glue of creation, by one's belief. Without the belief, the object does not exist.

Now, for example, in many ways it happens with a person—not that particular way, not that refined, perhaps, one might say. But a person at one time in their life, they will believe something so strongly that it will have an effect upon their life. Would you not agree?

Right.

Yes. All right. Now, time passes. Changes take place. And the belief does not have the effect upon the consciousness of the life of the individual as it had earlier. Is that not correct?

Right.

That happens with everyone. All right. Now what actually happens within the consciousness? For varying reasons, a person has these things or those things, is attracted to these people or those people. And in keeping with the laws they establish, they believe. And they believe that this is good and this is necessary. You see, first we start off—we believe this is good for us, whatever it is. And we believe that. And the more we believe that, the more we have to have it. And the more we have to have it, the more we must protect it. Because that which we judge we have to have is indispensable for our good [and] must be defended or protected.

Now in keeping with those levels of consciousness [there] are established what we call these false kings, judges that sit on thrones—these kings on their thrones. So then time passes and this that we *did* believe was very good, was absolutely necessary to the continuity of good in our life, that must be protected, defended and the armies, judges—because judgment is what defends, you understand. Truth needs no defense. It takes form or judge or judgment to defend. All of that starts its natural process of disintegration. And slowly but surely, we become more and more aware that it's not as strong as it used to be. Would you not agree? We're talking about beliefs in anything or anyone. And then the next experience we have is that it disappears; we're not thinking of it all the time. Then the next experience is like a shadow—once in a while a shadow comes across our consciousness. Is that not true?

Right.

In time, even the shadow disintegrates. As we evolve and broaden our horizons, the dawn becomes brighter and the clouds and all the shadows, they disappear.

Now, in reference to your question, the very same principle is taking place with what we call a physical object. Now in order to sense this object physically, the sensor, in this case myself, must have identification with the functions or sense process of the vehicle in which the person is in at any moment. Consequently, it not only has to disintegrate within the consciousness, but the sensing or identification with the form that does the sensing has to be transformed. Does that help with your question?

Yes. Thank you.

All right. Yes.

Along those lines of vibrations that we are identifying with—perhaps I'm saying that wrong. I'm thinking in terms of if our vision is failing, if we can change our rate of vibration from what we are looking at, if there's some way of doing that, would our vision improve?

No, no, no. No, that's an entirely different area in which we're now discussing in reference to a person's health, in reference to their sight. Your discussion in reference to the—you're stating that if a person's vision is failing, is that correct?

Yes. It is not doing as well as it did before.

I see. Now this is most interesting. Health is such a very important thing because it's the greatest wealth we'll ever know here, hereafter, before, or whenever. Health is the number one thing, for health—harmony is health.

Now, first of all, as we progress along this old world of creation, we have new experiences. Older experiences seem to pass along the way; once in a while, there's a shadow or two. And our hair starts to change a little bit, perhaps. And we don't seem to be quite as spry as we used to. And all these different things start happening. If we do not permit our self to grow graciously, which is harmoniously—for without graciousness, there is no harmony—if we do not permit our self to grow graciously and accept various changes in a positive way within our consciousness, then we simply serve to aggravate the growing process.

Now I find it noteworthy that everyone is interested in growing, as long as it's not growing old. You see, we're interested in the flowers growing. The trees—we love to see an old oak tree, fifty, sixty years old, real old, or an old redwood. We much prefer to see a giant sequoia compared to a little sapling. Yet, when it comes to us personally, that's the one thing we don't want. We want everything else to grow old, but not our self.

Now this is the area, I think, in reference to health, that we should consider. Consider why. What is it in our mind that wants a very grown or aged fine wine, that wants other people to grow old, but not our self? Because there's something there that can be used in a most beneficial way; that is being used, through the error of ignorance, in a most detrimental way. Now anyone that fights or bucks the inevitable is bound to lose someday. You know, it's trying to, like, fight taxes and death. You might as well forget it in old creation because you're going to lose. So we're fighting, unfortunately or fortunately depending on how you view it, a losing battle, a losing battle.

Now why are we fighting a natural process? Why are we doing that? Why are untold millions of people fighting a losing battle? Although there are other untold millions, many over in Asia, who don't fight it at all. They move along the stream of consciousness along with it, you see. Well, it has, of course, to deal with tenacious judgments within our consciousness. Deep in our consciousness are judgments that do not find joy, happiness, goodness, supply, and all the nice things of life—and enjoyment, you see—as a person gets older. And those judgments are the ones that are causing us to fight a losing battle and making life truly miserable, instead of enjoying life as we grow in consciousness and in the old forms that we carry around, you see.

See, if we believe we're the foot and the foot doesn't move the way it used to and it doesn't move exactly the way we demand it does, then we have problems with the foot. But we don't need those problems with the foot unless we insist on identifying with the form and all that the form has to offer. But we should ask our self those questions. Why do we want everything to grow old except our self? Why don't *we* take the view that we wish to grant to the universe and grow old graciously? And we'll always, in that respect, stay young, because we won't have to keep fighting.

Now, in reference to vision, well, if a person—you see, first of all, there are no accidents in the universe. First of all, the physical body is a direct effect of the mental body and the discord between the mental body and physical body. You see, here you have the spirit, the formless free being that you are. When there is harmony, when there is harmony between the physical material world and this mental world of yours, when that is in perfect harmony, then this divine, infinite, intelligent Energy can flow unobstructed. If you have problems in the consciousness and thinking about growing old and you don't want that to happen here in your mental world and yet it's happening in your physical world, then you have discord.

Now we understand in the Living Light philosophy that discord is simply disease. That's what, that's what disease is: it's discord. It's discordant. It is not harmonious. And therefore we understand that health is the effect of the Law of Harmony and disease is an effect of the Law of Discord. So whatever the battle is that is going on within your consciousness, if you will awaken to the battle, first awaken to it, that you may control it, and cast the light of reason on it, then you won't have to fight inside of yourself. And when you stop the fight or frustration within the consciousness, then the healing will take place.

Many people come to the church for healing. Some people, at the moment, are very receptive, and some are not. It isn't someone or something outside. They must let that Infinite Healing Power in. That is allowed in when there's a stillness here and there's no longer this battle, you see.

So the purpose of the philosophy is to help us to awaken to these many levels of consciousness. Then, in that awakening, we can adjust our priorities. Instead of working so hard to get something done with a level that we are frequently in and then slipping off into a level that we're not in too often, but when we get in it, it's totally contrary to our endeavors in life. That does not bring harmony, you see.

All philosophies have taught, "Man know thyself and ye shall know the truth and the truth shall set you free." But the process—we alone, only we alone, in our consciousness, can make that effort to be honest with our self and, through that honesty, to know our self.

First of all, when you understand—and I know you've heard before—nothing's either good or bad but thinking makes it so. Good and bad, in that sense, exist where there's judgment. Well, there's judgment only in the mental realms of consciousness. We understand and we know that our understanding of God, the divine, neutral, infinite intelligent Energy—it can't judge. Because in order to judge, you have got to have something to defend. And in order to defend, you must have falsehood. For truth, demonstrable, cannot be defended. Truth just *is*. You cannot defend that which is. [Do] you defend the air? No, you don't defend the air. You say the air changes or it's polluted? The air is still air. It doesn't matter if there's chemical changes within it; it is still air. You cannot defend that which is not defendable. Truth cannot be defended. It just is.

Now, you can—and, Lord knows, millions try—you can *try* to defend what you judge to be your right to your truth. That, you can defend, because you are then defending a mental form in which you have placed your portion, that you have earned in your consciousness, of what you call truth. That's defendable. And, Lord knows, untold millions work diligently to defend it. And that's why we have wars.

But any other questions before we conclude class? Yes, the gentleman here, please.

My question is, What question were you going to ask earlier in the evening?

I was going to ask a question of my student who is *[Rather than name the student, the Teacher clears his throat.]* and she hasn't asked yet. So I'm giving a few more minutes before I ask her. Thank you. Yes.

You've often made reference that Earth is the fifth planet in our solar system and it's the planet of faith. And I'm wondering how is it the fifth planet in our solar system, if you could explain. Because I know it's not the physical solar system.

Oh, you do?

Well, in our understanding of this planet, anyway.

Well, how many planets in this solar system?

Nine, that I know of.

And it does have a sun and a moon, doesn't it? All right. Well, getting right down to the point. You want to know why faith is number five?

No. Why the Friends picked . . .

No, nobody picked Earth as the fifth planet of faith. It just *is*. You see, it wasn't somebody [that] allotted it that. It just *is*.

No, that's not what I meant to—

Oh, what's your question? Excuse me.

I just—I—it—what I've always been taught in school is that it's not number five in the order of the planets. And I thought maybe there's another reason why the Friends referred to it being the fifth planet.

Well, if you're referring to the class that was given years ago, I don't feel, in fact, I know, it was not stated in the order of the planets, Earth is number five, if you will study that particular class. You will hear, however, that Earth is the fifth planet; that there are nine planets in the solar system of which they were speaking and that Earth is the fifth.

Now, the question, as a student of some time now, I would like to ask you to see if you know, why it is five. Do you know why?

Five is the number of faith.

Yes, it is the number of faith.

And it does seem to be that is what we are learning here.

Yes, we are learning that.

I can under—I understand that much, but beyond that I...

Well, all right. Let's, let's look at it a little, perhaps a little differently. In keeping with that same teaching on numbers, we understand that nine is the number of totality; that it is infinite eternity, if you look at the number. Now half of nine that—if you must number it, is one, two, three, four and one, two, three, four—it's number five, isn't it? That's half of it. Right? There is four on this side and there is four on that side. So you have four and five, which is nine or you have this Earth planet right down through the totality of *this* solar system, of *this* solar system.

Now, where does life exist, as you know it in your identity, in this solar system?

Here. I mean, that's all I'm aware of, as far as life goes. I really—

All right. Now we're going to move along with that. This planet which we revealed to you was the fifth planet, the number of faith; that we had entered this planet in our evolution. In reference to faith, it is the power of faith that evolves the forms. It is the power of faith. Now all the planets in this solar system of which we're speaking—now that you've open that door—are in the process of evolving. They are in the process of evolving. Science will find, as they are gradually beginning to find, that the planet Earth can easily be studied in its beginning stages by studying the planets around it. And so it is with all universes: that which is the pivot or the balance point in anything is the most evolved.

Now you can take that macrocosm to the microcosm. You can take it to a thought that you have or you can take it to anything in which you are interested. Everything has a pivot. It has a balance point that keeps it in form, you see. Now that pivot or that balance point is the power that is contained within it. Now long, long ago that same truth was revealed in many ways; one of which is, if you have the faith of a half a grain of mustard seed, speak to the mountain: tell it to move and it shall move.

Now that faith—you have that faith, but the awareness of how to use it, that's where we stumble along the way. We stumble because we must free our self from the force of belief in order to use the power of faith. And as long as we permit our minds to tell us that we believe we have this need or that need, as long as we permit belief, that controlling force in our universe, then we cannot speak to the mountain and tell it to move and the mountain shall move. Now someone may say, and I have heard many say, "Well, they were speaking on some mountain in your head." Well, of course, they were speaking of some mountain in your head! When you look at a mountain, where is the mountain? The mountain is in your head! Of course it is. You are the viewer. It's there for you.

Now if you have someone else or many people who are trapped in belief, you ask all of them and they'll say, "Yes, you do see a mountain because I see a mountain." And then you ask twenty people, "Now, do you see that tree up there?" And they say, "No, there's no tree there." "Oh, that tree right up there." "No, no, no. That's not a tree. That's a bush." And then someone else says, "That's not a tree or a bush. That's a great big stone up there." So, you see, it exists in the consciousness. That's where it is. It is clouded and it is controlled and it is moved and it is disintegrated by your own consciousness.

Time is up. Thank you very much.

FEBRUARY 16, 1984

CONSCIOUSNESS CLASS 235

This evening's class will be a discussion of the cause and control of experience.

Now you've already had teachings concerning the balancing of the soul faculties with the sense functions. And some of you are aware that all soul faculties are electric in nature and all sense functions are magnetic in nature. And when, through control, the sense functions, the magnetic field of our being is brought into balance with the electric field of our universe, our being, then we are free.

Now because electric power is the motivator and magnetic force is the reactor, then it is necessary first to become aware of the soul faculty that corresponds to the particular sense function that we find our self out of balance with. Now that is brought about through an awakening and an awareness of these corresponding functions and faculties.

The heart is the seat or center of all soul faculties. The—what you call the reactor or the magnetic field, located in the water center, or emotional being of the sense functions is the seat of what we know as creation. All creation is brought about through an amalgamation between the soul faculties and the sense functions. And all experiences in our life are an effect of the imbalance of those two particular fields: electric and magnetic.

Now when you pause to think on anything, in that moment in which you pause—for pause is a stillness, a refrain from reaction and, being such, you are, in that moment, in control of any particular experience or form that is in the process of being created through directed energy and the reaction of that directed energy by your magnetic field. Therefore, all experiences, in keeping with your communication within your own being, is what is actually taking place. Now a person makes a decision. When they make their decision of something that they want to do, they communicate in their consciousness and direct energy to the corresponding function which, through an amalgamation of the faculty and function, brings about the experience. If a person does not pause and in that pause have the control in the moment to direct the intelligent energy for the magnetic field to react or to create, they ofttimes experience something far contrary to what they consciously choose to establish or to do. Now many people are excellent starters and known as very poor finishers in many, many endeavors. That reveals a severe problem of communication within their own consciousness.

Whatever it is that you decide to do, you have to understand that in making the decision you must maintain the original control of the idea—the thought that motivated you in the first place. The reason we find so often in life that that is difficult to do is because we do not pause. Therefore, the direction of the intelligent energy going to different sense functions is not in balance with the faculties that we are expressing at any given moment.

Now we'll pause for just a moment here [to] give you an opportunity to assimilate what you have heard and also an opportunity to ask your questions in reference to it.

Now everyone has heard the teaching that a house divided cannot stand. However, very few people seem to understand what that means. The division is in the lack of understanding, communication, and its absolute necessity to creation. For without communication of the intelligent power or energy that flows through the electrical field, through the soul faculties to the corresponding, reacting magnetic field, there is no creation.

Now if you have any questions, you may feel free to speak it at this time. The lady over there, please.

At the time we pause, do we go into the electrical field at the pause?

Yes. Whenever you pause, whenever the mind is stilled, you pause. That is when you are identified with and, therefore, complete in consciousness with the electric field. Now the electric field is where the faculty of reason is. That's where all the soul faculties are, including, of course, the faculty of reason. So when you pause, in the moment of the pause, you are in control. It is there, where an intelligent decision is made and then communicated to the corresponding sense functions. That help with your question?

Yes. Thank you.

Now the lady back there has been waiting. Yes.

I would like to know about rejection in terms of what you're talking about as far as success.

Rejection? Yes. What we understand as the experience of rejection—a person feels rejected when they permit their consciousness to feel guilt. Now we cannot experience or register within our consciousness rejection without preceding it with guilt. Therefore, it is necessary for a person who experiences within their consciousness rejection to free themselves from guilt. Now a person feels guilty and, following that guilt feeling, they experience what they call rejection. However, usually a person thinks that that feeling of guilt has followed their experience of rejection. But it is the state of consciousness known as guilt that establishes the law through which the experience of rejection takes place within the consciousness. Does that help with your question?

Thank you.

You see, a person feels rejected and in the feeling of rejection is always the thinking, "What have I done? What could I have done and etc.?" It's totally self-related. And it blatantly and clearly shows the guilt of the consciousness that established the law through which the rejection was experienced within the consciousness.

Now the lady here was waiting for us.

Yes. When we use the conscious mind and the pause to communicate with the corresponding sense function, how are we aware what the corresponding sense function is? And how do we carry on this communication?

Yes, well, in order to carry on the intelligent communication with the corresponding soul faculty, the essential requirement, in order to be aware of what the corresponding sense function of the soul faculty is, is the absolute freedom from what is known as need. For, as we have explained in other classes, when you permit the consciousness to dictate what is known as need, then you have established the Law of Denial. And in the establishing of the Law of Denial, you are not in the light of reason or in the electric field, but are in the magnetic field through the Law of Denial that has been established. Therefore, a person first, through communication within their consciousness, declares the truth so that they do not have the feeling or dictate of need. For need is denial and that is far from the light of reason. You see, denial does not exist in the light of reason. Denial only exists in the magnetic field of the sense functions. Does that help with your question? Yes.

It does. And could you please give us an example what this communication would sound like when we do this?

Well, is there some specific area or subject that you are interested in? *[After a short pause, the Teacher continues.]* Well, for example, if a person wants to bring about a balance between the, say, the soul faculty of reason—for that's one of the finest soul faculties; it certainly transfigures us—and they want to bring about the light of reason over the sense function of fear, then they pause and they communicate. Through an awakening that they are not the limit that their mind is telling them they are—because, remember, fear can only be experienced when you are identified with limitation. If you are identified with limit, form, which is limit—all form is limit—then you have this feeling of fear, because you have need to protect the limit that you identify with. Do you understand?

And because, you see, that's a part of a sense function, then one, in having that feeling, that sensing of fear, must make the effort to cast the light of reason upon that particular function by declaring the truth within their consciousness: that they are not the limit that they are temporarily identified with; that it is, in truth, an error in their consciousness that offers to them—try to remember, friends, that fear offers to your consciousness denial, need, suffering, and all of the things that are discordant. Because, you see, discord cannot exist in a realm of consciousness where there is no limit.

Discord is dependent upon limit or form in order to express itself. So when a person, through an effort to communicate within their consciousness, declares the truth, through the declaration of the truth and a process of communication that takes place within the consciousness between the soul faculties and the sense functions, a person is brought into balance. Being in creation, they are no longer a part of creation, for they have declared the truth within their consciousness that they are not the form, which is the experience of any given moment. Does that help with your question?

Yes.

But, you see, my friends, that effort has to be made daily. It isn't something you make a declaration and it's all done for, when you consider that you have forty soul faculties and forty sense functions and the identification or that which we identify with is predominately limit or limitations. If you want to know how identified you really are with creation or limit, with denial and despair, then all one has to do is to listen objectively to their conversation in the course of a day. And they will be greatly surprised how many times they declare denial, despair, from an over-identification with the sense functions. Does that help with your question?

Thank you.

Yes, the lady back there had a question, please.

Yes. When one notices oneself going into despair, let's say, is there a process that you can—it seems so strong—is there a process in which to call yourself back out?

Yes, I just explained it to the student here.

I heard it, but somehow, I guess, it didn't get through.

Well, first of all, in reference to the experience of despair, which can only follow denial of the truth within the consciousness—for one does not despair without fear, does one? One does not despair without over-identification with limit, does one? So despair only follows one's lack of effort in refraining from over-identification with themselves because we believe we are the thought. And because we believe we are the thought, we have accepted we are the form. We have much to fear. And the reason we have much to fear is because we have so much to defend. Now if we didn't have so much belief, so much force of belief in the thought that we have at any given moment, we would not have despair, we would not have fear, we would not have judgment, and we would not have to work so diligently to defend and to protect that which, by the Law of Evolution, is destined to return to the source from whence *we* have created it. Yes.

Well, why—this may seem like a silly question—but why is it so easy, sometimes, to be in that "scene" and then, other times, just so difficult? It just seems like it's impossible not to, you know, get pulled into the fear and denial and limit.

At any time that we, through errors of ignorance, do not make the effort to know beyond a shadow of any doubt who we are and, therefore, what we are, the price, then, must readily be paid for over-identification with that which has been created and is in a process of return unto its source.

A thought is created within our consciousness. A judgment is created within our consciousness. And because we create it, through our own errors of ignorance, we identify with it and make the final step down by absolute belief that we are it. Then we pay the price repeatedly until the day comes, through the Law of Disassociation, through an absolute perfect balance between the soul faculty and corresponding sense function, we are in it and not a part of it.

It is the very nature of life to be in creation. It is the very Law of Life not to be a part of it. The effort must be made daily to look at the thought and the judgment within the consciousness as you look at a coat, a jacket, or a dress: you put it on and take it off when you choose to do so. Now when we, in our consciousness, put on the cloak of any thought, of any judgment and we take it off when we choose to do so, knowing full well, when we're wearing the coat, that we are not the coat—you see, my friends, in our ignorance, we have forgotten. And in that forgetting, we believe we're the thought. But we don't yet believe we're the coat that hangs in the closet. Some of us are very close to believing we are the coat. When something happens to it, that tells us how much we, through over-identification, have entered the realm of belief: that the coat, designed to be worn, we forgot and became.

Now that's what's happening in our mind from our lack of effort. We believe the feeling that we have at the moment that we wear it. And yet days, months, or years pass and we no longer wear that coat or shirt of feeling. We no longer believe that we are that coat that we wore at one time. But while we were wearing it, we certainly did believe that it was us.

So the homework to be done—and to be done daily—is to look at the apparel of your mind, to look at the many garments that are hanging in the closet of your consciousness. Many of them have served their purpose. They've long waited to be discarded, to return to the source to serve their purpose once again. But we have not cleaned the closet of our consciousness and therefore we cannot see clearly in that closet. There are too many garments that we are trying to wear all at the same time.

Think. You awaken in the morning; put your house in order before confusion sets in. Go to the closet of your consciousness. Choose wisely the garment that you shall wear. Shall you wear the garment of self-control for your outer coat? Shall you wear the dress or the trousers of gratitude? What garment are you choosing to wear moment by moment? For the garment that you alone are choosing to wear is the one that's bringing to you the experiences that you are having. Because you are not balancing that particular garment with the functions of creation and so the house is divided.

How many of us are pausing to think, to become aware of what garments we're wearing at any moment? And many of us change them thousands of times in the course of a few hours. One moment we say we feel just great; the next moment we feel terrible. Yet we alone are making those changes in our consciousness. We're doing that. We are doing it and we just seem to be the victims of it happening. That's like walking into your closet in the morning and certain clothes come off the hangers and drape themselves around you. Perhaps they're going to be too warm. Perhaps they're not going to be warm enough. It's quite ridiculous when one pauses to think that that's what happens.

You walk down the street. You go into a store and in a second, you strip yourself naked and put on a different garment depending on whom you encounter. That's what we're really doing. That's what we're doing all the time. We wear this garment for that person, a different garment for another. But we are not consciously choosing. And so we are stripped naked thousands of times a day because the effort is not being made to consciously choose what we're going to wear in the closet of our consciousness.

Are there any other questions? Yes, the lady over there, please.

If we're aware that we put on garments that are not right, but our mind doesn't identify what the garments are, as long as we pause, does the balance between the faculties and functions take place automatically?

The potential of the possibility takes place.

How can we try to make the potential a possibility, if we don't have an awareness of the exact function or faculty that we are dealing with?

The awareness comes through honesty in one's consciousness. Long ago I stated that honesty will lead us through. Well, it is honesty that reveals to us the corresponding sense function of any soul faculty. Does that help with your question?

The lady here, please.

Does the positive communication, after the pause, have to be verbalized or vocalized?

No, no. Because it's taking place in the realms of consciousness, it does not have to be given the spoken word of life-giving energy to create a form in that realm, because it is taking place within another realm of creation. It does not have to be verbalized. It is just as effective in that realm of consciousness. It's just as effective, absolutely.

The lady there, please.

If you call on the light of reason at the pause, well, it's my understanding that that will take care of the other soul faculties if you're trying to search what the soul faculty is and haven't found it.

Thank you. In reference to calling on the light of reason, the pause, the light of reason *is* the pause. There's no need to call. You see, that's what the pause is, the sense to pause. The consciousness enters the light of reason in the pause itself.

I see.

And, as I explained to the student over there, honesty will reveal the corresponding sense function. You see, there's a part of us that knows beyond a shadow, a shadow of any doubt. The part of us that knows beyond a shadow of any doubt is that part of the consciousness that *is* the electric, that *is* the Light itself. But in that pause and in that light of reason, there is no need; need does not exist. Need cannot exist where there is no Law of Denial. And in the light of reason, there is no denial. Therefore, there is no shadow.

The gentleman here, please.

Yes. You said when we pause, the corresponding sense function will be revealed.

The corresponding sense function is revealed in honesty, yes.

Would that be the same thing as our motive?

Oh, we all know our motives, yes.

That would be the same—the corresponding sense is being revealed, would that also be the same as motive?

It will reveal itself and therefore you will know beyond a shadow of any doubt your true motive. You see, motive, that which moves us, is ofttimes clouded, clouded by the sense functions. Therefore, when we pause and enter the light of reason and honesty leads us directly to the corresponding sense function, our motive is clearly revealed. That's why without honesty, we cannot see the corresponding sense function. Does that help with your question?

Yes, sir.

See? You see, ofttimes a person will do something contrary to a rule or regulation. The first thing that is spoken, if they're caught, is the defense, the justification of why they did it. That reveals the guilt. That also reveals the rejection. It also reveals the fear. It also reveals the denial. It also reveals the need. And therefore, one is working in a state—with a state of consciousness that is clouded: the true motive is not clear within the consciousness of the individual who finds it necessary to defend and to protect. Because truth needs no defense, no protection, no justification. I've tried for years to help my students to see the folly of justification, for it is a defending, a defending of that which is destined to go within the student's own consciousness. Because only truth is eternal; form is temporal. It's brought into being—comes from a source to which it's destined to return. Therefore, when we make so much effort to defend, to justify, and to protect, we are striving to defend and to protect that which is not true in our consciousness. Does that help with your question? Yes.

Once we reach our motive and, OK, and get this balance, is that a so-called correction or is there a step that we take? What do we do then, after we reach our motive?

There is no need and there is no step, because, you see, when you enter the light of reason that transforms a person's consciousness—because they enter the full electric field and honesty reveals to them the form or the function through which they are moving in consciousness, there are no steps to be taken outside of the pause to awaken. And from that awakening, one no longer experiences need, as I said before, for they experience no denial.

It is difficult—we make it difficult. The demonstrable truth that total acceptance is God; total acceptance is the Light. Yet, we spend much of our time defending, denying, and expressing intelligent energy contrary to the demonstrable law that the divine will or the movement or power of God or goodness is total acceptance. Does that help with your question?

Yes, sir.

See, when you speak the truth that the divine Light, the will, the power, the movement of goodness is total acceptance, that success in any endeavor is ever in keeping with the flow of the soul faculty of duty, gratitude, and tolerance, the first soul faculty—and yet, we ask for success as though it's some special technique, like becoming a mechanic or something; some technique, some type of manipulation that the mental world, in which we identify, can move and manipulate. It doesn't work that way. There's no possible way. As gratitude is indispensable and essential to the continuity and increase of any endeavor, that duty to the original motivation is essential, and total acceptance, the absolute broadening or expansion of the soul faculty of tolerance—those three simple faculties, the triune faculty, the very first step on the path of light and freedom is yet to be taken. The first step. Now, I gave to you so many years ago, duty, gratitude, tolerance—step one, soul faculty one. Faith, poise, and humility—step two. Two steps: essential, absolutely essential in moving through creation. But only you can apply duty, gratitude, tolerance, faith, poise, and humility.

Where is humility, if there is no wisdom of patience? Where is faith? Where is poise, balance, and harmony? They are nonexistent without duty, gratitude, and tolerance. It is so easy. We have it made so easy to believe; so difficult to express our faith.

Now, we seem not to have any problem in expressing our fear, for we believe so many things and have so many things to defend, to protect. Think. Everything you touch, everything you see, everything you hear, everything you sense, everything you taste is in the process of leaving your universe. Where is security in holding to that that, by its very nature, is leaving your world? That's not a very secure place to be. Because we cannot hold that which, by its very nature, is destined not to be held forever. And yet we hold to the form of thought. We hold to form of feeling. We hold to the throne of a judgment. It is that holding in our consciousness that is the suffering. That's where the suffering is.

We want something. We have a desire. Desire flows through our consciousness as the divine expression, the expression of the Divinity. We form it. And in our forming of it, we dictate its fulfillment. And in our dictating its fulfillment, we establish the Law of Limit. And in our establishing the Law of Limit, we suffer the Law of Discord, for we establish the Law of Fear. We establish the Law of Denial and that great Law of Need to protect and to preserve. That is not the path of abundant good. That is not the path of joy.

We decide we want something and it does not come into our universe and we get upset because it does not come. Does the upset demonstrate to us the wisdom of patience? Or does it demonstrate to us the foolhardiness of dictate? Which does it demonstrate to us? Of what benefit would it be to have the fulfillment of a desire at the cost of the goodness in our life? If we consciously, through mental manipulation, could bring God or goodness into our life, we would be filled with God or goodness! But we—our minds—do not know what goodness is, only in the sense of the limited dictates that we will permit it to enter our lives. And so we go searching the world to find God or goodness expressed in keeping with the few avenues that we have left open for it to enter our consciousness.

And then, when we find this need in our consciousness for goodness, the abundant good of life, and it doesn't come and it doesn't come and it doesn't come and we are upset, revealing to ourselves there is no wisdom, for there is no patience. What good would it be for a person to have the fulfillment of a desire of a new automobile if, after an hour of receiving it, within an hour, they drive along the highway and their life, which had yet much time to go, was ended? Then of what benefit would it have been? So stop and think when you have so many desires and your desires do not seem to be filled and it seems that it's taking so long to fill your desire. Pause in your consciousness and desire God or goodness as much and, yea, more than you desire the limited form through which you will allow God. And when you do that, you won't have the frustrations of impatience for the little God that you will allow in through a particular dictate of your mental substance.

Are there any more questions before we conclude class this evening? Yes, please.

I had a question dealing with when you were talking about pausing and how honesty will lead you through and to recognize the sense functions or soul faculties. As students, we haven't earned yet being given all the soul faculties and sense functions. So do we recognize it on a higher level of consciousness, not to the intellectual?

When you, in demonstrating entering the light of reason and you are lead, with honesty, to the corresponding soul function [faculty], you will have no need. Therefore there'll be nothing to discuss. When truth is permitted to enlighten the consciousness, the need for system disappears.

Yes, the gentleman over here, please.

How do we clean the closet of our consciousness?

Through a conscious effort, one, to be aware of the thoughts one entertains moment by moment and, two, to take control of those thoughts or garments, making an intelligent, conscious decision which ones have served their purpose and send them on to some charitable institute that may find use for them in others perhaps not yet so evolved.

Thank you. Good night.

FEBRUARY 23, 1984

CONSCIOUSNESS CLASS 236

Good evening, class. This evening's class will be on the parallel law of life, the power of will or the force of will.

Now, belief generates the force of will and moves images in the consciousness of mental substance. The effect [or] sensation of that is known to us as emotion. The identification with the movement of images in mental consciousness is the bondage or the obstruction to the freedom, which is the true being. Now that same teaching has been given for many, many, many centuries. Belief, which generates the force of will and moves those images, has been known throughout ages as the tree or life of knowledge. Man is not affected in mental consciousness by anything that man does not know. Because if man does not know, man does not have created in mental consciousness an image through which, by belief, he identifies and generates the force of will in order to have the effect or the return of the movement of the image.

Now, I'll give you a few seconds to absorb that and then we can have some questions. *[After a short pause, the Teacher continues.]* Just leave the recorder on, because that was a few seconds. Yes.

I'd like to hear more about the path of least resistance, in relation to what you were speaking of.

Yes, of course. Now the path of peace or the path of nonresistance—for example, when, through belief, you generate this power into what is known as force—for will, you must realize, is the power of the soul and the force of the mind; it is the lord or the law of our life. And depending on whether or not we identify with a mental world or a spiritual world, depends on whether or not we use power or we use force. Now in reference to your question on the path of least or, more properly, the path of nonresistance, the nonresistance or the generating, through belief, a force of will, to combat an image in consciousness frees one in consciousness from the battle or the struggle, which shall return to them as an experience. Does that help with your question?

Could you give an example?

Well, for example, you decide that something did not work out the way that you thought that it would. Do you follow me?

Yes.

Now when that happens, what takes place within the consciousness is, number one, you first made the judgment that something would work the way you had judged that it would work, in keeping with the images in consciousness that you called forth to fulfill what you judged would be fulfillment in any particular area of interest. Consequently, by calling forth these images to do what your force of will had judged would be done and were not successful, you experience the return of the images within your consciousness, for these images, they go out into the universe to accomplish what we are sending them to do, whether we send them by the force of will or we send them by the power of will. So when they return, you have a sensation or experience known to you as an emotion or mental upheaval. Would you not agree?

Yes.

All right. That clearly reveals to us that the use of the force of will is the karmic wheel of just return. And so man continues to revolve upon this cause and effect, or karmic wheel, as long as man insists on believing that he is the thought or the form that he creates in mental substance. That is one of the two paths of life. That is the path of the functions: belief and identification with form. And then you have the path of the faculties, which is the expression of the soul. Does that help with your question?

Yes . . .

Well, if one does what they know within their being is right to do for them and is not concerned with their fruits of action, they will not have to pay the price of the return of forms in mental substance, for they did not send them through the generating of force, the effect of their own belief.

So would that fall in the same lines of not caring what other people think or do?

One must not be concerned with what reason reveals one has not responsibility for. Responsibility, of course, being the ability to respond. For example, if you are concerned with what someone else does, then you must be in a position to control what someone else does in order to be able to intelligently respond. Now matrimony, usually, reveals this process quite clearly. One tries to establish the right to have another person do what they believe the other person should be doing and consequently, they experience, usually, from that type of thinking, a very difficult life.

Thank you.

You're welcome. Yes, the lady back there, please.

So, what would be the best way to create? Is there a way in which to create the images that serve you the best? How would one go about—perhaps I missed that part of what you said.

I under—I think I understand your question. And the question being, How does one create images that would be beneficial and constructive to one's own evolution? Is that correct?

Yes.

First of all, if we will pause and accept the demonstrable truth that all form, which is nothing more nor less than images—they serve their purpose of their original design. They have birth. They have death. Their life is totally dependent upon the continuous flow of intelligent energy. That whereas we are the creators in keeping with our evolution and by our own choice, we, therefore, have the power to create images intelligently to serve a useful and beneficial purpose, knowing that they will endure in keeping with the motivation or the law established at the time of their birth; that they will serve their purpose and that we never forget that we are not the image, the form that we have created.

It is when we forget that we are not the form created by our own choice, that we are not the thought, when we forget that we are the power that moves the form, we are the power that moves the thought, but we are not the thought—therefore we are not the form. It is when we forget that demonstrable truth that we have what is known as the experience or sensation of the return of the images that we alone have created.

Now the first step in remembering that great truth is to pause and to remind oneself that whatever enters our consciousness we alone, we alone have chosen to permit it to happen. For like any child, it knows its place of birth. All feelings, all thoughts, they all know their home. So when they return and when we grow up and accept what, in this philosophy, is known as the ability to personally respond to all experiences in life, knowing full well they are the return of what we have sent out. And being the return, we have the wisdom, the reason, and the power to place them in their proper perspective and to return them to the substance from which we alone have created them. Does that help with your question?

Yes.

You're welcome. Yes, please.

Could you speak on the power of will in relation to eating and not eating?

Yes, of course. First of all, the experience or sensation of eating or not eating is subject to and dependent upon the force of will, for eating or not eating is not the expression of a soul faculty. The soul is not dependent upon the physical process or the physical world. That is something that has been generated, of course, that force of will, by our belief. Now if we have images within our consciousness that we permit, through our lack of effort, to dictate to us how much we must eat in order to feel a certain way, in order to have a certain emotional experience, as long as we permit our self that error, that error of ignorance, of the lack of effort, which is over-identifying with the created form in our consciousness—or forms—[then] we, through our belief, are being controlled.

So the first thing to do is to separate truth (that which we are) from creation (that which we believe we are). Now experiences are revealing to us constantly, as we identify with that which we believe we are, experiences are constantly revealing to us that what we believe we are is in a constant state of change. It's in a constant process of evolution and refinement. Therefore, we clearly see that which we believe we are is not dependable, is not reliable, and we never know for sure when it is going to change. Now, in reference to eating or any other sensation—for it is an expression of the functions of creation—we first must make the effort to be consciously aware when we first experience the sensation, the sensation that we call hunger. Now we first have a sensation; a sensation takes place within the being, would you not agree?

Yes.

Followed by the conscious awareness of the thought of food. Is that not correct?

Yes.

Now, when we examine that, we find that the form or the thought impinged upon the consciousness, made the first registration, and we became aware of the sensation; then, we became aware of the thought. You see, because it is the return of a form that has been generated through belief by the force of will—its return is an effect. The effect is a sensation or emotion, followed by a conscious thought to fulfill the return of the image that we have sent from our consciousness. Therefore, a person in an effort to gain some degree of control—for without control, there is no freedom—a person first goes to work on the returning images entering their consciousness. It is known as conscious dining.

There are very few people that consciously, consciously dine. Very few. They dine or eat with the experience of a thrill or a sensation of varied, so-called emotions. But a conscious choice, a reasonable discussion with one's own consciousness—"I choose to dine this particular way. I choose to consume this particular food. I consciously choose to consume this amount, and no more."—is the first step in gaining control. Now therefore, a person can have a little of many things that are good and beneficial. It is when we close our eyes to the faculty of reason that we enter belief, where need is offered to our consciousness and instead of a little going a long ways, it takes a lot to go a short ways. Does that help with your question?

Yes. Thank You.

You're welcome. Yes, the gentleman here, please.

How does belief enter into the picture when one sets out on what they consider to be a successful endeavor based on past experiences and the prior experiences of these same endeavors were successful in the past.

Yes.

Yet, at another time, the result of these endeavors fell apart.

I understand.

What is the relationship between belief—and this person thinks they're doing the right thing. They feel they're setting the right laws into motion.

There is a contradiction between the conscious mind and the subconscious mind. There is a contradiction between the two minds. And that requires an honest, sincere effort to communicate with one's inner being. Now, for example, a person, from past experience, consciously choosing certain laws, reaping the harvest of success from those laws that they have consciously chosen, at a later time in their life, chooses consciously identically the same laws, expecting, of course, identically the same exact results, and that does not happen. That reveals that the conscious effort, the conscious choice, is not being accepted by the subconscious mind or computer. And contrary results are the effects.

Now a person, making those decisions, having already had the success with the experiences in the past, must make the change in consciousness to find out where, what variable has been introduced into the emotional being—what variable. Because, I can assure you, there is something that has been introduced that is different or there would not be a different experience with the same conscious laws being chosen. Emotionally, there is something different; there is something different in the subconscious. Now once that is found, once one communicates with oneself honestly, they will find what that variable that has snuck into that area of their consciousness and in rooting out that variable, they will find that the same laws will bring the same success.

Ofttimes a person does not relate, you see, in the sense of they separate their business endeavors from their emotional and personal experiences. They consciously believe they are separating it, but that is not what is happening in the magnetic field in the subconscious, where their emotions are in control. That is not what is happening. Something else is happening. So, you see, this is what—through an honest effort of communication, that will be revealed to anyone. Does that help with your question?

Indeed. Yes, sir.

Because there is a variable that's been introduced. And the variable has to be in the magnetic field where that is being returned, you see? There is a variable. And working with something like that, taking ten to twenty minutes a day, more than once a day, perhaps three or four times a day, especially prior to establishing the conscious law for the success, that's very important, because that will reveal itself. It always does.

Thank you very much.

You're welcome.

Along a similar line, if you have done something consciously and you are set on a path—this is regarding business, too—on a path that felt successful up to a point, but that most of your life you had an attitude of rejection that has always tried to trap you and keep you from going in that direction—I'm aware that the armies do come in close to the gates of victory to cause problems. But how, if you have these two separate drives going on, how do you, well . . .

I'll come back to your question as you give it a bit more thought. I want to speak to the gentleman who just asked a question.

All right.

If you will remove need from your consciousness, you will find the variable will no longer bring those experiences.

Thank you, sir.

You're welcome. Now, in reference to your question, of course, it can be simply stated, as you have already stated, that a house divided cannot stand. And so there is a division within consciousness of what one believes has been, of what one believes in reference to rejection etc., etc. And it is the identification with those beliefs that established those laws of force, you see. So we do have, of course, at any moment, we have the conscious choice to remove from our consciousness those images that have not brought to us, from past experiences, the success and the constructive good that we are seeking. Yes.

Is that removal by separating truth from creation?

Yes, but the separation of truth from creation, you see—for example, when we spend our time thinking of what we're doing, then, of course, we are generating, through that process, that belief, we're generating this force of will. And those are the forms that are sent out. And, of course, with that sending is the hope of return and the need of expectation.

Thank you.

And I think that one often finds in life that the real experience rarely, if ever, meets the expectation. Yes.

Thank you.

Rarely ever. Because, you see, stop and think why that which returns unto us rarely meets the expectations that we sent out. Well, to that degree and extent, of course, reveals how great we believe we are. Not how great we *are*, but how great we believe we are. Therefore, of course, the expectation far exceeds the return, because only such great expectation could we possibly have, believing, when we send that out, that we are so great. So it never does measure up, you see. It can't measure up, for no one is as great as we believe that we are, you see?

You see, you can look at the world over and you can find a lot people that are similar, similar. They may have brown hair. They may have red hair. They may have blond hair. But they could never possibly measure up to how we feel about our self. Now, there's everything good about feeling good about oneself, oh, but what a woe it is to believe that that feeling good is the greatness that we believe we are. You see, we are greater than we know. And thank God for that, because if we knew how great we really were, we would not be able to permit our self to see our image, because the image, we would have to destroy.

In other words, until the light of reason is cast upon the human ego and it becomes educated, there is no way possible that there can be any image that even comes close to our own. Because if an image gets close, we become afraid. We fear. And the reason we fear is because there is no security, there is no reliability, there is absolutely no stability in an image. So what we believe we are is an image, but what we *are* is the power of infinite intelligent energy.

So we stop and talk to our self a little bit, that we may become a little bit more aware that we are greater than we know and we are grateful that we don't know the truth of how great we are. Because if we did, in our present state of evolution we would not be able to live with our self, let alone permit a reflection thereof. I hope that's helped with your question. Yes. The lady over here, please.

You've been talking about the force of belief, the force of will. Can you use the power of will when you're dealing with form and creation and setting laws into motion?

Power of will is not subject to limit. All form, all thought is limited. The Light cannot, and never shall, serve creation. It is not subject to the laws of creation. Creation is subject to the

Law of Life. And the Law of Life is the Light itself. It is creation that comes and goes. It is creation that knows and has birth and death. It is creation, the tree of knowledge. That is not Life. That is not Light. That is not Truth. Yes.

So then is it wiser not to try to set these laws of the force of will into motion and to try to open up your soul faculties and not try to dictate what's going to be?

In reference to your question of wiser, there is a path of wisdom and then its opposite, of course. Now in reference to that question, one must honestly ask themselves, "I am here. I am changing. I have experienced many changes. I do not believe that I am so great that I can no longer identify with self, therefore, no longer experience belief in form, therefore no longer express the force of will. I am an evolving soul. I still think and by my thinking, I believe I am. I have not yet evolved to the state of consciousness where I am, therefore I am. I am at the state of evolution where I think I am, therefore I believe I am. And by so believing that I am, I generate the force of will. And I am creating. And in that process of creating, I am experiencing. Therefore, in my state of evolution I still have, and know, what is emotion and feelings, attachments, rejections, and all that creation has to offer."

The purpose of this school is to help those who are seeking, in their evolution, is to help them, if only for moments in the course of a day, to have moments of freedom from a redirection of intelligent energy, by identification, not with creation, but the I that they are, not the I that they think they are. It is the thought of I that is the force. That *is* the force. For without the thought I, there is not belief. It is the thought of I that is the force; it is not the I.

So, man makes effort in his evolution, as he continues to evolve and to return to the Source from whence he has wandered. Man works on a broadening of one's horizon and, therefore, no longer has this belief that they are very special and very unique, for they are beyond specialty. We are beyond the unique. That which is everything, everywhere, never absent or away cannot be bottled up and limited by specialty and uniqueness. That is for those in stages of evolution who still have the need of comparison.

And without judgment, there would be no comparison. So that is for those on the rung of the ladder of eternal progression who still are evolving and have not yet risen in consciousness to what is known as the will of God, the power of life. There is, of course, in total acceptance the Light and the awareness thereof, for there are no forms to battle, for there are none rejected. You see, there can be no rejection unless there's a judgment. There can be no judgment unless there's a comparison. There can be no comparison unless there's a uniqueness, a specialty. That is all force. That is the karmic wheel of continuous illusion and delusion. Does that help with your question?

Yes.

Yes, the gentleman there, please.

Yes. When we are physically affected by something—well, I'd like for you to explain what is happening when we are physically affected by something that's happening in our con—everything that's happening in our consciousness and our subconsciousness.

Yes, we are physically affected ever in keeping with what we are doing mentally within our consciousness. But we and we alone have the power to bring about the changes that we choose to make. If we are not happy with experiences that we encounter physically, which is nothing more than an effect of experiences established mentally—the return of forms that we alone have chosen—then the place to go to work is in the realm of mental consciousness where the cause is. The physical body is an effect. It is an effect.

Now when you work and do something with the physical body, you bring about or introduce a change in the mental body. For example, if a person has their hand amputated, there is a change within the mental consciousness or mental body of the individual. If you have what you call a cold, there is a change within the mental consciousness: the images are changing. The images are moving ever in keeping with the force that is generated by our own belief. We *believe* we have a cold. We have many images within the mental consciousness who dutifully go to work to prove to us, at any given moment, how absolutely right we are.

You see, my friends, we cannot keep the balloon of the uneducated ego inflated unless we constantly puff air into it. Well, the air we puff into the uneducated ego is how right we are in anything that enters our mental consciousness. Now, for example, it is the images within our consciousness, whether you call them colds or flues—we all go through this. Some more than others. And some [of us] finally grow through it in our evolution. It is the images in mental consciousness that go to work, in keeping with the force of will, generated by our belief, to prove to us how right we are. And so we are in a constant process of proving to what we think is our self how right we are. Because if we don't continue in proving to our self how right we are, then we've got to make the next step in evolution, which is freedom from the thought of I and returning home to the I that we are.

So as long as we insist on believing that we are the *thought* of I, then we shall continue the experiences generated from belief by the force of will and their return into our mental consciousness. Does that help with your question?

Yes, sir.

You see, look what happens to the consciousness if we're not constantly on guard. Our mind looks around, through our senses, and says, "Whoops, that person's got a cold. Thank God I don't have that!" But then we don't—sometimes we don't go to work on it within our consciousness. Then the next thing we know, "Oh, there's another one that's got a cold!" And the next thing you know you hear someone say, "Well, it's like a hospital downstairs. It's like that Marin General Hospital down there." So many people have colds down there. And if you don't go to work on it, the next thing you know everybody's got a cold [and] there's a part of you that feels left out. You don't have a cold like everybody else. Now everybody else is getting sympathy: "Oh, you poor thing. Well, it will pass." But you don't have one yet. Well, the next thing you know, no uneducated ego likes to be left out. Because you must realize it takes an uneducated ego to believe that it is left out. The true I knows that it is everything. Therefore, how can it be left out of anything, because it is everything. So, it takes an uneducated ego to feel left out. So you feel left out. And next thing you know, that goes through this computer here in this magnetic field, "Left out. Left out because why? Why? Well, everybody's getting attention but me. They've all got colds. That's why they're getting attention. Ah, I'll get a cold!" Next thing you know, you've got one.

Now, the thing is, you don't consciously think that way. But what did you do when you were a little child? What did you do to have what you thought you needed when you were a little child? If you thought you needed some love and some attention, you did whatever you were able to do in your little mind. Well, it's that little mind that we're all working with all the time. You see, the five-year-old is five years old. The five-year-old is still within the mental consciousness. The five-year-old didn't change. No, no, no, no. A six-year-old was born. And then a seven-year-old and then an eight-year-old. But the five-year-old, the four-year-old, the three-year-old, the two-year-old, they all exist in mental consciousness. And when you think of yourself, you open up that door down there. And unless you have honest communication between the Light and the lesser light and you see clearly what is taking place, you never know which one's going to come up from the basement: a five-year-old, a two-year-old, a sixteen-year-old. You never know.

And so it is the purpose of the Living Light to help you to show you the law that you may apply it. And therefore, it becomes your truth, your freedom, which, of course, all truth is individually perceived. It is not individual, but it is individually perceived. And through your own daily effort, you, slowly but surely, gain control. And when you want to use that five-year-old that's still in consciousness there, you use them. And when you don't want to use them, you don't use them, for they are creations. They are what *you* have created. You are their mother and their father. You are their authority when you stop, when you pause, and you no longer spend the life-giving energy of the power of the universe in what is known as the thought of I.

Thank you. I see our time is up. Thank you.

MARCH 1, 1984

CONSCIOUSNESS CLASS 237

Now this evening we'll continue on with our discussion on belief, faith, creation, truth. Now prior to individualization, which is the effect of the Law of Identification, there is the state known to man as bliss. And so through the Law of Identity, man forms or separates—individualizes—and, in so doing, becomes self-aware. And so it is in our evolution, as we gain more and more awareness of self, it is ever at the cost or expense of the state of consciousness known as bliss or heaven.

Now will power, which is intelligent energy, and total acceptance, which is the will of God, reveals itself to be intelligent goodness. And so man, being intelligent, and man, in truth, being good, ever seeks to return to that which he is in truth.

The difficulty is in man's own evolution, his own individualization, his own identity. To the awakened, will power (intelligent energy) is director; to the sleeper, it is dictator; and to the dreamer, it is despair. And so this eternal process of evolution is not something that a wise man looks forward to or backwards from, but looks at it each moment of conscious awareness. Now will power (intelligent energy) is the lord or the master of our universe. This master, to the awakened, is director and goodness. To the sleeper, it is dictator and disaster. To the dreamer, it is despair and hopelessness. And so we find to return to this awakening that has never left us—only through the Law of Identity have we, at times, blinded our self to this great truth within us.

And so through a process of denial, denying our divinity, denying our own ability to respond to all that we create, known as experiences—[and not] to respond to them intelligently, to respond to them with an impartiality, which energy, intelligent, truly is—we react by creating, through the Law of Identification, other forms and the battle within our consciousness continues on.

We seek, with our minds, to control. And in that effort of seeking from our mind, which is individualized and, therefore, limited, we ever search for knowledge, for ways to manipulate, which is to control our destiny, to control the experiences that we encounter in life. Because in that effort of seeking knowledge of how to manipulate, of seeking knowledge of various techniques, we must pause in our consciousness and awaken that we are using mental substance, the effect or the form created by our own limited minds; we are using forms that can only battle forms of like kind. Consequently, the effect is a house divided, which has no substance, and offers, in the final analysis, no goodness, for we are using intelligent goodness in a limited and self-destructive way.

The denial of our ability to respond to our attitudes of mind, to respond to our emotions, to respond intelligently to our experiences, reveals to us a difficult path, to say the least. Therefore, wisdom, which is the effect of the Light which we are—which, like truth, cannot be formed, cannot be conceived, for it just *is*.

And so in these classes, it behooves us to first become aware of our thoughts, which form our thought patterns, which, in turn, through the Law of Identity, are individualized within our consciousness and, in that state of growth of individualization, are separated from the true being which we are and act upon our consciousness strictly, wholly, and completely in the purpose of their original design.

And so we go along in life. We wish to make certain changes in our lives for we reach various decisions and do not wish to continue on with some of the experiences that we have been having and we seek to make changes. In order to make a change, we must use intelligent energy. We must use intelligent energy wisely. It is intelligent. It is energy and it is impartial and absolutely neutral. Our will power, that is, the energy (intelligent energy) that we choose to direct, acts upon that within our consciousness to do what we send it to do. If, however, in our efforts to make changes in our life, we direct, through an awakened consciousness, we direct this intelligent energy to accomplish and act upon the forms within our mental substance and if we believe we are the forms on which we are directing intelligent energy to act upon, then we react through the magnetic attachment, which, of course, is our own belief.

Now this same truth, of course, has been given to you so many times in so many different ways. Not until we awaken to the truth can we use this great power, which man calls faith, not until we awaken to the truth that we are not what we believe.

Now we have spent many years believing that we are this way and we are that way. We have spent many years believing that we feel and have experiences because of what someone else is thinking or doing. That type of thinking reveals to us our bondage of creation. That is the life of the sleeper. And so our minds are ever seeking, looking outside for the cause of why we are, where we are, when we are, ever looking outside to find something or someone to blame for any experience that we judge is not beneficial or good in our life.

And so the early steps of evolution to return to the truth and freedom that we are is daily effort to honestly ask our self, first, "What, in truth, is this experience that I am having?" Second, the acceptance that it is created by our own mind through our own error of ignorance, for we do not consciously choose to direct intelligent energy to forms that we judge will not bring us goodness and things that we desire. There is no awakening without that daily effort.

The bondage of creation is the denial of truth. And when we, by conscious choice or through omission, deny the truth, which is, "What I experience is taking place within my mind. My mind is a vehicle designed by the Great Architect to serve the goodness which I am. By my denial, I am destined to the dual Law of Creation. Through my over-identification, through the great awareness of self, I believe I am the experience. And because I believe I am it, I become it through the error of my own ignorance." Whenever a student denies the truth, I am well aware of their suffering, for the law is indeed impartial.

However, in keeping with our teachings to suffer senses not in vain, for a freedom of the soul is gain, I am well aware that we have made, through our denial of personal responsibility, *we*—not goodness, not God, not intelligent energy—but we, in the twilight zones of ignorance, have made suffering the path for our truth and our freedom. Suffering is not a path designed by the goodness of life. It is a path that has been designed and created by denial—the direct opposite of total acceptance. And we know that total acceptance *is* the will of God; it *is* the Divinity. For nothing (no thing) is left out from the sustenance, the intelligent energy, for its own fulfillment of its purpose of design. Therefore denial *is* the night. Denial *is* the direct opposite of the

Light. For all of life reveals clearly to us that even the sparrow is sustained, in its journey through creation, is sustained by intelligent energy, God, or goodness of life.

And so it is our evolution moment by moment. When we view evolution, we should view it in the moment of our conscious choice, for only in the moment of one's conscious choice is one receptive to the power of God. Only in that moment, the moment of conscious choice, is the director guiding us on the path of goodness.

The forms or thoughts, that some of you might prefer to call them, are not you, but they have been created by a vehicle, a mind, a mental body that, in your evolution, you have earned. It is a vehicle that is fully qualified to serve the purpose of the goodness that you are. One will not become receptive to the goodness they are by annihilating the vehicles that they have earned in evolution. One will be receptive to the goodness that they are by awakening the vehicles they have earned to be used, not abused, in their evolution.

Each and every experience in life is serving, to the awakened, a good and beautiful purpose, for in each and every experience, intelligent energy, the power of God, is sustaining it. Now when you use the power of God to bring about a change in your life, you must remember that it is the same power of God that is sustaining the patterns of the past that you are working to be freed from. Therefore, if you insist on believing that you are those patterns of mind, those attitudes, those forms that you are trying to change, then you have two armies of equal strength on the battlefield of creation.

Now this chain that binds us, called belief, of course, is nonexistent when we no longer identify, therefore, individualize and are freed from creation and limit and are above and beyond, therefore, are not affected by.

Now we'll pause a few moments for your questions. If you wish to raise your hand. Yes.

We've been told that there is no time in truth. Would that indicate that there is always sunlight or daylight in the spirit realms?

Well, in reference to there is no time in truth and the question is, Does that indicate there is always sunlight or daylight in the spiritual realms? Time is dependent upon the Law of Identity. That which is spiritual is formless and, therefore, is free. Now some of us shudder at the possibility that we should lose our identity. But how can we shudder at demonstrable truth? That which begins is that which ends. So if you believe that you began, in keeping with your belief, so shall you end. If you believe you are the vehicle that you're presently using, then in keeping with that law of belief, shall you lose the vehicle that you are using. For that which we gain is that which we lose and that which begins is that which ends.

Therefore, the struggles of life and the difficulties and the suffering are ever in keeping with the insistence of our mind—our mind, a vehicle that we're using—from its insistence that we are this limit, that we are this form. However, when our mind wants something that this limited form cannot accomplish, has tried and has failed, then it seeks to turn to that which is formless and free. Those are the moments, in great suffering, that our minds will accept the possibility that there is something greater than that which we believe we are. There are those rare moments in life. And it is this wonderful process of suffering that helps us to return home to that which we are.

Now something cannot come out of nothing. Then the question arises, Are we something? Or are we nothing? We believe we are something and indeed we are something for a time. So many years of our life, we identify, we believe we are that. The illusion called time marches on and then we believe we're a little bit different. And it's a constant process. And so what is it that came out? Nothing; no *thing* came out and no *thing* returns. *We* have always been. *We* will always be. If you believe the "we" is what you believe you are this moment, then it is guaranteed to change, for that is the identification. That is the limiting. That is the individualization. As long as you need to believe that you are the limit, you shall be the limit. But we cannot believe that we are the limit forever. Because limit is an effect of a dual law and like all laws that are dual, they are equally balanced in so-called time in eternity.

Now in reference to your question, Are the spiritual realms all light? The spiritual realms, beyond creation, are not realms that contain the Law of Judgment. Now the Law of Judgment is dependent upon comparison, and comparison is dependent upon the Law of Duality. Therefore, that is creation. That is not the spiritual realms of truth and freedom. So one cannot say that it is light in comparison to dark, for it is that which sustains both in our thoughts of comparison. Does that help with your question?

Yes. Thank you.

You're welcome. Yes, the lady here, please.

Could you speak about personality in relationship to disassociation or what you're speaking about?

Well, in reference to personality, one, pausing in that question, would see that, first, there is a need within the consciousness seeking, in mental substance, to be fulfilled. Personality, the over-identification with self, is known in this philosophy as self-love. It offers to any person the fullness of the functions of creation, of course, including the effects of need in a world of function known as envy, jealousy, and greed. We experience need as an effect of a grounding in self. The grounding in self, of course, is our denial of personal responsibility and therefore, we separate our self in consciousness from the goodness that we are. And that separation, registering in the consciousness of self-love, is known to the mind as need. We are lacking and yet, we desire. And we look out and we judge through comparison, for two eyes see two things simultaneously. And so we look out and see that what we think we desire, someone else has and we start to feel envious through our over-identification with our self-love. We start to feel jealous and we begin to become greedy.

There is no benefit to this over-identification, known as personality. You cannot experience personality unless you first deny the truth that you are. You see, we cannot experience need without denial. We cannot experience jealousy, envy, and greed without denial. When we over-identify with our self and this self-love, within our mental substance we become greater than God. That's what happens in our mind. We become, in a mental identification, greater than God. Therefore, whoever believes they are greater than God, goodness, guarantees the law to prove to themselves a little something about goodness of life.

So when you turn your view horizontal in life instead of vertical, then you must pay the price of that denial and experience, through your own self-love, personality. Does that help with your question? Yes.

How do we move through this world without it?

Without personality?

Yes.

By being in this world and never a part of it.

So then we don't need to use our personality?

You don't need to use personality in the sense that I accepted the question of personality. In this philosophy, personality or personalities means a conflict, a manipulation by one mind, an attempted manipulation of another mind. That's personality. That's turning to creation, instead of God. You see, whoever depends upon their mind for the goodness of life must joyously accept both good and bad. So when you depend on personality, which is a vehicle and a device of mental substance, you must be willing to pay the price. If you're willing to pay the price, then that's your growth in evolution. Does that help with your question?

Yes.

You see, many people—I spoke a little earlier on techniques and manipulation. The more you depend on techniques, manipulation, the more you become a victim of personality, the more you become a victim of the forms of your own mind. The mind is limited. It can learn many techniques and it can manipulate many things. But it cannot do everything. And using a dependence upon mental substance to accomplish the goodness of life, one must accept the demonstrable truth: they must pay the price of the Law of Duality. And ofttimes in life, using personality and our mind to gain what we think will bring us goodness, we are so grateful, as time marches on, that it didn't stay in our life too long. Would you not agree?

Yes.

So, you see, the mind is limited and being limited, it cannot see beyond the forms of its own creation. And when you cannot see over the hill, a wise man doesn't go that way. So use your mind to climb the hill. But that's when you best come out of your mind, for the horizon beyond is not subject to mental substance.

You said when you can't see, then you—

The mind is a limited vehicle. It is form and, therefore, limited. And when you use your mind, it only looks so far. It cannot see beyond the hill. It cannot see beyond the form of your own creation. Therefore, it is wise to use something far beyond the mind: to use the intelligent energy that sustains the mind. Why use a form when you can use the power that is the life of the form? One thing is an effect and the other is a cause. Does that help with your question?

Thank you.

Yes, the lady in the back was waiting first. Yes.

It sounds so simple and an easy accomplishment and yet, daily, it's very difficult. And if one isn't familiar with—it's like being in an unknown forest. And you're used to operating in one way—it just sounds so simple and easy and yet it's not that simple and easy.

Truth is simple and unconcealed. It is as simple as you permit it—or anyone permits it. The simplicity is ever in keeping with what anyone is depending on at any given moment.

But what if you're just used to using—it just seems exasperating that it—to the ear, it sounds so easy and so simple and yet, the practice of it or the putting into accomplishing it—at least, you know, maybe, maybe I'm only speaking from my own experience, but it, so far, has not been so easy.

A wise person speaks only from their own experiences and growth in life, of course, for it would be foolhardy for one to speak for others, were others not present to speak for themselves.

Difficulty is dependent upon the contradictions in consciousness. No matter what duty or job we have in life, it is as difficult as our over-identification with our self will make it. We have all had experiences when a person says, "Why, that was no problem at all. I went to rehearse that song—the first time it came out like that, just beautiful. Absolutely no difficulty whatsoever." Same song, at another time, when the singer is in a different rate of vibration with varying dependencies on mental substance, singing of the song is extremely difficult. So it reveals to us, demonstrably, that difficulty in anything in life is dependent upon the Law of Identification. And we and we alone choose our identifications in life. Does that help with your question?

Well, I hear the words and they make sense to me, but somehow I can't seem to accomplish it. So it's—I'm experiencing an exasperation with it.

I see. I see. Now may I say one thing? Intelligent energy or will power, one uses to declare what they cannot do; one also uses it to declare what they can do.

Now the statement of truth is very clear, very clear: to God, to goodness, to that which we are, all things are possible. Only to denial do we find things impossible. And what is denial, the destiny? The obstruction in consciousness to accept we are the ability to intelligently respond.

Now, to that which we are, all things are possible. And when you take that light throughout your consciousness, you will find those certain things, those certain obstructions that you tenaciously believe that you are and therefore, in that area of consciousness, God is nonexistent. For to you, in keeping with your belief that you are that obstruction that you have created in consciousness, it does not work. And so we hear and the next step is to listen. For whoever listens absorbs, like a sponge, into the consciousness, guided by the light of reason.

Now the light of reason that transforms us, that transfigures form, this great soul faculty known as reason is the vehicle through which intelligent goodness, God, energy flows. So when we use this faculty, this soul faculty of reason, when we awaken and have a director, an awakened consciousness, and we direct this vehicle known as reason to the form of our obstruction that we hold to through our own belief, the effect of our own over-identification with self, the obstruction is removed from our consciousness. But we must be willing to do that; we must care enough for truth and freedom and the goodness that we truly are. And when the goodness and truth and freedom that we truly are rises in our consciousness in an awakened mind and faces that which we believe we are, that light shall remove that obstruction from our path in evolution.

One may show the way and reach, through the spoken word, which is life-giving energy, the faculty of reason within another being, but one can only show the way. One cannot remove another's obstruction, for that is contrary to the Law of Individualized Evolution of Form. I hope that's helped with your question.

Yes, the lady here, please.

When one's trying to gain control over the forms of their mind, is it necessary for them to face the emotion that was used in creating the form?

In reference to freeing oneself from the creations in mental consciousness, Is it necessary to return to that which created it, the form? Is that correct? *[After a short pause, the Teacher continues.]* The law shows us the way out of a thing is the way we got in.

In reference to that, with many endeavors that we make, sometimes we're successful. Sometimes we quit. Sometimes we play around, you see. Rarely are we the director. We're usually the dictator and the dreamer. The dreamer plays around and the dictator goes high and low, like a roller-coaster.

Well, anyway, we came into what we call belief, as I explained earlier, through identification. And the way we see what it has offered us and does offer us—it offers us many limits, many thrills, and many excitement of the senses and, slowly but surely, we begin to turn our true being back to that which we have wandered from. And we find, in our efforts to return home to that which we are—not what we believe we are and think we are—we find an ever-increasing amount of creation in our life. What it is—it is not ever-increasing. We are only experiencing the many chickens who come home to roost. For we're going back home the way we left home. There's one way out and there's one way back. The path is straight and the path is narrow. So the way you got into it is the way you get out of it.

So if you are working to accomplish some endeavor in your life and you have struggled with it a year ago, ten years ago, twenty years ago, you must face those forms created. You must face them with the lamp of honesty, for it is a dark way through the realms of the mind of mental substance. And it offers—the hissing hounds of hell stand before the gates of victory.

When our mind entertains for a moment the thought of the annihilation of what we believe we are, when what we believe we are is constantly being annihilated and we're constantly gaining new forms, new, new, beliefs—so here we are constantly annihilating what we believe we are and constantly gaining these changes, for that is the Law of Evolution. That's the law through which all form is bound. There is no escape as long as you're identified.

And so it is the forms that we believe we are that are petrified, because they know their existence is wholly, totally, completely dependent upon you. For they have no soul, for they are not truth and they are not light. That's why there is no soul: they are hollow. They are created forms of a mental world. Without you to live off of, they no longer exist.

And so when we hear our mouth say, "It's difficult. Oh, it's impossible. Things are so bad and it's someone else's fault," try to remember that is not you, but you are responsible for them using your mouth. But they are not you. But you must never forget it is your denial of being responsible for your mouth that permitted them that control in the first place.

Thank you. Good night.

MARCH 8, 1984

CONSCIOUSNESS CLASS 238

Good evening, class.

One might say that we're starting early this evening, which, of course, is to our benefit and our opportunity to see what takes place within our mind based upon reason or judgment. And, of course, that's in keeping with the two paths of thinking that we are constantly using.

Now these two paths of thinking that we live by, that we choose to live by—one of which is our mind looks out: it sees and it compares and in so doing, it judges what we have and what we have not. And in that process, it reacts and we begin the type of thinking that's known as wishful or wishing, not thinking, but wishing. Then there is the other path of thinking. The path of going within our own consciousness, viewing, with the light of reason, what we have made available to us and what changes we can make to bring about what we desire in life. However, most of our time and our energies are spent in the former, known as wishful thinking. Because in looking outside to see the world, we establish, through our judgment of what we have and have not, our destiny, for we identify with what is known as denial, through the process of comparison that guarantees the limit known as judgment.

We all have a great deal of experience with that type of thinking. We all have a great deal of experience in the frustration that it offers. For example, that type of thinking is revealed when we permit our minds to say how difficult something is. The reason we say that something is difficult is because we are in a realm of consciousness of comparison. So based upon what we think we have available to us, what we desire to obtain, we view the obstruction and call that struggle or difficulty.

Now we have stated many times that whoever views the obstruction shall not find the way, for when we place our attention, which is the vehicle of directing infinite intelligent energy, to the obstruction, the obstruction becomes more solidified within our own mind. And through that process of solidification, we believe that we are denied what we desire.

Now many, many people have taught positive thinking. It goes far beyond positive thinking because one thinks many, many things and they call that positive. When, in truth, it reveals itself to be wishful thinking. Now we know, because we have accepted, that we have brown hair and brown eyes, blonde hair and blue eyes, red hair and brown eyes, or go on down the list. And we reinforce that belief every time we look in the mirror and every time we think of our self.

We believe we are getting old and in that belief do we age. If that belief is based upon a creation within our consciousness of beauty, of harmony, of goodness, of benefit, then that is the way, of course, that we will age. Because aging, as we know aging, is nothing more and nothing less than a change in form. Now, change of form is taking place all the time. We help the change along or we make the change most difficult. And so considering many experiences in our life we find distasteful because they are distasteful to the type of thinking or realm of consciousness in which comparison exists.

Try to understand one cannot compare until one identifies with separation. There must be separation in order to compare and separation exists, of course, in a world of creation. If truth were possible of separation, it could no longer be truth. Therefore, when we permit our self this luxury of separation in consciousness of what we are, what we truly are—the separation between that and what we believe we are—then we have this battle and this struggle of a house divided. The only thing that can bring us to the wholeness of that which we are is to begin the process consciously, daily upon inward thinking. That takes a lot of effort because it has taken a lot of effort for us to gain this outward thinking.

A person says, "Well, I would like this and I would like that and I would like something else." And our likes, sometimes they last awhile and sometimes they don't. Because to any mind that looks outside, there is such a diversity and such a temptation of so many things that no one person could possibly entertain all of them at any single time. When we find that we feel struggle, we find that we feel difficulty in any area of our life, then we must pause and awaken that we feel that in keeping with outward thinking. In keeping with our judgment of what something and someone out there is doing, not doing, having, or not having compared to what we think we have or don't have. That, of course, is the struggle that we permit; the luxury—for it is a luxury—that we permit our self to have.

Now I've said many times, and will say again, that all the good there is, is wherever we are. If at any time we cannot see it, it is only because we will not allow our self to think and, therefore, to see it. We will not allow our self because we are not pausing and, in that pause, awaken inside of our self. Whenever we look outside, which is most of the time, we see what we think we desire ever, ever beyond the horizon of our present attainment. Because no one can think outside (can deny that which they are) and have in consciousness that which they are. Because, you see, we look out to attain; we constantly look outside to attain and we experience a need to attain only from a consciousness of denial.

You cannot attain what you already are. You already are truth. You already are freedom. You cannot attain that because that is what you are. Now you can think and, therefore, believe that you desire that and you do not have it because you're looking outside and it doesn't exist outside. So as long as you look outside, which offers you comparison, as long as your mind—you permit your mind to do that, then you will continue on with the destiny of your own denial.

Because anyone who denies what they are, and being motivated by the truth that they are, will experience the need for it. When a person knows beyond a shadow of any doubt and, once having known anything beyond a shadow of any doubt, goes to sleep in the realms of satisfaction and, in so sleeping, forgets what and who they really are, has that deep inner knowing. Although they deny they have it, there is something inside of them that always knows. For no matter what it is in life that we have ever had, we still have. You cannot remove from the consciousness that which the consciousness has experienced. You can deny that you have it and in a physical sense, that is true: you no longer physically have it. But the physical manifestation of anything is only the solidification of the mental substance, which is the cause of it.

Because you have moments of goodness, there is no way, except through your own denial, that you can no longer have those moments of goodness, for they exist within your consciousness. They were formed by your consciousness, solidified within your consciousness, [and] made manifest to your physical senses. Therefore that which they truly are—the essence of a thing is the principle of anything—that, you can never be without. Now a person ofttimes has great difficulty—that awakening—because they think this way: through over-identification with the mental image of what we call self, there is the physical manifestation that is extremely solidified. Being identified with self, one says, "I have had and have not." And one, therefore, in their consciousness, looking outward, experiences the comings and the goings of creation. And we all, in that type of thinking, feel loss because we are over-identified with what we call the gain.

Now when we work for something and finally attain it, a part of our mind already, from the effort of working for it, becomes attached to it. Now that attachment, being an extension of the solidification of form created by our own mind, becomes the force that brings us the experiences that we interpret to be loss. That's where those experiences come from in our own mind.

Our classes for many, many years have spent, and continue to spend, much of its energy and time on understanding the vehicles through which our true being is expressing. For when we understand the vehicle through which the formless, free being that we are, when we understand the vehicle, we can guide, control, and use it more intelligently. If we do not understand the principles that a vehicle, an automobile, is subject to, then we cannot use it to its full benefits.

If we do not care properly for any vehicle—the vehicle of intelligent energy passing through form, known as a thought, known as an attitude, known as vibration, a law established—if we don't understand it thoroughly, we cannot reap the harvest or the benefit from it. So it is of the utmost importance that we understand our vehicle, our human mind; that we understand its physical manifestation, which is the effect of a solidification of mental substance. Because that's what it is. Oh, we call it flesh and bone and we call it many things, but it is the solidification of mental substance. In the final analysis, it is subject to the laws that govern mental substance.

As we look in our life at what we think we want, we, slowly but surely, in time become aware that we think we want this for a time, only to think that we want that for a time. Because that thinking is only a denial of what we are. We are seeking to express. We know what we are. We know who we are. The difficulties we have created are limits and obstructions to the free flow or expression of what we, in truth, know that we are. And so we go through life working along to attain that, for we ever seek to express more fully the being, the freedom, the truth, the abundant good that we know deep in our heart that we truly are.

Now some people, in their efforts, will express it through art, through singing, through painting. Others, they will express it through the many different jobs that they have. But there's always that something that's missing. And that something that's missing is that feeling within our consciousness there has to be something better. That something better, that something greater is the message, the voice knocking at the door of our conscience that we are indeed greater than what we think we are and what we believe we are. But to make that step, we must give up what we think we are in order that we may be what we truly are. Because you cannot have both. You cannot have the limits of mental substance and serve it through believing that you are this and that and that and that and have the truth that you are fully expressing itself.

Now we'll pause for a few moments. If you have any questions, you raise your hands, please. Yes, the lady in the back, please.

Could you be more explicit about looking in, that process, like, literally?

I'll be happy to share with you in reference to the type of thinking, the path of Light, of looking in.

First of all, to look in, one must become aware of something to look into. Would you not agree? Then a person pauses and thinks, "What do I have to look into?" And in that type of thinking, they're not yet looking in, but they're on the path. They look and they say, "This is the way my life seems to me. These are the difficulties that I see. These are the struggles I see. These are the things I wish I had that my mind tells me I don't have. This is what I want to be. I haven't got there yet. It doesn't look like I'm going to get there in keeping with my impatient schedule. And things don't seem to be the way I want them to be for me." Now that's a start, because what we have done is take a look at the mind that looks outside.

So as we start on the path to look in, we first view the mind that stands in the way. We see, first, the obstruction to what we desire. Now if we take a look at anyone who wishes for anything, we will find, quickly and easily, all the struggle. We'll find all of the obstructions in the way. Oh, the desire is there. And the mind rises up and justifies why it is not so advisable to work our self so hard to attain that: there must be an easier way. You follow me so far?

Yes.

That's beginning the path of looking in. Now if a person, in sincerity and honesty, continues on the path inward and is not sent back to outward thinking by fear—for fear is faith directed to mental substance and it is that faith directed to mental substance, that force, that keeps us from what we are. But that only takes place through over-identification with form, limit, or mental substance. Do you understand?

Yes.

So we go through all that this outward mind has to offer. We go through all of the seeming obstructions, all the things we don't have, all of the things we want to have, all of the questions of, "Why did this happen to me?" all of the questions of, "How did it happen to me? What mistake did I make or was it the mistake of someone else?" And we go through all of that. And if we keep our eye single—that means we do not let go of the light of reason. We do not forget for a moment our purpose and motive for stepping on this path of looking in to return to that which we truly are and be freed from what we thought we were. We will pass through those realms of consciousness. We will experience the seeming struggles and difficulties and the years, just like pages of a book, will start to turn.

And we'll go back, so-called, in time and experience, which is only a passing through this computer of the mind. We will once again reexperience the frustrations and emotions. Therefore, we must keep our eye single. For if we do not keep our eye single, carrying the lamp of honesty, guided by the light of reason, we will forget. And forgetting for a moment, we will believe we are an experience that has passed long ago. And that's where we will stop and in stopping, someday again we shall rise to start the journey all over again. Does that help with your question?

Yes. Thank you.

Now, there is no way to get out of anything that we find our self in except through the very door we passed through to get in, in the first place. The way out of anything is the way we got in. There is no other way. There is one way into the mental world: it's known as the Law of Identity. There is only one way out of the mental world and it's known as the Law of Identity. That's how we got in and that is how we get back out.

Now, you take just any recent experience that you find disturbing. If you take a moment and be at peace, keep your eye single, relive the experience that your mind, in its outward path, viewed as such a great trauma in your life, you will find, with the light of reason, the experience was of nothing, for it was only creation. Something that came in keeping with laws that we alone set into motion. Something that has passed in keeping with laws that we alone set into motion.

Now the purpose of these classes is to help us to understand the laws and, in understanding the laws, to be inspired to use them that they may free us, for that is the purpose of law. The purpose of law is to free, not to bind. The purpose of law is truth. It's not falsehood. Now man makes many laws and the laws that man makes limit, restrict, and bind. Those are man's laws. The laws of God are laws infallible, infinite, eternal, that free. They do not bind. Does that help with your question?

Yes. Thank you.

Yes, the lady here please.

In that process of looking in and reviewing what experiences have passed, if we find that we're attracting negative experiences by this process—I understand because it is associated with self-pity. How do we maintain the light of reason and put God in it to examine it on a different level?

Yes. For example, a person, in the process of that path of objectivity and review to free themselves from those realms of consciousness, finds they are attracting similar experiences in their life reveals to the person, in their efforts, that they are over-identified with self and, through that process of over-identification, are once again reactivating laws that were established before. Now no one can stop us from thinking about our self. But *we* can stop that process and we have the ability and we have the conscious choice moment by moment.

Now the purpose here is to help us to see these laws so clearly that we will be inspired not to bind our self to them as we are working to be freed from them because of our over-identification with our self. Does that help with your question?

If you choose to over-identify with something and through the process of over-identification believe you are it, then you establish the law to, once again, relive the experience in keeping with that law established. That is what you don't want. Is that correct? Then only through control of one's own mind can they be freed from over-identification, the magnet which pulls it to us.

You see, all these laws we have set into motion, once we re-activate them, they are great magnets, because, you see, we are pulling them up out of a realm of consciousness in which they have solidified and we call that emotion or magnetism. So once we call them up, if we do not, as I said earlier, use the light of reason, if we do not keep the light of reason shining and keep our eye single, then we will, once again, have those experiences in principle. Yes.

Could you give us some guideline as what to say to ourselves or what to do?

Well, it's not what to say; it's a matter of what we do. You see, we consciously choose, moment by moment, to think about our self and how we feel and what we're doing or not doing. Usually we, we think about our self in respect to what we don't have and what we desire. Now, that is—you see, so often when I speak about over-identification with self, people don't relate to it. They say, "Well, I'm not thinking of myself all the time." No, no, no, no. They're not stopping and calling their name constantly into the universe. No, no, no. All they have to do is think, "I wish I had that. Oh, why didn't this happen? Oh, I don't know what I'm going to do." And be so concerned about their life. You see, one cannot have self-concern without self-love. And one cannot have self-love without over-identification.

For, you see, the over-identification is the denial of what we are. The over-identification creates within our consciousness what we think we are and what we think we are deprives us from what we desire, because what we think we are looks out; it compares and sees what we don't have. Because what we think are is separated from what we are. And because we have separated that which we are, we believe what we think we are and through that belief establish the force and the magnet pulls it into our universe—the Law of Denial.

So it isn't—there are no words that you can say, "I stop thinking of myself and therefore I am freed from myself." No, no, no. It does not happen that way. Because you see, every time you permit your mind to be concerned about what's going to happen, what's not going to happen, "How am I going to take care of this? Will I be happy or won't I be happy? Is it going to work out? Isn't it going to work out?" That's total over-identification with self. And that's where all the struggle of life is. Because that's separation from truth, that which you are. And therefore you ever seek to attain through denial. You see, if we don't deny, then we won't have to work so hard to get what we think we don't have. We have to struggle so much to get what we think we don't have because we deny what we are. Does that help with your question?

You see, when we permit our self to deny, then you must realize, we're looking outward and we're constantly comparing. And that judges—we have, we don't have, we're happy, we're not happy, all of that is taking place in those realms of denial. Because we are, at those times, what we think we are. And we think what we think we are based upon comparison, based upon what someone else has or does not have. This is how we *think* what we are. And when a person believes that what they think they are is what they are, then they must pay the price of the Law of Creation and the Law of Duality. For each moment of happiness, they must experience its opposite. For each moment of good, they must experience its opposite because that is what they have chosen: believing what they think they are. Whoever believes what they think they are must pay the price of the Law of Comparison, must pay the price of the Law of Dependence.

You see, when we think we believe we are what we think we are, then we are constantly dependent upon getting what we judge we don't have because we are constantly looking at a world of comparison. We do not have happiness, because our happiness is dependent upon judgments made by our mind as an effect of comparison of looking outside. Therefore, when those judgments are satisfied, we are happy—we *think* we're happy. And we believe what we think and therefore we are happy. That is an illusion created by our mind. But it's only for a time, for form is in a constant process of birth and death. It is constantly rising only to fall.

So all these experiences are rising and falling, offering to you goodness and its opposite: day and night, happiness, unhappiness, joy and sadness constantly. But, you see, that's a total lack of control. It's a total lack of the mastery of life. It's a total denial that you are captain of your ship, you see, that you are captain. It is a total denial of the truth, for it is dependent on what other people do or don't do. And because we cannot control what another person does or does not do, we are constantly the victim, through our dependence for our happiness upon their fickle minds. And their fickle minds are constantly dependent upon some other fickle mind.

There is no joy, there is no happiness in believing that you are creation. There is no happiness or joy in believing you are the automobile that you drive. Though there may be temporary moments of thrill when it's brand new and working just fine, but time marches on, this great illusion. The day is guaranteed when it starts to fall apart. The day is guaranteed when it stops when you want it to start. And so that's creation.

Now we have taught repeatedly, separate truth (that which you are) from creation (that which you think you are), for that which you think you are offers you belief, comparison, dependence, and ever the victim of what someone does or does not do because you view them in keeping with the fulfillment of the judgments solidified within your consciousness. And when those solidified judgments are not filled, then they, like the great puppeteer, are controlling your mind. Does that help you with your question?

Thank you.

You see, we have not come to Earth to be manipulated by what some mind does or does not do, but *we* give that to them through our dependence upon them. It is our error of ignorance. It is a very unstable way to live. Our emotions, our magnetic being constantly reveals to us how unreliable and how unstable it is. It is not the mastery of creation that we are designed for. It is just the opposite.

The Light that we are is the very essence; without it, creation does not exist. When we believe we are the thought, which is creation, then we ever seek to force the Light to be the victim of the form that we create. That is not possible. It is contrary to the infinite divine laws of life. There's no way possible. It offers nothing but frustration. Does that help with your question?

Yes. Thank you.

You're welcome. The lady here, please.

In that the way out of a thing is the way you got into it.

Yes.

As we're going through the reviews—as we keep working on ourselves through life, does that mean we will constantly be reviewing and then finding that pattern of that particular level we're dealing with?

Well, the purpose of reviewing—because, you see, we have to go out of a thing the way we got into the thing. You see, the purpose of reviewing—you can do it now consciously; make the effort. If the Light is too bright, 'tis best one see it not now. One must go ever in keeping with their own efforts of directing their will, for the will is the lord of our universe.

Review or return to that which we are is inevitable. It takes place consciously to those who are awakened to the process while still in the physical flesh. It definitely takes place as we move on into these other realms of consciousness.

You see, there is no, in our understanding—I have never experienced any judgment in the sense of any being that passes judgment upon us. If one can say there is any judgment, it is their reaction to the process that is inevitable: that is, passing through the creation which they have spent time believing that they are. And, of course, we cannot free our self from what we believe we are until we make the effort and *be* what we are. And so we do, in leaving the earthly realm, we move on through these many forms that we have created, these things that we believe that we are because we must shed them, you see, in order to be what we are: the freedom and the truth and the Light.

Now it isn't what we need to add to our mind that frees us. It's what must be removed from our mind that frees us. And that's the process that takes place. Now in principle it takes place every day of your life. It's taking place all the time in principle, for you find some type of attachment to something or someone and the next thing you know, it has physically left your life. And the next step is that it leaves your consciousness in the sense that you finally accept that it is not your God and, therefore, in that acceptance, you are freed from it.

You see, acceptance is the will of goodness. The movement, as I have said, the movement of goodness through the consciousness is total acceptance. And so when you find that, in error in evolution, you have placed your faith in a created form in your consciousness that is solidified and made manifest out there in the world, you see, then through your own total acceptance are you freed from denial which manifests itself as dependence upon it for your goodness, you see.

You see, if we don't deny, we cannot depend. We are dependent ever in keeping with our denials. So if you find yourself dependent upon money, for example, you find yourself dependent on people, for example, then you can be rest assured you are dependent in keeping with the law and the extent and degree that you express the Law of Denial. Man depends on what he denies and therefore he creates his destiny. Does that help with your question?

Yes.

Anyone else have a question? Yes, the lady in the back, please.

Would—any time that fear comes up into the consciousness and you replace it with God, would that be the same thing as reviewing?

No, no—

You still need to review?

—No, no. Fear is a direction of intelligent infinite energy, directed by the will of man to a mental world. Now it is man who chooses to direct it to a mental world and experience what he knows as fear or to direct it to the Source from whence it comes and be transformed by the light of reason, which is the expression of the power of God. Now that's up to man. Man chooses to do that. He chooses to do it in keeping with the Law of Denial and that, of course, is manifested in his life through over-identification with self.

You see, think. When we permit our self to over-identify with self, we separate our self from the stream of consciousness that we are. And in separating our self from the stream of consciousness, we get a trickle, instead of a flow. That's what we do. We don't have to do that. We do that through error. We do that through error of ignorance. It's entirely up to us.

So, if you experience fear, then be aware in that moment: "I fear. What am I fearing? I'm fearing . . . " Because something will rise within the consciousness. You can look at it that way. Or, having the fear, you can say, "Now I am experiencing fear. Ah, yes! I am directing intelligent energy to my mind. Why am I doing that? My mind is a vehicle. It is not eternal. My mind came. It grows. It serves its purpose and it goes. For that that comes returns. That is the law." All of life reveals that to us.

But that which we are has always been. And because it has always been, it shall always be. And so it is not wise, nor is it healthy, to identify with what we *think* we are when we know very well that's in a constant process of change. And in this process of changing what we think we are, we experience fears and threats and all these different things we experience through our dependence, which is the effect of our denial, which is brought about by our over-identification with self. Does that help with your question?

Yes. Thank you. So would one still have to go back to the root of . . .

No. To remove fear from the consciousness one does not have to go into review at that moment, no. But in order to free oneself completely and to return to that which they are in truth, one must pass through all of the things that they have created that stand in the way, like clouds in front of the Light. Yes, they're *our* clouds. It is *our* will power directed to mental substance, which created force, through belief, that brought them into being. Therefore, they are ours. We have a responsibility to return them to the source from whence we have gathered them. For if we do not do our job, we do not complete it—we called them forth; we created them to serve a purpose. It's like the glass: it serves the purpose to contain liquid. *[The Teacher takes a sip of water from a glass.]*

Yes? That's fine. I know. *[The Teacher responds to a signal from the technician recording the class.]*

We created it, you see. And whatever we create, we are responsible for. We created it to serve a purpose. We don't just throw it out into the universe, for it will go out in the universe and ever return to us, because it knows its creator. As we know that creation is limit, that which is limited knows what created it. Therefore, any of those things created, the creator is responsible for. And you can't just throw them out in the cold, for they'll come back someday to be warmed up again.

Yes. Now we have, perhaps, a moment for one more question. Then it looks like our class is over. Time passes so quickly in this world. What is it, please? Yes.

This is a little different than what you were speaking about, but I've noticed that—

All my students are different. Thank you. Yes.

I'm sorry. But I've noticed that in my studies I seem to reach periods where the absorption of learning kind of stops for a while.

Yes, that's most understandable. It's—we notice that with all beings, whether they are four-legged or two-legged: the attention span is limited and controlled by the fickleness of the human mind, which is ever tempted by its weaknesses to a multitude of desires. I do hope that helps with your question.

Thank you very much. Good night.

MARCH 15, 1984

CONSCIOUSNESS CLASS 239

Looks like this is class number ten, which means next to the conclusion of this particular semester.

Now this evening's class is on the eternal search. It offers to all people freedom or frustration. That, of course, is dependent upon what we choose at any given moment to identify with. To identify, for our security, with knowledge, we guarantee the experiences of frustrations. To identify with wisdom, we then guarantee our freedom.

Now emotions are an expression of our own mental attachments. They are the unenlightened defenses of the human mind. For example, we find no need to defend with our energies and effort anything that our minds are not attached to. We do, however, find a great need to defend that which our minds have chosen to be attached to. That is what knowledge offers to us. It offers the need to defend. For when this eternal search registers in the human mind, the human mind ever seeks to know, for it believes what it knows it has the possibility of controlling.

And so when we place this great eternal path of ours into the human consciousness, we find many things that we place our security in. In a physical and material world, it is only natural for our minds to seek their security in material substance. And so when we permit our minds to decide that our security is threatened, we defend what we believe is threatened by our emotions. That is the path of knowledge.

The path of wisdom knows beyond a shadow of any doubt. For in the realms of knowledge, there can only be doubt. For our minds only know what our minds have been programmed to. Our minds are programmed to the beginning of things. Our minds, by the very nature and principle of their design of limit, know the ending of things. Therefore, whoever relies upon their mind for this eternal search, which is an evolutionary process, shall ever be frustrated and shall continue to suffer until such time as a choice is made within the consciousness to identify with that which cannot be controlled, which is beyond fear, beyond doubt, beyond need, and beyond denying.

The need to know is a frustrating experience for anyone who is over-identified with a mental world. For it offers to those who are over-identified a constant process of doubt. We have already experienced our reliance and dependence upon what our minds know and, in knowing, believe they can control. It has already proven to us to be a path of frustration and struggle.

And so it is not what we need to add to the mind; it is a matter of consciously choosing at any moment to free our self through the direction of our will power, the intelligent use of the power that flows through our consciousness, to choose at any moment the light of reason rather than the lesser light of knowledge, emotion, defense, doubt, fear. The greatest step that is made by any form in evolution is the step of awakening that you are not the thought. And because you are not the thought, you cannot possibly be the form. Until that step in consciousness is made, there is no freedom from the karmic wheel of cause and effect. For it is through the identification with limit that you experience the constant need in mental substance of the eternal search.

Security is indispensable to the abundant good, to the health and welfare of any form. Without harmony, there is no health. For many years I have taught that health is the effect of harmony. For many years we have taught the healing vibration of flowers. And yet, the question has not risen that flowers are the spirit of harmony. For many years we have taught the study of nature, for you are an inseparable part—your form—of nature. What affects nature is affecting you and what affects you is affecting nature.

It is a matter of returning to that which we have wandered from. And we are far from returning to that which we have wandered from when we permit, from lack of effort, from lack of control, we permit the unenlightened defenses of falsehood. And that is the expression of emotions to defend our mental attachments. When we permit ourselves to defend falsehood, we are not in a level of consciousness that is receptive to truth. When we rely upon what our minds can gather, we are far from secure. When we permit ourselves to feel good when our mental attachments are serving us and we permit ourselves to feel bad when our mental attachments are not serving us, then we are far from the truth.

It simply means we are not applying what we have already received. Now the Law of Receiving is in keeping with the demonstrable Law of Giving. Nature abhors a vacuum and will not tolerate an imbalance. Therefore, because we are an inseparable part—our form—of nature, it is our duty and our responsibility to maintain balance. The maintenance of balance is dependent upon the faculty of reason, and the faculty of reason is ever available to us at any moment of our choice.

When you pause to think, be conscious and be aware. Are you thinking or is there something within the consciousness that is thinking for you?

Look at all of nature. See its demonstrable efforts and successes in maintaining balance. Because it does not depend on a thought passing through a mental world, it does not experience what man knows as need and frustration.

As we continue on the path of freedom, many things will distract you. The many things are what you are passing through. And what you are passing through are the forms of the thoughts that you believe are you.

We have given a few classes here, recently, on the benefits and wisdom of faith rather than the bondage and the frustrations of belief. The multiplication of our beliefs is ever dependent upon the degree of our identification with the original belief called self.

You see, when, in our process of evolution and in our service to the Light that we are, when we entered the image, the image—that is what we unfortunately believe we are. You see, we look into a mirror, a reflector, and we believe that that is us. That is the original belief. That's where it all started. That original belief is an effect of over-identification. Whenever we permit our self to over-identify with any*thing*, that is, form, in that moment, in that moment we believe that we are it. And in that belief we lose what we are. And so we are going through this process of believing that we are so many different things. Consequently, we lose, for a time, we lose in our consciousness our conscious awareness. We believe and therefore we lose what we are.

We look at our life and see that we have believed this and then we believed that. We look at the course of one short day: we believe we feel good, only to believe we feel the opposite. We believe we are secure in that which we have, through our ignorance, depended upon for our security. We get a paycheck; it is in keeping with our judgments and, for that moment, we feel secure, only to move in the next moment to total frustration and insecurity, which, in turn, in time, will be the very instruments to free us from belief, that we may move and do the work that we have come to Earth to do.

For example, when you look at anything, you have, at the moment of your choice of viewing, you have, flowing through your being, the intelligent energy necessary for the evolving of whatever you view. That is a grave responsibility. And yet, we look at many things and we do not pause to serve the purpose of our being.

The human species is the most evolved animal species, known as human, on the Earth planet. Because it is the most evolved of the animal form, it has, by the very Law of Evolution, the greater responsibility to the forms of the planet on which it is expressing. You consume food and drink; yet, you do not pause that this intelligent power may flow unobstructed through your being that you may serve the purpose of *your* being, which is to be the instrument through which all creation shall evolve harmoniously.

The creatures upon your planet that you have responsibility for no longer are you in communion with. So few people on the planet communicate with the varied creatures that they are responsible for. Man is responsible to all forms of life. He is responsible by the very process of evolving through them. Those who have passed through anything in life establish the Law of Qualifying, for they have, through their efforts in evolution, successfully freed themselves from the bondage and the limit of the form through which they have evolved. Consequently, of course, they have established the Law of Qualifying.

I note that some of my students, during class—and we only have one class left for this semester—seem to be sleeping. I note that. I note that as I have noted it many times with great interest, for I find that the content, sometimes, of the class is not in keeping with that which some of my students have chosen to identify with. Therefore, it is not graciously accepted. Therefore, one who does not graciously accept what they receive uses many devices to free themselves from it. One of the many devices, that we learn early in life, is just like it is when we went to our schools: to close our eyes and go to sleep. That's fine if, in closing our eyes and going to sleep, we remained mentally in consciousness in the class. Then it would be, of course, extremely beneficial. But that, unfortunately, with some of my students, is not what happens.

The strongest desire that we are serving at any time becomes the vehicle of transporting our eternal being, known as our soul, to wherever it chooses to take us. It would indeed be frustrating for some of my students to have their automobile take them wherever it decided and they woke up where they didn't want to be. I say that to help those who have stated that they're unable to help themselves.

Now try to remember this, my good students: when you say that you are unable to help yourself, what you are really saying is that you believe that you are controlled by something beyond your ability to intelligently respond. That's far, far from the truth, for it denies the very basic principle of the Living Light philosophy: that basic principle being personal responsibility, the ability to personally respond to any experience that, by the law of like attracts like, you have called forth into your universe.

To some of you, I realize, over these past weeks, I may have seemed to have spoken a bit strong. But what is strong depends, of course, upon what *we* individually think. Strength is an expression of conscious choice of what is available to us at any moment of our choice. We are as strong as that upon which we depend and find our security. So we find that in many areas of our life, we are very strong, and in other areas of our life, we are very weak. So all we need to do, while we're in those realms of need, is choose wisely what we're depending on.

And so I'm going to give you a few moments here for your questions. And perhaps you might think a little more deeply about emotion, the defenses of that which anyone chooses to be mentally attached to at any moment. Emotions being defenses of mental attachments, the expression thereof, cannot demonstrably be truth. They are the opposite; they are falsehood. For truth needs no defense, for need does not exist in truth. Need only exists in falsehood. So when you tell yourself you need this and you need that and you need something else, pause in all the telling in your consciousness and declare the truth. Will you die if you don't have this and you don't have that? You have everything. Everything that is of good that you could possibly desire already is waiting for your acceptance. But it cannot enter your universe until you permit it to do so by following the path of wisdom, instead of relying upon the path of knowledge.

Now, one says, "Well, what is the path of wisdom?" The path of wisdom is self-evident. It is self-evident. We already know what knowledge, what knowing a thing has to offer. Oh, it is true, for a time it seems, for a time, that we control what we know something about. But it's only for a time. For there's always over the horizon a broader knowledge, a brighter light. There's always another mountain beyond the hill that we have just climbed. And beyond that mountain, there's another one.

And so in the realm of knowledge, there's always something to know to prove to us what we did know, no longer can we rely upon and feel secure, for there is, yea, a greater mountain of knowledge. And we're just beginning to view that one. So in knowledge, there's always doubt. And in doubt, there is always fear.

That's what belief in self has to offer—a constant process of surprises. To those whose senses have need for stimulation, rely upon knowledge; you will constantly be surprised, disappointed, frustrated, doubtful, and fearful.

Now it's time for your questions. And for those of you who don't know yet, after my many years of visiting with you, how to control a yawn: rather than embarrass yourself with yawns, simply swallow when you find the need and you won't have to sit and yawn. *[After a short pause, the Teacher continued.]* Well, I think that in these classes no question means no answer. Yes, the lady there, please.

Yes. When the spirit, when the spirit gives us forecast on weather conditions, is that subject to akashic records, just like those things with people?

Well, in reference—if you are referring to our annual forecast, we have said for over twelve, fourteen years now that we read from the Book of Cause and Effect. Now I think we have covered that many times. If you choose to call them akashic records, that's fine. That's a term used by other philosophies. But we have stated clearly many times that we do read from the Book of Cause and Effect.

You see, all things, mental, physical, are ever dependent upon what they, as forms, depend upon. Now dependence, of course, directs energy, for one cannot depend on what one does not place attention upon. And so as one places attention upon an object of their choice, they depend upon it. And depending on their identification with the object, they enter the realm of belief and become the victim of the object of their choice. For example, you depend upon a job for your livelihood and you dictate what the job is, the next thing you know, you believe that that is your security. And in keeping with your belief, it is your security for a time. It offers bondage, frustration, disappointments, and fear and doubt and everything that that realm of consciousness offers to anyone. Does that help with your question?

Yes, the gentleman has a question, please. Yes.

I would like for you to speak more on emotions in so far as the conscious, I guess, the conscious recognition of how they reveal themselves in different parts of our anatomy. And in so far as if you're trying to work on a law or something that is happening—you are trying, I guess, to control creation or say an affirmation and you have an emotional reaction. It must be emotional because it happens in a certain part of your anatomy. And you don't know what it is—of emotions.

Yes, well, in reference to your seven questions there, I'll try to take them point by point.

One, you are asking for the location of emotion. I have already given in these classes that the stomach is the seat of the affections.

Now pause for a few moments and think. We defend to the degree and extent we believe necessary that which we attach our self to by believing that we are that which we have identified with. Now if you place your attention upon what you judge is right or wrong and you permit yourself to over-identify with it, you enter the realm of consciousness where you firmly believe it. Now that belief exists within your consciousness. Whenever your mind alerts you that your belief on what is right or wrong is being threatened from without, then what you call emotion rises as a defense of that which you believe you are. Now you are not what you believe is right or wrong, for if you were what you believe is right or wrong, you would have annihilated yourself many times over in just a few short years. For what we believe is right or wrong is in a constant process of changing.

Therefore, unless we grant our self the opportunity for the lion's strength—the pause to think—then we are controlled by the realm of knowledge and we are frustrated and bound. We are not freed—*[The Teacher sneezes.]*—excuse me—we are not freed by the light of reason. These emotions have, these defense mechanisms have a most detrimental effect upon the physical and mental body. And because they have such a detrimental effect upon the physical and mental body, they create a discord, which is contrary to the Law of Harmony, which is the Law of Health.

Now, say, for example—and we have given this to you also—the coating or covering of your form, this flesh, the skin, represents the sensitivity of your universe. That's what skin represents. It's the covering; it is that which registers. It is the first registration. The sense of touch is the original sense. Now—and so the skin, which represents and is used by the sensation known as touch, is very evolved and highly sensitive.

When, for example, that which you are greatly attached to and really believe you are, your mind says is threatened, then you will experience problems with your sensitivity, and emotions will rise to defend and to protect that which you believe you are. That is the nature, the design, and the purpose of the human mind: to preserve and to protect. So through a belief that you are the form in which you are presently expressing, you have these many different experiences with your health until such time as you pause and awaken that your form is not you.

And when you truly awaken, you will not only see clearly that your form is not you, but you will see clearly that your thought is not you; that your emotion is not you; that you are that which uses your body. You are that which, in truth, is designed to use your mind and not be used by it.

The problem created by an over-identification with the image, the original image, is that we believe the limit, for the limit is all the mind knows. Now that which by its very nature is limited can only experience limit. So as long as we insist on believing that we are the limit, then limit is all we can justly expect. It is when you believe that you are the emotion, which by the nature of the human mind is defending that which you are mentally attached to, then the price is extracted.

But look at life: one time you're mentally attached to this, only at another time to be mentally attached to something else. And this process is taking place all of the time. You don't have to go through this illusion known as years and centuries to awaken. You have earned the opportunity in evolution to awaken this very moment and any moment of your conscious choice.

And so when, through laws you establish, you have the return of experiences that you don't like, pause and learn to cast the light of reason upon belief. Until a person is willing to consciously communicate with themselves, until they're ready to make that step, they cannot separate truth from creation. You see, if you sit down when you feel the sensation known as emotion, if you pause in that moment and you start to talk with what you think you feel, you will, slowly but surely, gain objectivity by entering the faculty of reason, which will transfigure you. Now that's where the line is drawn to separate truth from creation.

However, if you are not ready to make that effort to communicate, that simply reveals that you are still at a stage of evolution believing that that feeling, emotion, and experience is you. And you must continue to pay the price until you're ready, through communication within your own being, to separate truth from creation. Does that answer your seven questions?

Yes, sir.

You're welcome. The lady over there had a question, please. Yes.

Are there positive expressions of emotion?

Are there positive expressions? That is an excellent question. And I have an answer through my question to you. Are there positive, and therefore guaranteeing the opposite, known as negative, expressions of truth? [That] is my question to you.

Well, truth just is.

Thank you very much. Therefore, that which you are just is. Then one must ask oneself the question, "What am I interested or concerned with, emotion, positive or negative? That is not me. That is what my mind uses to defend that which I am attached to, but that is not me."

You see—I'm so happy that you brought up the question. Because, you see, the question reveals, you see, the question reveals clearly and demonstrably that that which desires emotion to have a positive side is that which we believe—those emotions—which we believe we still are. But we are not the emotions! They are creation. They are something that is created. Of course, there are positive emotions; of course, there are negative emotions. But that is not what you are. But as long as you believe that is what you are, then you will have to defend them. Do you understand?

Yes, I do.

Because, you see, it is falsehood, belief, that requires defense, not truth. Truth needs no defense. Only falsehood must be defended. But a wise person does not choose to believe and suffer the payment of falsehood when truth is constantly available.

Thank you.

And it should be of great interest to you that fear, of course, we know is faith in the human mind. But fear, you see, the emotions, the defenses of mental attachments in consciousness, are afraid. What are these things afraid of? What are they? That's the question we must ask our self.

First of all, stop believing that you are them. When that happens, you understand, then you can choose consciously whether or not you will direct any sustenance to them through attention. A conscious choice—not their choices—your choice, you see. It's a child that has been created by the human mind. That's what it is. The mental attachment is something that the human mind has created. And it is the human mind that uses the senses, what you call emotion, to protect that which it is attached to. It cannot be truth.

It fears, however. All thoughts fear. For all thoughts are form created by mental substance, which offers to them the very ingredients of knowledge, doubt, fear, control, and this eternal quest of security.

So one simply takes a look at the path and they say, "I really believed that was me a year or so ago. I really did believe that that was me a month ago." And, of course, while they believed it, of course, it was them, for they made it so. Belief makes it so. So when you have an emotional outburst, you feel the experience in keeping with your belief that that is you. But you only believe it for a time, because it is governed by this great illusion known as time.

The only man that fears death is the one who fears birth. And the one who fears birth is the one who believes life and does not demonstrate it. There's a great difference between a demonstration and a belief. The demonstration of life is the freedom from the bondage of belief! If the lily of the valley believed it was only a lily, if the lily of the valley could look and compare and see the giant sequoia, then the lily would not be happy anymore. That's our problem, my good friends: we know too much!

Anyone else have a question? The gentleman over there, please. I know.

When we become aware of a pattern that was established in early childhood, how can we enter memory par excellence to confront that pattern?

It is not necessary to confront that which has been unless, through lack of effort, we permit that which has been to control that which is. Now it's quite a simple thing. That which has been exists within consciousness. When we pause, we are aware of its existence in consciousness. Is that not correct?

Yes.

When we pause. So when we don't pause, it happens. Is that correct?

Yes.

Fine. So what does wisdom reveal? That we pause more often. Correct?

Correct.

So when we pause, we are aware. When we are aware, then we make an intelligent, conscious decision and we choose not to serve it if we do not wish to serve it. Is that not correct?

That's correct.

Then there is no problem, is there?

There is no problem.

You see, one is a slow painful process and another is taking control over one's being and choosing wisely what they will do at any given moment.

You see, when you stop believing you are the emotion that rises to defend that which you are attached to, when you stop believing, it will stop controlling you. Destiny is not at our command, not until we enter the light of reason. Destiny is at the command of that which we believe we are at any given moment. And if you believe you are the emotions, if you believe your security is dependent upon a piece of paper, anytime you believe that, the piece of paper is in command. You have given freely this great being that you are to a form that you, for a moment, believe that you are. [Has] that helped with your question?

Yes. Thank you.

Now, see, what the mind says—I know a little bit how the mind works—it says, "Well, when I don't have this piece of paper, I feel terrible because everything goes kaput." My good friends, as long as you believe it, so be it, for that is the law. That is—man is a law unto himself. Then a wise man pauses and he says, "It is demonstrably true that I am a law unto myself. What am I doing with the law that I am?"

The law has no emotion. Why does the law have no emotion? For the law, a servant of truth, just is. There's nothing to defend in the laws of God. They just are. The laws of God, the movement of goodness, just is. There's nothing to defend. Only falsehood can you defend. And so you are a law unto yourself. Choose wisely and do with the law, consciously, what it is designed for you to do with it. I hope that's helped with your question.

The lady here has a question, please.

What is acceptance? How does it work and how can we be more accepting?

Well, first of all, the question—How can a person be more accepting?—is demonstrable: how can one be more accepting is by being more godly. Now nothing in the universes is denied their sustenance. Life demonstrates that sustenance is something beyond the control of our thought, for even our thought is sustained by that sustenance. Therefore, we see that demonstration around us constantly, everywhere. And it reveals to us the will of goodness or God. So man wishes to be more accepting, then man must be more godly. And to be more godly, one must take control of that that one believes that they are that stands in the way of the goodness that they truly are: that's controlling our thoughts and not permitting our thoughts to dictate that we are them. Does that help with your question?

Yes, sir.

Because, you see, the flower, God does not leave out, nor the human nor the animal nor the ant that crawls the ground. It is all sustained, you see, impartially. Think: nothing is left out. Nothing in the universe is judged to be unworthy. Not even a thought that you permit within your consciousness that denies the right, even that denial is sustained by the power of goodness, by the light of God. Think of that. The law established by the mind of man, that returns. And that's known to man as a bad experience. His denial goes out into the universe and returns as a bad experience to his mind. Do you understand?

Yes.

Yet, man denies because he believes. He believes he's the limit and therefore his search for security keeps him on the path of a constant frustration because he believes. And he changes his beliefs constantly, constantly.

So if one truly desires the goodness of life, then one makes the effort to be, just be what the demonstration of goodness is: the denial of nothing, the acceptance of everything. For it is not possible to deny until we judge, and it is not possible to judge until we compare. And it is not possible to compare until we depend. And it is not possible to depend when we be the truth that we are.

Yes, is there someone else that has a question now? I thought for sure there'd be questions on why some of my students sleep in class. *[The Teacher pauses for a moment, then continues.]* No one? Yes, yes, the time is getting close. *[The Teacher addresses the audio technician who is recording the class.]* Who knows, we may go longer; we may go shorter. Yes.

When I first learned to meditate, I was taught to meditate sitting on the floor, cross-legged. Is that not—and then I heard that we're supposed to, in this philosophy, sit in a chair.

That is correct.

Straight backed.

Yes, we have evolved. You see, people are taught ever in keeping with what someone else taught them. Well, here we have this philosophy in this school and someone else has a different philosophy, a different school. And we have reasons why we have instructed our students to sit properly and keep the spine erect and not to ground their electromagnetic fields from crossing. Yes, we have demonstrations of the just reason and benefit of the way that we teach. However, we do not have any compulsorily regulations governing such things.

And one believes many different things and receives, of course, temporal benefits therefrom. The goodness that is available, as I've said so many times, is ever subject to what control one makes sincerely with the obstructions that are standing in the way.

I say if you insist and must believe, in keeping with overidentification with the illusion, what some philosophies call maya, if you insist that you must believe, then choose something beneficial. If your days must be spent in believing in your various stages of evolution, then let the laws of belief serve you well and stop serving them. See, a person believes if someone does this and someone doesn't do that, then they will feel certain ways. Pause and think. There are many things you can believe that aren't dependent on what someone else does. And when you consciously choose what you're going to believe for the moment or the day, then simply stick to it, if that's what you want.

I'm trying to help you and guide you and show you there's something greater than that realm. I mean, a person can believe in a new car and establish the law. At what cost? That remains to be seen. You see, these things in realms of belief—they have payment and attainment. All of them. They are creation. They are two-sided, for the law is dual.

I'm trying to help you to help yourself to move from either side to the divine edge. For the divine edge, though, is very narrow, it is the path on which freedom casts the light of goodness on the eternal journey. But it is a narrow edge and it requires a single eye—you see?—a single eye. That means you do not look to the left and you do not look to the right. You do not interest nor concern yourself with positive emotions, for you guarantee negative emotions, for you have moved beyond that in evolution to the divine edge. You are not interested in right, for you are not interested in wrong. For nothing's either right or wrong, but thinking makes it so. *Thinking*, thinking makes it so. If you believe you are the thought you think, then you guarantee the doubt and the fear, then you guarantee the experience. If you believe that money will bring you happiness, you guarantee happiness for a time, unhappiness for who knows how long. For those are the realms. That's what creation offers. Left side or right side, that's what it offers.

If the goodness that you seek contains dependence, then you are bound, for dependence reveals the lack of security. And that's what knowledge offers. It offers the constant frustration. To rise is only to fall. To have is only to lose. To get is only to give. Ofttimes in the getting, we do not have the choice of what is given. Ofttimes the giving in life, the Law of Giving, takes place without our gracious acceptance. So whatever we seek, we must remember, oh, we shall find. But shall it be a dead end? And if so, how many dead ends do we want to go to, when there's something far greater than all of that?

As I've said, to forget is very human. Ah, to forgive, that's divine. Now I know that I have said to forgive is human and to forget is divine. But I want you, when you listen to this class, to review that several times and see its application in the content of the class in which I am giving. I have, over these many years, always enjoyed my students who, after hearing class, have reminded me that I made a mistake. For it is always a wonderful doorway of opportunity for further enlightenment for myself. If one cannot learn from a student, then one is not qualified to be a teacher.

Do you have any other question?

I don't know how to put it.

Well, I won't tell you how to meditate.

Right. So uncrossing the legs keeps the electric field free or . . .

You might study basic electricity and I'm sure it will benefit you. If you don't have time to study, I'm sure that you could ask someone who will help you with that.

All right. All right.

You see, truth needs no defense and I'm not about to defend the type of meditation that I have given for so many years, my dear.

I just wanted to understand it, that's all.

Well, one cannot understand anything until they pause and are willing to first think. "This is what they offer here. That's what they offered over there. Now which philosophy do I want to be in or do I want to straddle both?" That's the question, wouldn't you say?

Yes.

Now one who rides two horses never reaches his destination in life, wouldn't you agree?

Yes.

Well, let one horse go; make a choice and you'll get right to your goal.

I understand.

Oh, my, yes. I know that you do. I know that you do. That's what that's all about. Yes. No problem. Well, considering I've gone overtime, I might as well stay around for awhile. *[Many students laugh.]* Yes, the gentleman here, please.

Yes, in the beginning when you're trying to introduce a change, such as, talking to your—making a conscious effort to communicate with one's consciousness and you have—

Well, let us, let us be a little more specific: a conscious effort to communicate with the different forms that one has created from intelligence (essence) and placed in their consciousness. Because, you know, we are the ones who place them there. Why, I wouldn't want you to think or dream for a moment that somebody else put them in there. Yes, go ahead.

Would you recommend to us an example, I guess, would be the best word, in trying to do that communicating?

Oh, most happily! I would be more than happy to do so, especially for you, a young married man with a family and everything. Well, now the first thing is, of course, a conscious awareness.

And, now I would say if a man was married and had a wife and the wife said that you refused to communicate with her, that would be my first step on making some effort. I would say, "Now let's see, this is my wife. She says I don't communicate with her. Now I want her to tell me exactly her view of where I don't communicate so I can, possibly, make some intelligent choices in my life to make some effort to communicate." You see, one who does not communicate with himself is far from being qualified to communicate with another. So you are a very fortunate young man that you have a wife who has, on more than one occasion, registered an official complaint that you don't communicate. Does that help with your question?

Fine.

Good. I'm sure you'll make some effort from now on. Could one have a better merit system than a wife who is revealing the truth about a husband's lack of communication with himself? *[After a short pause, the Teacher continues.]* Pardon?

No, sir. I may not communicate with her, but—

Well, of course not. One does not communicate with another if one does not make the effort to communicate with oneself.

Yes.

For they have not qualified themselves.

So I should talk to her first?

Oh, no, you can't possibly talk to her until you first talk to yourself.

Well, that's what—that's what I was asking. I always had the judgment that talking to myself is silly or ridiculous.

Why, of course, because to do so, you're bound to separate, in time, truth from creation. And when you do that, you're going to find out who you really are, not who you thought you were. That's most understandable.

OK.

Do you believe you're the foot—your foot?

No, I don't believe I'm my foot.

Do you believe you're your finger?

No, I don't believe I'm my finger.

Do you believe you're your head?

No, I don't believe that either.

I see. Do you believe you are the name that you are?

No, I don't believe I am the name I have.

Do you believe you are the emotions that you freely express at times?

No, I don't.

If you do not believe you are the emotions, do you believe when you express those emotions that the experiences you encounter after the expression are joyous and beneficial to you?

They have joys and they are beneficial . . .

All times?

All times?

Yes. At all times?

I feel that they would be more joyous and beneficial if I adhered to them or apply them, but—

When you get angry and upset, do you believe that is you?

When I get angry and upset, most of the time I'm not even conscious of it.

You're not conscious of it. That's most interesting. Now if a person expresses anger and emotional upset and they are not aware of it, what, in those moments, would one be aware of?

Probably has-beens. Probably identifying with some, some of these forms.

I see. Well, if one so believes something—and that is how our minds can work. We can so believe something that we're not even aware of what is happening because our belief is so solidified in being what we think we are. And that's where all our problems are, whether or not it's the lack of communication or it's a dollar bill.

Now I like to work with things that I find with my students have high priority. I find money, ego, and sex have very high priority in a world of creation. Don't you?

Yes.

Well, if I do not communicate on that which has high priority with my students, then I cannot establish an intelligent rapport. Could I?

No, you couldn't.

So, what do you think? Which function do you believe is necessary for you? Which one causes you the most problems?

I, I feel money causes me the most problems.

Very good. Very good. It's number one on the list—causes you the most problems. Why do you think money causes you the most problems?

Because I direct so much energy to the lack of it.

Knowing the law, why do you place so much attention on the lack of it? Knowing the law, why don't you place your attention on the abundance of it? Why choose to place your attention upon the lack of something when you can consciously choose to place your attention upon the abundance of it?

It takes effort and it takes continuity.

Are you telling me that it takes less effort and it takes less continuity to think about the lack of something than it does the abundance of it? Is that what you're telling me?

No, sir, I'm not. But if I am, I know better.

Well, you did tell me that it takes less effort. And I just simply asked you, Do you mean to tell me that it takes less effort to think about the lack of something than it does to think about the abundance of something? Now just stop and think. Because it's either money, ego, or sex. And this money-sex thing is totally dependent upon what is known as the human ego, the uneducated part of it. Now think about that.

Now, a person [is] controlled by their belief that they are the thoughts that are in their consciousness—you hear?

Yes.

And the thoughts that are in the consciousness, dependent upon intelligent energy, that is, the continuity of its flow for their existence, rise up within the consciousness to be fed. They are fed through your direction of attention to them. And the energy flows and they continue to grow and to flourish, just like a blade of grass.

So, if in your life you have created forms of the lack of sustenance, as you're saying, you're discussing money, and you have created forms of the lack of money, and they feed on that energy and they grow stronger and stronger, and you keep placing attention on the lack of money and they grow stronger and fatter and bigger and then, changes take place in your life and you start to experience a little trickle, a little flow of money. And you place more attention upon that flow and that trickle of money and more money comes! And you place more attention—through the Law of Gratitude, you know, when we're grateful for the crumb, we guarantee the loaf. You see, it's like the crumb of the lack of money. You put a little attention on there and you keep your attention, which is the flow of your energy, on that and it starts to get bigger and bigger and bigger and bigger and bigger.

Now, as I was saying, they got all nice and fat. They're just as happy as can be: absolute total lack of money. They've now just had a feast! And they're all laying down taking a nap. And while they're taking a nap, you're moving around in creation and over here you start to get a little trickle of money. You keep your attention going on that little trickle there and the trickle soon becomes, from those crumbs, a loaf! The next thing you know, the loaf gets bigger and bigger and bigger.

Then, all of a sudden, those money-lack entities wake up from their nap. And they're starved! They rush into your consciousness and the next thing you know, they tell you, you have very little money. And they keep telling you that until they tell you, you have no money. And you keep placing your attention on them and the next thing you know, you *believe* you have no money. And the more you believe that you have no money, the more you prove to yourself how right you are until you have no money at all! Because you alone establish those laws from the lack of conscious effort, where the faculty of reason and the Light flows. Do you understand that?

Yes, sir.

Now, is that the way you want to live? Now if you have established this in your life—the flux and the flow, the skinny ones and the fat ones, the fat ones and the skinny ones, and back and forth and back and forth—and if you believe that that is you, it's a rather exhausting evolution. Rather exhausting. There's—you miss the beauty. You cannot enjoy the flower. You cannot look and contemplate the architectural design—how beautiful it is. You see, you miss all of that, for the only thing you can see are pieces of paper, you see. They don't have any feelings. They don't have any life. They've got some ink, yes. And they're just plain made of wood; it's paper. But is that life? Is that life?

And if you believe what those things you've created over here tell you—that if you don't have this and you don't have that, you're going to have this pain and that pain and all this other stuff, and as long as you believe that, you've got a wasted life ahead. Is it worth it? Is that really what you want?

It's not what I want.

Then you have no problem. You have no problem whatsoever. Because if it's not what you want—and try to remember this: we always get what we really want. No matter what anyone says to us, we always get in life what we really want. The only problem is when it comes around we want something else. But we always get what we really want. I have yet to meet a person in all of the universes that does not get what they really want. Now a lot of them and in a lot of those places, they swear on *anything* that they didn't want what they got. But they just forgot, temporarily, when they did want it, you see.

We want many things, and many things is what we get. The thing that we—we always get what we really want, but in our wanting, we're not honest and we don't even consider what it's going to cost. So when the cost comes due, you see, you've got to pay the bill. When that comes due, you swear up and down you never wanted that. No! You only wanted what is there for your desire. But you never considered that's going to cost, you see. That's the thing in life: we don't consider the cost. We only consider the fulfillment of the desire, you see.

It's like going to the store. You see a coat; you want it. Do you walk in and take it? That would be wonderful! But someone else is going to take you if you try that! So, you see a coat—that's what you want. Do you not look at the price tag? All creation is a price tag. Your thoughts are creation. Each one has a price tag. They require so much energy. That's their price. Take a look and see how much they require. Shop intelligently in the playpen of creation, for everything has a price tag.

Thank you. Our class is concluded till next week.

MARCH 22, 1984

CONSCIOUSNESS CLASS 240

Good evening, class. This is our final class and tonight's class shall be "The Fullness of Life, The Joy of Living."

Whoever seeks pleasure shall ever find pain. For pleasure and pain, like birth and death, are the movement of mental substance formed by belief and solidified in the consciousness by your dependence upon it. For you are, in truth, the I of eternity, the eternal I. It is when you permit yourself to believe that you identify that you temporarily place the cloud of illusion over your view. This process is known as a denting or i-dent—identifying. The cloud of illusion, that which you, by eternal spiritual design, are to view and, in so viewing, to guide and, in so guiding, to control, has been revealed throughout all ages. It has been repeatedly stated that you have been given charge over all creation. And whoever in evolution has earned the responsibility of charge over all creation must place their duty to their eternal responsibility above and beyond all else.

And so you view many things and in the viewing, you lose the truth that you are, temporarily, through believing that you are what you view. Now we may liken that in your world to going to a movie. You see and you understand there are actors that are playing parts. They are not reality. They are not truth. They are playing on a stage. You know beyond a shadow of any doubt that they are simply acting. You know that the story is fabricated from mental substance. You know that it is a fantasy. You know, in truth, that it is an illusion. And so it is with your daily thinking. From your efforts of some time in believing that what you see, that what you hear, that what you sense, and what you feel is what you are, you establish the Law of Denial of what you are and you become what you believe and, from that process, depend upon that which is pleasure and guarantee pain. That which is conceived is that destined to deceive.

So it is in this our final class of this semester that you have earned in evolution the opportunity to separate that which you are from that which you believe you are, for belief is something that comes and goes. It is a great force in the universe. It is the king of all creation. Without belief, the curtain of illusion would not exist. It is the indispensable ingredient of form and it offers to anyone who, through error of ignorance, denies what they are to believe what they see. That, in turn, is known as the karmic wheel of cause and effect.

And as long as you permit within your consciousness what is known as need, which is the effect of belief—one of the many effects, for belief, as I said, forms from the illusion, and dependence solidifies the form within your consciousness. And whatever man depends upon, man must pay the price, for the very nature of what illusion is: a coming and a going, a beginning and an ending.

And so you experience the force of emotions, the moving of mental substance, and you experience the so-called struggles of life, when life is a joyous experience to those who make the conscious effort to stop the process known as illusion. To stop the process of illusion, one must first make the conscious effort to control the illusion. To control the illusion, which is movement of mental substance, one must first still the vehicle through which mental substance is able to move. And that, as I have taught you in years past on your Earth, is a stilling of your mind. And so at this stage in your evolution this effort must be made before you can free yourself from the illusion that you temporally believe that you are.

You have, in the course of a day, a limitless number of opportunities to free yourself from this illusion in order that you may truly serve the purpose for which you have entered the earth realm. Those opportunities come to you in your various works and duties in your association with people and things. And so the curtain of illusion, you are ever viewing and therefore you are never without an opportunity to declare the truth and, in the declaration, take control of the vehicle through which the illusion is made possible.

When you feel an extremely strong emotion, that indeed is a golden opportunity whether the emotion records within your consciousness through your belief—which is the forming and your dependence, the solidification of—whether it brings you pleasure or it brings you pain. When you truly no longer are aware of a difference between pleasure and pain, then you are freed from the illusion and you shall not know birth nor death. You are, by your own evolution, greater than that which, through error, you have permitted yourself to become.

The application of anything is ever in keeping: when the illusion that is being served no longer serves you in the way that it brought you so much pleasure that it now brings you so much pain, there is a neutralization that begins to take place within your consciousness. For that which has been formed as pleasure forms, when they no longer serve, there are the pain forms. And they are contradictory or in discord with each other. So what takes place within the consciousness to one who has identified and, through that identification, clouded the eternal I that they are, what takes place is known as the war of the emotions. When the war is over, the soul, in that moment, in that experience, is freed. And the experience of the freeing of a soul is a joyous experience. That *is* the fullness of life. That *is* the joy of living. For the illusion called creation, that goes, for it comes. It is not reliable. It will always bring what is called temptation.

We are tempted by pleasure; we are not tempted by pain. Yet, pain and pleasure, in truth, servants of illusion, do identically the same thing to what is known as the senses. Both pleasure and pain stimulate the senses. The stimulation of the senses is a movement of mental substance. And so it is only in the judgments that we depend upon that we discern that a pleasure is an experience that we seek and a pain is one that we fear ever experiencing. Those judgments, those forms exist within your consciousness. And whenever you believe, you are limited to that which is already existing in your consciousness. And so this is the step in evolution that you, as students, all have the opportunity to make. If you feel you are not ready, be rest assured, pain, like pleasure, shall continue to have you work for it. For that *is* limit, that *is* creation, that *is* form, that *is* birth, and that *is* death.

Now I'm going to give you a few moments for your questions. And to those students who have been with me so many minutes—for in the universal clock, some of you have been with me ten minutes, some twelve minutes, some two minutes, some four minutes, some six minutes. For your Earth year is equal to, on the universal clock, one minute. And so it's time now for your questions on this our final class of this semester. *[After a short pause, the Teacher continues.]* We have no questions; we can have a short class. Yes.

Yes. In light of this class tonight, could you please discuss how this relates with what was said in an earlier class about our responsibility to monitor our thoughts that they are really serving the purpose for which they are intended?

Indeed. We are filled with good intentions: intent in our consciousness to experience goodness. We seek to experience goodness for we know we have denied it. And because we have denied it—we deny what we are, the goodness that we are—we have created blemishes on the purity of the Light that we are, for we are the I of eternity. Because we know deep within our consciousness that we have permitted our self to believe that we are what we view, because of that, we seek to, once again, experience what we truly are. And so we seek goodness. We seek what the illusion permits us to call goodness, because what we call goodness is dependent upon our experience.

Think of this, now. As long as you believe that you *are* and what you *are* can be defined, as long as you believe that you are that, then you are controlled by the illusion, for that is what the illusion offers. And so because we believe that we are limit, because we believe we are a body, which is form, which is limit, because we believe that, when we seek goodness, that is dependent upon experiences that we have already had. What we really mean to say, in truth, is that we seek pleasure for we have experienced enough pain. Do you understand?

Now this philosophy is an evolving, broadening horizon. And you move in consciousness slowly but surely. No one awakens from a sound sleep, the total victim of this illusion called creation, no one awakens joyous, for they awaken with the belief of the moment that they are awakening. Do you understand?

And so in reference to good thoughts, good, of course, we understand is God, the Light; that's what we are. Now we have recorded within the illusion, within mental substance, certain guidelines. And in recording those guidelines or teachings, we have, in the illusion, established certain judgments, which, through our identity, we *believe* is goodness for us. And because we believe it and because the philosophy is guiding ever a return to that which we already are, then, of course, it is beneficial as stepping stones to the truth that we are. You see, no one can give you what you are: you are truth. The only thing that any teaching can do is to offer to you a path: guidelines to return to what you are. It cannot give you what you are because you are already that, but it can certainly guide you to return to what you are. Does that help with your questions on good thoughts?

The lady—yes, the lady there, please.

So would it be best not to seek goodness?

That is not what I just said to the student here when I answered his question. I do feel when you listen to the recorded, magnetic tape that you will have a much clearer understanding. I did not say that at all. But I do see that it does require another listening. So you be sure and listen to that when you hear your recording of your class.

Yes, the lady here, please.

Could you please explain the purpose of the universal clock?

Well, the purpose of the universal clock, that moves what you might think, of course, much slower than the clock that you have identified with—it is a universal clock and it is the monitoring of the illusion of a particular universe. For, you see, all universes, like all people, like all things, are illusions. And illusion offers, through movement, stimulation, which you call pleasure or pain. Does that help with your question? Yes.

And also, what governs the speed of this so-called time?

The movement of the illusion. In other words, in perspective, the universal clock, the movement of the illusion, the movement of mental substance, known as illusion, moves much slower than it does on your particular Earth planet. But try to remember you are only one planet of many in a universe. And therefore it is understandable: an individual moves faster than a mass.

Thank you.

Yes. Yes, the lady back there, please.

Could you—this isn't really in line with what you've been speaking of, but could you give a definition of friendship?

I gave a definition of friendship long ago, but I will, once again, restate it. True friendship—I see that's what you're asking about is true friendship.

Yes.

True friendship, being use and not abuse, respects the rights of difference and will weather any storm.

Yes, you're welcome. *[After a short pause, one of the students sighs and the Teacher continues.]* Is that a question?

No, sir.

It is?

No, sir.

I see. Well, there are two things I find in class: questions and statements. So if it's not a question, it had to be a statement. *[Some students laugh.]*

Yes, the lady there, please.

If you haven't already completely covered it, could you speak further on the difference pleasure and good?

Well, in reference to pleasure and good, you see, pleasure is dependent. Would you not agree with that?

Yes.

Goodness, being God, has no dependence, for goodness, God, Truth just *is*. Because it just is, there is no dependence, you see.

Now, pleasure is not something that just is. Pleasure is dependent; creation is dependent; thought is dependent. Whatever is dependent is not truth. It is illusion. That which is truth *is*.

There's no dependence. You see, whatever is dependent denies, and it is the denial that is inseparable from the dependence.

You see, you are truth. When you permit yourself to depend, then you deny that which you are. And from your denial of that which you are you establish your destiny. And so, you are truth. You permit yourself to depend on pleasure, then in that moment, you are no longer truth. And therefore, by denying what you are, you experience pleasure and depend upon it and guarantee its opposite, called pain. Your belief is what does that. No law but the law of those who, through a clouding of the I of eternity which they are (by believing that they are what they view), become dependent and experience the pain and pleasure, the struggle and strife of life—when you are the joy of life, when you are fullness of life. But no one can bring about that evolution within your consciousness. Only you, with your own light, the truth which you are, can free yourself from the lesser light.

Belief offers the lesser light, for it is the forming of illusion. Truth is the Light which you are. And so when you permit yourself to tarry too long in this great infinity, when you permit yourself to be tempted, that's when you establish the laws, believing that you are what you're viewing. Just like I stated earlier, like you view a movie. And the longer you view it, the greater your chances of believing that you are what you view because, you see, you are tempted.

Say, for example, you go to a movie and you see a young lady that you would like to be like. She seems to have everything and your mind seeks everything. So you are viewing the movie of a person who is playing out that part which you have permitted your mind in its evolution and temptations to believe that is what you want. Well, before you know it, you believe that you are what you are viewing. When that happens, you identify. And in that process, you cast a blemish, the cloud of illusion, over the eternal truth which you are, that I of eternity, and the purity, the Light, that wonderful purity, you lose that temporarily. It's a temporary loss. It is a temporary loss because that is the nature of illusion.

Therefore, it takes a person still tempted by the lesser light of illusion, it takes a person tempted by the lesser light to believe that they are the lesser light. Does that help with your question?

I think that there's a matter of semantics. People say, "I feel good." Now, are they saying, actually "I feel pleasure," rather than good when they make that statement?

Well, when you say that "I feel good," are you speaking an illusion, which is dependent, or are you stating truth, which you are?

Now if you say "I feel good," you are dependent on that which is causing you to have that experience. If you say you are good, then you are! Because that's what you are: the I of eternity. You *are* the truth. It has nothing to do with dependence. But, you see, you often find people say, "I feel good." Well, as you're working with that state of evolution, that's far preferable than hearing them say, "I feel bad." Wouldn't you agree?

Yes.

Now we all seek to hear how good everyone feels, for we seek to feel good. Do you understand that?

Yes.

Now we seek to feel good because we have already denied the goodness that we are. That's why we seek it. And because we do seek it, when we hear someone say "I feel good," there is a moment there, just a moment, that we feel that goodness they feel. Just an instant. It doesn't last, because, all of a sudden, we deny our right to feel that goodness. And we say, "What right have they to feel so good and I feel terrible?" Do you understand that? So it only lasts—we only permit it to last for a split second within our consciousness because then all of these defenses rise up, called envy, jealousy, greed, etc., etc., and the whole panorama of this curtain of illusion.

So you *are* good. That is what you are. You feel good because you believe you're something else. And what you believe that you are, that curtain of illusion, it has its cause and effects. You understand? But remember, it's dependent. You see, the illusion is designed to be dependent upon you, for without *you*, it does not exist. Without you, the illusion doesn't exist.

Now you are that which, through your evolution, has charge over the illusion. It is your purpose and your design to guide it, to control it. That is your destiny. That is your purpose in evolution. However, because you have forgotten your duty, your eternal duty, and you've gone to the movie house and you believe that you are what you're viewing, your purpose, your true purpose is not being served. But that's only temporary, for the movies come and the movies go. Just like thoughts, they come and they go, in keeping with our denial, which is absolutely necessary for our experience of need. The more denial, the more need.

Now one who over-identifies with the limited form known as self has much more denial than one who is not so over-identified with the little, limited form known as self. Does that help with your question?

Yes.

So the greater the self-identification, the greater the experience within the consciousness of need, for it is equal to the denial of truth which you are.

Yes. You have a question there.

As we raise our rate of vibration in our consciousness, do we also increase the speed, the rate?

Yes, let me follow you here. You are speaking in reference to the illusion, the movement of mental substance?

I'm trying to understand the correlation between raising our rate of vibration—

Then please—Thank you.

—becoming first in our consciousness.

Yes, then please explain your understanding of raising your rate of vibration.

Like a higher level of consciousness, to get out of self, more universal in our consciousness.

Well, now, thank you. A higher level of consciousness is ever equal to and subject, of course, to one's efforts of freeing themselves from the over-identification with the self, you see.

Yes.

And so as a person, through their efforts, spends less time in believing the forms that they view, then, of course, there is less identification with the form, or limit, of self, you see. And through that process, the rate of vibration of the person, the I of eternity, which they are, in that respect, is indeed a much higher—of course, it is *the* rate of vibration and in reference to what you were referring to as speed is a very high speed.

Now I see what you want in this correlation here. The higher the speed of an object, the more stationary it appears in the veil of illusion. Does that help with your question?

Thank you.

Yes. And remember, that which so many people believe that they are is not what they are at all.

Thank you.

Never was and never can be. Yes, the lady there, please.

Does the Law of Expansion and Contraction that runs the universe, is it correlated with the universal clock?

Yes, indeed it is.

And we have—do we have our own clocks and our own laws of expansion and contraction and as we change our rates of vibrations and our levels of consciousness, does the rate of our clock change in relation with the universal clock?

Yes, until such time as it stops.

OK. Thank you.

And in that realm of mental substance, it's called death. It begins and it ends. Yes. This is why a wise person makes greater effort to stop thinking about themselves, because the more they think about themselves, the more they believe the forms in mental substance, the more they're dependent upon them, until such time as life indeed is very weary. Yes.

If we got to the point where our clock stopped, wouldn't we be out of self?

Are you now speaking of eternal truth, that which you are, or that which you believe you are?

I was thinking that we might go beyond what we believe we are to what we are.

Well, when that happens, there is no starting, for there is no stopping.

Thank you.

You see, truth *is*. Light *is*. God *is*. You don't start and stop truth; it just is. Crushed to earth, it raises again, for it is only crushed in mental substance, that is, your awareness of it.

So, now some time ago, in guiding you to this class, this very evening, to this final class, years and years ago on your Earth planet, we gave to you: awareness belief become. So there you are. You view, you are aware. You believe and you become. And from that process you are bound and from that bondage you are freed.

You see, all of that is dependence, for all of that is denial. Remember, the more identified you are with self, the more you deny, for the more you have to protect, the more you have to defend until you're totally exhausted from all of the forms of illusion that you have created by denial and belief that you are dependent upon. You see, you protect and tempt to defend that which you believe you are. So the more you think about yourself, the more forms you have to look after. The more forms you have to look after, the more you have to defend. The more you have to defend, the more exhausted you become. Does that help with your question?

Yes, the lady there, please.

Then in going out of that thing, because the way you get into it is the way you get out of it, is—do you go backwards in that procedure then? Or where does belief become? You have to become belief and then you're aware of what you've been doing. Is that how that works?

Well, as I've stated before, it's not what you need to put into a vehicle called mind; it's what you really have a need to take out of it. Because there's plenty going in there all the time. In other words, you're constantly adding to your need to defend the multitudes of thoughts or forms that you believe that you are.

Now, should you make the effort daily to pause to think more deeply, which is beyond the realms of creating forms and beliefs and more things that you're dependent upon and more things to defend, should you make the effort daily to pause and to truly think, then you will, slowly but surely, awaken and once again view and, through viewing, guide and control, instead of believing and be guided and controlled by the forms solidified within your own consciousness. It is these many forms that we have solidified through this process that we depend upon for the various things that we seek because, from our dependences, we have denied. And so the vicious circle goes round and round.

Now we've always taught that selfless service is the path to spiritual awakening. Now perhaps you may have a broader understanding on what selfless service really is.

And in our conclusion of this final class, as time in your world is marching on, I think it would behoove you, as students, to have a bit broader perspective of what it is to be a prophet in your world of illusion. What it's really like—not what you believe it is like, but what it is really like. A true prophet must know beyond a shadow of any doubt, go beyond those realms and see clearly and, therefore, in so doing, be an instrument through which truth may shine through the veil of illusion and, in so doing, being in the illusion, must constantly work consciously with the bombardment of forms that exist in the veil of illusion. And this is why prophets have always been taken away from the veil of illusion.

In our philosophy, it's known as auric pollution. They've always been taken away from the veil of illusion, for the forms created by belief, solidified by dependence, ever seek sustenance for their continuity. And they seek, being forms of the lesser light, they ever seek the brighter light, for the brighter light contains purer energy. It doesn't have the blemishes on its purity. And so it, therefore, is a much higher quality of energy than the lesser light. And so the battle is moment by moment for prophets who expose themselves consistently to the great veil of illusion.

Now if you look around your world of illusion, you will see people go to what you call healers. And they go to prophets. And some are prophets. Some are true prophets; some are false prophets. Some are true healers; some are false healers. That is ever dependent upon the prophet, whether or not they are making conscious, moment-by-moment effort. For if they do not, they soon become the victim of limitless numbers of forms of illusion who not only have a great feast of the energy until that channel of energy is so contaminated with the blemishes that its purity becomes highly questionable—like a battery that serves things that need charging.

Therefore, this type of school is not only rare and unique in your world, it's very continuity is, in your world of illusion—for here is a physical, material world, that's a world of illusion. This type of school, its continuity and existence, being in a world of illusion, is totally dependent upon the daily efforts made by whatever students are allowed to attend it.

Thank you very much. And I do hope that your questions, at least some of them, have been cared for.

Good night.

MARCH 29, 1984

CONSCIOUSNESS CLASS 241

Good evening, class. Welcome to our new classes, monthly. And so this evening we will begin with the origin of the species, the evolution thereof.

The Principle of Good perceives the consciousness of intelligent energy and the law conceives the evolving form. Be that planet or be that man.

Now man, in belief, is an evolving, hybrid animal. Man, in truth, is the Principle of Good. And so man awakens to the animal or he awakens to the truth. The animal of man is the bondage of intelligent energy and the Principle of Good; it is the creator of creation. And so in keeping with the laws that govern creation, man pays, through the laws of payment and attainment, in keeping with man's own belief.

[In] the evolution of the form on this planet Earth the so-called missing link, of which we spoke so many of your years ago, will never be found on your planet Earth, for it does not exist this day on your planet Earth. For many, many eons ago on your planet, in the early evolving stages of the animals, intelligent beings from a sister planet visited your Earth and you are the effect of that conception, of that creation, today in your form.

However, you find in your experiences in life, you find a continuity of the seeming struggles of life, experiences that do not appear to bring to you the goodness that you know is justly and rightfully yours. For man being, in truth, the Principle of Good, man, therefore, is the perceiver and therefore, by the Law of Perception, the receiver of the good that he, in truth, is.

In these classes and in this school we offer to you the opportunity to make intelligent decisions rather than to make ignorant judgments. For the function of belief, its very nature is to make judgments, as the faculty of faith, by its very nature, makes decisions. We will once again share with you our understanding of the difference between making a judgment and establishing a decision in your life. The difference between judgment and decision is that judgment offers to us no possibility of change. Decision, being a faculty of faith, offers to us the possibility and probability of evolution, which is subject to the Law of Change.

We know at any given moment whether or not we are free in faith or we are bounded in belief, for our days are filled with the opportunities of making changes. Our experiences (or effects of those opportunities) reveal to us clearly whether or not we are bound in those moments or whether or not we are free.

Man and man alone, in this evolutionary process, is serving what he experiences in life. And so when we look at life and we see and we experience the goodness that is justly ours, then we know beyond a shadow of any doubt what it is that we are serving.

We have, each and every moment, this wonderful opportunity. This very class scheduled this evening was your opportunity: your opportunity to choose intelligently that which your mind established in its belief or that which your soul, ever moving on the peaceful path of light and truth, [established]. You alone had those experiences. For the greatest growth that anyone can ever make is from the personal experience from the laws that they personally establish.

In this evolutionary process of the human being, we are destined, by the very laws of evolution, to return to that which we truly are and to be freed from that which we think, therefore, judge, desire, therefore, believe and be bound. We have those moments ever with us—belief and bondage or faith and freedom.

How graciously we accept changes which appear to be beyond our control reveals our growth at those times. And so when we find difficulty in letting go, then we know why we have difficulty in holding. We have difficulty in receiving, for we have difficulty in giving.

A thought that is permitted to entertain the mind of man becomes solidified by intelligent energy being directed to it. The solidification of any thought is known to man as a judgment. And so man, through lack of effort and conscious awareness, permits a thought to entertain his consciousness to stimulate his senses. The longer the thought is permitted to entertain and stimulate the animal being of man, the more solidified is the judgment as an effect of that directed, intelligent energy. And the more solidified the thought, the greater the bondage of the judgment through man's belief that he is what his thought is saying to him.

And so through that process, solidification of the thought through the bondage of the judgment, through the belief that he is that creation of his, through that process, man's desires are stolen from the godhead, limiting the goodness that he truly is and [he] suffers in keeping with that error of ignorance. That, however, is necessary for the evolutionary process of the hybrid animal.

And it was here recently that I was asked in reference to the evolution of form on your planet, At what state of evolution were birds on your planet? You already know from the study and your education in your mundane schools that birds have evolved from the reptiles; that the reptiles have come from the element water of your planet. And so birds, in their state of evolution, are in the final stage of the manifestation of form on your planet. For they are, through their own demonstration, the effect of being able to use the element earth and to experience the freedom of the element air.

And so man long ago, in his awareness to express the freedom, the truth, and the goodness, put wings, the wings of birds, to depict the angels of heaven. And so we find, in keeping with our teachings and the teachings of the ages, that those who make the effort to enter in consciousness the element air are free. They are free from the bondage of that which your planet has to offer.

However, man does not enter into those stages of evolution without the price that he has set for himself by his own beliefs. And so in order to enter that element known as air, in order to experience that freedom, we must pass through the element that purifies all things that enter it. That's known as the element fire. And so all beings, in their stages of evolution, experience what the element fire has to offer: the change, the purification of form.

Man, while in belief, does not consciously choose to enter the purifying fires of freedom. No, man tells himself that "Because of circumstances beyond my control, I am suffering at this time. I am not able to fill the desires in my life. Because of circumstances beyond my control, I am not able to do just exactly what I want to do." This is the great deception. For that is in keeping with our unwillingness to accept the inevitable evolution, known to our mind as change.

The awakening of the spiritual being that we are is not something that can be manipulated by that which covers and clouds it. It is not within the nature of conception to perceive. It is only in the nature of conception to create and, therefore, to bind.

Personal responsibility—the ability to personally respond to all things that take place in our life—that ability we find great difficulty with only because we are waiting to accept whatever happens to us at any moment in our life is directly caused by us. Through an acceptance of that demonstrable truth (that man is a law unto himself) through an acceptance of that truth, man begins to walk on the path of freedom and to experience the joy of living. For it is then that man awakens to what he truly is and no longer serves what he believes he is.

It is not in the keeping of the evolution of the human being on your planet to turn your back on creation, for being a part of creation, you bear a personal responsibility to use it. Also we bear a personal responsibility not to be used by it. We are used by that which, by the law, is designed to serve us when we permit our self to experience discord, the opposite of peace and harmony, the opposite of health and goodness. When we permit our self to be disturbed, to be discordant, it reveals to us in those moments that we are serving the half of us that, by its nature, is bound to destruction and decay.

And so in our evolution, whoever sees the good in all things and, in so viewing the goodness in all things, broadens their horizon, refrains from the weakness or temptation of the animal part of our being and knows what it has to offer, is not deceived by it and, being not deceived by it, cannot be tempted to conceive with mental substance a way to experience the Principle of Good that we truly are.

Acceptance is the will of God. And that which we accept within our consciousness flows harmoniously, peacefully through it. That which we deny in our consciousness we become destined to and, therefore, the victim of. And we find our self, in order to protect and to defend our beliefs, we find that we deny many things. And each denial adds to our bondage. Each denial supports and increases the energy directed by attention to the rightness of our own beliefs.

Everyone has, in truth, great faith. Everyone has great talent. Everyone has great strength. Everyone *is* the Principle of Good. No one has more dedication than anyone else. No one has more ability than anyone else. We choose what we want to be dedicated to. We choose our allegiance in life. We choose what *we* want to believe. We choose what we want to do. Now we do that consciously at various moments in our life. The sadness is when man does not make the daily effort to know himself and, therefore, to know the truth and, in knowing the truth, to establish the Law of Freedom. Man consciously, in his life, desires something, limiting the divine expression, which is desire. Man uses the divine expression as an effect of fulfilling his belief in his judgment, which is, in truth, the solidification of a thought that entered his consciousness at some time in his life.

Unfortunately for man, from one view (fortunate for man who knows beyond a shadow of any doubt that he is, in truth, the Principle of Good), man having, through laziness, permitted a thought to entertain his consciousness and stimulate his senses to solidify to a judgment of which belief demands the fulfillment thereof through the expression of limited, divine expression called desire. Man experiencing a desire, not consciously, seemingly, being unable to fulfill it. Seemingly, it no longer is in his mind. No, my friends, it's no longer in the mind. From laziness, it has solidified itself and entered the basement of the water center where it can go to work and grow, like a mushroom, in the darkness or in what is known to us as the lesser light. Only to rise someday to demand its service to it, only to rise within the consciousness to possess the mind and obsess the being. That, my friends, is the just and rightful payment for laziness. That is a just and rightful payment of the falsity of belief. And it serves a good, rightful, and just purpose. For when, through the laws of repetition, it offers to the human mind sufficient deprivation, sufficient struggle, sufficient pain, then the minds of men begin to pause to think and, with the faculty of reason, make necessary changes within their mind that they may experience the goodness of life. For that awakening to being in truth the perceiver of good fulfills itself in keeping with the divine law to be the receiver thereof.

Like anything in life, man requires sustenance and requires harmony and support in whatever endeavor that he chooses. And so those who choose in life the path of being—for the path of being is the path of truth and freedom—those who choose the path of being require, as they stumble along that path, the support and the encouragement of those who have succeeded, to some extent and degree, along the path that they have chosen.

For we are the living demonstration. We are the demonstrable proof that we are all extremely successful. We succeed in whatever we choose to succeed in, in keeping with the law that we have established. The problem and the confusion to the mind is quite simple: we choose to do one thing at one time in our life and then, supposedly, it doesn't work and we forget that we have chosen that. Years pass by and we move on to different things. And we tell our self, our impatience, our ignorance tells us we failed in that and we failed in that and we failed in something else. We are not a success; that's what our minds tell us. The mind that serves the ignorance of laziness tells us the many times we have failed in the filling of our desires.

However, wisdom reveals to us that those desires, that we supposedly no longer have, have been working diligently in the basement of our consciousness; that they have been growing and that someday they do rise and we wonder what's happened to us: we only have another failure to add to our list. Yet wisdom reveals it is not a failure at all. It is a success of something that we desired, [and we] made no true effort, true effort to fulfill, did not maintain or sustain the light of wisdom and reason. And so when it rose, we moved on from what we were doing and returned to that which had risen from the basement of our consciousness demanding our energy to fulfill itself. And so this goes on with us all the time.

And so all prophets have shared with you that great truth, "O man, know thyself, and ye shall know the truth, and the truth shall set your free."

Whoever permits themselves discouragement is serving a shadow of the past. For they are, at that time, in the realm of belief and that shadow has risen once again.

Temptation is what all philosophies teach about, the freedom from temptation. The prayer, so common to all, "Lord, lead me not into temptation." Knowing what the Lord is—the law of the universe, our universe—we can understand that we asked the law not to lead us to our weaknesses. We asked the law, through the demonstration of our faith.

For temptation is not a faculty of that which you are. Temptation is a function of that which you *believe* you are. The weaknesses that man says that he has—and a weakness is nothing more nor less than our belief that we are the victim of something that we cannot control. That's what a weakness truly is. It is a belief. But who made the belief? Who is it that created that? Who created the judgment? Who solidified the thought? We did it. And therefore we, being the one who created it in the first place, we have available to us the intelligent energy, the power to change it. So no man is controlled by a weakness until man believes that he is the weakness. And that is the fine line of separation of truth, that which you are, from creation, that which you believe you are.

And so in this wonderful evolution through this planet, for from other experiences you have come, to other experiences you are going. And heaven is ever available to those who are willing to give belief that they may gain faith. But for man to give belief, man must first refrain from denial. And by refraining from denial, man will no longer be destined to need. For we alone establish the Law of Need by denying the truth that is. So through our denial of what is, we are destined to what is not. "To those who have, yea, even more shall I give. To those who have not, even that shall I take away." The Law of Good never fails us, for being the Principle of Good, it is not possible to fail us. So a wise man does not deny, for a wise man chooses not to be in bondage from belief, which only serves the solidified thought at some time in his life.

Now I do want to give a few moments to those of you who may have questions in reference to the origin of the species and the evolution thereof. I realize that there are many questions entertaining your consciousness and you have a responsibility to you to ask them. And so we'll take those moments and you be kind enough to raise your hand.

I would rather have the birds flying towards me than away. *[On the table in front of the Teacher is a glass of water. On the glass is a depiction of birds flying. As the Teacher speaks these words, he turns the glass so the birds face him.]* Yes.

By what was said tonight, are the birds more evolved than man?

Is your question, Are the birds of the planet more evolved than man?

Yes.

The birds of the planet in the evolution and the demonstration of what they are capable of doing with their form and if you believe you are your form, in that sense, they are more evolved. To those who believe, the birds are more evolved. Because if you believe you are the form, then you are limited in your evolution and you are not able, at this point in your evolution of form, to enter freely the element of air without assistance. Does that help with your question?

Yes. Thank you.

You're welcome. *[After a short pause, the Teacher continues.]* I thought sure perhaps some of you would like to ask about the need to sleep during class. Yes, please.

Could you explain further what it means to deny—what that exactly means?

When a person believes they are the solidified thought in their mind, when they believe they are their mind, then they must, they believe, protect and defend it. For believing that they are the judgment, they must protect that, for that is them. Do you understand?

Yes.

If you believe you are your thought, then you certainly believe you are your judgment. And if you believe you are your judgment, you surely believe you are your desire. And if you believe that you are your desire, you must protect it and defend it, for in keeping with the degree and extent of your belief, you permit the basic nature of the animal, the instinct for survival, to take control of your being. And so in keeping with the basic nature of the animal form which you believe at any moment that you are, you certainly will do whatever is possible and capable in keeping with your belief to protect and to defend it. Does that help with your question? Yes?

So that's where the denial lies?

Well, in keeping with the defense of any judgment or any desire, man denies the possibility of change. You see, my friends, when you believe you are the desire or whatever it is that you believe you are the desire of, you deny the possibility of change. For the possibility of change to the instinct—Yes. Thank you—to the basic nature and instinct of the animal which you believe that you are is survival. And you will protect and defend your survival. Thank you. Turn it over, please. *[The Teacher speaks these asides to the audio technician who is recording this class.]* We'll pause for a moment. *[After the audio cassette was turned over, the Teacher continues.]*

Have you passed that through there? All right. Fine. Now, does that help with your question?

Yes.

All right. Fine. The lady there, please.

Yes. In the light of reason, is that pause helping us separate truth from creation and separating the thought from us?

The possibility is in the pause. The probability is dependent upon, of course, one's own values.

Thank you.

Yes, the possibility is in the pause. Yes, the lady there, please. Do you wish to ask your question, yes?

No.

Fine. *[Addressing a different student, the Teacher continues.]* Yes, please.

What is the effect of laziness?

Bondage.

Is that . . .

Bondage to whatever you believe that you are. If you believe you are miserable, laziness supports that belief. If you believe that you are a failure, the lack of effort supports that belief. If you believe you are suffering, the lack of effort supports that belief. And that's known to man, of course, as laziness.

You see, my friends, it takes energy to be lazy. Have we not yet awakened to the demonstrable truth that it takes a great deal of energy to be lazy? Have you not experienced a day when you felt you would just lay in bed and be lazy? And then finally a desire to eat struck a blow to your mind and your body tried to react. And have you not found difficulty in moving after lying in bed for fifteen, sixteen hours? Pardon?

Yes.

It takes energy, intelligent energy to be lazy, for it takes intelligent energy to believe and a person is tempted to laziness by some thought in their mind. Would you not agree? An so in order to solidify that thought, in order to serve the bondage of that judgment and its limited expression known as desire, that takes energy. Yes. And so a person can accomplish, in truth, twice as much by doing something that they can look at, after, and say, "I wisely directed intelligent energy and this is an effect of that direction of intelligent energy." That help with your question?

Yes. Thank you.

You're welcome. Yes.

Can you tell us further about the being that inhabited the animal form when it came from another planet?

What would you know—what would you like to know about the intelligent being that you are? What would your beliefs like to know about that? What is it you would like to know?

What motivated their coming to the earth realm?

The law.

The law?

It is the nature of goodness to express itself. And so the Principle of Good, as I have already stated, the Principle of Good—that's what you are—perceives the consciousness. Do you know what that means? The Principle of Good perceives the consciousness. Do you know what was said? Do you recall what was said in our opening of our class? What is it that the Principle of Good perceives? The consciousness of what? Of intelligent energy.

Oh.

Do you accept that you are intelligent energy?

Yes, I do.

That's what you are. And so the being that you are—that mingled with the being that you believe you are—is greater than the animal that believes. For faith is far greater than belief, for that which leads to freedom is certainly superior to that which leads to bondage.

You can only be the evolving, hybrid animal, you can only be that through your belief. Now you don't have to believe that you are the animal. All you have to do is to *believe* whatever form you create. And if you *believe* the form that you create—you believe that that form is you—then, at those times, you are the hybrid evolving animal of your planet, that knows birth and knows death. Birth and death are only experienced by the evolving animal. Birth and death, the servants of creation, are not known to that which you are. They are only known to that which you believe you are.

Thank you.

You're welcome. Yes.

You mentioned discouragement is based on shadows of the past.

Correct.

So when one is discouraged, then [do] you need to trace it back to what, in the past, is causing that?

Yes. That's a fine question and requires a little discussion. Whatever we—whatever experience in our life that we deny personal responsibility for, we guarantee and establish the law for the repetition thereof. For example, if a man, in his life, experiences what he calls love with another person and experiences the pleasures and stimulation of the senses that it has to offer to the evolving animal, and change, the Law of Evolution, he crosses along that path and that which he believed for a time that he loved is no longer harmonious or in accord with him and if man, at that time, does not accept personal responsibility that it all took place, in truth, within his own consciousness, that it never was, in truth, dependent upon what another did or did not do, but was wholly and completely dependent upon how he chose to view it in keeping with what judgments, what solidified thoughts, he chose to believe in, if man, in those experiences, accepts the demonstrable law and personally expresses his own ability to state the truth, "All of this I have brought into my life. All of the seeming good, all of the seeming bad, I alone, O God, in keeping with the law, have established those experiences. They have nothing to do, in truth, with what someone else does or doesn't do. They have to do with what I alone choose to do with the forms, the thoughts that I create in my mind," if man accepts the truth at those times, the principle of those experiences will not repeat themselves in his life. And the benefit from that is freedom from discouragement. Does that help with your question?

However, for all of us that takes daily effort to declare the truth: "I use the form known as my mind. I use it. I am that which moves the thought. I am the power behind the thought. Without me, the thought cannot be. Without me, it cannot solidify. Without me, it cannot bind me. So I am that intelligent energy that can, at any moment, choose the goodness of life, for that is what I am. When I permit myself to fall and to believe that my goodness is dependent on what something beyond my control does or does not do, then I must pay for the denial of the Principle of Goodness." For man gives so freely, so freely that which is and works so diligently to manipulate that which he will never be.

So man will never be the animal—only through the deception of belief. Man will never be another eternal soul, for man *is* his own soul. So man therefore, in that awakening, does not seek nor search to find God limited in person, place, or thing. Man pauses and awakens and sees God or good in all things regardless of appearance. For appearances affect only belief. Appearances do not affect that which you are. Appearances only affect that which you believe you are.

And so when you find yourself reacting to that which appears across your consciousness, then you know in that moment, in that moment you have entered the realms of belief and, therefore, are destined to pay for your bondage. But man is never left without that wonderful opportunity to choose this power of faith rather than this force of belief. For, you see, force is the strength of the animal, but power is the very Principle of Good or God. Remember, power controls nothing beyond its just domain. Force ever seeks to control everything that appears before its view. Does that help with your question?

And it is, of course, when we believe and enter the animal being, the form that we are temporarily using, of course, it is understandable that we want to experience that which we are. So we ever seek the good in life. But the payment is very great when we believe we are the thought that tells us how to get it. The payment is more than an intelligent being cares to make.

Any more questions? *[After a short pause, the Teacher continues.]*

I see, by one of my students, that you would like a description of the beings that entered this planet eons ago, this planet Earth, mingled with, in keeping with the laws of evolution, and their service to that which they are. Of what benefit will it be to describe, in order that you may create, through belief in mental substance, a limit to intelligent being? Of no benefit at this time in your evolution.

Now this is the one and only class for December. Next class will not be, you know, until the new year—January. And so, of course, it would behoove you to have your questions formulated, because, I assure you, when class is over, I'm not going to stay around to answer your questions over a cup of coffee. So I would like you to understand that rather than be weakened, known as tempted, after.

Yes, the lady here, please.

Throughout history each generation seems to be more, not only physically, larger, but more evolved. Is that the pattern and is . . .

I understand your question in reference to people seem to be physically larger throughout the ages. That depends and is subject to many factors. It is subject, first, to the factor in the evolving of the species whether or not intelligent energy is predominately directed to belief or to faith. That is one factor. For the more intelligent energy that is directed to belief, the more the form is affected. All right. Then, of course, there is, on your planet, the environmental factor. If through generation upon generation these species are exposed to certain temperatures and climatic conditions, the form adapts and adjusts. Then, of course, there is the factor involved of the tendencies of each and every form in keeping with the original commingling with the animal on your planet.

Now the question arises within the consciousness and the minds of men, well, did they commingle with just one particular species of animal? Then I present with you the reasonable, logical question: Is there such a thing on your planet as crossbreeding? Pardon? Then you would agree, of course. So what thought in the minds of men would believe that intelligent energy, intelligent beings would only commingle with one particular species? No. No more so than it takes quite a limited mind—one filled with denial—to make the judgment that there's only intelligent beings on one planet and that's known as Earth.

Whenever and wherever the negative poles of nature on your planet come together, there intelligent energy enters. You call that soul. At that moment, at that moment intelligent energy enters at the very moment of conception. It is not limited to the commingling as you know it, for the days dawn very quickly on your planet when your so-called test tubes and all this shall take place in your laboratories and what you now call cloning is not some type of fiction. These are realties that limited minds have yet to view. Does it help with your question?

Yes. Thank you.

You're welcome. The gentleman back there, please.

Ofttimes it seems that the force of the animal being is so very great.

Ever in keeping, my friend, with your belief. There is nothing that is subject to something else that can be as great or greater than that which it is subject to. And so force is subject to power. Without power, force does not exist. Without a mind, thought is not created. Therefore, when you accept the demonstrable truth that you are the mover of the mind and not the mind, then you enter faith and experience power. But as long as you insist on believing not only that you are the mind, but you are the thoughts that pass through the mind, then you have to pay, like anyone must pay, for the bondage that you create. Yes, go ahead with your statement. *[After a short pause, the Teacher continues.]* Your statement was it seems that force is so great.

I was just going to ask you to speak on that.

I see. On what?

On—what—how it gets to be so great.

Man's belief. It is the child of man's belief. Man becomes in keeping with his own belief. If you believe that you are poor, through your belief that you are, you will establish all the laws necessary to prove how right you are. All animal beings, by the instinct for survival, fight to prove they're right. Does that help with your question?

Yes. Thank you.

And so if you insist on believing, then choose believing that may bring you a little bit smoother and, hopefully, less payment in life. I tell you there are moments when you no longer believe and in those moments, you are free. That's in between what my students call their trips. That's the pause, they say, that refreshes. Yes.

On that, I think we will have refreshments. Thank you very much.

DECEMBER 13, 1984

CONSCIOUSNESS CLASS 242

Good evening, class. We'll continue on with our class on evolution.

The prince or principle of peace is the power of God. Now the evolution, which is, in truth, the expansion of limit, known to man as the evolution of form, which is limit, is made possible by this expanding-contracting principle of limit. And so harmonious evolution is ever subject to and dependent upon the wise use, and not abuse, of the first and second soul faculty of being. The first, as most of you are aware, being duty, gratitude, and tolerance; the second being faith, poise, and humility.

Man's seeming struggles are ever dependent upon the efforts of limit or form to control the power which sustains them. And so we are tempted in our efforts in evolving by our beliefs that we are what we think we are, in keeping with the evolutionary process of what we know as self-awareness. We are, in our present evolution, self-aware. We are self-aware and, therefore, dependent upon belief, which is limit, which is force. For belief has boundaries. Having boundaries, it is limit. Therefore man is bound by his own beliefs through his own identification with his own awakening to self-awareness.

As we continue to evolve, we experience discord and disease, health and harmony depending upon our needs to control that which we are by directing energy to that which we believe we are. So we find in this process struggle and suffering. We find also in this process a constant awareness of obstruction to the divine expression known as desire.

The reason that we obstruct the divine expression known as desire is because we tempt to control the power by the force that we believe that we are. Now force is force, for it demonstrates a resistance or an obstruction to the fulfillment of the divine expression known as desire, for man, forming the divine expression by the limits of mental substance, believing, through identification, through experiencing need from denial of what he is and choosing to believe what he is not. The suffering process, the struggle and frustrations are ever with the limited consciousness of the human being until such time as we move in our evolution from self-awareness to universal awareness, known to you as cosmic consciousness.

Because limit has awareness of something greater than what it is, because it does have that awareness—and it has it because it is the effect of cause; it is the form or personality of principle—because of that awareness, it is tempted to be what it, by the divine architecture, can never be.

You cannot fill a vessel with more than what the vessel can contain. And so it is man's responsibility to ever increase the vessel that he believes that he is and, in so doing, the broadening of that horizon awakens within his own limited mind the advisability of following the path of nonresistance in consciousness. Many prophets have revealed to you to turn the other cheek. However, because man is identified with his cheek, man chooses not to turn, for man ever experiences need. As long as man insists on his efforts to control power and, in those efforts, deny what he is, his path and destiny shall be lack, want, desire, the needs of force.

Now we'll pause for a few moments for your questions on the first few words that have been spoken. Yes.

Could you give some other examples of when a person thinks he is something that he really, truly is not?

Yes. In reference to a person thinking that he is something that he, in truth, is not, reveals to all minds the insistence of the mental world or limit that man has identified with. It reveals to man that because he thinks, he, therefore, believes. And he believes what he thinks because he identifies with limit. And through identification with limit, man experiences the force of belief at the temporal cost and loss of power.

Man thinks many things and he thinks them with all of the force that need has to offer at any given moment. Therefore we find that man thinks many things, that man's thinking and man's believing do not endure. Only power is forever. All thought, all limit is change, for all thought reveals to man limit. And all limit reveals to man force. And all force reveals to man a constant changing process, known as evolution.

That which we are does not evolve. That which we believe we are does evolve. And so in man's efforts to control, man is frustrated by his own beliefs. When man gives his greatest gift—that's known as the gift of self. Now the gift of self—my little student may be excused, please. *[The Teacher excuses a parent to attend to their child.]* Now the gift of self is everything that we believe we are. And so when we give, in consciousness, everything we believe we are, we free that which we are from the bondage of our own beliefs and in so doing, we experience what we are, which is freedom from want, need, and desire. For that which we are does not change. Change is subject to our own needs. Our needs are the effects of our own denials. Does that help with your question on thought?

Yes, the gentleman over there, please.

I am confused about the value of thinking since it seems to tie us to limit and judgment and desire and those limited things that—how can one think and not get into those problems?

In reference to your question on the value of thinking, let us pause and speak one thing: "I believe that I am for I am. Therefore being I am, I believe." Now when we enter in our evolution this world of creation, when we enter the mist of force, which is controlled by mental substance, the effect of the very principle of opposites or duality, we, at that moment of identification, we establish the Law of Denial of what we are through identifying with what we *think* we are. Now when we think we are something, in order to maintain that what we think we are, we are, in order to maintain that delusion, we believe. For if we did not believe in that process, then we would not long be what we think we are.

Now the value of what we think we are is a principle of the very realm of consciousness of limitation or creation. And so we enter or identify with—for that's how we enter anything, is by first denying, experiencing need, and tempting to control what we believe that we need. So when we enter or identify with that world, world of creation, the world of limit, when we believe we are that, we form thoughts. And we form them from a dual law, the Law of Creation. Through this awakening process, the expansion of a thought or a form, we, slowly but surely, are the true instruments of the evolution of limit. And by so doing, forms are refined, evolved, and, in so-called time, in eternity, form, limit, will accept the possibility and, accepting the possibility, will expand its own limit. And the purpose of the free spirit entering the bondage of belief, known as creation, shall be served. Does that help with your question?

Yes, the lady back there, please.

How do you give what you think you are? How is that done?

How does one give what they think they are? One, through an awakening process, chooses the power of faith, the principle of peace, the Law of Good, and sees clearly, "What I think I am is dependent upon the bondage of belief, is dependent upon my denial of what I am, that I experience the lack of what I desire." And through that process and through that awakening and through the use, not abuse, of the first and second soul faculty of being—duty, gratitude, and tolerance; faith, poise, and humility—through that process, man, humanity, has no problem in giving up that which is frustrating and limiting and suffering for that which they are: faith, poise, humility.

When we find within our consciousness the thought of being a servant distasteful, when we find in our consciousness the thought of serving without conscious gain [distasteful], then we must, in keeping with that law established, we must pay a very high price to give the gift of self. For when the thought of serving without gain is distasteful and to the degree of how distasteful it is to our mind reveals to us the bondage of our belief that has grown from our denial of what we are. Does that help with your question?

Yes, the lady there, please.

Can you describe the principle of peace?

The human mind has for eons—in fact, there never was a time when the human mind did not desire to limit power, which only reveals the mind's efforts to control it. To define, to limit the Limitless is the desire of mental substance. To define God is to limit God. And to limit God is to choose false gods of clay feet. I know that you, as a student, would not be tempted to limit the Limitless. Therefore, faith being the avenue through which the prince or principle of peace, the power of God expresses itself, it is faith that frees man from the bondage of belief. Man, any man, can define or limit belief. In truth we define or limit belief and we continue to build the prison of our true being. So man, when he gives *all* that he believes he is, when man gives all that he *believes* he is, in that moment man will know beyond a shadow of all doubt: man shall awaken to what he is. The prison doors shall open in that moment; man shall leave as long as he makes the effort to sustain and to maintain his being in the faith. For faith is what man *is* and belief is what man thinks he is. Does that help with your question? Yes.

What is the purpose of desire and how can it be used for a positive end?

Thank you for your question. What is the purpose of desire and how can desire be used for a positive end? Desire is beyond end. Desire is beyond positive or negative. Man's attempt to control desire, man's attempt to limit the expression of God is where man enters his own bondage.

Now, first of all, in order to experience the need of the limit or control of the divine expression known as desire, man must first deny what he is in order to experience the need for what he is. We experience the need for good. Good, God, the principle of peace, power, faith is not a luxury to the consciousness. Peace, power, good, God is indispensable to the very existence of all life, for that's what life is. It is only when we, through this process of identification—which is totally dependent upon our efforts to direct energy to controlling what we truly are by believing we are something else. And so by that process of believing that we are the thought of the mind at any moment, we experience need. We only experience need as an effect of denial.

And so the good of desire, the principle of desire, having no limits or boundaries, for it is the divine expression—the flower does not experience need, for it does not deny that which it truly is by believing the limit through which that which it is, is expressing itself at any moment. Man experiences desire—that is, the formation of desire, the limit of desire. And by his efforts to control the divine expression, man experiences resistance to that. And that resistance, an effect of belief, an effect of need, that resistance is force. And force is governed and controlled by a dual law. Does that help with the question?

Thank you.

Go ahead with the next one.

Well, what I'm trying do is understand, I guess, what— because you speak of, of divine desire. I—

No, my dear, I do not speak of divine desire. I speak of desire, the principle. That's what desire is: the principle, divine expression. It is the principle of God. Man's effort to control it, man's own effort to control the divine expression known as desire—it is man's effort to control it that man suffers. Man suffers from his own temptation. Man is tempted by what he denies. Man is never tempted by what he accepts. Acceptance is the will of God. And denial, therefore, is what? I ask you the question. If acceptance is the will of God, the harmonious flow of good, that which God is, then what is denial? Have you an answer to my question?

The rejection of good? The rejection of God?

The rejection of good. Can one control good? Is the air you breathe, is it good? Without it, would you say it was bad?

It would be awful unpleasant.

Very unpleasant. Would you consider that which you consider unpleasant to be good?

No.

Possibly beneficial, not necessarily good. Many things are beneficial that our minds say are not good. So there we are. It's all relative.

What we're speaking of [is] our resistance to God's will. It is our resistance to God's will. That resistance is from our own experience of need. We deny good and from the denial of good we experience the need for it. And the experience of the need for good is subject to the limits of our own evolution of self-awareness, for it is our own mind that dictates how good or God shall enter our lives. Therefore we find, having no control over our own mind, we find that one moment we experience good, for we have fulfilled, in mental substance, the necessary demands of past patterns, forms that we have created, belief that we are the judgments we have created. However, man moves on and he finds there are times when he is not able to fill these limited mental forms that he has created in past time. And when he is not able to fill, to satisfy, to serve these limited forms through which he has permitted God or good to enter his consciousness, then man, as he continues to evolve, experiences less good, less God and more suffering and more struggle.

However, there's good in all things. And as man continues to suffer and man continues to struggle and man continues on the paths of frustration, he, slowly but surely, begins the process of accepting the possibility that he has limited good or God in his consciousness and begins to broaden his horizons, to expand his consciousness. And through that expansion, resistance is not as great, for there is nowheres near as much limit to the God he will allow into his life. Does that help with your question?

Yes.

You're welcome.

Thank you.

[After a short pause, the Teacher continues.] Now I don't want you to ask why the little magnetic tape down there is silent, because no one seems to be awake here. Now, now, we know why it's silent. Yes.

Could you please give a definition on character? What is the principle of character? And, I guess, just speak on character.

First, I would like to ask you a question.

Yes.

What is the purpose of your question, for it reveals a need? What do you think is the purpose of your question? What do you think the motivation of your question is?

Well, so that I can use it.
In what—do you—yes, go ahead.
It's a soul faculty. I know that much. And . . .
Is it the first?
No.
Is it the second?
No.
In one's efforts to become what they desire to become—first having denied what they are—in one's efforts to become what they desire to become, does not life reveal we first crawl before we walk?
Yes.
Surely, wisdom reveals it is best to walk before we run. So would it not behoove us to consider, having stated character being a soul faculty, having also stated that it is not the first or the second, would it not behoove us to consider upon what all soul faculties rest? To surely consider faculty one and faculty two? Would you not, therefore, in learning a musical scale, be then qualified to possibly play a tune that is reasonable? Would you not consider that to be of greater benefit at this particular time?
Yes.
First of all, if we will stop and pause and think: "What does character mean to me? Which faculty is it? Do I begin my education and learning of a musical scale with mi or do I begin perhaps with do re mi? Is there something ahead of mi that I begin with in order that when I get to mi I may be a bit more qualified?" Do you not feel that it would be in your best interest? For by the time you reach the soul faculty of character, you may no longer find a need therefore.
Yes.
Is one dissatisfied with what they believe their character is? Does one feel, believe, and judge that through character greater good or God can enter their lives? These are questions, I think,

you would find most beneficial. For whoever expresses duty, gratitude, and tolerance, faith, poise, and humility shall be freed from all concern of self, where limit truly is. I see my little four-legged student there found his way through the door. *[The Teacher refers to Reddy, who is a dog.]* Yes.

Would you speak on poise?

Pardon?

Would you speak on poise?

Poise? I'll be happy to share my understanding on poise. Tell me, in the triune second soul faculty, what proceeds it?

Faith.

Now do you find anything in your world, poised, lacking faith and humility? Tell me, would you say that humility has any acceptance in it?

It would be all acceptance.

Would you say without value of duty, wisdom of tolerance, one could experience gratitude?

No.

Therefore poise—a poised mind is a mind that is controlled, as a vehicle, by the driver who knows they're not the vehicle and is not tempted to become it. So a person interested in being, *being* what they are, a person interested in that is a person of peace; the principle being, that expresses without concern, without need, without want, for they are what they are and are not tempted to be what they are not.

Many times I have spoken on the faculty that lights the lamps in the mist and the dark realms of old creation: the lamp of honesty. For it is in the lighted lamp of honesty that the Philistines shudder, for nothing can stand against the power of peace. However, the power of peace cannot express itself without honesty. We cannot control, and therefore a wise man cannot be tempted to control, the power of peace. One does not experience temptation except from denial. So if one does not deny what they are, one does not experience need to be what they already are. We already are the good that is. It is only our denial of it—I know. It is only our denial of it that causes us all of the problems.

Yes, the lady back there, please.

To use the example of a flower being what it is, it just is what it is, and it doesn't tempt to be anything other than that. So is being a man or a woman below that? Are you speaking of a higher purpose or—my question is, Does it have something to do with one's own nature or being male or female or above that—in being true to what, as the flower?

Well, tell me something. Does the little flower, its form, when it requires water, say to you, "Water? No, no, no. I don't like that person. I don't want that person to water me." Does the little flower express the first soul faculty of duty, gratitude, and tolerance? It's certainly tolerant: many people water flowers.

Now water is water, you see. Even the form of the flower knows water is the value; water is the priority. The necessary ingredients for the vehicle to express so that the Infinite Intelligence, God, expressing through it, that little flower accepts that water from you or you or you or you. It does not go into an emotional reaction because it does not express its personality in that way. Now there are, of course, various species of flowers that certain humans, in extremely negative type of thinking—now what is negative thinking, first, while we are talking on the flower? Negative thinking is the expression of the denial of God. You see, we think negatively and what does that negativity say? It says, "I don't have this. I don't have that. I don't have any money. I don't have any of all the functions," that we are over-identified with, you see. So when you're speaking of negative thinking, you are speaking of your expression of your denial of God.

Now it is true, there's certainly—there are certain species, even in the plant kingdom, who, through their own sensitivity, through their own awakening of their form, through their own self-awareness, have a greater struggle through the refinement of the form—you understand, the expansion of their limit—have an emotional reaction to certain personalities and their negativity or denial of the very sustenance the flower requires for its own survival.

So, you see, that, you call in your world, a hybrid. A hybrid is an expanded limit, you understand? It's refined. So the more refined the form, the more expanded its own limit in consciousness, the greater the struggle of the form for survival. For by its own expansion, it exposes itself to what, by its own refinement, are now alien vibrations and frequencies and indeed [is] difficult for the flower, for the human, for the animal, or anything else. Does that help with your question?

And you well know there are certain flowers and plants and trees that, being very refined, very expanded in their limits and indeed very beautiful, as all flowers in truth are, but more appealing to the mental substance from their own complexities. For the mental world prides itself on complexity and abhors simplicity. You see, we—the mind takes pride in that which is mysterious, for we take pride in that which we believe that we have that others do not, for that offers unto us an avenue through which we are tempted to control. Does that help with your question?

The lady here, please.

Will you please speak on the responsibility and the damage we do to our pets and our children, little children, when our vibrations are not healthy for them?

Well, I think, first, we perhaps, in reference to your question of damage that is done to that which is exposed to us, for we, in our evolution, have earned the ability to respond to other creatures, to be instruments through which greater good may flow, and therefore, having earned that ability to respond to the will of God known as total acceptance, we bear, of course, that responsibility.

Now in reference to your question, we offer to the world what we first offer to ourselves. We cannot offer to another, including an animal, a plant, or anything else, what we do not first offer to ourselves, for we are not qualified, then, to do so. We are only qualified by what we offer to our self. So we, knowing—as students of the Light, we know—whether or not we accept is another thing; whether or not we apply is still another thing—but we do know. We know from our own life that the effects of harmony are health and abundant good. We have already had those experiences. We also know that discord, discordant thoughts in our mind, discordant judgments in our mind, that we alone put there, that we alone call forth—the effects of those things, we've already experienced, are the lack of ease or known to man as disease. For man is not discordant and man does not lose the lack of ease—and peace, the power that healeth all things—healeth: bring into harmonious action all things. So, being aware of that, we know what our responsibility is. We know what we have the ability to respond to. And, of course, if we offer to our self disease, the lack of peace, the lack of power, the lack of health, wealth, and happiness, of course, that's what we offer to whatever we, in our evolution, have called forth into our care. As those who we are attracted to are attracted to us are nothing more and nothing less than the mirrors of our own denials of what we are, we therefore become dependent not upon those we attract into our life, [but] dependent upon our belief that what we have attracted into our life, oh, we cannot live without. Does that help with your question?

Thank you.

And so we find this seeming struggle in life. Here in old creation, things, they come and things, they go. Only God, only the principle of peace, only the power of good is ever with us. Now whether or not we wisely choose to deny or to accept, in time, in this great illusion called time, we will. Be rest assured, we're already in the process. When we no longer find sufficient good in that which we have, by our own law attracted into our life, we move on in consciousness. And in time, we move within, through the expansion of the limit of our own judgment.

And so whoever lives in the shadows of the mist must pay the price that is extracted by the shadows of the mist. For a shadow has no soul. A shadow has no spirit. It is only a shadow, the reflection of the obstruction to the Light of God. So whoever identifies with the shadowland—and please remember, the shadowland is that which has passed, be it a moment, a century, a week, a day, a month, or an hour. The shadowland is that which has passed—the price is very great, for the shadow is the effect of an obstruction in consciousness to the good, to the Light, to the truth that we truly are.

And so we are being. And being is the moment of conscious awareness. All feeling, all emotion is based upon the effect, the effect of a shadow. Do you understand—

Yes.

—what I mean by "feeling"? First, we must, through our own denial, experience need. Experiencing need, we experience emotion. Experiencing emotion, we experience feeling. For we identify with limit and we lose what we are and become what we are not. So if the hand is removed, where are you? Are you the foot? Are you the toe? If you are, you are bound and serving a shadow, an effect. Whoever serves effects does so at the cost, at the great cost and the sacrifice of what they are.

The only thing that tempts the consciousness, the only things that ever tempt the consciousness are shadows. They tempt us through the law that we establish by believing, *by believing* that that moment in which they were created, that moment and the way they were created is the only way we experience God. And because we alone, we alone created that limit, when those shadows rise across the consciousness, through the identification and awakening of self-awareness, we are tempted. We are tempted by our weakness. We are tempted by our unawareness of what we truly are.

You cannot tempt that which does not need. How can you tempt that which has no consciousness of need? You can only tempt what denies. And what denies must pay its price, for the laws, divine laws are very just. They do not fail. The principle of peace does not fail. Man fails in his efforts to control his own mind. Man is not patient. And the reason man does not often express the wisdom of patience is because he believes what he is not. I hope that's helped with your question.

Yes.

What is the process of identification?

The process of identification?

Yes, sir.

We cannot identify and, therefore, become until we deny what we are and believe what we are not. You see, by denying what we are, we experience need to *be*. By experiencing need to *be*, we search, we identify, we become, and we are bound by our own beliefs. Now that isn't a subject you've got to think about [from] eons ago and the evolution there[from]; [it is] the evolution of the moment. In your mind, you often tell yourself, "I do not have this. I do not have that. I do not have that. And I don't see how it's possible I'm going to get all those things that I need." Do you understand?

Yes.

Now some time ago, we revealed to our students how to free yourself from need. The same truth we again reveal, a bit more expanded perhaps—different vehicles through which to express the same light; different vehicles, different words, same teaching. You take and you steal—the mind does—the divine expression called desire. You steal it by putting boundaries around a principle. Then you look around the world of creation to get it filled. Because you have put boundaries on it, you've emptied it. That's how you empty the divine expression called desire. You see, the moment that you put a limit on a principle, you experience the need of a personality. Do you understand that?

Yes.

So our mind looks around and it says, "I need this and I need that. And I need that and I need that. And I need that because I desire it." Is that not true?

Yes.

"And I desire it because I believe I don't have it." One does not desire what they have. So what has happened, you see, in that stage of evolution, that's when you give back to the Divine that which you have stolen. Say, for example, that you want a new chariot, all right?—an automobile. And you have this desire. You first justify why you don't have it. You must first justify that to your mind. You must first tell yourself, "I need a new car." You tell your mind you need a new car—justify—"because the one I have is not doing such and such and such and such and such and such. I am weary of the color." And go on down the list.

So, you see, the human ego (uneducated) must justify all its thoughts, acts, and deeds. For if it does not justify all its thoughts, acts, deeds, desires, if it does not justify them, then it has no defense to support its judgment, the effect of its own denial, the experience of need. So it brings up all of its troops, its armies of mental substance, to protect the judgment it has made—its own denial.

Now to give all of that to God, to give back what we have stolen—stolen in the sense that we have put a fence around the divine expression called desire—and to give that to God, to the power within you, and to use the faculty, the wisdom of patience, in keeping with your own laws of evolution, you shall experience the day when the principle, the principle of the desire, which you stole by fencing in, shall be fulfilled. You, however, cannot dictate to the Divine that your new chariot shall be red, gold, green, yellow, or white. But a new chariot it shall be in keeping with your giving that gift of self to God and not loaning it.

So many people pray for things. I would not like to be awakened and awake to the force that answers the call of dialing up for things, for the domain of limit is something that is the domain of the fallen angel of the principle of peace, the Light, the Infinite Intelligence. So whoever prays for things dials up on their little telephone of communication to that fellow that chose, by his own denial, chose need and who, by that own choice, fell from the right hand of good. And God, the Light, sustains the realm of limit, of form, of need.

And so, though we bargain with people who believe they are limit, though we give and take—little give, lot of take—when it comes to dialing up for things, for limits, be rest assured, that realm that answers the call takes a lot more than what it's willing to give. I think perhaps you can best relate that to what they term loan sharks in your world.

Now, I think it's time for our refreshment. Thank you.

JANUARY 10, 1985

CONSCIOUSNESS CLASS 243

Good evening, class.

Tonight's discussion will be on defilement of the temple of God. Now throughout the ages the prophets have taught and forewarned all humanity not to defile the temple of God. And how do we defile, and what is, the temple of God? We all, I'm sure, agree that the temple of God to which we are personally responsible is the body in which we now live. Therefore, whoever goes against the purpose of design is defiling that purpose and, in so doing, is defiling the temple of God to which they are responsible.

Now what are the reasonable, self-explanatory results of the defilement of anything? To go against the purpose of the design of anything is a defilement. And the results of that defilement are a degeneration, for degeneration is simply going against the original purpose of design.

None of us consciously choose to defile or to degenerate ourselves. None of us do that as a conscious effort. We do it in a lack of understanding the purpose of design. When we use a saw that has been designed to part a piece of wood and we use it for a hammer, we are going contrary to the purpose of design. We are defiling the saw. And therefore we have degenerated the purpose of its design. When we use a knife to pry open a can or a jar instead of that which is designed for that purpose, we defile the knife. And therefore *we* are degenerate in our act, in our thought, and in our deed.

We so often question why there is such struggle in our life and in our world. It is because we are not pausing to consider. Our eyes are designed for a purpose. Our feet are designed for a purpose. Our nostrils are designed for a purpose. The light of reason, which contains as an indispensable ingredient of reason, contains total consideration. We would not consciously desire to be defiled. We would not consciously desire to defile anything or anyone. For in knowing the law, we must first defile and degenerate our self.

The temple of God is the house in which the Principle of Goodness, by divine design, flows. When we seek goodness—we seek it, for, through our errors of ignorance, we have denied its existence within us. We cannot seek nor search for anything that we have not first denied the existence of within our own being. And so as we seek and we search for good, it is only the effect of denying the good that we are in truth. And the payment of that error of ignorance, for everyone, is very great and very high.

Sooner or later in our evolution, when we have sought and we have searched, when we have struggled and we have wandered far enough and long enough into the worlds of creation to find the goodness that we first denied, we stop the search.

We stop the seeking. And when we stop, we pause. And when we pause, we gain control over these multitudes of forms in our consciousness. And when we gain control over that, we find the goodness that we are. We no longer are deceived by the denial of what we are by believing we are what someone or something tempts us to believe they have that we need.

Everything that we think we need, everything in life is the effect of denying its existence within our own consciousness. To the degree of our faith is it made manifest unto us. We always get what we really want. And we must begin to question, If it is demonstrably true—and indeed it is—that we always get what we really want, then why do we cry in the frustrations of our mind that we do not have what we really want? It only reveals to us that we *believe* we want this and we want that. But that isn't what we want at all.

Our faith is equal: we have great faith. None of us have more nor less than the other. We use it in different ways. And the greatest faith a person can possibly demonstrate in their life is to thank the Principle of Good, called God, for that which they *believe* they want and, from that belief, experience the lack thereof. Therefore, in seeking this goodness, the effect of denying its existence within, to declare the demonstrable truth, to thank God, this Principle of Goodness, for having it, you rise in consciousness and live to see the day in your mental world that you have it, for you refrain from denying what you are by the demonstration of gratitude and the manifestation of faith.

We so often limit faith to religion and yet, we demonstrate faith in so many different ways. It takes this great power flowing through us, directed by faith, to a judgment, a form—it takes this great power directed in that way through our channel of faith to the form of the judgment to be convinced, by the created mental form, that we are it. That, my friends, takes great faith. It takes great faith to convince the human mind that it is the judgment of any moment. It takes that great power. And God in his divine mercy has granted us the divine right of choice—to choose to degenerate the purpose of the temple of goodness, to choose to be, temporarily, the prince of darkness, when the angel of Light is ever waiting for our own awakening.

And so each time that we permit our mouth to speak, an effect of our mind to think, that we have not and we need, that we are emotionally upset and frustrated that things don't go our way, remember that it takes this great power, the direction of it, through the avenue of faith, to be convinced and, therefore, to believe that you are the denial. You see, we convince our self that we are the denial, for we constantly convince our self that we are in need. We do not permit a day to pass in our lives that we do not permit our self to believe we need this and to believe that we need that. And so look at this great power that is ever available to us, never absent or away. We, however, restrict, usually, this great power to the lack of supply of the goodness that we seek by denying that we already have it.

No one seeks anything in life that they do not first deny and, therefore, experience the lack in consciousness of. A person says, "I need love. I need affection. I lack love and I lack affection." We lack it for we deny its existence within our consciousness. And by denying its existence within our own consciousness, we, therefore, experience within our consciousness the effect of that denial and, therefore, go searching, ever looking for what we believe will bring us the goodness, the God that we seek. Therefore, we become dependent on people, places, and things. However, it is a dead-end road. There is an end to it. There are many detours before the end, but it is, in truth, a dead end.

Now many of you are not aware what is meant by dedication. Dedication, as I've stated before, is dead to everything but that which we choose to believe we are. And so if we wish to be dedicated to something better than what we have already experienced, let us then be loyal, loyal to our self. Let us be loyal to what we are and stop being so loyal and so dedicated to what we are not.

Now we'll pause for a few moments for any questions that you may have in reference to the payment of the transgression of the law, the demonstrable law, the will of goodness, known to you as total acceptance. For whatever you accept in life, you do not deny. And what you do not deny, you do not experience the need of. We all have the power within our consciousness to accept. That *is* the will and the unobstructed flow of goodness. It is available to us every moment. It is never absent from us. We do not experience it in the moments that we deny its existence.

In order to judge, we must deny. Therefore the Principle of Good is free from all judgment. This goodness that you seek as an effect of denying its existence, of denying what you are, flows unobstructed through the flower and the tree, the plant and the animal. It has, and *is*, total acceptance. God or goodness is the greatest servant you will ever know, for no one is ever left without.

And when we accept what we really are and stop believing what we are not, then we will accept everything, the right of all expression. Whoever accepts totally the right of all expression is freed from the frustration, the struggle, and the suffering of the errors of ignorance and the transgressions of natural law. Because we accept the right of everything, we are freed from all obstruction. And when we are free from all obstruction, life flows harmonious. And the effect of the Law of Harmony is health, the health of our temple of God, the health of our mind, the health of our wallet, the health of our purse, the health of the principle of joy. It is only the denials that build obstructions.

Because you accept the right of all expression does not guarantee you must experience the right of all expression. You accept the right of it and do not pretend to be greater than the Principle of Goodness. For whatever, as you well know, that we cannot tolerate in another is waiting to be educated within our self. Whatever we find our self, through so-called pride, adverse to, we guarantee to become attached to. For the Law of Adversity guarantees the attachment to what we are adverse. For we over-identify with the obstruction until we guarantee the day when we believe we are the obstruction. That's called the bondage of attachment.

And so what is it when we permit our mind to say we have not? What joy, if any, do we experience from the suffering of that belief of ignorance? What thrill could we possibly, possibly be tempted to, to deny the goodness that we are and believing the opposite? What possible sensation can be greater than goodness? What possible thrill can be greater than the abundant health, wealth, and happiness that is what we truly are? What possible thing could tempt us to be the victims, through dependence upon the forms of limit, upon the forms of denial?

Our physical body, in keeping with the physical laws of limit, we are not. When we believe that we are, we suffer. We use the limit for the purpose of its design and experience the goodness that is. We go contrary to the purpose of the design of limit in a world of creation and we pay the price. And the final effect, that dead-end road, is that we wrench our self free.

Now long ago I spoke to you to spend some time each day—a few moments—and tell yourself the demonstrable truth, "Thank you, God, I'm getting just exactly what I want!" Because, sooner or later, you are going to say to yourself, "I don't like this experience and I'm getting exactly what I really want?! I have got to awaken within myself and stop believing that this is what I want and that's what I want. I must," as you would say, "clean up my act and get a different perspective. Because that's not intelligent thinking." To experience frustration, deprivation, degradation, and deprivation and know the truth—that you are getting what you really want—is indeed a difficult pill to swallow.

Now it's time for your questions, if you will raise your hands, please. Yes, the gentleman in the back, please.

How is the denial—what would—that seems like a great degradation. How did that first enter into our experience?

First of all, if you will review within consciousness the many, many teachings that you have already had long before coming to this particular school—many prophets have spoken forth over the eons of time. The Principle of Goodness, the effect of total acceptance, freed from comparison—of course, you cannot have judgment without comparison—freed from the Law of Duality, expressed itself freely without limit. Now in the evolution, in what you would call evolution of time—there is no time. It's something that the mind, mental worlds have created. It does not exist in truth. It exists only in mental worlds where limits are. What you know as the spiritual world is limitless. That which is limitless is therefore free.

When this Principle of Goodness entered, through design, the realms of limit known as form, the law, in order to accomplish that, is known as the Law of Duality. For in order to have limit, you must establish the principle of comparison. And in order to establish the principle of comparison, you must have opposites. And so creation is governed by the Law of Duality, the principle of comparison, through which pride expresses in what is known as judgment.

Now you wanted to know how it became established and of what benefit is it.

Think of the great responsibility that we all have. First, in accepting that which we are—the free, formless Principle of Goodness, known as God. Then think of what we believe we are. We cannot levitate. That is, most people in your world cannot levitate because they believe they are the limit of their form. Therefore, through that belief, they are governed and controlled by the Law of Creation, which is the Law of Duality, which is subject to comparison, which expresses through what you know as judgment or bondage. However, there are those while yet in form who remain free because they do not believe that they know who they are and, therefore, are not governed by, at all times, those laws of limit, duality, or creation.

What you know as suffering does not exist to that which you are. It only exists to that which you believe you are through the laws of identification with the Law of Duality, the principle of comparison, the bondage of judgment. Need or denial does not exist to what you are. It exists only to what you believe you are. And it is through an over-identification with what you believe that you are that you suffer and that you struggle. For identifying with what you believe that you are places you not only under the laws of duality, the Law of Comparison, the bondage of judgment, but it places you in what is known as a flux and flow tide of creation. You rise in creation, only to fall, only to rise again, only to fall again, only to rise again. If that were not true, you would not have so many marriages and divorces in your world.

So you rise up with one desire, perhaps you fulfill it for a moment or a time, only to sink again, only to rise again. You call that the spice of life, I think, known as variety. We know it in our world as license, the degeneration of the principle of liberty.

And so when you, in ignorance, defile the purpose of anything, you must pay for that defilement through the degeneration of the purpose of the design, through the depravation and the degradation. And so by believing you are the limit and by over-identification with your belief, you experience the lack, the limit, for you have identified with the limit to such an extent that you believe that you are the limit. And so you look at your hand and you believe that you are hand—you are your hand. The hand is cut off and you experience the suffering thereof. And yet the hand still exists—the hand of the body that is responsible for the gross physical effect that you look at and call your hand.

Now, the domain of limit is the domain of the fallen angel. It is the domain of Lucifer, who fell from the grace of God. By believing that he was the limit, he became the limit and, in so doing, experiences, as the payment of that belief, as the payment of that over-identification, the lack of goodness in life. For whatever goodness limit experience[s] is totally, wholly, and completely dependent upon the Law of Duality, called payment and attainment. And so you pay dearly to attain little and then you fall to pay more to attain less.

Now some of you say, "Well, the experience never did meet the expectation." Well, of course, it can't meet the expectation. We always expect more than we're willing to pay for. That's what the world of duality and limit has to offer. We expect more because by expecting more, we are greatly tempted. And so as long as we continue to expect much and experience less, it serves a very good purpose to stop looking outside for what you have readily available to you inside. Does that help with your question?

Yes, sir. Thank you.

You're welcome. Yes, the lady there, please.

Is it as simple as it sounds to change it over, that search for the love you talk of? Or is it a longer, slow but sure process one goes through?

Well, in reference to a slow, but sure process, that depends upon what a person judges within their consciousness how great their need is. You see, there's one thing about the denial of God—the need becomes so intense that we finally turn back to God. And so therefore when we teach, "O suffer senses not in vain for freedom of thy soul is gain," it is through that process.

Now, if you believe you are the type of a person that doesn't care for long durations of suffering, then, to that type of mind, one is inspired to make the suffering as short as possible. And one awakens within their consciousness: "I'm going to work very hard. I'm going to stop trying and I'm going to start doing." So it depends, of course, upon the desire of the individual and their particular mind, their particular bondage of belief and also how much thrill they experience from pain and suffering. Does that help with your question?

Yes. Thank you.

Yes. Some people, you know, they receive a great deal of energy, you see, as an effect of their suffering and pain, for they solicit it. They have something within their consciousness to justify their solicitation for more attention and, therefore, gain more energy from others. Yes. That help with your question?

Yes.

Yes. *[After a short pause, the Teacher refers to the church dog as he continues.]* Well, long ago we said that God, the Principle of Goodness, is like a flea; you never know when you're going to find—where you're going to find them. *[Many students laugh.]* But I'm sure that they know their home and they'll stay in his aura.

All right. Are there any other questions this evening? You know, I—yes, the gentleman here, please.

So when you speak of denial, that's the effect of need or you say—

No, need is the effect of denial.

Need is the effect of denial. So if you feel that coming upon yourself—

Need?

A need.

Yes, then you know you are denying what you are and tempted to believe what you are not and can never be.

So at that point, what is the best thing to do?

Well, at the point that one begins to experience—first of all, one has to become sufficiently identified with what they are not. And we become sufficiently identified with what we are not by thinking of what we call self. We think of our self. And when we think of our self, we direct intelligent energy to limit. We direct intelligent energy to what we are not. We direct intelligent energy to what we are using, a body, a temple, a mind. We direct intelligent energy to that limit to the extent that the limits, the thoughts of the past and the patterns of the mind of past experiences rise up, receive the intelligent energy, are activated, and begin to control our being.

Now when they begin to control our being by draining sufficient intelligent energy from what we truly are, we become convinced that we are those forms that have—we have awakened through over-identification with them and we convince our self—they convince us, those shadows, that that is what we are. And because they are designed by the principle of limit, they offer to us only limit. They support our experiences of limit for they were designed by us for that purpose.

So where does one put the brake on? One puts the brake on when they find that which they are, this formless, free abundant goodness, when they find that they're beginning to think of limit, they're beginning to think of what one calls themselves. And, you see, when that happens, the principle of duality enters; the principle of neutrality, the divine free spirit leaves. So one puts the brake on in those moments of awareness by putting God in where self is trying to gain a foothold. For self is only the expression of the bondage of belief and that is not what we are. And if we permit the identification to continue for any length of time, then we are directing, through this great power, this great avenue called faith, to that bondage, to that limit, and we must pay the price to wrench our self, once again, free.

Now we all know if any of us were, or are, what we believe, we wouldn't be here this moment, for we have believed so many different things in our life. So we all know that we are not what we believe. We all know that. You see, there's a time in our life when we say, "I believed, I believed with all my heart." And some people even go so far—some minds—"With all my body, heart, mind, *and soul*." Well, that realm doesn't even know what a soul is. It denies its very existence. So it only shows its own ignorance. And we really believe, you see, and we say, "Yes,

I really, I really did believe that I was in love. I believed I was in love, body, mind, and soul." Whatever happened to that belief? "Now I don't believe now, not now. Oh, that was years ago."

And then time passes. Something else happens in our life. And once again that belief—it's now a different person, different place, different circumstance, and yet, oh, we're absolutely convinced. We totally, totally believe! And yet we are not awakening to the demonstrable truth that the duration of the belief is dependent upon the belief that preceded it with another person, another and another and another. And so time marches on. And so the duration of the belief is for this length of time and that limit. And then it gets shorter and shorter and shorter, as man and woman say they get older and older and over. And then finally that doesn't seem to work anymore. And they turn, finally, to the possibility in believing in the Principle of Goodness called God. And then, you see, they transfer that to what they call God. And then, all those false gods of the mental world rise up and then finally, some even become atheists, only to turn to the true God that does not demand, does not dictate, and does not judge. Does that help with your question?

Thank you.

Yes. You're more than welcome. The gentleman here, please.

Why is it, when we experience a denial, therefore a need in one area of our life, say, the personal, it seems to permeate all our entire life, such as business and all the other facets of our life? Why does it spread and contaminate the rest of our life?

Yes, that is very individual and it reveals to any individual that has the contamination spreading out through their business world that the original law established was directly related to and affected by the emotions of the person very early in life.

Now sometimes that is a hereditary tendency, you see, and sometimes, of course, it is not. Not all things are hereditary. I'm not here, of course, to give personal discussion on that matter, but I would like to say in reference to that, if we will go back in time in our life, we will see that in reference to our business enterprises that, as an indispensable part of the business enterprise, our social life was always, shall we say, the frosting on the cake after such hard day's labor. Does that help with your question?

Yes, sir.

And through that, you see—in other words, you see, our mind says to us, "Now, I've just about killed myself working like a dog, you see. And I have a right to entertain my senses and have some joy here." More properly, of course, satisfaction. And so early in our business endeavors, you see, in life, the Law of Association is established. Consequently, you see, then when things are not harmonious—they are discordant in our personal, emotional life—they have a direct effect, through the Law of Association, over many years of experiences, with our business life, you see. So it not only affects our personal emotional life, it has a direct corresponding effect upon our business life, for we have made it so in those early days of ignorance as part of our payment for working so hard. Does that help with your question?

Indeed, yes, sir.

For we have many businessmen in all worlds, of course, and their personal life is over here, and when it comes to the dollar bill, that no longer exists within their consciousness. They have it absolutely, totally separated and their waters are totally parted in reference to those things. They will not permit them to mix. But should one have that particular pattern and through those laws of association, then one should make great effort, great effort within their consciousness to be very considerate and very kind with the individual and tell them that if they're interested in you, of course, then they must show more consideration for harmonious, happy, and joyous time. Otherwise, there will not be the money for them to enjoy anymore. Period. That's it. Now if they have any sense at all, they will make great effort, because otherwise, it means they won't get to go any place, at least with you. Does that help with your question?

Indeed, yes. Thank you.

Yes, I would correct that, you see. A little bit of balance. A little healing. Yes. Thank you. What is it?

Yes. When the forms are repeating—

Yes.

And they're repeating full swing, let's say, and a person has trouble wrenching himself from it from time to time and more regularly than not, if it is a form that has duration from a past event, what is the way you break free from it so it doesn't hold you in that duration without just capsizing?

Yes. I can answer your question with one word, but I would prefer to—a little more explanation. So it'll take longer than what's left on there. Turn it over. *[The Teacher instructs the technician recording the class to change the audio tape so that the class can continue to be recorded.]*

That's fine.

Now in reference to the great struggle of wrenching oneself free from that which they have, of course, created in their life, it is a simple thing. Indeed it is. Redirect the attention. You can only open the trapdoor to those realms through your—anyone's identification with themselves, for that's the only place they exist. They do not exist anywhere else. They do not exist anywhere else.

Now ofttimes a person will say, "Well, I'll stay away from that person or I'll get all polluted." Well, what they are telling all of us, of course, is that, through that strong vibration in the atmosphere of self, self, self, self, that they are weakening themselves from overexposure. You know, you lay out in the sun, you see, for enough hours—in a strong enough sun—and you're destined to pay the price. I think you call it the burn of the sun, you see? So all things use wisely in keeping with the purpose of their design.

So if you find yourself entering that realm, you don't fight down there. Because, you see, down there, you're absolutely convinced that's you. And tell me—a house divided cannot stand. So you don't battle with what you believe you are until, through effort of not identifying, [not] over-identifying with yourselves, you experience what you are and not what you believe you are. So in order to go down there, you first, you see, you must permit, through over-identification with that trap, you must open that trapdoor. Then, while down there, the only way you can stay down there—there isn't any other way except by believing you are what's down there. You won't like it. So you don't fight down there.

When a person desires in life to win a battle, they battle on their own front, not on someone else's. So you don't go down into that realm [that], by the divine law, the false king of creation rules. The prince of darkness, that's his realm. And when you're down there, you believe what's down there [is] that [that] you are. You wait until you've crawled, exhausted, up from the prince of darkness' realm. And then on your home front in the light of reason you make the necessary changes not to be tempted so easily.

You see, a wise person knows from eons of experience it is a very expensive luxury to think of what one calls self. It is indeed a very expensive luxury. It would be far better, in old creation, to think of the tree, a favorite tree you have. A dog, a cat, a person is more difficult. You're more easily tempted to enter the realm below in thinking of a person. But, you see, to the uneducated ego, it's much better to think of a dog, because we have that wonderful ability to believe that we're smarter than the dog. And by believing that we are, we have, let us say, a better opportunity of staying up out of those realms.

Now the dog knows very well that you're not smarter than him. He is so smart, he permits you to believe that because in believing that, he can get his own selfish desires filled. And so, many animals, you know, they seem very humble and very passive—it's called passive resistance—and in the final analysis, through objective observation, we see that they do exactly what they want to do, when they want to do it. And because we believe we're smarter than they are and they, in truth, are really smarter—for they are better con artists than we are our self in that respect. Does that help question?

Yes. Thank you.

You're welcome. They have the smarts to appeal to our weakness, for they know that we are convinced of how right we are.

Are there any other questions in this evening's class? I wouldn't want you just to sit and fall asleep or to waste all that nice tape over there, with so many things of importance to discuss. Yes.

Could you please discuss about defiling our body by our thoughts?

Any thought that is—any thought that contains need is defilement of the temple of God.

Thank you.

For it is denial of the temple of God or the house of the Principle of Goodness. So any thought that contains within it need. Therefore, you see, when we permit those thoughts, we are defiling that temple of goodness and we will, of course, pay the price.

We must ever be aware, awake, and alert in our acceptance of what we are and on guard with the weakness and temptation, which, of course, is nothing but weakness, of what we are not. See, the truth of the matter is that all things we are, can do, and be. But that takes one thing: that takes the will of God and that is total acceptance.

You see, when a thought enters our mind of what we want to do, there are many thoughts that rise up in the emotions. To those who are aware, they know what those thoughts are.

They hear them clearly within the consciousness. To those who are not, they feel them as emotion. For that is—we have identified with the Law of Duality. So for every good thought that rises, there is equal and ofttimes more of the opposite. And for everything that we want to do and we believe that is us, there's always the—because we are depending on limit.

To put God in it or forget it is a basic principle of a good businessman. Because when you put God in anything, you take self out. And when you take self out, you take limit out. And when you take limit out, you have the limitless. And then, you see—for there are many things the mind desires. Well, when we give it to God or forget it, it enters our universe for we took limit out. You see, our belief is the limit. We identify with self and then we are bound by those laws. So it's only good business practice to take limit out and let limitless in.

Yes, the lady here, please.

When you say put God in it, is that a part of disassociating yourself from yourself?

Yes. You no longer—well, you are not the limit. You see, you never were the limit. There's no way possible that you can be the limit. You can only believe that you are the limit. That's as far as you can go. You can believe that you are the limit. You can believe that your eyes are a certain color and that those are your eyes. No, those are eyes that you use. You are not the eyes. If you were the eyes, when the eyes go, you would no longer have awareness that you are you. You are not the hand. You are not the foot. The foot is removed and yet you still are you. [You] have different feelings about being you because you believe that you've lost a hand or a foot, but you still are you. Therefore, you are not, *you are not* the limit. You are not the eyes. You are the formless, free being that uses the eyes in a world of limit.

But you are not the world of limit. And therefore when you put God, which is the Principle of Goodness, which is—the very movement of the Principle of Goodness is total acceptance. That is, the will of the Principle of Goodness, that's its movement. And so when you put God in, you remove the limit. And when you remove the limit in anything, the limitless flows and you experience the good. But when you do that, there is no dictate, there is no limit, there is no mental activity, there is no panting and suffering and waiting for the effect, for it is manifest in the moment of your own awakening. There is no experience of need. There is no experience of lack, for you are no longer in it.

You see, only God can make a tree grow. Only God can make a blade of grass grow. Only God can cause a flower to bloom. Now, you see, that's what you want to put into the business of living. Only God, the limitless can do it. Now our minds do many things, but only God can bring the goodness. No limit can bring the goodness. It can bring an experience in which we believe: "There's goodness!" But it's so little. It's so small. How long will it last, you see? "Will tomorrow's business be real bad? Will the holidays bring me the abundance that I am seeking?" Holiday comes; holiday goes—didn't bring us the abundant good that we were seeking at all. We were in it (the very principle of limit), and the limitless was not allowed in. This is why anyone in their living puts God in it or forgets it.

Yes, as the lady asked, back there, it is so simple. It is so simple, you see. The one thing—and some time ago you received a lovely hymn and it states in a few of those words, it says, "God"—Principle of Goodness—"free me from the needs of glory . . . Honesty will lead me through." *[The song is "Humble" and it was given through the mediumship of Mr. Goodwin.]* You see, the needs of glory exist only in the laws of limit. They do not exist in the limitless, only in the laws of limit.

Now what are the needs of glory? The satisfaction of the limits, the limits of desire. And it is so fleeting. It is a thrill, a satisfaction for a moment. And its payment is very high: it's called, in your world, regret. The sleep of satisfaction is the waking, the awakening of regret. So show me a mind that's been satisfied and I will show you a mind that experiences regret: regret that it wasn't more; regret that it didn't last longer; regret that it costs so much. Give me your list of regrets, they cannot possibly (the satisfactions) balance the payments. Does that help with the question?

Thank you.

A mother, she raises her children. She experiences, depending on her own evolution in consciousness, she experiences the satisfaction of her pain. For she believes *that* is hers. She *believes* she has had the experience; that is, in her mind, the fruit of her womb. And therefore, ever in keeping with the belief that she is her womb is the attachment to the fruit thereof. And so that is an experience of the needs of glory. That is an experience of the thrill of satisfaction. And the years roll by and the regrets grow into great mountains. And finally a mother looks along her path in life and sees this great mountain that she must climb—or remove—in order to continue on the path of her life.

For things, they come and things, they go. And forms are things. The body is a thing, a temple of the Principle of Goodness. It is what the—it is what the Principle of Goodness uses. It's not designed to use the Principle of Goodness. The Principle of Goodness is to use the body. The body's not designed—your automobile's not designed to tell you where you're going to go. Your automobile that you drive is not designed to tell you whether it'll start or stop or it's tired: no, it's not moving today. And yet, through lack of effort, we permit *this* vehicle to tell us that all the time. Does that help with your question?

Yes. Thank you.

You're welcome. Yes, the gentleman there, please.

When we deny and believe we are dependent, do we—is that dependence on the belief or is that dependence on the person, place, or thing outside?

Oh, no, the dependence is on the belief that we are the limits of the thoughts that we permit to enter our mind. It is all taking place within our own mind. We become the victim of our own denial. That takes place within our own mind. And because it is our mind, we can, at any moment, do something with it in *our* mind. Do not be fooled nor tempted to do something about it in someone else's mind, when you have everything available to do everything about it in your mind, where it was born.

You see, we, in these beliefs, you see, in this bondage, we believe that God enters our life by this person, that person, by this thing, that thing. And when this person and that person, this thing and that thing doesn't do what we desire, we lose this goodness in our life. And because we experience the loss of that goodness and through our own denial that we did it to our self, we're the last ones in that belief to admit we did it to our self. We're the last ones to see the divinity in disaster. We enter the karmic merry-go-round of blaming outside, for we're not yet evolved to accept it all took place inside. Does that help with your question?

Yes. Thank you.

Yes. So the first step in being free and experiencing the abundant good of life is to constantly remind the mind, "All right, this is my thought. This is my mind. It doesn't matter what he does. It doesn't matter what she does. It matters what *I* do. It matters what *I* think because it's my mind. They are my judgments. And they are affecting *me* first," you see. And you can do something with you; you can do nothing with someone else. You can be an instrument through which reason may flow or stupidity, but you cannot—care less what they do with it. For the moment you care what they do with it, then you are controlled by something outside in keeping with your belief and you pay a very dear price. It is a luxury that no practical person could possibly afford.

Thank you.

You're welcome. And if you will make the effort more often, daily, to say, "I was thinking of that person. Every time I think of that person, I get all upset. I shall stop thinking of that person or I shall change the judgments that I have concerning that person, because I do not desire for that person to become my god. And that can only happen by my laziness in consciousness and not making the change that I know is necessary and that is possible for me." It's called personal responsibility—the ability to respond to all personal experiences. And no one can possibly deny in their suffering and struggle and deprivation and degradation that it's not a personal experience. It's very personal. Yes, indeed.

Yes, the gentleman there, please.

Would meditation help us get rid of our needs in general and if so, how?

Yes, indeed, that certainly, certainly can. It contains that possibility and absolute probability. In fact, it's very demonstrable.

First of all, to properly meditate takes control of one's mind. It takes effort to control the mind and therefore the law is established in that particular respect to control the mind no matter what desires are tempting to distract us, no matter what weaknesses we believe that we are. It's time for meditation. That time is set aside. It is repeated each and every day, seven days a week, 365 days a year, year after year after year and establishes the law of the control of the self. It puts one's house in order before confusion sets in.

Therefore, an intelligent person, usually their intelligence says, "Now, I shall give that a try, to gain control of my mind, if nothing else. To once again be the captain of my ship and the master of my destiny." They establish that law of the control over the self. By so doing, in the course of any day, they can, through the Law of Conscious Awareness, once again bring that to their conscious awareness, that discipline—morning meditation time—and gain control over the weakness that is tempting them at the moment. And so in that way, it is extremely beneficial, most beneficial to anyone and to everyone.

And this is why we find one of the most difficult things for the human being to accomplish is the twenty-minute-a-day, daily meditation. If they begin to meditate at a certain time, the first thing that goes is the certain time. That's the first break, you see. That's the first leak in the dike, you see, in the dam. The next thing to go is, "No, no, no. I can't do it on Friday. Could do it on Saturday, though." And that's the next thing that goes. Then the next thing: "This twenty minutes seems more like an hour! I've got so many things I've got to take care of!" That's the next thing that goes. And then you finally see that that's all broken down. And once again, one is a victim of those realms, you see, of those limits. Yes. Yes.

As the years pass by, day in, day out, ten, twenty, thirty, forty, fifty, a hundred, five hundred, a thousand, ten thousand, etc., one experiences that freedom from those limits and then one can say, "I think I'll go back down to see what the limits are like. I'll stay down there for ten seconds." And you go down for ten seconds and you've seen it. "Yes, oh, yes. I remember what it was like." And you come back up again, you see. See, then you can consciously enter and leave limit, creation, need, suffering, health, wealth, and happiness, you see. Then you can consciously do that, you see. That is what we all strive for.

For, you see, we have this great responsibility as formless free beings entering limit and form to, through expression of that which we are, to raise the rates of vibration of the forms of limit. In other words, it is an educational process that is taking place, you see. And that is how all limit evolves and returns more refined to come out again. These are the laws of refinement of evolution. They have been going on for eons and eons and eons and eons of time.

It's just like if you have what you call a pet, an animal, a plant, or anything. You see, what you do with it and what discipline you offer to it, you are serving that which you are, not that which you believe you are. Then you become an instrument of goodness through which the plant, the animal evolves. And your purpose is then being served. You see, and when we don't do that, we go against the very purpose of being. And when we go against the purpose of being, we are tempted, weakened, and believe what has been, what is to be. And we—because we have gone against the purpose of being. Our suffering only exists on those two ends of the pole. Yes. So you bring what has been and what is to be together; that's called, "When our hindsight becomes our foresight, we gain insight." And that insight is the awakening of what we are.

One need not hope for tomorrow, for by bringing yesterday and tomorrow together, they are. And then for them, there is no yesterday, there is no tomorrow, for their consciousness is serving the purpose of their being and they *are*. And when you *are*, that's eternity, that is infinity. That's what you are. There is no three minutes. There is no five minutes. There is no thirty years nor sixty years. For you are all of that and, yet, not controlled by it. That's being in it, not a part of it.

See, God is *in* creation. God is not a part of creation, for God is not limit. But without God, that does not exist. It exists only as long as it serves the purpose of its design. When it goes against the purpose of its design, it goes through the decaying process and returns to the source from whence it rose. And so thoughts, like flowers and all other limits, they rise and fall and rise and fall. And so we can already look and see, "Oh, yes. This thought has risen and it is in the process of falling. This thought has risen before. It's much more refined today than it used to be. It's become cunning and clever, devious, etc., for that's how limit works." For it learns from the intelligence that we are, you see. That's where it gets its learning.

So remember, when you are working with the thoughts, first of all, separate truth from creation. Look at the thought objectively within the consciousness. And in so doing, listen to it. It will tell you—and it's very intelligent. It has access to the intelligence that you have permitted it to have access to. And you remember one thing in life: that which they do not know does not harm us.

And the battle never ends, for the war is never over. As long as there are vehicles through which formless, intelligent energy is to express in keeping with the very design and purpose of the world of creation, the battle never ends; the war is not over. For without the darkness, there is not the awakening of the Light. For in a world of duality, there must be comparison. And so man walks along a very thin, thin line, ever tempted to the warmth and satisfaction of the darkness, ever looking to the sunlight of reason. And if we believe we are the senses of the world of creation, then to the warmth, the satisfaction shall we fall, only to rise again, only to fall again. And so as we rise in regret, we grow in reason. And it is reason that transforms us.

Thank you. I see that our time is up. Thank you. Good night.

FEBRUARY 14, 1985

CONSCIOUSNESS CLASS 244

Good evening, students. This evening's class, we'll carry on with our discussions: faith and belief and the Principle of Good.

Now all of us have heard, from various philosophies, that to God all things are possible. And yet, ofttimes in the course of our daily experiences that doesn't seem to be what we ofttimes experience. However, if we accept that God is the Principle of Good and that to God, which is the Principle of Good, all things good are possible, therefore, why do we not experience this God or goodness throughout our daily activities in our life? Well, when we look at the reason why we ofttimes do not experience goodness is because we censor what goodness is.

Goodness or God, for us, ofttimes is dependent upon the dictates of our own mind. And by believing that we are the thought in our mind, God, the Power, the Divine Principle, which sustains the mind and the thought thereof, is not and cannot be subject to that which is, in truth, in its own evolution, in its own growth and expansion, subject to that which it depends upon for its own existence. For example, we believe that we are the thought of our mind and in so doing, our thought, our mind, which is dependent upon experiences of limit of past events, dictates what good is. So when we dictate by our thought of our own mind and we believe that we are that thought by over-identification with our mind, then we do not experience that Principle of Good and, therefore, cannot expect that all things are possible to it for us, for we have chosen, through our own error of ignorance, to believe we are the thought of our mind.

The step in evolution to make, in that respect, is the separation of truth, that which we are, from creation, that which we believe we are. As we insist, in this error of believing, that we are limit or creation, we suffer. We suffer the pangs of so-called frustration. We all know from our own experiences what frustration is like. We cannot help but agree that it is not a harmonious or beneficial experience. And yet, we find ourselves frustrated because we believe the thought in our mind that says to us, "Things are not going my way." When we say that, we reveal to our self that we believe, at that time, that we are the thought in the mind at that moment. And yet we all know that we have many thoughts in our mind and that those thoughts change. Gradually, slowly but surely, they evolve. They expand. We broaden our horizons by expanding our consciousness. And so we know from our own past experiences that we are not what we thought we were in times past.

Ofttimes, in times present, one moment we believe we're this, only to turn around and believe we're something else. Now how do we do that? We tell our self, "This person to whom I am attached or this thing to which I believe I am attached is not responding in a just and fair and loving way. This thing, this person, this place, that place is not justly treating me." We reveal, therefore, at those times, to our self, that we believe we are that thought. We project upon another what we have bound our self to. It's known in this philosophy as reflections from within. Someone smiles, and if we believe that we are the thoughts of our mind, which we are yet to demonstrate control of, then this smile means to us that they're happy with us or, in truth, it's not a smile; it's a grin and they're making fun of us. And so all of this is taking place within what we temporarily believe is us.

Now the goodness that is in such experiences, over a period of years or centuries, is that we do become weary of those experiences. Ofttimes in our evolution, we become very suspicious and we become very cynical. We enter the depths of despair. We begin to believe that everyone in the world is out to get us. We look in our consciousness to find a justification for that temporary belief. When we want something and we believe we are the want of the moment and we don't get it, then we justify in order to bring some degree of balance or stability to our mind. The only way that we can bring about a freedom from that type of bondage is to accept, as I have stated before, the possibility of our right to the goodness of life; that in that possibility we are not dependent upon anything, anywhere that is beyond our own control.

For when a captain of his ship of destiny gives charge to the first mate, the captain must accept, in so doing, that he is not the first mate. Therefore, in giving charge to his own ship, he must, in the light of reason, accept the possibility that his first mate has a mind of his own. And so it is the captain's responsibility, personal responsibility, being the captain of his own ship, to accept that possibility of such an experience and to once again, should the ship go off his course that he has charted, to once again take charge of his own ship. The first mate may or may not like it. The first mate may justify and blame outside, because he has attached himself to that which is the just and sole right of the captain of the ship.

Now you are captains of your ship. If you choose, at any time, to take what you call a break or a rest from your duties and responsibilities and you look around the world and you make the judgment, "That will be a good first mate to take over my ship while I'm resting," should you be tempted to do such a thing, then be rest assured that rest is not satisfaction. Whoever rests in life is aware, awake, and alert. Whoever is tempted to be satisfied is lulled to sleep, to a state of consciousness where the light of reason does not shine. And so should you choose to be satisfied, instead of to rest, then you must pay the price of the sleep of satisfaction. You must be willing to pay the price for what will take place with your ship by your own choice to go to sleep and turn control of your ship of destiny to someone else.

Therefore, a person who considers their personal responsibilities in evolution may close one eye, but never both. A person considering their own life—and each of us are responsible for our own life—weighs out whom they choose at any moment to take charge of their ship, puts their faith in the Principle of Good and not in the temporal pleasures of satisfaction. The price is great to those who believe that satisfaction is fulfillment. For there is one thing we have all experienced in the tempting to be satisfied: there is never enough. If there was enough, if fulfillment, that soul faculty, did in truth exist in satisfaction, then there would not be such a thing as temptation. For when a cup is filled, there's nothing left in the fulfillment of it but the overflow. So we can see from our own daily experiences that fulfillment is not satisfaction, that satisfaction leaves our cup ever empty.

And so when we are tempted, let us remember, our cup shall ever be empty, for there shall never be enough to fill it. And yet we know beyond a shadow of any doubt that the cup overfloweth by the very Principle of Good.

And so it's our own perspective. It's what we choose to do with our own mind. We alone choose what we believe. We choose it, ofttimes, to satisfy what we call a desire. And we go from one moment to the next believing that we're that desire or some other desire. And yet it is our own mind that is speaking. But our own mind is not us. Life has already revealed that to us. No one being freed from the temptations of unfulfilled desires would ever say that they truly believe they are need, they are constant want, they are constant unfulfilled desire. For to believe that we are that discord and disaster is to accept within our own consciousness that God, the Principle of Good, in truth does not exist.

And so we will find, at times, the mind says, "I don't believe in God anyway." Well, when we speak that forth, we are revealing to our self that we are firmly convinced we are the opposite of good. Therefore the Principle of Good in truth, for us, at that moment, does not exist.

What we cannot control by our mind, as I have stated before, we diligently work to destroy. Whoever believes they are their mind and the thoughts thereof works diligently to destroy what it cannot control. That law is self-evident. Therefore, if we believe a thought, that creates a thought pattern, becomes a judgment, and an insatiable desire, and if we truly insist upon believing that we are that insatiable, unfulfilled desire, then we go out into the world to fill that desire. And because we have already deluded our self by believing we are that desire and by believing that it is filled only by a victim—someone to fill it for us, not God, not the Principle of Good—some person, some place, something, we therefore are driven, by our own uneducated ego, number one, through the law that like attracts like to search it out in the universe and to find it. For the law will not fail us. Once having found it, we are controlled by that obsession to control it.

And whenever the moment awakens within our consciousness that we cannot control it (that which we judge is the instrument through which our goodness is coming into our life), then there is no stopping our efforts in those realms that have no light that we believe we are, there is no stopping in our efforts to destroy it. For it becomes, within our own mind, a threat to what we believe we must have. And whatever threatens what we believe we must have is threatening the very basic instinct—the instinct of survival.

And so when we permit our mind to tell us that God and goodness is subject to a dictate of our mind, then we are driven and possessed to go into the universes and find that thing, person, or place that we believe will satisfy our desire, will fill our life, and restore in our consciousness the God or goodness that we cannot live without.

Nothing exists in creation without the Principle of Good. Without God, not even the ant that crawls the ground remains in the form of what you know as an ant. Therefore, human beings, ants, flowers, animals, must have, by the very Law of Survival, must have and must experience God or goodness. And when the form, at any time, judges that it is not experiencing God or goodness, it is driven and compelled to experience that which is absolutely essential to the continuity of its form. And so those are the prices—some of them—that we must pay in our error of ignorance. In believing we are form, we must pay the price of form. But in paying the price of form, let us awaken and not deny the demonstrable truth.

If we believe that in order to experience goodness we must have pieces of green paper and we do not have pieces of green paper sufficient to our belief of our own judgments, then we are experiencing the absence or the lack of the Principle of Good and we cannot long endure it. And so we are compelled and possessed to get it at any and all cost, for we must have God or we cannot survive.

The great danger in believing we are the mind, in believing we are the form is that we have lost control. And by believing we are our mind, we open up Pandora's box to all the shadows of experiences in our life. If we are trained as little children that we must have so much green paper for the goodness of life, then, when we do not experience in our evolution that much green paper, we lose God, we lose goodness, and we cannot bear it, for we cannot survive without God.

And so in your evolution if you accept the demonstrable truth, you will begin to broaden the avenues through which your mind will permit you to experience good or God. And in so doing, you will no longer be restricted to such few avenues of choice. And so when you do not have green paper, you can turn, with your mind that you believe you are, to experiencing your God as you view a flower, to experiencing the goodness, the God that you must have to survive, in a breath of air, in the viewing of the ocean or the waterfalls. And in so doing, in the broadening of your horizon, you will not destroy yourself by your own denials, which we have all lived to view are in truth our destiny.

If you have restricted your mind, that you believe you are in your stages of evolution, to green paper, to other people, broaden those horizons for your own good. For no mind is greater than the power that sustains it. And no thought is ever more forceful than the person who believes it. So our thoughts do just as much damage or just as much good as the bondage of our belief that we are them.

We pause, sometimes, and tell our self that God is everywhere, that there is no place where God is not. Now if we truly did believe that, then we could touch the tree and experience God or good. If we truly did believe that—for we know we believe we are our own thought, usually—if we truly believe that, we could look at the plant and we could experience God. And we would not have the frustrations and the dependence upon another species, like our self. We would not have the victimization of a piece of green or yellow paper. We would not have the frustrations from not experiencing the Principle of Good.

And so we must not permit our self to tell our self that we believe that God is ever present, never absent or away, we must not permit our self such a luxury of hypocrisy. We must not do that to our self. If in that statement that God is everywhere in everything and when we look and see that our wallets are getting thinner, in our own judgments, and we cannot look to the flower and be freed from the frustration of limiting God there, then we demonstrate unto our self that we are speaking forth one thing, demonstrating the opposite, and guaranteeing the frustrations of failure. For we are determined to be successful and I never ever saw a person that wasn't successful.

We may say that "I have failed in this and I have failed in that." We were very successful in the service to our own judgments of what we were going to accomplish. Therefore, we indeed and in truth demonstrate that we are successful in whatever we choose to be successful in. Even if the final experience from, or effect from, our own success of serving our own judgment is what our own mind tells us was a flop or a failure, we have accomplished that failure. And in that truth, it is demonstrable we have been most successful. Show me your failures, I'll show you your judgments that you may see how successful you really are.

That is encouraging, my friends. To show to you in honesty and truth that you are a great success, it's only a matter of being honest with our self. For when we look in honesty at the many successes in our life, then we can pause and we can say, "Yes, I got rid of that one out of my life when I chose to do so. I brought this one into my life when I chose to do so. I managed to accomplish more attention and more pity of myself because I set the laws necessary into motion to have less money. Therefore, I did and I was successful!" But, you see, my friends, we must be honest with our self. When we permit our minds to tell us that we are the need of a moment, we work diligently to fulfill the need and we are indeed most successful.

The problem is, a few moments later, some other need rises up [and] we believe we're that and it's contrary to the need prior to that need. And therefore we end up believing what a failure we are. We are not failures! We have evolved in evolution and, as forms in mental substance, we are the most successful, in that respect. We have evolved [and] we have available to us, consciously, infinite intelligence to direct however we personally choose to direct it. So when you say that things are difficult and not going your way, be honest with yourself and take a good look at the way they're going and say, "Now just a moment. Let me be honest. Why, I'm getting exactly what I set into motion. I forgot that that is what I wanted." Because you're going to see how right you really are.

You know, it's like, ofttimes I have found in your world of creation, it's like people come together and sometimes get married and [have] relationships and they're, they're so happy. And they say how beautiful life is and how great God is and how wonderful everything is going. And it lasts, oh, varying times. Sometimes, with some, it's a few days; others, it's even weeks. And there are even those who it spreads out to be months. And then—of course, we mustn't expect a miracle, perhaps a little improvement, as one of my students once said—there are some cases that possibly even go into years, though very rare in your world. And then we sit down and we say, "What was the matter with her or him? What happened to them? Everything was so beautiful and now it's all falling apart. What is this that they've done that I'm experiencing this disaster and failure in my life?" That's the lack of honesty—the total lack of honesty.

Whoever makes no effort to pause and be honest with themselves does not consciously face the fickleness of the human mind and, through a lack of honesty, refuses to see, from that lack of honesty, how fickle the human mind is without the light of reason. And so it has always been the advice of the Light to winter and summer anything before you spring and fall it. And yet, we do not see that happening, for the light of reason does not flow. From a lack of honesty, there is an unawareness of the fickleness of the human mind. Yet honesty will lead us through to the faculty of reason and there, we will clearly see: "Why, my goodness, in the course of one hour I have just experienced a hundred desires of which 99.9 percent are not harmonious or in accord with each other." Would one call that stable or fickle? I'm sure we would all agree that is fickleness.

And from our lack of honesty to look at our mind and demonstrate the truth—it is an instrument we use, but it is not what we are. Our own uneducated egos will not permit us to view that we are, in truth, extremely fickle. And whoever is extremely fickle is easily and extremely tempted.

And so we find these various relationships, and from a lack of honesty with oneself, fickleness begins to have full sway. And it shoots out there and there and there and is tempted and then it wonders, someday, "Whatever happened? Whatever happened? Why is there a failure in my marriage? Why is there a failure in my relationship? Whatever happened?" Why, we have proven beyond a shadow of any doubt how successful we truly are with the fickleness of our mind that we refuse to be honest and face the way it really is. For in so doing, we would force our self to accept the demonstrable truth: "That's the mind. That's what I use. That's not what I am."

Now just because we are not the mind does not exempt us from our responsibility of it. We are not the car we drive, but we are responsible for its care, attention and understanding it, that we may take care of it. And so because we are not the mind, we are not freed from the responsibility of being aware of how it works and aware of what it's doing just because we don't want to face the fickle mind that we insist on believing that we are. To do so is to separate truth from creation, to separate that which we are from that which we believe we are. One is power; that is what we are. The other is force; that is what we believe we are.

So no one wants the light to shine upon the shadows, for in the shining, the shadows disappear. And as long as we insist on believing we are the mind, we will not permit the light of reason to shine upon it, for in so doing, there will be no more shadows. For a shadow is only the effect of an obstruction to the Light of eternal truth. And for us to permit the light of reason to shine over the fickle mind, we must accept the truth that we are not it. We don't have to wonder or worry or concern our self about loyalty or fidelity until we're willing to grow up and be honest with our self.

If every thought we permitted our minds to express in consciousness were thoughts of good, then only good could we possibly experience. Whoever makes no effort to control their car guarantees the day when they're controlled by it. The demonstration is quite clear: what we do not value in life, we guarantee to lose. So what we take for granted, we establish the law to lose. That's demonstrable truth. So if you want something in your life to continue, then do not forget the law, for the law will not fail you.

And encourage yourself in the great success that you truly are: successful failures from successful minds and small people from small minds. Our minds broaden in one minute and our minds contract ever in keeping with our own efforts to be honest with our self.

Now we're going to take a few moments to pause for your questions in reference to our little class tonight to see how you think you really feel. From the truth, do you feel discouraged? From the truth, do you feel encouraged? From the truth, do you feel frustrated? How do you feel from your exposure to the truth? For how you feel reveals, of course, to all of us where we are. So we don't have to ask anyone where we are. All we have to do is ask our self how we feel.

Does a person—and this is a good question to ask oneself—does a person say, "I now feel poorly," or does one suddenly awaken to feeling poorly? Does anyone have an answer to that question? If you do, raise your hand. Which comes first, the chicken or the egg? Yes.

I think you suddenly awaken to feeling poorly. I think you feel that way first.

Why certainly, when we feel we're poorly, there's no question that we feel that way. How did we feel that way? What is feeling dependent upon?

Self-thought.

Very good. We first have to make a judgment of what we think and, in so making the judgment, experience the feeling. We must first make the judgment. In our reacting to anything we sense, hear, see, feel, or touch, we make a judgment. The effect of the judgment, our feeling when we are identified with the limit known as self, is dependent upon that judgment. So if you feel poorly, pause and go to the next step: "I feel poorly. I must find the thought pattern, the judgment within my mind, that I react to and experience feeling poorly. I can change my feeling by finding the cause of it." And so that's our right. That's awakening, for poorly cannot be considered, by any mind, as feeling good. Therefore, we must feel good: we have no choice, for we are dependent upon God for our existence.

And so when we feel poorly, the opposite of feeling good, we best find out what judgment in our mind is responsible for the feeling. And when we find what judgment is responsible, then we can look at the judgment, see what it is based upon, and see what it is dependent upon. And I guarantee you that any experience of feeling poorly is totally dependent upon a judgment of the mind that is telling us that something outside of us, beyond our control, we are somehow the victim of—a total denial of personal responsibility. It's like a person saying, "Well, I don't have enough money today. I feel poorly because I don't have enough money. And my God and my goodness and my good feelings are dependent upon me having a certain amount of money in keeping with my judgment. Now I don't have that money because—I guarantee you it is something that has happened—or happening—that is beyond your control. It must deny. A feeling of poorly or bad is totally dependent upon the denial of personal responsibility. And because it is dependent upon the denial of personal responsibility, it is something beyond our control. Our mind can tell us nothing else. Does that help with your question?

Thank you.

Thank you. Now we have time for the rest of your questions. *[After a short pause, the Teacher continues.]*

So because we know we must feel good to survive, then it is only reasonable that we start telling our self how good we feel. To those who make that effort, greater goodness, a greater God enters their consciousness. We have a choice to tell us what a good day it is. We have a choice to tell us what a terrible day it is. We have a choice to tell ourselves our God is dependent on what someone else does and therefore, "They're not doing what I judge will permit my God to enter my life. Therefore, I'm the victim of what they're doing." How sad. And yet, we insist, at times, on being successful with those types of experiences.

Did you have a question there? Yes, please raise your hand. You go right ahead.

Thank you. I've experienced feelings of regret and, to me, when that creeps in there, it's sort of like a con artist getting in there with justifications. And I was wondering if you could speak a bit on that—how that works.

Yes, of course. If you are experiencing regrets, then they—you must be rest assured the debt has come due and it must be paid. It's known as the chickens coming home to roost. Regret is the payment that all minds must make for the pleasure of satisfaction. You see, in a world of old creation, when we are tempted to believe that we are it, we find that we're tempted by the thought that says we have a need; the need must be satisfied. And so we establish all laws necessary to fill the need. We think it's getting filled. We accept that it is, through the temporary experience and the thrill of satisfaction.

As I have stated to my students before, it is much more economical and certainly more practical to take a short ride on the roller coaster for a thrill than to pay such an expensive price by the limits of the mind to receive any thrill, if it's a thrill that you need, dependent on someone else that you can't control. A roller coaster you can put in your money, a few pennies or whatever they charge you, you can sit in the seat, hold on for dear life, and get the thrill of your life, if you go on the right roller coaster. Then you can step off, if you're still able to walk, and have that wonderful experience that you had the thrill that you judge that you needed. You're only regret will be a temporary imbalance, perhaps, in walking for a few moments. But your price and your payment is so much more practical and economical.

And so a person who permits their mind to experience regret is over-identifying with the debt that they themselves chose in their moments of ignorance and they must pay. The collection agency has come to your door and they're going to collect their just due. You had the thrill; you had the satisfaction. The debt must be paid. Now the debt can be paid graciously or it can be paid with a great deal of emotional pain and suffering and frustration, but it shall be paid, for the law will not fail you. And in that respect, you only demonstrate how successful you really are. And so a person who has regrets over anything—you know, be honest with yourself and say, "Well, I had the thrill. It wasn't worth it. I really don't think that the debt that I owe can possibly be just and fair, but it was my thrill, my satisfaction. I got it and, like it or not, I have to pay for it." The chickens have come home to roost.

And if you look at it that way, you won't feel bad at all. In fact, look at the good that it offers your life. The next time that you're tempted, you will take a look at the price tag.

You see, creation—long ago I stated that to you—creation is a price tag; choose wisely what you buy. For the truth of the matter is, you're only making payments; you'll never own it. You know the word *buy* or *purchase* means that it is something that you're able to possess and control. That's not what it's like in creation. You see, that's why you must choose wisely. When you believe that you are the need to be satisfied by thrill, there are so many of those playgrounds in which you could be thrilled and pay your little pieces of green paper or in coins—very reasonable, very practical. And if you feel that you need a thrill two or three times a day, you could ride them two or three times a day. So all you have to do—or if you found it more economical or convenient, well, you could even get a horse to ride and experience the thrill if it'll go fast enough, you see. It depends on what you judge you will accept for your thrills of your senses.

And I can only say it's better, in these judgments and these beliefs of need for thrills and satisfaction, it's certainly much more wise, of course, and practical to choose something that you can pay for. It's started and it ended and you're free and clear and no chickens to come home to collect. Does that help with your question?

Thank you very much.

Any other questions? *[After a short pause, the Teacher continues.]* I'm so happy to see I have such illumined students. It makes me feel much better, because like does attract like and I am here in keeping with that law. Yes, do you have a question?

Yes. How is the spoken word life-giving energy?

How? That's your question?

Yes, sir.

How? You want the mechanics of the process, is that what you're asking for?

Yes.

Do you believe that's you that just asked that question? That's a question I have for you. Do you believe that's you? Did you believe that was you?

Yes.

It's a spoken word, isn't it?

Yes, it is.

You believed it was you.

Yes.

That which you are, the Principle of Good, the power of God, you have formed and, through your belief, solidified the form and given unto the form your very breath of life. And by that very process, your spoken word is life-giving energy. For you not only gave it your breath of life, you formed it by your own mind and you solidified it by your own belief. It is, therefore, your child, your form. You have given it birth. It shall return unto you ever in keeping with the way you sent it forth. And the manifestations in our life, known as our experiences, are ever in keeping. Speak forth and, in so doing, accept. It's yours, for that is the law. It is yours. It shall return unto you from the very level that it was given birth in keeping with your own belief. Does that help with your question?

Yes. Thank you.

Indeed. And so we speak forth many things and in so doing, we believe in varying degree. And those are the forms we have given life to. They cannot die, for they have been given the breath of life. And so whenever we believe we are the mind, they all come in. Some of them—hungry, tired, demanding their care, knowing, by the very law of birth, that we're the father, we're the mother. And we have a responsibility to care for that which we have given birth to. The law does not fail us.

So choose wisely what you give the breath of life to. God, the Principle of Good, unto you has given the breath of life. And you, in keeping with the law, have given the breath of life and continue to do so. That which you are, the Principle of Good, has given the breath of life. To what will you continue to give the breath of life? As we, having been given the breath of life by the Principle of Good, known as God—and we are the children of God, for God is our father. We are destined by the very law to return to that which has given forth that which we are. And so you, in keeping with demonstrable law, [having] given the breath of life to the thoughts of your mind, they shall return unto you. And as some of my students have said over the years that that goes around, comes around. No longer concern yourself with what's coming around. Awaken to what's going around in what you believe is your mind. Does that help with your question?

Yes, sir.

Go on. Yes, the lady here, please.

What is the purpose that God did give us the breath of life?

The purpose of form is the evolution and the awakening of limit to the limitless, which it, in truth, is dependent upon. And so when the human mind (limit) accepts it cannot and does not survive without the Principle of Good, then the human mind is awakened in consciousness through its own acceptance. And therefore, God, the Principle of Good, is fulfilled.

Thank you.

You see, the limit of good is the belief of denial. We believe we are need in keeping with denial of what we are. We deny what we are in order to become what we believe we need. And so man experiences need and frustration and everything that goes along with it, as his mind insists on denying that which he is. And the longer we continue to believe that we are the need, the effect of our own belief and denial—whoever believes they are separate, unique, special, individual, great, supreme, the one and only in all the universes, is far from the demonstrable truth of the good that they are. For they are dependent upon the limits of need.

We believe we are great in keeping with the need, the effect of our denial that we're not so great. For there was, in our own evolution, a moment when we knew beyond a shadow of all doubt that we are the Principle of Good that serves *everything*. And we look at that and do not take pride. And so pride, born of an insatiable need, the effect of denial, must take pride in what it can control. And so we go through the universe in our efforts to control something out there and wake up someday and find out what we made such great effort to control was, in truth, controlling us.

So often we look at the little critters and the little creatures and we say, "Wonderful dog—does exactly what I tell him to do. Just wonderful. Very dedicated, very loyal, very independent. I'm the only one that can feed him." And we enter that great deception, delusion, that puffivation of our so-called pride. Someday we look and we see, "What am I doing here? What am I doing? I'm a regular nursemaid. I have to drag her here. I have to drag her there. I've got to be home at certain times. I've got to do this. I've got to do that. Who's in charge here? Who really is the victim? I thought all the time I was controlling that lovely animal and now I realize it was so smart and so intelligent it gave me exactly what it observed that I believed that I needed." "I gave it the illusion that it was controlling me. And I'd better go someplace else now because that human has just woken up that I've been controlling them all this time." Now in your world, when that critter is a two-legged one, you call it a divorce. *[Many students laugh.]* I hope that's helped with your question.

The gentleman behind you, please.

Yes. What part of our anatomy is—does our soul lodge or live or exist?

Well, in reference to the limit of which you are speaking—because, you see, your finger cannot exist without the Principle of Good. Now if you cut your finger off, do you lose your soul?

We have these limited views, I think, of soul. The heart is the expression of the soul. Does the finger live in the human anatomy without the heart? If it is true, how does it get its blood and its life? No, it's the heart that pumps it there. Therefore, is the soul only in the heart? Good question that you have there.

Now this soul enters at the moment, the instant, the very instant when the negative and positive pole comes together. The soul has awareness of all life, all time, since its moment of individualization. Now so often we think of the soul as limitless. The soul, being individualized, is not limitless. It is the spirit, that which we are, that is limitless. The soul is an individualized expression of the Allsoul. We are spirit and being spirit, we're formless and free. Now this spirit that we are, formless and free, is individualized and that we call soul.

Now because we are spirit, formless and free, and that which is formless and that which is free is not limited by, for its own existence and continuity, to any form. That includes the individualized soul which, of course, is formed by its own process of individualization. Therefore, you have—some of you—awareness of what psychologists call split personalities, multiple personalities, etc., etc., etc. You have in various philosophies, studies, and literature what is called possession, demons. You have, also, your own understanding of what you call soul.

Now the question that you have brought up through your question of, In what part of the human physical anatomy does the soul reside?—you have opened up the door and we will take a few moments for that.

How does a soul leave a physical body and another soul get in? Ancient philosophies have taught that. Christianity itself teaches it, based upon the very principle of exorcism and driving out what is known as the demons. It is important in your evolution to first separate truth from creation. To understand the comings and goings of the soul, one must first accept, by separation [of] truth from creation. As long as you insist on believing you're the mind, the hand, the finger, then you have a ways to go in understanding the evolution of the individualized soul.

I can state this, in your present state of evolution, the soul comes and goes in keeping with the laws that you alone have established and continue to establish. Ofttimes I have stated to you—some of you, as students—you're out to lunch. Sometimes you're out to breakfast, lunch, and dinner! The soul with which I am working is not present at that moment. It's somewhere, but it's not in the form that you believe it is. It's out.

Now because spirit is formless and free and because we already understand that we have various thoughts and that we believe we're that thought or this thought or some other thought at a time, when you're out to lunch, someone else is in. And if you are not aware that you are out to lunch, breakfast, dinner, or supper, that is no fault of the Principle of Good or God. You have a responsibility to yourself, to your own eternal evolution, as an individualized soul, to know who's inside your vehicle at any moment. That's a responsibility that you have. But you cannot face that responsibility in honesty and truth until you begin on the path to separate truth from creation and stop believing you are these things. For as long as you believe you are the foot, then you are limited by that own darkness, that error of ignorance and, therefore, are not ready for further understanding of where you are when you're out to lunch or how you get out to lunch or who comes in to use your form for however long or what are they going to do with it.

You see, my friends, if you insist on letting someone drive your car, at least be honest with yourself and find out who it is that's driving it. For when you return to it, you are responsible for it. And ofttimes I have seen a soul return and be very upset at the one who just left, for they left them in a terrible mess. But that is not the fault of the soul that came in; that is the fault of the soul that left without facing personal responsibility of who was going to come in and what were they going to do with their old form in their life.

Now I speak to you not only from personal experience in my own evolution, but I speak to you in reference to my own channel. Don't think for a moment that he stepped aside graciously. It took a lot of work. He wanted a lot of assurances of what I was going to say. And he also wanted guarantees that it would not be contrary to what his mind told him was him. It takes a lot of effort and a lot of faith.

And yet, I speak to students over these years on Earth and I find they not only go out to lunch, they go out on vacation. And the one that's getting in there, they would never, in the light of reason, choose to permit them not only to use their body, but to mess up their whole life. And so I find students on the earth realms, now and then, waking up and saying, "What's happened? What a mess! How did this all happen?" and then, in keeping with the errors of ignorance, must justify what someone else has done to them, when it had nothing to do with someone else at all.

Now these particular things I have not spoken much upon to the group of students on Earth. To one or two, I have discussed it and how it happens. And so we will see what our next class brings in keeping with the law not only of your interest or curiosity, but in keeping with the Law of Personal Responsibility.

And when you're told you're out to lunch, try to understand it's a very serious, serious thing. Your world no longer works consciously with the masses through the processes of exorcism. Your world has entered the depths of delusion and deception that it doesn't exist. And yet, eons, centuries and centuries of your great philosophies have revealed repeatedly what happens. Your body is only a vehicle. You are not it; you are responsible for who is in it. You cannot be aware of who is in your body until you accept personal responsibility. It's a vehicle you're using. The abuse of it is your lack of awareness. If you insist on believing you are the thought of the vehicle, you have no control of who is in it at any time.

Thank you. And look towards the days ahead when you are ready—and remember, should that law be the path we go with our teachings, be rest assured I will not permit, as your teacher, to accept the grand cop-out that "Something possessed me for a moment." You will not be permitted to deny personal responsibility. It's your vehicle that you are using. It's your mind. You are not it; you are responsible for it. It's just like the moments of thrills and satisfaction: when the debt comes due, don't tell me it isn't fair.

Thank you. And good night.

MARCH 14, 1985

CONSCIOUSNESS CLASS 245

This evening we're going to discuss the step-by-step process on the path of freedom.

Now a long time ago you were given a little saying that is most applicable to these necessary steps. And that little saying is, "O Love divine, a servant be / 'Til selfishness imprisons me / And warps the reason of my mind / Into the madness of the blind, / When truth cries out, 'Not mine, but Thine' / And frees my soul with Love divine." [Discourse 25]

Now that seems to be a beautiful little saying, but it is much more than just a beautiful saying. It clearly reveals the path and the laws that are necessary to apply in order to accept what is known in this philosophy as personal responsibility. Now in speaking over these many years of personal responsibility, there appears to be great difficulty in applying that law. Whenever we permit ourselves to think that our experience, whatever it may be—an experience that we judge to be good, an experience that we judge to be not so good—whenever we permit our mind to think that way, we deny that law that frees us. And it is the denial of that law that causes us to suffer. The suffering is the experience of the belief that we are the thought of the moment. Because by believing that we are the thought that we think, we, therefore, bind our self to limit, to form, to what is known as creation. We, of course, know that we are responsible for the thoughts we choose to think. To permit our mind to tell us that the experience or the effect of the thought that we think—that someone or something beyond our control is responsible for them is a denial of the very truth that frees us.

There is no freedom until we make that effort each day to begin to talk to what we call our self. For what we call our self in our mind is our mind. It is not what we are, but it is what we, at times, think that we are. And because we think that we are these thoughts that we have in our mind, instead of accepting the demonstrable truth that we are the creator of these thoughts and that these thoughts are vehicles through which experience, in keeping with the demonstrable law that like attracts like, we deny what we are and accept what we are not. That is the suffering that we have in life. That is not the design nor the purpose of living. It is, however, the purpose and the design of bondage.

And so a person understanding that simple truth and in considering it each day, many times a day—for it is many times a day that we have experiences. We have many varied experiences. The ones that we judge that we like, we take credit for. The experiences that we judge that we do not like, we deny credit for them. And so we are, in that respect, of course, a house divided.

However, we must ask our self the question: Why do we— what is it within us that takes credit for the experiences in our life that we judge to be good? What is it then that denies responsibility for or credit for the experiences in our life that we judge to be bad? We, therefore, contradict our self. And in so doing, we reveal to our self that what we believe that we are is—demonstrably true—a contradiction. For you cannot take credit for experiences in life that you enjoy and deny credit for experiences in your life that you do not enjoy. For experiences in our life, the very principle of the law is that we alone, and nothing beyond our self, have established and created those experiences.

It's a process, of course, of growing up. Once accepting personal responsibility, we begin, first, to take credit not only for what we judge to be good, the experience thereof, we take credit for what we judge to be bad in our life. The difference between taking credit for what we judge is good in our life and denying credit for what we judge is bad in our life is very simple: what we judge is good in our life, as an experience, glorifies what we call—and believe we are at times—the self. And so the denial or acceptance of experience, ever in keeping with the censorship of our judgment, is a servant of what is known in this philosophy as self-glorification.

And so we go now to these triune functions, known as a mess and indeed a mess it makes in our life, called money and sex, both serving to glorify what we call our ego.

Now for many years we have taught that ego is designed to serve a very good purpose. Without it, man does not express initiative. Without it, we do not evolve the form in which we find our self on the planet. Therefore, to attempt to annihilate or to submerge what man calls the human ego is to go against the inevitable Law of Evolution and it is to deny the purpose of the soul's incarnation in form. Its purpose being to evolve the forms through an expansion-contraction process.

All form, all limit, evolves through an expansion-contraction principle. And so one must not make any effort to deny, suppress the human ego. One must learn, through an acceptance of the demonstrable Law of Personal Responsibility, to accept all experience in one's life as effects of laws that they alone have set into motion. And in doing so, one then begins to have the initiative to bring about the changes in keeping with what they judge is good or bad. No one in any world at any time chooses consciously to be the victim of what someone else is doing, is not doing, will do or won't do. For to do so is to turn one's back on what one is and make the effort to be what one is not.

Each and every person has evolved to where they find themselves at any moment. The purpose of growing is inevitable. We cannot—no matter how much we try—we cannot stop growing. Growing being an expansion and contraction process of evolution. So in spite of what we think we want or what we think at any moment that we do not want, we are growing, we are evolving. We do not have to experience so much frustration and so much discord and so much suffering. That is not necessary. It is only the effect of not applying the infallible laws of the Divine.

Like anything in creation, when we believe we are creation, we are the victims, at those moments, of what is called patterns or attitudes. We are the victims of patterns and ways of life, for we, in establishing those patterns and those attitudes, at the time of establishing them, through ignorance of attachment to our fruits of action, we believe we are them. That is the difficulty in making changes, which are inevitable in our life. That is the difficulty in accepting the freedom of personal responsibility. Yet, regardless of the difficulty, we find ourselves evolving; we find our self suffering from believing we are the patterns that we have become familiar with. And being familiar with the patterns, we have found emotional security in them.

But emotions, just like your hand, are vehicles designed to be used. Emotions, in and of themselves, you are not. You are, however, the one that, by the divine Law of Evolution, may use them wisely or unwisely. If you use them wisely, they will serve you (that which you are) very well. If you do not use them wisely, when the tools no longer serve the worker, the worker begins to serve the tools. So if you do not use the tool known as emotion wisely, you will someday awaken that the tool that you thought you were using is, in truth, from your lack of effort and awareness, it is now using you.

And so it is when anyone awakens to the truth that they are being used, they awaken with a great deal of resentment, a great deal of irritation. And if, in their evolution, they have yet to accept personal responsibility, then everything around them receives the blame for their experience of the moment. But in so doing, when we permit our minds to blame outside for our unwillingness to grow inside, there comes a time when we become very weary—that everything we touch does not work out the way that we judged it would, that everything we do seemingly, in our minds, begins to fall apart. That is a process that everyone goes through who denies personal responsibility. But the final result of that, after ofttimes years and centuries of exhaustion, is the acceptance of the inevitable: that blaming outside is, in truth, a process of creating false gods with clay feet; that false gods are destined to go. For they have come into our life and having come into our life, they are destined to go from our life. But those gods are not someone outside. Those gods are what we've created inside in our days of ignorance of the truth that frees us.

And so in keeping with these laws of like attracts like—and I stated at our last class in reference to obsession and possession, we certainly—some of us—have grown to that point where we have some awareness of thoughts and feelings that, at times, seem to possess our mind—that, as hard as we try to free our self from identification with these disturbing thoughts and these disturbing feelings, the harder we try to free our self from those disturbances, it seems the worse we get. And it is true, the more we battle with them, the greater the struggle for us.

And why is that so? Because we believe that we are the realm in which we are having the experience. You see, we believe and, through that belief, are solidified to our own judgments known as self. We believe that's what we are. And because we believe that's what we are, when these disturbances return to us in our life, we find great difficulty in freeing our self from them. We don't like the experience. We battle with it in our own consciousness. And yet, in that battle, we blame someone else for the cause of it. And because we blame someone else, we deny the law that frees us. Someone else did it to us. And as long as we insist on protecting this throne of self-glorification, then we must pay the price of that belief. And indeed, we pay that price.

And when we have enough experiences of discord, enough experiences of frustration, enough experiences of these distasteful forms that we don't like the feeling of, let alone the thought of, when that moment comes and, instead of battling them, we accept responsibility for them, we accept personal responsibility and in so doing and in that moment, we are then qualified to tell these children we have created in our ignorance exactly what to do. That's when they listen. They listen when we declare the truth. When we tell them, "You're my children. You've come home in keeping with the law: what I send out shall return to me. I, being the father of them, I, being their creator, they have come home. I don't like their looks. I don't like what they say. I don't like how they act. I alone have created them. If I permit myself to believe that I am creation, then I am one of them and have denied the authority of being the father of them."

And so when we allow our mind to tell us that the cause of the distasteful experience is what someone else has done, is doing, or has not done or will not do, then we become, through that, one of the children. And we fight with them. We will not win.

Now we may go to a counselor, a therapist, or someone else. If they have any awareness of the law, they will have objectivity. And if they have understanding of the spiritual laws, they may be instruments through which the light of reason may dawn in your consciousness. And when that light of reason dawns in your consciousness, your experience of those forms and that obsession and possession, you no longer have. For you, through the light of reason, have been transformed. You have been transformed through the light of reason by an acceptance of personal responsibility. You no longer are denying the truth and therefore, he who does not deny the truth cannot be bound by the lie. So in acceptance of the truth, the bondage of the lie, we are freed from. For the lie is a lie unto our self. And because it is a lie unto our self, it is only our self that suffers. For whoever establishes the law to lie, to deceive and delude themselves shall pay the price for that effort.

So when we discuss obsession and possession, it does not mean that you must suffer from those experiences. You have been granted, in keeping with the laws you all have established, an awakening within your own consciousness. The step is the application that that awakening has offered to you.

Life is indeed a joy to behold. It isn't a joy one moment and a terrible grief and sadness the next moment. That's not what life is. Life is a joy to behold. Now life is not a joy to possess. Life is a joy to behold. For it is in what we know as possession—the expression of the belief that it is mine, the denial of the truth that it is Thine, the Divine Spirit—that's where the problem truly is.

And so, you see, no one wants to hold to that which is distasteful. If you can and are willing and ready—because you certainly can if you're willing—declare the truth when all seems well: "Not mine, O God, but Thine." If you establish the law that it is not yours, but it is the Divine Intelligence's, you will state the truth. Now the most difficult time is not when things are going bad that you declare that truth. No, no, no. That's the easiest time. It is when things are going what you say good and well. For that is the time—that's the most difficult time. When things are going really well and you state the truth, "Not mine, but Thine, O Divine Spirit," you free yourself from the denial, which is a need for the glorification of self. For it is the glorification of self that is the greatest bondage you'll ever know.

So when things go so well, don't let the throne of self receive the glory. Then you will have no problem when you slip and things go what you say terrible in your life, things go really bad, in stating the truth: "Not mine, O God, but Thine." For no one wants to hold to that which is distasteful. And they have no problem giving it to anyone or anything they can find to give it to. So work when all things seem well. When you feel really good, declare that truth: "Not mine, but Thine." For then, you will place yourself not only in the light of reason, you will open the doors wide of supply. For you have become an instrument through which the Law of Gratitude is unobstructed in your life.

It is difficult for the mind to accept when one feels they're short of anything. It is more difficult when we believe we're short and we believe that we need. That's difficult. But, you know, we can't believe that we're short and we cannot believe that we need until we deny what we are. And in denying what we are, we blame the cause of that experience on something we cannot control.

Wise is the man who controls all experiences in his life, for that is the man who has accepted the demonstrable truth of personal responsibility. For all experiences, you are the captain of. You and you alone can change them. You and you alone can control them, for you and you alone have created them. Accept that truth, be free, and stop the denial and the suffering. For there is no benefit except its final destination; when you hit the bottom, that's when you're willing to try anything. And in keeping with your own effort to maintain and to sustain that willingness shall you remain free. It's when we hit the bottom and we're willing, then, to try anything that anything begins to work. Then we easily slip back to the patterns of mind that we are so familiar with, only to fall again, to rise again, to fall again. The rising and falling, the flux and flow is ever in keeping with the acceptance and the denial.

Now it's time, a few moments, for your questions. Yes, please.

You spoke last week on when the soul goes out and you're out to lunch and something else comes in and takes over the body. And I'd like to know, Is the one who enters equal to the level of consciousness expressing at the time of departure? And does the mental body go with soul? Please explain.

Yes. First of all, the individualized soul—the Divine Spirit, which you are, has a covering, what you would call a covering, of individualization. That's known as the individualized soul or the soul body. Then, of course, you have a mental body, an astral body, a universal body; there are several bodies that your soul expresses through.

When that which you are, Divine Spirit, covered in the vehicle known as individualized soul, leaves your physical body in either the soul body or the soul and astral body—as you want to try to understand these bodies are all like layers of an onion. They are only bodies, only forms. When this, that which you are, Divine Spirit, individualized by what is called soul, leaves your physical body, it can leave with an astral body, a mental body, or can leave only with the astral body and the universal body. And so in that sense, there are times that, upon return, that you are shocked or greatly surprised at what you may have said or what you might have done. That does not, of course, free you from responsibility: you are responsible for the vehicle that you have earned in your evolution. You are responsible for your physical body. You are responsible for your mental body. You are responsible for your astral body. You are responsible for your soul body.

And so it does not free anyone from the responsibility of what the bodies may do, for we are responsible for what they do.

Now if you choose to leave one of your bodies and you do not establish the necessary laws of responsibility to put it in the care or charge of someone that you can trust, then whoever finds the body vacant will enter in keeping with the law that like attracts like and becomes the Law of Attachment.

Now does the form that uses your body when you go to lunch, so to speak—is that in keeping with the vibration at the moment you left your body? Is that your question?

Yes.

Not necessary so. It has to be in keeping with the basic vibration that you have established for the body that you have left when you went out to lunch. And because you have denied personal responsibility for your body by going out to lunch or leaving it not in good care, then you, ofttimes, that is, you, your soul, have quite a struggle and quite a battle to get back in. If you will try to understand, the wandering souls from the realms of what some philosophies call purgatory, of what the Living Light philosophy calls the astral realms, if you'll try to understand that these bodies, these mental bodies expressing—and astral bodies—expressing in mental and astral forms, being over-identified with physical bodies, are still hovering, as earth-bound spirits, hovering as earth-bound spirits with an insatiable drive in their minds to have a physical body through which to experience their self-gratification and self-glorification.

Now these truths, known for ages of your world, have unfortunately been set aside. As far as the masses of people, they are completely ignorant, or the masses would be much more alert of where they are at any moment or any time. For no one would leave their home with all their valuables in their home without making some effort of responsibility for proper security. And so an intelligent person, surely, would not leave their home (their physical body) without taking the necessary steps to properly secure it. So that a thief may not come in the night, the night of unawareness, and take over your home. Does that help with your question? Yes.

Can you express a little more about how to secure it?

Well, first of all, if you are going to go out to lunch, you have to use some degree of intelligence and consider where you're going for lunch, how long you're going to be gone, who you are going with and what you're going to do, how you're going to get there and how you are going to return. Then make some intelligent decisions in reference to who you can trust to take care of your home while you are gone. And therefore, until you have, in your efforts in life, made those proper arrangements, then, of course, it is wise not to leave your home. And when you are tempted to do so, consider whether or not there's going to be any valuables left—that you've worked so hard for—when you return.

You see, what are the valuables of the home in which you are, that physical body and that mental body? It has many valuables. It not only has many experiences which were good and beneficial—and [required] great effort on your part in evolution. And so when you leave that home and these difficult patterns that (some) you have out grown, so to speak—you must understand it is only through your conscious mind and your conscious effort that you have freed yourself from patterns and attitudes of mind that have proven to your conscious mind to not be beneficial to you.

And so when you leave your body, you take with you, you understand, that conscious mind where the faculty of reason is expressing itself. And when you do that, you leave a body that is subject to, in keeping with the laws of the predominant patterns in your life of like attracting, and that type of entity is attracted. It finds a house in which they can fit, you see, because it has to be like attraction. And you return and wonder what's happened that patterns you spent years in controlling and, hopefully, educating and growing through, have, once again, taken over your mind, your body, and now your little soul.

Now what does that reveal? It reveals that in a person's efforts of freeing themselves from patterns of mind that have proven beyond a shadow of any doubt to be detrimental, it only proves and demonstrates that the patterns of mind were not put through a process of education; they were suppressed, no matter how many years they were suppressed. Or they would not continue to be there and so easily activated by a discarnate entity from the earth-bound realms of a spirit world. Does that help with your question?

Yes. Thank you.

Yes, the gentleman here.

Is there a difference at all between the soul and the spirit?

Yes, yes, yes, indeed there is. There is quite a difference in the sense that you cannot individualize God. God is the Divine Spirit. The Divine Spirit, known as God, Infinite Intelligence, cannot be contained by limit. Therefore, the difference between the Divine Spirit and the individualized soul is one is limited by the process of division, individualized, divided.

Now I know that is, perhaps, a bit difficult to understand, but here we are, that which we are, Divine Spirit, that *is* God. That is not limited. That is what we are. We, the Divine Spirit, God is expressing through form known as the individualized soul. Now that that is divided from an Allsoul or individualized, that is limited by the very Law of Individualization. In other words, individuals are form; therefore, individuals are limited. So the soul evolves as the forms evolve.

Now you cannot educate God. You can only educate that which is subject to learning. The human mind is a vehicle of mental substance. It is the instrument that may be educated; it is the instrument that may learn. The soul, though individualized, cannot learn, cannot be educated, does not learn. The soul, individualized, expands. The soul doesn't learn. You cannot educate soul, for the soul is of soul substance, not of mental substance. So the education process is limited to a mental world of the human mind. Now the soul expands, expands—the individualized soul, it expands as the restriction of the mental body is educated. As the light of reason floods the mental world of limit, the soul expands and, therefore, is more free to express itself through a mental body. Does that help with your question?

Therefore, we, that which we are, Divine Spirit, expressing through individualized soul, bear a great responsibility. Now responsibility is not the Divine Spirit. Responsibility, the ability to respond, is the soul body, the mental body, the astral body, the physical body, for that which is affected responds. Do you understand that?

Yes.

That which cannot be affected cannot respond. Do you follow me there? Therefore, responsibility or the ability to respond is limited by the laws of limit to that which is composed of limit, which is mind, body, and soul, not, however, Spirit. Spirit-God does not respond, for Spirit-God is not affected by that which is an effect of its very essence and not the cause thereof. You see, you cannot have an effect without a cause. God *is*; the Divine Spirit *is*. There's no beginning to God. Because there's no— for there's no limit to God. Because there's no beginning to God, there is no end to God. To define God is a waste of time and energy, for to define is to limit.

So man can only define or limit that which is subject to the laws of limit. That which is subject to the laws of limit is that which limit creates. So the Divine Spirit [is] not created by limit, for God is not created. You cannot create something and through the very Law of Beginning not experience its own ending. That which is created is that which has begun. God did not begin. And because God did not begin, God cannot end.

Now man tempts to define God. Man tempts to confine or imprison God. Man does that from a realm of denial of God, for it is the mind that denies God and it is only the mind that is tempted to define God or to confine God, to control God.

You see, God, the Divine Spirit, is the greatest servant man will ever know. But it is God in this sense: the Divine Spirit is a servant subject to no master. So we cannot control God. We can only control the mind, our mind, which permits us to experience God. No one can experience God for us. Everyone can, and does, experience God for themselves.

If we tell our mind that "I experience God when I do that. And when I want to do that and I don't get to do that, then I lose my God," that is a great bondage, for it is a great control by mental substance over the divine right of the individualized soul to experience, to enjoy the good or God that is. However, man does not have to suffer that terrible censorship and depravation in life, for man, turning to that which he is, the Divine Spirit, declaring the truth: "My goodness comes only from God. My goodness, my God, my joy, my happiness, my health, my wealth, and all the goodness I can possibly experience is not dependent on what my mind says for my mind is a tool, subject to my soul. My soul is an individualization or covering of that which I am. It does not have want, need, or desire. So my job in life, in order to have the abundant good of life, is to educate my mind." Does that help with your question?

Thank you. The gentleman back there, please.

Why is it that man is nearest to God when he's in a garden?

Why is man closer to God when he's in a garden? Does not a garden represent Nature herself?

Yes. [The student speaks very quietly.]

Pardon?

Yes.

Yes. When man is in a garden, in that sense man is closer to God in a garden than any place else on Earth. Well, as I have stated some time ago, you know, that God is like a flea; you never know where you might find him.

When we look at nature, we enjoy that which we judge is beautiful. And one thing about nature—it has such a variety, even the most prejudiced of minds can find something they judge is beautiful. To look at nature and to experience what we judge is beautiful or interesting, without having to give anything but our eyesight for the enjoyment, we don't seem to mind doing too much. We don't mind, it seems too often, to look at the beauty that surrounds us in nature. We judge that to look at the flower and to think, "My, how beautifully that grows. Everything's so different," doesn't cost anything. Of course, it does cost. It costs our energy. It costs the use of our eyes. It costs the use of our senses. But because we put so little value upon our senses, being so addicted to their abuse, we no longer consider that they are valuable, that they do have some worth.

You see, when the tool no longer serves us, we begin to serve the tool. That happens often with our senses. So here we go into the garden of nature. We see these things. And they interest us for a time, some of us; to some, they interest even more. But everyone, if only for a moment—they may hate flowers, but they just might find a tree. There's something possible there, that for a moment, if only a moment, they judge is really something. Oh, they may not call it beautiful, but they judge something and they experience a good feeling in that moment. Well, they let God in there.

You see, nature is variety. Each flower is just a little bit different. You can't get bored in nature. Each tree is just a little bit different. Each leaf of each tree is just a little bit different. That interests the human mind that seeks unendingly for something just a little different. That interests the human mind that is so quickly bored with the same thing, for the uneducated ego must ever have something a little bit different. Nature's forms offer us that. And it doesn't, in the judgment of our mind, cost us anything.

So for those moments, as our minds are so interested in all the variety, we forget, in those moments, we forget the needs of self. We forget in those moments. And in those moments that we forget, we experience something much greater, much greater. We forget the disturbance, the seeming problems, the frustrations. And in forgetting, what it really means, we are not identifying with the limits of our mind. And by not identifying with the limits of our mind and how poorly things are in our life, by not doing that, we are, in truth, doing something else. And that something else is where God gets in. Does that help with your question?

Yes. Thank you.

You're welcome. Well, now if there are any more questions, we'll get to them. Otherwise, it looks—we should conclude because everyone is so sleepy this evening. Yes.

In line with what you spoke of before, regarding leaving the body in the care of someone, should we go out—we shouldn't, but should we go out—is it leaving it to the Divine Spirit that would take care of it?

If you have experienced the Divine Spirit, then you would, of course, then be satisfied that, number one, you can trust the Divine Spirit. But I would suggest that you first—what do you call it in your world?—make a dry run, I think they call it, a test. *[Many students laugh.]*

Thank you.

Are there any other questions? Yes, certainly.

Many religious groups say when you pass on, you go straight to heaven or you go straight to hell.

Well, of course, that's most understandable. They have to offer them some kind of a carrot. Thank you, go ahead.

And many others—[The student laughs.]

Well, isn't that what you offer rabbits? Carrots.

Carrots.

Yes. No offense to any religion, but I'll say some carrot has to be offered, because, you see, remember, man is tempted by the carrot and through that temptation makes effort to stay with anything. Yes, go ahead with your question.

I think you answered it.

No, no. Please, please go ahead with your question.

And others—religious groups, Christians, non-Christians— say there are other purification processes—purgatory, astral realms. And I was just wondering how such a split of such an important issue ever occurred.

Yes. Well, if we try to understand that some founders of various religions and philosophies in your world have various needs—you have founders of religions who have firm beliefs and conviction that quantity is best. You have founders of religions and philosophies who are firmly convinced that quality is best. And so you have these different religious organizations. Those interested in quantity offer the larger carrot to the rabbits. Those interested in quality offer something different. And personal responsibility isn't even a carrot at all; it's just a cabbage.

[Many students laugh.]

And so try to understand that and you won't have any problem with why they offer these various things, you see. If you note, those who promise the most have the most masses. Those who promise work and effort, they have the less. Yes. But the guardians of the astral realms wait with open hands for the souls to enter. And they do have many carrots for the temptation.

I think if you will reexamine what is called The Lord's Prayer, which Lord, being law, the law of our universe, of course, is the lord of our universe. If you will study that and reexamine it, I think that you will find that man is only tempted by denial of God. Man is never tempted by an acceptance of God.

And so we are not the temptation. And when we believe we are the temptation, then we know what we're doing: we have denied what we are in order to experience what we are not. And one does not desire forever to be what they are not by the expense and the cost of denying what they are. That help with your question?

Thank you.

You're welcome. Gentleman in the back there, please.

Could you speak on the Law of Entropy, please?

Some time ago, many, many years ago, I spoke on the Law of Entropy and perhaps at some time in the future—in fact, I delivered a paper through my channel many years ago [in] another country at another time and perhaps in keeping with the evolution of the class, someday, may be delivered.

Yes, do you have another question? Yes.

What is the principle by which the demons are driven out?

First of all, it is not possible for one to experience a self-exorcism as long as one believes and, through that belief, cements the identify with form. In order to drive out the demons that have entered the temple of God, your body, your mind, it has to be through the Law of Disassociation. A person using the practice of what you know as exorcism cannot be aware, in any sense of the word, that they are their thought or their mind, their body. For to so identify places them as a willing subject for the possession of the demons that have control of another body.

And so if God is not in it, forget it, for no good shall come there from. And the process of removing or, more properly, depolluting the temple of God, is one that few people are willing to tempt. For those who have tempted to do so, end up with the demons they've tried to drive out of another body. For God was not in it. God does not get into our consciousness by saying, "God in my thought." My, oh my! It takes much more than that. It takes the effort of your being to wrench yourself free from the belief that you are that person. That help with your question?

Yes. Thank you.

And I'm sure you will find in your world, for many, many, many years the process—so helpful to the souls—of exorcism is no longer practiced. There are so few willing to pay the heavy price for the initiation process of years to be an exorcist in the first place.

No one wants to be around anyone who is possessed by the demons. No one wants to. And the reason they don't want to is because they believe they are the limit. They believe they are the form. They have yet to separate truth from creation. They still believe they are creation. You see, we know whenever we believe we are creation, whenever we permit our self, our mind, to tell us we need—when we permit our mind to tell us that we need anything, then we know beyond any shadow of any doubt that we have denied God and believe that we are creation.

Creation is something designed for your use, not abuse. It's designed for use. And so anyone believing they are creation doesn't stand a chance in exorcising demons from anyone, for they don't stand a chance of exorcising demons from themselves. And so physician, heal thyself. That help with your question?

Thank you.

Yes. The greatest danger in the process of driving demons out—anyone learning that process—is to permit their mind to believe that they have need. You see, it's a pollution that takes place when the demons have control. The demons express themselves through the spoken word, through transmission of thought, through transmission of feeling, and all the senses. And if you believe that you are creation, if you are a servant of the false gods that control creation, the vehicles, if you believe that, then you will pay the price of that belief.

So in driving the demons out of another, one must first drive the demons out of themselves by not serving creation. You see, creation is designed to serve what we are. We are not designed— our individualized soul—to serve creation. But, you see, when we believe we are creation, by denying God and experiencing need, then we must pay the price.

When we love God as much as we love self—only equal—we shall be free. For creation is not something that should not be loved. Creation is a vehicle. One should love and care for the vehicle that they, in evolution, have earned. One should love and care for it, not at the expense of denying what they are and believing they are what they are not. For one can only believe what they, in truth, are not—they may only believe it for a time. For to believe what you are not is the principle of the Law of Delusion. Time is an element of delusion. And so you can only believe what you are not in an element of time. And so in your world they say sooner or later, you will wake up.

No one goes to sleep who does not awaken. You might think in other ways, in mental ways, someone went to sleep and they died. Why, they, they did not continue to sleep; they woke up. Death to one world is birth to another. And I'm sure you will all agree there's a lot of things that we have we wouldn't mind dying to and being born to something better. No one minds dying to a cold or misery to be born to good health and happiness and joy. So there's always something that we can look forward to being born into. When a person says they're short and in terrible need, why, they would love to be born into its opposite of wealth and freedom from lack and need. It is possible in the moment we choose in our own consciousness.

We must learn to choose wisely our dedications in life, for our dedication is absolute death to anything and everything that we are, by our own choice, not dedicated to. When you choose to do something you want to do with all your mind, you do it. You are ofttimes unaware and dead to everything else that is taking place. Yes, dedication is death to all distraction.

I hope that's helped with your question.

Thank you very much. Have your refreshment.

APRIL 11, 1985

CONSCIOUSNESS CLASS 246

Good evening. The class this evening will continue on with our understanding of the creation in our life, our world and how we make it.

Now the length of time or duration of any event or experience in our lives, its duration of stay, of course, is dependent upon the amount of energy that is directed to it. And this is why we have often said to place your attention or energy upon the way and to remove your attention from the obstruction. And so we find that some events never seem to leave our lives, while other events or experiences seem to leave far too quickly.

And we still wonder how can we control them. For we think that we ofttimes are making that effort and the results appear to be opposite of our intent. However, that is only seemingly true, for we direct energy to any event or experience from many levels of consciousness. And energy directed from one level of consciousness ofttimes is absolutely contrary when directed from another level of consciousness. And so a person having those experiences, not having the results that they thought were in keeping with their efforts of directing energy through attention, ends up usually quite confused and makes the judgment that they are the victim of circumstances or the fickleness of another's mind. And in that type of thinking, of course, there is a grain of truth: one is the fickleness of a mind. However, the mind is our own—the part that we don't seem to want to accept, let alone to recognize.

Now I'm sure that we'll all agree that what we understand as greed, the function of greed, is only the uncontrolled expression of what is known as need. So when, through lack of control of our thoughts, we judge that we are in need of anything—and the more we identify with that judgment that we have made, the less control we have of its expression. And we, sooner or later, find our self the victim of that function known as greed.

Now we've spent many years in showing to you, through discussion and example, the obstructions in life. And in so doing, one, through a little effort, quickly learns how to place their attention upon the way. For only in understanding an obstruction can one ever be in a position to find the way. That does not mean that we continue to identify with the obstruction, for then we find the obstruction (the molehill) is greater than the tallest mountain. It does mean that we should make a little effort in understanding how we create, through a lack of effort to awaken inside our self that we alone create these obstructions, how we create them. Remember, an obstruction within our consciousness cannot exist until we first experience need. And we cannot first experience need until we first deny what we are. And in the denial of what we are, we believe and accept what we are not. When we believe what we are not and we understand how our mind works, then we can certainly understand by believing in what we are not we are destined to experience need. For we are trying diligently, in that belief, denying the truth and experiencing what denial of truth has to offer.

Now in this earthly time, we all are in the process of preparing ourselves for the experiences not only of the moment, of the tomorrows, but we are preparing ourselves, qualifying ourselves for the realms in which we will spend our future time and the length of time we will spend in those realms.

Now all philosophies teach that there is a so-called heaven, a so-called hell. Some philosophies, they teach, also, there are places in between. Well, I'm sure that we'll all agree that our days, at least a good portion of them, are in those realms that are in between. Some philosophies call that a purification realm, a purgatory. And in that sense, of course, it is true. We often find our days in realms of consciousness that can be easily considered in between: not sure of this, certainly not sure of that, doubtful about this and, of course, questionable about that. We frequently spend much of our time in those realms of consciousness known as in between. In between because that is what fear offers anyone.

When we have experiences that prove to our judgments that we should use more caution, we soon begin to awaken within our minds what is known as the function of suspicion. We find difficulty in trusting anything. And anyone who does not make the effort to thoroughly investigate anything in their own mind should, for the sake of survival, be suspicious, for being suspicious, of course, reveals that we have had experiences in life: not understanding ourselves, we have exposed ourselves to experiences that we consider not in our best interest. And when that happens, we find that, from a lack of understanding our own mind, we must be suspicious of our mind. And, of course, we offer to the world that suspicion. For one is suspicious of another in keeping with the qualification of being suspicious of oneself.

We have experiences in which we feel that we are tempted. We do not like to be tempted, for we already know the effects of temptation and it clearly reveals a level of consciousness in which we encounter an experience that we cannot control. And so suspicion serves its purpose for survival of anything. But it is only one of the many functions that prove, in time, to be detrimental to one's own awakening unless a person makes the effort to understand those realms within themselves.

Now it appears to some minds that change, for them, is not only difficult, it is next to impossible. Well, everything changes in everyone's life. How long it's going to be is dependent upon the laws they alone have established and continue to do so.

When there is an awakening within our mind that we should make a change and we know that we should and we find one justification after another to postpone the change or changes that we know we must make, we, in that type of thinking, establish laws to bring about circumstances and conditions in our life through which we become forced, seemingly forced, beyond our conscious choice, to make the changes.

We don't like—no one likes (their minds) to make changes that way. So when you begin thinking about making a change in your life, the sooner that you do it, the happier you will be. For once that awakening takes place in your mind in keeping with your own effort of growth, to postpone it is a very difficult path of struggle and suffering. And the change proves itself beyond a shadow of any doubt to be much easier, in that sense, than to pay the price of the laws you set into motion that are literally forcing you, seemingly so, to make those changes. So woe to one who knows the way and chooses to sit by the wayside and watch, so to speak, the world go by, for it's only much more difficult for them.

We'll take a couple of moments, here, for questions in reference to the class, in reference to the changes and taking control, taking control of one's life by taking control of one's thoughts. For there are moments in everyone's life when they experience the peace and the goodness that they are. Those moments, for some, appear to be extremely rare, extremely rare because we make those moments dependent upon a multitude of conditions before we can experience those moments. So if you will raise your hand now, I'll be happy to answer your questions. *[After a short pause, the Teacher continues.]* I don't know whether there's no energy to raise one's hand or no incentive to wake up. Yes.

It seems after a long struggle that when you discover, I'll say, "the way," in quotes, it's as if you've been asleep and it's a strange sensation. It's like suddenly it's daylight. Can you explain that please?

Well, in reference to accepting one's responsibility for their life, if one has denied it for some time and then finally begins to accept the responsibility for their life, it could, to some, seem to be a strange sensation, for it is contrary to what we're used to. And anything that is contrary to what we're used to, we ofttimes consider strange. That, of course, which we are familiar with is not strange to us at all. But that which we are not familiar with, we do judge to be strange until we become familiar with it. So in that respect and in that sense, in awakening to responsibility for our lives and all the experiences contained therein could indeed be a very strange sensation to many minds. Yes. Does that help with your question?

Thank you.

Yes.

When you spoke of the intermediate planes, I understand, like, on the other side, that souls merit through their fear—Did I understand that correctly?—of not making a decision one way or the other through their fear. What governs the length of time that they will be in those particular realms? And is there some procedure by which they go through—of investigation—to find out for their own benefit so they're no longer so indecisive?

Thank you. In reference to that question, the length of time spent, the length of time of any event in anyone's life, the length of time in any plane of consciousness, in any realm, and in any experience is ever dependent upon the energy which has been directed or continues to be directed to it. For time, the illusion, is subject to energy, as all events, all forms, all limits are subject to the same law—the Law of Directed Energy. For example, as long as energy is directed to any limit, then that form or limit exists. When there is no longer energy directed to limit, then that form or limit disintegrates and returns to the source from whence it has been taken, formed, and limited or separated from the whole in the realms of illusion. Does that help with your question?

You see, because truth *is* and because truth *is*, there is no division of it. It just is. One cannot justify truth; one cannot define truth, for to be tempted to do so is to limit that which is. And when we tempt to limit that which is, we experience that which is not. Does that help with your question?

Yes. Thank you.

You're welcome. Yes.

Are there any very important laws of nature on Earth that can be applied to the length of time that things exist?

In reference to the laws of nature and the length of time that anything will exist, for example, what you call the element air exists. Now to look at what you call air, the mind says it does not see it. Would you not agree?

Yes.

So in reference to the laws of nature and in reference to something that one could apply for their own benefit in viewing or understanding a law of nature, then the element of nature that it would behoove one to identify with would be the element air. Formless and free, man is not able to limit it. He is not able to form it. It just *is*. It is the closest thing in a world of creation that could bring you to an understanding of what you are in comparison to what you are not.

And so when you permit your mind to think, "Air, that's what I am. I'm formless. I'm free, like air. I'm here. I'm there. I'm everywhere. Nothing can hold me. Nothing can shake me. Nothing can imprison me. Only that which I am not can be held, can be imprisoned, can be limited." You see, only that which you are not—and therefore, not being, shall never be—can be limited.

So man identifies and believes in what he is not. Therefore man, by believing what he is not, experiences need, for he's trying to be what he cannot be. And whoever tries to be what they cannot be, by denying what they are, must pay the price for believing what they are not. Now the price we all have to pay in insisting on believing what we are not is known to our minds as need. You see, whoever denies is destined to experience the need as the price, as the payment for denying. The will of God, the Principle of Goodness, is total acceptance. And whoever believes for a time they are greater than the will of the Principle of Goodness must pay the price. And the price indeed, to the human mind, is very high. It's known as uncontrollable need, which man experiences as a function called greed. Does that help with your question?

Yes. Thank you.

You're welcome. Yes, the lady here, please.

I have found—you had mentioned tonight, when you said, when it's time to make a change, to make it as quickly as possible.

Yes . . .

I have found in making changes, sometimes there is a lot of self-concern, which seems to be the opposite effect of what I desire. You know, the self-concern goes so much into making the change, instead of, maybe, awareness.

Yes. Well, don't you think it would be advisable to have a little understanding on what you call self-concern?

Yes.

When one finds that they are concerned over making a change in their life—what, what are we telling our self when we're concerned over making a change? Would you not agree that we are telling our self that there's a possibility that in the change that we are making we may not have as much control as we thought we had before making the change?

Yes, sir.

You see, you see, this, this business of concern over whatever changes we are making and etc.—we are concerned because we are revealing to ourselves the fear that possibly in this change we are making there may be something in it that we can't totally control. And because we believe that we have so much control over what we presently have and to trade that in for what we are thinking of having and not have at least as much control as we have over what we think we already have, we start to experience what is known as self-concern.

We only guarantee again and again and again that we, not being the denial that we insist on believing that we are, called need, and ending up with greed, that, sooner or later, we are not controlling any*thing*, but every*thing* has been and continues to control us.

A thought rises in our mind and we are unhappy. You cannot possibly say you are controlling that thought. You are the victim of the thought for you now feel unhappy. So you do not have control over the thought; the thought has control over you. You did not sit down—in a minute *[The Teacher addresses the sound technician.]*—you did not sit down and say, "I choose to have this thought for I recall how miserable I was the last time I had it." No. Seemingly out of the depths of the deep you have a thought and you're miserable. You did not consciously choose a miserable thought. The truth of the matter is, you didn't think about any thought; it just seemingly appeared. Correct?

Correct.

My dear friends, when you aren't doing anything, everything is doing you. And sooner or later we shall awaken: when you do nothing, everything does something with you. Now that's the difference between being the master of your destiny and the lackey of someone else's. So either you choose to do everything or everything chooses to do you. Now that's the choice that man has made for himself in his evolution. Whoever is too lazy to be the doer must graciously accept being the done. *[A few students laugh.]* Does that help with your question?

Thanks.

Some people are done well. And some are done not so well. But all appear to be done. Yes.

Is our fear of losing control the reason why we establish a pattern of postponing facing our responsibilities?

It is one of the many devices that the human has in reference to believing that it is what it is not. You see, if one can postpone any inevitable change, which they know is coming in their life, and they simply continue to postpone it, well, they just don't have to face, as you stated, that possibility that they might not have quite as much control as they have with that which they are already familiar. And the longer we postpone the inevitable in our life, the more difficult it is, of course, for us to face it. That help with your question?

Thank you.

Yes. You're welcome.

I would think my students would be a little bit more interested in being—in doing instead of being done. So many cry when they're awakened that they've been done. Yet, I hear no cry for doing. So the choice is simple: Do or be done. There are no in-betweens. There is—creation is a duality: it's either do or be done. Now if you choose to be done, then you have no right to cry. If you choose to do, you have every right to cry with your joy and happiness, for the workers win. Yes.

Is that not in the same vein as being the leader, instead of a follower?

Yes, indeed. You see, anytime, any moment that you permit your mind—you permit the true you not to be alert to your vehicle, your mind, then you are serving your mind. So either you are taking control moment by moment of what your mind shall do or you are serving what your mind chooses to do.

And so often in life we reach that point of saturation where we really believe the thought in our mind is us. And then time passes and we wonder how we ever got such a thought, let alone to believe that that was us. Now one divorce after another tells mankind that he is not and could not possibly be the thought in his mind. No, that something happened. Some thought got in there, but that was never him! So many seeming mistakes in our lives—we awaken and say, "No, no, no, no, no. Some strange alien thought entered my mind. For a short time, I was possessed. But I am not possessed anymore. I made the right decision." Would you not agree?

So, you see, it's quite simple: either *we* tell the mind—our mind—what it's going to think, what laws shall be established—either we do it or it does us. And we look through our experiences over the months and the years and say, "Just a moment. No, I never told my mind to cause me to feel like that, let alone make those mistakes." Would you not agree?

Oh, yes.

Yes. You see, so either we tell it what it's going to think and what it's going to do or it does it to us. That's the separation of truth from creation. Awaken in the morning and put your house in order. Tell your mind what it's going to do. Don't even give it a chance to tell you what it's going to do, because when it tells you what it's going to do, it does the same old thing: the same old mistakes, the same old experiences.

So that's how we know whether or not our mind is telling us or we are telling it. If our experiences reveal to us we are repeating the same old pattern year after year after year, we can be rest assured we're not telling our mind anything. It is doing everything. You see, we awaken and we don't like what our mind has done to our life. But, you see, look at the positive in it. Sooner or later we're going to awaken so much that each and every moment, when we open our eyes, we'll say, "Mind, this is what you're going to do today. Don't give me any flak. If you do, I'm going to let you have it."

You have to make conscious effort. If you don't do that, then you must accept a repetition of past experiences, for that's all your mind can offer you. That's all any mind can offer anyone. No mind can offer any person anything new. It can only offer them everything that has been. The human mind is a has-been vehicle and we must understand that it can only offer us, being a has-been vehicle, it can only offer us, in truth, that which already has been. So regardless of appearances of something different, it is only the deception of the human mind to tempt us to something different when it shall ever prove to us it's the same old thing. Does that help with your question?

Thank you.

Otherwise, it could not tempt us to—for us to serve the repetition of its pattern. It must put on the facade of something different, something unique, something special. It must do that to us in order to tempt us. Now remember, it's our mind and we're letting it do it to our self. That's how the mind works. Yes. Yes, please.

Is there any dependence on the mind at all?

There's total dependence on the mind, my good friend. Absolute, total dependence on the mind by the eternal soul in the sense that from a lack of effort of awakening inside, man has reached a state of believing he is the mind. You see, when you depend on anything over a period of time, you reach, someday, the point in which you believe you are that which you depend upon. Did it help with your question?

Yes.

I don't think so, yet. *[The Teacher laughs.]* You have, you have a thought. Do you understand that?

Yes, sir.

You believe you're that thought.

I do. Sometimes.

That reveals the dependence, you see? How can man discern whether or not that which he thinks is that which *he* thinks or whether or not it is that which has been, that's trying to deceive him into believing that's what he thinks, when he's not thinking that at all? That is a question one must ask themselves. From whence cometh this thought? From whence cometh this thought?

You see, we cannot test the spirit that they are of the Principle of Good, called God, for we have yet to test the thought to see where it comes from. So until man has awakened to test the thought, a mental realm, he's far from qualified to test a spiritual realm. We must first test that which we're familiar with. And so the testing must begin with our own thoughts. From whence cometh these thoughts? Test them that they are of the Principle of Good.

Yes, the lady there, please.

So could you also say that in relation to change that one should say, Where does this come from, like, if one is considering a change?

Yes, because ofttimes one thinks that they are considering a change when, in truth, it is only another avenue through which old patterns may expand themselves in one's consciousness. Yes. One must learn to test. You test spiritual values with the truth that you are the vehicle of its expression, known as the soul. Now you test mental values with a faculty of your soul. And which faculty, of all the faculties, would you use to test a thought that it is from the Principle of Good?

Reason.

Reason! That's why: Keep faith with reason; she will transfigure thee.

Yes, the lady here has a question, please.

How do you let your mind have it?

How do you let your mind have it? By first separating truth from creation. You see, a house divided cannot stand, for it exists in discord. Therefore, there has to be one captain of one ship. Now a person is one ship. They have the responsibility of being captain of that ship and making conscious decisions of where their ship shall go in this great sea of life. Now when you do not make—Yes, I know—the conscious choice moment by moment as a captain of your ship, when you do not make that conscious choice, the crew begins to mutiny aboard your ship and you do not reach your port of destination. Turn it over, please. *[The Teacher instructs the audio technician recording the class to turn the audio cassette over in order to continue recording the class.]* Thank you.

Now when you awaken in the morning and you decide what it is you want to do with your life and you make your decision, then you're going to be aware of thoughts in your mind that will justify and that will rise up with varying emotions that you're not going to do that. Have you not already had that experience? Pardon?

Yes.

Well, who's in charge? Are they in charge? Are you in charge? Now had you demonstrated charge over the years, they would not even be tempted to be so blatant. They would be far more devious and certainly more subtle than to rise right up in your consciousness and tell you the things that are contrary to what you have decided to do. Do you understand?

Yes.

And so those things that rise up—after you make a decision, you experience thoughts rising up in the consciousness contrary to the decision that you have made. Is that not true?

Yes.

That reveals the lack of effort and it also reveals phenomenal need to take charge of one's own mind. Now what happens when one begins to make the effort to take charge of their own mind? They do not rise up as blatant. In time, they will not dare, those forms, and tell you that which is contrary to the decision you have made. They will become much more subtle. They will appeal more to your weaknesses for, having been created by your own mind, they know all your weaknesses. They know everything that is available in your mind. And that is known as man know thyself, ye shall know the truth and the truth shall set you free. And that's where we must begin.

And so when you have something to do, you make a conscious decision. You do not speak it forth into the atmosphere. You do what you have to do and at least give yourself the necessary seventy-two hours to complete the decision that you have made. For, you see, if you, in making a decision—stop and think—in making a decision to do something and you already have the experience of the negatives rising up, the doubts, the fears, and etc.—would you not agree?

Yes.

Can you imagine what happens to a person who makes a decision to do something and then tells their best friend? When their own mind does those things with all those negative forms—*in their own mind*—what do you think those things are doing in their best friend's mind? My goodness, my students. My, oh my, oh my! Secrets of the universe are never given to blabbermouths. No, no. When you have something to do, to a person who has not made the daily effort to control their own mind, it's difficult enough just to get it done. But to have something to do and having reached a decision and then telling your best friend, that's like telling your worst enemy. That help with your question?

Yes. Thank you.

Because being your best friend, they're certainly in rapport with all your negativity. Otherwise, how could they be considered your *best* friend?

Yes, another question there.

Last summer at a seminar, you spoke of when we're creating new forms to go do something for us to tell them how long that should take. How do you perceive that? And how do you know that it is the new forms anyway and that you're not just creating some more old ones?

By knowing oneself, one knows the truth and there is no problem.

With both—

But only each individual can know the truth that is within them.

Thank you.

And when you know the truth, there is no question of how long it takes for a job to be done, for you will have already done the job yourself and, therefore, been qualified. You see, one must first qualify themselves. One does not have a question in how long a job takes once one has qualified themselves in doing the job.

And so if you want anything done in your world, first do it yourself. Then you will qualify yourself for it to be done by that which is responsible to you in keeping with the laws established. That help with your question?

Yes. Thank you.

Certainly. Yes, the gentleman back there. You have a question?

How can we—

I thought you were going to ask a question on what is it that causes a person to roll their eyes? But, how can we what? Yes?

What does cause a person to roll—

We'll go to your question first and mine second. *[Many students laugh.]*

When a person is so identified with their own judgments—

And something runs contrary to their judgments of which they are so identified with, they roll their eyes. Yes, now go on with your question. *[Many students laugh.]*

How can we begin along the path of truth and freedom to make that separation and perceive it as a judgment?

First of all, as you stated, how can one "so identified with their judgments," implying that one is truly over-identified with their judgments. First, what causes one to over-identify with a judgment of their mind?

Self-thought.

Wouldn't you consider need?

Yes, sir.

Well, what do you think one benefits in their life by experiencing a great deal of need?

The glory of self.

The glory of self, certainly. Now if we accept the possibility, just accept the possibility, as I've stated before, that we are not perfect—absolute perfect beings—if we'll only take a few moments each day and accept that possibility, through the accepting of that possibility, we will begin to refrain from denying the truth that we are. We first must accept the slightest possibility that we are not perfect.

You see, there's a part of us that has absolutely convinced us that we are perfect. And it is that part of us that is so convinced that fills our universe with need. You see, when a person believes they are perfect in anything, there is no thing they must do: no effort to be made. Now there are many, many married people and there are many wives and mothers who will tell you that their husbands absolutely believe in their perfection. And therefore they do nothing. You see, there is no thing to do when you're perfect. And if you permit, in any area of your life, the belief that you're perfect, then in that area, no change is necessary; no effort is necessary. Everything is wrong outside, for no one can understand your great perfection.

And so there is a level in all minds known as laziness. And so in those levels of consciousness, any thought that enters there has to be perfect, for only perfection can endure in those realms of laziness. You see, imperfection cannot endure in the realms of laziness, for imperfection would cause a disturbance in those realms to perfect itself. For there is a lack, therefore a need: it causes discord. So *only* thoughts, forms of absolute perfection can survive in the realms of laziness, for there's nothing that a perfect thought has to do.

And so by that absolute belief that you are perfect—therefore there's nothing to do, no effort to be made, no changes—one remains sleeping in the realms of satisfaction. For the realms of satisfaction are the naps of laziness. That's all that they are. You see, the sleep of satisfaction is nothing but laziness. So in anything in your mind, you want to believe you're perfect, be rest assured, you will not move a finger, let alone an eyelash. That help with your question?

Yes. Thank you.

See, you have nothing to do when you believe you're perfect, except look out and see that everyone else has a long ways to go to reach the realm where you are. And yet, one believes in their perfection at great cost, phenomenal cost. For one can only sleep for so long. The very laws reveal they periodically awaken. Yes. Irritation—periodically, they are disturbed. It's known as irritation. It awakens the soul in the sense it disturbs that realm of laziness. And that's why a person, in that awakening from the realms of laziness, they believe they're irritated for a time.

Yes, the lady there, please.

Then a person who believes in their imperfection, are they ruled by the same need as the person that believes in their perfection?

Well, a person who accepts the possibility that they're not perfect is a person who is willing to accept the possibility of making a change in their life.

All one need do, if one needs, is to look at nature and see if everything in form is perfect. But then again, one must also ask oneself the question, "Now let me see, who is going to judge? Is everything different? Is everything the same?" One quickly sees everything is not the same. It's just a bit different. Well, which difference is perfect?

So, you see, you have all of this taking place in a mental realm, far below the Divine Light where the Principle of Good *is* and there's nothing, *nothing* to judge. Judgment is the domain of the realm of Lucifer, for it has to see opposites. God is Divine, one united whole, known as the Principle of Goodness. Therefore, God sees no difference between the sparrow and the lily of the field. Only Lucifer sees difference, for only Lucifer knows difference. For Lucifer knows what he is and Lucifer knows what he believes he is. So only Lucifer is capable or qualified of judgment, not God, the divine neutral intelligent energy that is. For those who judge *must* view difference. Does that help with your question?

Thank you.

Otherwise, there is no comparison. Without comparison, there is no judgment. Without judgment, there is no death. Judgment is based on believing that we are what we cannot be. And whoever believes that they are what they can never be must ever experience the lack of what they are. And that's called need; the uncontrolled expression thereof is greed. Yes.

I was going ask what the best method for motivating people is—or good methods.

Yes.

But maybe the question really is, is, What's the best way to motivate yourself?

Survival is the greatest motivation man shall ever know. It is an animal instinct. Man believes he is the animal. Therefore, to move the animal, that which he believes he is, survival is the greatest instinct, for survival will move the animal. So to motivate a person, you must work with what the person believes is their survival. And when you work with what they believe is their survival, you will be amazed how motivated a person can quickly be. Does that help with your question?

Oh, yes. That's very good. Yes.

And, of course, a person believes they are many things. So there are many areas of consciousness which one can work. When one believes they are the paper that does the thing they believe to fill their desires, their wants, and their needs, then when it is threatened, the instinct of survival rises and they're quickly motivated. Would you not agree?

Yes.

Yes. We have time. We have time for one more question. I think you should have that question. Yes, the lady here, please. Very important question.

What is God consciousness?

You already know what is God consciousness. I know that you know. And it's a very, very important question. What is it to you?

Being in God.

Yes. Well, is it not being free from needs and wants?

Yes.

And that which is discordant to, to one's being.

It's true.

It is only in one's own best interest to make a little effort every day, every morning when one awakens. For it is quite a simple thing: either we do it or something does it for us. And so often in the course of a day, we don't like what that something has done for us, for it did such a poor job, for we quickly judge what a miserable day it's been—what terrible experiences. So that reveals that we have not put our house in order the first thing on awakening. You see, some time ago we gave to you, "Awaken in the morning, put your house in order before confusion sets in."

Well, be rest assured when you don't awaken and put your house in order, those various realms of consciousness and all those forms that have been created on them, *they* set confusion in, because they all want a piece of the action. You're the action; you're the energy. And they all want a piece of it. And they're going to get it if *you* don't take charge of the situation when you first awaken each and every day. All the way. That doesn't mean you just awaken and say, "I put my house in order. That's it!" Why, five seconds later you may find confusion set in. "I've got to put my house back in order again." Put your house in order and experience the joy of living.

Thank you.

MAY 9, 1985

APPENDIX

The Divine Healing Prayer

I accept that the Divine Healing Power
Is removing all obstructions
From my mind and body
And is restoring me
To perfect health, wealth, and happiness.
My heart is filled with gratitude
For the Divine Law of Acceptance
That is healing both present and absent ones
Who are in need of help.
Peace, the power that healeth,
Is guiding my thoughts, acts, and deeds
As God and I go hand in hand
Living a life of joyful abundance.

The Total Consideration Affirmation

I am the manifestation of Divine Intelligence. Formless and free. Whole and complete. Peace, Poise, and Power are my birthright.

The Law of Harmony is my thought and guarantees Unity in all my acts and activities, expressing perfect Rhythm and limitless flow throughout my entire being.

Without beginning or ending, eternity is my true awareness and sees the tides of creation, as a captain sees his ship.

As the Light of Truth is sustained by the faculty of Reason, I pause to think and claim my Divine right.

    Right Thought. Right Action. Total Consideration.

        Amen. Amen. Amen.

Divine Abundance

Thank
(Gratitude)

You
(Principle)

God
(Divine Intelligence)

I'm
(Individualizing)

Moving
(Rhythm)

In
(Unity)

Your
(Realization)

Divine
(Total)

Flow
(Consideration)

www.ingramcontent.com/pod-product-compliance
Lightning Source LLC
Chambersburg PA
CBHW020054020526
44112CB00031B/100